D0118576

501
low-carb recipes

501 low-carb recipes

Pamela Clark

ELIZABETH HOUSE

Food director *Pamela Clark*
Food editor *Nancy Duran*
US editor *Suzanne Fass*
Senior home economist *Cathie Lonnie*
Home economists *Sammie Coryton,*
Benjamin Haslam, Elizabeth Macri,
Christina Martignago, Sharon Reeve,
Susie Riggall, Jessica Sly,
Kirrily Smith, Kate Tait
Editorial coordinator *Rebecca Steyns*
Nutritional information *Laila Ibram*

Editorial director *Susan Tomnay*
Creative director *Hieu Chi Nguyen*
Senior editor *Lynda Wilton*
Designers *Alison Windmill, Mary Keep*
Studio manager *Caryl Wiggins*
Editorial/sales coordinator *Caroline Lowry*
Editorial assistant *Karen Lai*
Publishing manager (sales) *Brian Cearnes*
Publishing manager (rights & new projects)
 Jane Hazell
Brand manager *Sarah Cave*
Pre-press *Harry Palmer*
Production manager *Carol Currie*
Business manager *Seymour Cohen*
Assistant business analyst *Martin Howes*

Chief executive officer *John Alexander*
Group publisher *Pat Ingram*
Publisher *Sue Wannan*
Editor-in-chief *Deborah Thomas*

Printed by Bookbuilders, China.

An Elizabeth House book
Published by ACP Publishing Pty Limited,
54 Park St, Sydney, NSW 2000, Australia;
GPO Box 4088, Sydney, NSW 2001, Australia.
Ph: +61 2 9282 8618 Fax: +61 2 9267 9438.
acpbooks@acp.com.au
www.acpbooks.com.au

Cataloging-In-Publication Data is available
from the Library of Congress

ISBN 1581732821

© ACP Publishing Pty Limited 2004
ABN 18 053 273 546

This publication is copyright. No part of it may be
reproduced or transmitted in any form without the
written permission of the publishers.

Photographer Prue Roscoe
Stylist Julz Beresford
Home economist Sammie Coryton

Front cover Teriyaki pork with wasabi dressing, page 125
Back cover (clockwise from top left) Cajun chicken with
chunky salsa, page 135; pork and veal sang choy bow,
page 125; sweet and sour grilled cod, page 210;
tom yum goong, page 41; salade niçoise, page 34;
hot and sour steamed fish with thai salad, page 222
Page 1 Cioppino, page 212
Page 2 Baked ricotta with tomatoes, page 14

contents

LOW-CARB VALUES of COMMON FOODS

	Carb (g)
almonds, with skin, 1 tablespoon	0.6
apple, granny smith, raw, unpeeled, small, 4½oz	10.8
artichoke, canned, in brine, drained, 3½oz	1.2
arugula, raw, 3½oz	2.2
asparagus, canned in brine, drained, 3½oz	1.5
asparagus, raw, 3½oz	1
avocado, raw, small, 7oz	0.6
bean, green, frozen, boiled, 3½oz	2.8
bell pepper, green, raw, small, 5oz	2.3
berries, mixed, frozen, 3½oz	8.7
bok choy, cooked, 3½oz	0.9
broccoli, boiled, 3½oz	0.4
brussels sprouts, boiled, 3½oz	1.9
butter, 1 teaspoon	0
butternut squash, baked, 3½oz	2.8
cabbage, napa, raw, 1 cup shredded, 3oz	0.7
cabbage, red, raw, 1 cup shredded, 3oz	2.5
cantaloupe, raw, 3½oz	4.7
carrot, raw, small, 2½oz	3.2
cauliflower, boiled, 3½oz	2
celery, raw, 1 trimmed stalk, 3½oz	2.2
cheese, cheddar, 1oz	0
cheese, feta, 1oz	0.1
cheese, mozzarella, 1oz	0
cheese, parmesan, 1oz	0
chile, red, raw, 1 teaspoon chopped	0.2
coconut milk, unsweetened, canned, ¼ cup	2.3
cream, pure, ¼ cup	1.7
cream, sour, ¼ cup	1.7
cucumber, hothouse, raw, 4½oz	2.3
curry paste, 1 tablespoon	1.8
egg, fried, 1, 2oz	0.2
egg, hard-boiled, 1, 2oz	0.2
eggplant, raw, small, 8oz	6
fennel, raw, small, 7oz	3.6
fig, raw, medium, 2oz	4.9
gai larn, cooked, 3½oz	1.1
garlic, raw, 1 clove	0.3
ginger, raw, 1-inch piece	0.5
ketchup, tomato, 1 tablespoon	5.4
leek, raw, small, 7oz	4.7
lemon juice, 1 tablespoon	0.5
lemon, raw, medium, 5oz	2.5
lettuce, iceberg, raw, 3½oz	0.4
lettuce, romaine, raw, 3½oz	1.8
lime juice, 1 tablespoon	0.3
lime, raw, 1, 3oz	0.8

mayonnaise, whole egg, 1 tablespoon	0.2
meat (beef, veal, lamb, pork)	0
milk, ¼ cup	2.9
mushroom, button, raw, 3½oz	21.5
mustard, all types, 1 teaspoon	0.2
oil, olive, 1 tablespoon	0
oil, peanut, 1 tablespoon	0
okra, raw, 3½oz	1.4
onion, raw, small, 3oz	2.8
passionfruit pulp, canned, 1 tablespoon	1
peach, raw, small, 4oz	6.3
peanut butter, added sugar, unsalted, 1 tablespoon	2.5
peanuts, unsalted, 1 tablespoon	1.6
pepper, 1 teaspoon	0.5
pine nuts, 1 tablespoon	0.7
pistachios, shelled, 1 tablespoon	1.5
poultry (chicken, turkey)	0
prosciutto, 1 slice, ½oz	0.1
radish, red, raw, 1, 1oz	0.7
sauce, soy, 1 tablespoon	0.6
sauce, tartar, 1 tablespoon	1.1
scallion, raw, 1, ½oz	0.5
seafood, oyster, raw, 3½oz	0.7
seafood, salmon, smoked, 1 slice, 1oz	0
seafood, tuna, canned in oil, drained, 3½oz	0
spinach, raw, 3½oz	0.6
squash, raw, 3½oz	3.3
strawberry, raw, 3½oz	2.7
tofu, raw, 3½oz	1.3
tomato, crushed, canned, 3½oz	3.2
tomato, raw, small, 3oz	1.7
watercress, raw, 3½oz	0.8
watermelon, raw, 3½oz	5
wine, dry red, ½ cup	0
wine, dry white, ½ cup	0.4
zucchini, raw, small, 3oz	1.4

HIGH-CARB VALUES of COMMON FOODS

honey, 1 tablespoon	23.5
ice-cream, chocolate, 1 scoop, 4½oz	25
lemon soft drink, 1 cup	27.1
mango, raw, small, 10½oz	25.5
milk, condensed, sweetened, 3½oz	55.3
papaya, raw, small, 1½lb	31
potato, baked, small, 4oz	50.5
raisins, ¼ cup	28.6
sweet potato, boiled, small, 9oz	30
yogurt, frozen, soft serve, fruit, 1 scoop, 4½oz	30.9

Low-carb eating

WHAT FOODS CONTAIN CARBS?

Carbohydrates are found in starchy foods and sugars. So all grains (flour, bread, pasta, rice, breakfast cereals), most fruits and many vegetables (especially root crops such as potatoes and carrots) fall into this category.

When starch is combined with sugar – in chocolate bars for example – this results in a very high carb count with almost no nutritive value.

Carbohydrates are used in the body as fuel. They give you energy. That's why athletes eat high-carbohydrate diets. However, if your grandmother wanted to lose weight, she'd cut out bread and potatoes for a couple of weeks – there's nothing new about a low-carb diet.

HOW TO USE THIS BOOK

Each of the three sections in this book – losing weight fast, losing weight slower, and maintaining weight – contains recipes for breakfast, lunch, dinner, and appetizers/snacks.

LOSING WEIGHT FAST

The first section is made up of recipes which have no more than 12g carb per serving. At three meals a day, that gives you a total of 36g carbohydrate. If some of the dishes contain much less than 12g, you can add a snack or two, to make up the 36g total. The limit of 12g per serving is not as restrictive as some low-carb diets, but you will lose weight on this diet without ever feeling hungry.

This diet contains plenty of vegetables, as well as protein, with a good balance of nutrients to keep you healthy. You won't suffer some of the common side-effects of the more restrictive diets, such as constipation and tiredness.

Unlike many low-carb diets, this section is full of interesting food ideas, so it's possible to stay on the 12g regime for longer and not get bored – and boredom is the reason most people come off their low-carb diet.

LOSING WEIGHT SLOWER

The second section contains recipes which have no more than 25g carb per serving. This increases the choice of foods considerably. Much more fruit is introduced and you can even have a piece of toast for breakfast.

This is the diet you go on after you've lost a considerable amount of weight and, although you want to lose more, you're content to do it more slowly.

There's a huge variety of delicious recipes to choose from, so many in fact that you could easily follow the recipes in this section all your life.

If you find you need to lose a bit more weight in a hurry, go back to the 12g section for a week or so.

MAINTAINING WEIGHT

The third section contains recipes with no more than 43g carb per serving. This is food for life. There are enough carbs to keep your diet balanced, but not so many that you gain weight.

With such a huge variety of recipes, all the family can enjoy the food in this chapter without ever knowing they're on a reduced-carb regimen.

A NEW WAY OF EATING

- Re-think your snacks. Don't go near the junk food aisle in the supermarket. Junk food is very high in carbs.

- Steer clear of carbs that put on weight without giving you any nutritive benefit. The worst offenders are potato chips, chocolate bars or any other sweets (very high in sugar), ice-cream (high in sugar), soft drinks, and any snack food made from flour, such as cookies.

- To lose weight you have to be prepared to spend more time cooking.

- The enemy of the diet is hunger. It's when you feel hungry that you reach for the quick fix – french fries, chocolate bars, cookies. Prevent hunger by eating enough food at each meal to satisfy yourself. Don't eat until you can eat no more, but eat enough to last you until the next meal.

- Be prepared. Take some berries to work with you, or a few slices of ham and a tomato. Eat these if the craving for 'a little something' comes upon you.

- Forget cakes, pastries, donuts. On a low-carb or reduced-carb diet, these are not for you.

Losing Weight Fast (no more than 12g carbs per serving)

arugula, canadian bacon and poached egg salad

PREPARATION TIME 15 MINUTES   COOKING TIME 15 MINUTES

Pecorino cheese, the generic Italian name for cheeses made from sheep milk, is a hard, white-to-pale-yellow cheese, traditionally produced when the sheep are grazing on summer pastures.

10 ounces canadian bacon, sliced thinly

5 cups (7 ounces) arugula

¼ cup coarsely chopped fresh basil

2 ounces pecorino cheese, shaved

4 eggs

GARLIC VINAIGRETTE

2 cloves garlic, crushed in garlic press

1 teaspoon dijon mustard

⅓ cup extra virgin olive oil

¼ cup balsamic vinegar

1 Cook bacon in large nonstick skillet, stirring occasionally, until crisp. Drain on paper towel; cool.

2 Meanwhile, make garlic vinaigrette.

3 Place bacon in medium bowl with arugula, basil and cheese; toss gently to combine.

4 Half-fill the same cleaned skillet with water; bring to a boil. One at a time, break eggs into cup or saucer, then slide into skillet. When all eggs are in skillet, allow water to return to a boil. Cover skillet, turn off heat; let stand about 4 minutes or until a light film of egg white sets over yolks. One at a time, remove eggs, using a slotted spoon, and place on paper towel-lined saucer to blot up poaching liquid.

5 Divide salad among serving plates; top each with an egg, then drizzle with vinaigrette.

GARLIC VINAIGRETTE Combine ingredients in screw-top jar; shake well.

SERVES 4
per serving 0.7g carbohydrate; 37.7g fat; 449 cal; 28.2g protein

zucchini and mushroom omelet

PREPARATION TIME 15 MINUTES   COOKING TIME 25 MINUTES

2 tablespoons butter

2 cloves garlic, crushed in
garlic press

4 ounces button mushrooms,
sliced thinly

1 cup coarsely grated zucchini

4 scallions, chopped finely

8 eggs

4 tablespoons water

1 cup coarsely grated
cheddar cheese

1 Heat half of the butter in a small nonstick skillet; cook garlic and mushrooms, stirring, over medium heat about 2 minutes or until mushrooms are just browned. Add zucchini and scallion; cook, stirring, about 1 minute or until zucchini begins to soften. Remove vegetable mixture from skillet; cover to keep warm.

2 Break two eggs, one at a time, into a cup or onto a saucer. Place eggs together in medium bowl with 1 tablespoon water; using a whisk, beat lightly. Add ¼ cup cheese; whisk until combined.

3 Heat 1 teaspoon of the remaining butter in same cleaned skillet; swirl so butter covers base. Pour egg mixture into skillet; cook, tilting skillet, over medium heat until almost set.

4 Place a quarter of the vegetable mixture evenly over half of the omelet; using spatula, flip other half over vegetable mixture. Using spatula, slide omelet gently onto serving plate. Repeat steps 2, 3 and 4 three more times with remaining ingredients.

SERVES 4
per serving 2.3g carbohydrate; 28.8g fat; 357 cal; 22.8g protein
tips You can use a regular skillet, but spray the skillet with vegetable-oil spray before adding the egg mixture.
The skillet and butter should be quite hot when the egg mixture is added, so the omelet base sets almost immediately.

smoked salmon omelet

PREPARATION TIME 10 MINUTES   COOKING TIME 15 MINUTES

6 eggs

⅔ cup heavy cream

1 tablespoon warm water

⅔ cup sour cream

2 tablespoons coarsely chopped
    fresh dill

1 tablespoon fresh lemon juice

8 ounces smoked salmon

1 cup (1½ ounces) baby
    arugula leaves

1   Break eggs into medium bowl, whisk lightly; whisk in cream.

2   Pour a quarter of the egg and cream mixture into heated lightly oiled
    9-inch nonstick skillet; cook over medium heat, tilting skillet, until omelet
    is almost set. Run spatula around edge of skillet to loosen omelet, turn
    onto plate; cover to keep warm. Repeat process with remaining egg
    mixture to make four omelets.

3   Combine the water with sour cream, dill and juice in small bowl. Fold
    omelets into quarters; place on serving plates. Top each with equal
    amounts of the salmon, sour cream mixture and arugula.

SERVES 4
per serving 2.9g carbohydrate; 41.1g fat; 481 cal; 25.9g protein

puffed egg white omelet

PREPARATION TIME 25 MINUTES   COOKING TIME 20 MINUTES

12 egg whites

4 scallions, chopped finely

⅓ cup finely chopped fresh chives

½ cup finely chopped fresh
    flat-leaf parsley

½ cup coarsely grated
    cheddar cheese

½ cup coarsely grated
    mozzarella cheese

1   Preheat broiler.

2   Using electric mixer, beat three of the egg whites in small bowl until soft
    peaks form; fold in a quarter of the combined scallion and herbs.

3   Pour mixture into heated lightly oiled 7-inch nonstick skillet; cook,
    uncovered, over low heat until omelet is just browned on the bottom.

4   Place skillet under preheated broiler until omelet just sets. Sprinkle a
    quarter of the combined cheeses on half of the omelet. Place skillet
    under preheated broiler until cheese begins to melt; fold omelet in half to
    enclose. Carefully slide onto serving plate; cover omelet to keep warm.

5   Repeat process with remaining egg whites, scallion and herb mixture
    and cheese.

SERVES 4
per serving 1.1g carbohydrate; 7.9g fat; 148 cal; 18.2g protein
tip Wrap foil around skillet handle to prevent it from melting or overheating
under broiler.

smoked salmon and roasted vegetables

PREPARATION TIME 15 MINUTES   COOKING TIME 20 MINUTES

2 large red bell peppers

6 baby eggplants

4 medium zucchini

5½ cups (8 ounces) arugula

7 ounces sliced smoked salmon

1 teaspoon finely grated lemon peel

2 teaspoons fresh lemon juice

1   Quarter peppers, remove and discard seeds and membranes. Roast under broiler, skin-side up, until skin blisters and blackens. Cover pepper pieces in cling wrap or paper for 5 minutes, peel away skin; slice pepper thinly.

2   Meanwhile, slice eggplants and zucchini lengthwise. Place eggplant and zucchini strips, in single layer, on oiled baking sheets. Place under broiler until lightly browned both sides.

3   Serve roasted vegetables and arugula with smoked salmon. Sprinkle with peel; drizzle with juice.

SERVES 4
per serving 11g carbohydrate; 3.6g fat; 147 cal; 17.6g protein

ham, roasted tomato and sautéed mushrooms

PREPARATION TIME 10 MINUTES   COOKING TIME 20 MINUTES

4 medium plum tomatoes

2 tablespoons balsamic vinegar

vegetable-oil spray

10 ounces button mushrooms,
    sliced thickly

½ cup loosely packed fresh basil
    leaves, torn

¼ cup loosely packed fresh cilantro
    leaves, torn

¼ cup loosely packed fresh flat-leaf
    parsley leaves

7 ounces shaved deli ham

1   Preheat oven to moderately hot.

2   Cut each tomato into four wedges; toss in medium bowl with half of the vinegar. Place tomato, in single layer, in oiled shallow casserole; spray with oil. Roast, uncovered, in moderately hot oven 20 minutes.

3   Meanwhile, toss mushrooms in same bowl with remaining vinegar; cook, stirring, in oiled medium skillet until tender. Add herbs, toss to combine. Transfer to serving plates with tomatoes; keep warm.

4   Place ham in same skillet; heat, stirring gently. Divide ham among serving plates.

SERVES 4
per serving 2.6g carbohydrate; 2.9g fat; 91 cal; 13g protein

bacon and asparagus frittata

PREPARATION TIME 15 MINUTES   COOKING TIME 45 MINUTES

6 thick slices bacon, sliced thickly

1 large red onion, sliced thinly

½ bunch asparagus, trimmed

4 eggs

4 egg whites

1 cup buttermilk

1   Preheat oven to moderate. Grease deep 8-inch square cake pan; line base and sides with parchment or wax paper.

2   Cook bacon, stirring, in heated small nonstick skillet until crisp; drain on paper towel. Add onion to same skillet; cook, stirring, until soft. Layer bacon, onion and asparagus in prepared pan.

3   Whisk eggs, egg whites and buttermilk in large jug; pour into pan. Bake, uncovered, in moderate oven about 35 minutes or until frittata is set. Let stand about 10 minutes before cutting into squares.

SERVES 4
per serving 8.5g carbohydrate; 11.6g fat; 322 cal; 45.6g protein

squash, zucchini and red pepper frittata

PREPARATION TIME 20 MINUTES   COOKING TIME 1 HOUR 10 MINUTES

1 pound butternut squash, peeled,
**   chopped coarsely**

2 large zucchini, chopped coarsely

1 medium red bell pepper,
**   chopped coarsely**

1 tablespoon olive oil

7 ounces feta, crumbled

8 eggs

½ cup heavy cream

1   Preheat oven to moderately hot. Grease and line base and side of deep 9-inch round cake pan with parchment or waxed paper.

2   Combine squash, zucchini and pepper, in single layer, in large casserole; drizzle with oil. Roast, uncovered, in moderately hot oven about 30 minutes or until vegetables are browned and tender. Reduce oven temperature to moderately slow.

3   Arrange squash, zucchini, pepper and feta in prepared pan. Whisk eggs in medium bowl until frothy. Whisk in cream; pour over vegetables and feta. Bake, uncovered, in moderately slow oven, about 40 minutes or until frittata sets and is just cooked through.

SERVES 4
per serving 10.7g carbohydrate; 40.3g fat; 514 cal; 28.3g protein

cucumber, celery, apple and spinach juice

PREPARATION TIME 10 MINUTES (PLUS REFRIGERATION TIME)

1 small hothouse cucumber,
unpeeled, chopped coarsely

2 stalks celery, trimmed,
chopped coarsely

2 large granny smith apples, cored,
chopped coarsely

1½ cups (2 ounces) baby spinach
leaves, stems removed

1 cup water

⅓ cup firmly packed fresh
mint leaves

1 Blend or process ingredients, in batches, until pureed; strain into large pitcher. Refrigerate, covered, until cold.

MAKES 4 CUPS
per 1 cup serving 11.1g carbohydrate; 0.3g fat; 55 cal; 2g protein

tomato, carrot and red pepper juice

PREPARATION TIME 10 MINUTES (PLUS REFRIGERATION TIME)

4 medium tomatoes,
chopped coarsely

2 medium carrots, chopped coarsely

1 medium red bell pepper,
chopped coarsely

⅓ cup firmly packed fresh flat-leaf
parsley leaves

1 cup water

dash Tabasco sauce

1 Blend or process ingredients, in batches, until pureed; strain into large pitcher. Add Tabasco to taste. Refrigerate, covered, until cold.

MAKES 4 CUPS
per 1 cup serving 6.3g carbohydrate; 0.2g fat; 37 cal; 2.1g protein

baked ricotta with tomatoes (see page 2)

PREPARATION TIME 10 MINUTES   COOKING TIME 20 MINUTES

2 teaspoons olive oil

1 tablespoon pine nuts

**2 cloves garlic, crushed in
   garlic press**

**5 cups (8 ounces) baby
   spinach leaves**

1¼ cups low-fat ricotta cheese

1 egg, beaten lightly

**2 tablespoons coarsely chopped
   fresh chives**

**1 pound baby vine-ripened
   tomatoes**

1 tablespoon balsamic vinegar

1   Preheat oven to hot. Lightly grease four cups of a regular muffin pan.

2   Heat half the oil in medium skillet; cook nuts and half the garlic, stirring, over low heat until fragrant. Add spinach, stir until wilted. Cool 10 minutes.

3   Combine cheese, egg and chives in medium bowl with spinach mixture; divide mixture among prepared muffin pan cups. Bake, uncovered, in hot oven about 15 minutes or until cheese is browned lightly.

4   Meanwhile, toss tomatoes with vinegar and remaining oil and garlic; place, in single layer, in small shallow casserole. Roast, uncovered, in hot oven 10 minutes. Serve ricotta with roasted tomatoes.

SERVES 4
per serving 4g carbohydrate; 11.8g fat; 164 cal; 10.5g protein

baked eggs with pancetta

PREPARATION TIME 15 MINUTES   COOKING TIME 20 MINUTES

2 teaspoons olive oil

1 small red bell pepper,
**   chopped finely**

4 ounces pancetta, chopped finely

4 ounces button mushrooms,
**   chopped finely**

4 scallions, chopped finely

⅔ cup finely grated
**   parmesan cheese**

8 eggs

2 teaspoons coarsely chopped
**   fresh flat-leaf parsley**

1   Preheat oven to moderately hot. Lightly grease four ¾-cup shallow ovenproof dishes.

2   Heat oil in medium skillet; cook pepper and pancetta, stirring, until pepper is just tender. Add mushrooms and scallions; cook, stirring, until scallions soften. Remove from heat; stir in half the cheese.

3   Divide pepper mixture among dishes; carefully break two eggs into each dish. Bake eggs, uncovered, in moderately hot oven 5 minutes. Sprinkle remaining cheese over eggs; bake, uncovered, in moderately hot oven about 5 minutes or until eggs are just set. Sprinkle parsley over eggs just before serving.

SERVES 4
per serving 2.5g carbohydrate; 20g fat; 284 cal; 23.9g protein

scrambled eggs with fresh chorizo

PREPARATION TIME 5 MINUTES   COOKING TIME 10 MINUTES

Chorizo is a sausage made traditionally of coarsely ground pork and seasoned with garlic and chillies.
If you cannot find fresh chorizo, substitute with any spicy sausage.

8 ounces fresh chorizo, sliced thickly

8 eggs

¾ cup heavy cream

2 tablespoons coarsely chopped
   fresh chives

2 teaspoons butter

1   Cook chorizo, in batches, in heated large skillet until browned all over; cover to keep warm.

2   Break eggs into medium bowl, whisk lightly; whisk in cream and half of the chives.

3   Melt butter in medium skillet over low heat; cook egg mixture, stirring gently constantly, until egg mixture just begins to set.

4   Serve scrambled eggs, sprinkled with remaining chives and chorizo.

SERVES 4
per serving 3.8g carbohydrate; 42.6g fat; 478 cal; 21.2g protein

scrambled eggs with dill and smoked salmon

PREPARATION TIME 5 MINUTES   COOKING TIME 5 MINUTES

8 eggs

½ cup milk

1 tablespoon finely chopped
   fresh dill

2 teaspoons butter

10 ounces thinly sliced
   smoked salmon

1   Whisk eggs in medium bowl; add milk and dill, whisking until combined.

2   Melt butter in medium skillet; cook egg mixture over low heat, stirring gently, until mixture is just set.

3   Divide eggs among serving plates; top with salmon.

SERVES 4
per serving 1.8g carbohydrate; 16.8g fat; 282 cal; 31.1g protein

tomato and eggs on corn tortilla

PREPARATION TIME 10 MINUTES   COOKING TIME 40 MINUTES

1 small red onion, chopped finely

4 medium tomatoes,
  quartered lengthwise

1 tablespoon balsamic vinegar

1 medium red bell pepper,
  chopped finely

4 eggs

four 7-inch corn tortillas

Tabasco sauce, optional

1 Cook onion in lightly oiled large nonstick skillet, stirring, until soft. Add tomato and vinegar; bring to a boil. Reduce heat; simmer, uncovered, 15 minutes, stirring occasionally. Stir in pepper; simmer, uncovered, 5 minutes.

2 One at a time, break eggs into cup or saucer, then slide into same skillet on tomato mixture. When all eggs are in skillet, return tomato mixture to a boil. Cook, covered, about 10 minutes or until eggs are firm. One at a time, remove eggs and tomato, using spatula.

3 Warm tortillas. Place tortillas on serving plates; top with tomato and egg mixture. Serve immediately with Tabasco, if desired.

SERVES 4
per serving 8.5g carbohydrate; 5.7g fat; 124 cal; 9.4g protein

fennel fritters with poached eggs

PREPARATION TIME 15 MINUTES   COOKING TIME 20 MINUTES

1 tablespoon finely chopped
  fresh fennel tips

1 medium fennel bulb,
  chopped finely

3 scallions, chopped finely

1 small carrot, grated

3 slices bacon, chopped finely

2 eggs, beaten lightly

½ cup ricotta cheese

¼ cup all-purpose flour

2 teaspoons baking powder

vegetable oil, for
  shallow-frying

4 eggs

1 Combine fennel, fennel bulb, scallion, carrot, bacon, beaten egg, cheese, flour and baking powder in medium bowl.

2 Heat oil in large skillet; shallow-fry heaped tablespoons of mixture until golden brown and cooked through; flatten slightly during cooking. Drain on paper towel.

3 Meanwhile, half-fill a skillet with water; bring to a boil. One at a time, break eggs into cup or saucer, then slide into skillet. When all eggs are in skillet, allow water to return to a boil. Cover skillet, turn off heat; let stand about 4 minutes or until a light film of egg white sets over yolks. One at a time, remove eggs, using a slotted spoon, and place on paper towel-lined saucer to blot up poaching liquid. Serve eggs with fritters.

SERVES 4
per serving 10.9g carbohydrate; 29.5g fat; 376 cal; 17.4g protein

poached eggs with bacon, spinach and pecorino

PREPARATION TIME 5 MINUTES   COOKING TIME 15 MINUTES

1¼ pounds spinach, trimmed, chopped coarsely

6 slices bacon

4 eggs

⅓ cup shaved pecorino cheese

1 Boil, steam or microwave spinach until just wilted; drain. Cover to keep warm.

2 Meanwhile, heat large nonstick skillet; cook bacon until crisp. Drain on paper towel; cover to keep warm.

3 Half-fill the same cleaned skillet with water; bring to a boil. One at a time, break eggs into cup, then slide into skillet. When all eggs are in skillet, allow water to return to a boil. Cover skillet, turn off heat; let stand about 4 minutes or until a light film of egg white sets over yolks. One at a time, remove eggs, using a slotted spoon, and place on paper towel-lined saucer to blot up poaching liquid.

4 Divide spinach among serving plates; top each with bacon, an egg, then a quarter of the cheese.

SERVES 4
per serving 0.8g carbohydrate; 13.1g fat; 194 cal; 18.5g protein

poached eggs with bacon, spinach and pecorino

grilled vegetable and ricotta stack

grilled vegetable and ricotta stack

PREPARATION TIME 20 MINUTES   COOKING TIME 30 MINUTES

2 baby eggplants, sliced
   thickly lengthwise
1 medium green bell pepper,
   sliced thickly lengthwise
1 medium red bell pepper,
sliced thickly lengthwise
2 large zucchini, sliced
   thickly lengthwise
four 6-ounce portobello mushrooms
2 cups ricotta cheese
2 cloves garlic, crushed in
   garlic press
½ cup finely chopped fresh basil
2 tablespoons finely chopped
   fresh chives
1 tablespoon coarsely chopped
   fresh oregano
1 tablespoon finely grated
   lemon peel
2 tablespoons toasted pine nuts

TOMATO PESTO

¼ cup sun-dried tomatoes, halved
½ cup firmly packed fresh
   basil leaves
2 tablespoons balsamic vinegar
2 tablespoons water

1 Cook eggplant, peppers, zucchini and mushrooms, in batches, on heated oiled grill or grill pan until browned and tender.

2 Meanwhile, combine cheese, garlic, herbs and peel in medium bowl.

3 Make tomato pesto.

4 Divide mushrooms, stem-side up, among serving plates; layer with cheese mixture then random slices of eggplant, zucchini and peppers. Drizzle with pesto; sprinkle with nuts.

TOMATO PESTO Blend or process tomatoes and basil until mixture forms a paste. With motor running, gradually add combined vinegar and water in thin, steady stream until pesto is smooth.

SERVES 4
per serving 10.9g carbohydrate; 17.6g fat; 288 cal; 21g protein

grilled haloumi, asparagus and arugula salad

PREPARATION TIME 20 MINUTES   COOKING TIME 15 MINUTES

5 ounces baby green beans, trimmed

1 tablespoon olive oil

2 bunches asparagus, trimmed and halved crosswise

1 pound haloumi or white frying cheese, sliced thinly

1 large avocado, sliced thinly

½ cup toasted macadamia nuts, chopped coarsely

5 cups (7 ounces) arugula

MACADAMIA DRESSING

1 teaspoon dijon mustard

¼ cup macadamia oil

¼ cup sherry vinegar

1   Make macadamia dressing.

2   Boil, steam or microwave beans until just tender; drain. Rinse under cold water; drain.

3   Meanwhile, heat half of the oil in large skillet; cook asparagus, in batches, until just tender.

4   Heat remaining oil in same skillet; cook cheese, in batches, until browned both sides. Drain on paper towel.

5   Place beans, asparagus and cheese in large bowl with avocado, nuts, arugula and dressing; toss gently to combine.

MACADAMIA DRESSING Combine ingredients in screw-top jar; shake well.

SERVES 4
per serving 6.5g carbohydrate; 67.4g fat; 758 cal; 33.4g protein
tip Haloumi must be browned just before serving or it becomes leathery and unpalatable.

avocado caesar salad

PREPARATION TIME 20 MINUTES

2 small heads romaine lettuce or inner leaves of 2 large heads romaine lettuce, torn

1 large red onion, sliced thinly

2 medium avocados, chopped coarsely

⅓ cup sun-dried tomatoes in oil, drained, sliced thinly

2 ounces parmesan cheese, shaved

DRESSING

1 clove garlic, crushed in garlic press

2 egg yolks

2 teaspoons dijon mustard

2 tablespoons white vinegar

1 cup extra light olive oil

1   Make dressing.

2   Combine ingredients in large bowl with dressing; toss gently to combine.

DRESSING Blend or process garlic, yolks, mustard and vinegar until smooth. With motor running, gradually add oil in a thin steady stream; process until mixture thickens.

SERVES 4
per serving 9.6g carbohydrate; 86.6g fat; 859 cal; 13g protein

sweet chili and lime mixed vegetable salad

PREPARATION TIME 20 MINUTES   COOKING TIME 5 MINUTES

**1 bunch asparagus, trimmed,
    chopped coarsely**

4 ounces fresh baby corn, sliced lengthwise

1 medium red bell pepper, sliced thinly

4 ounces shiitake mushrooms, sliced thinly

1 hothouse cucumber, seeded, sliced thinly

12 scallions, sliced thinly

4 ounces fresh bean sprouts

1 red serrano chile, sliced thinly

2 tablespoons finely chopped fresh cilantro

2 tablespoons fresh lime juice

1 tablespoon sweet chili sauce

2 teaspoons sesame oil

2 teaspoons fish sauce

1 clove garlic, crushed in garlic press

1 Boil, steam or microwave asparagus and corn, separately, until just tender; drain. Cool.

2 Combine asparagus and corn in large serving bowl with pepper, mushroom, cucumber, scallion, sprouts, chile and cilantro.

3 Place remaining ingredients in screw-top jar; shake well. Drizzle salad with dressing; toss gently to combine.

SERVES 4
per serving 10.3g carbohydrate; 3.1g fat; 92 cal; 5.2g protein

stir-fried cauliflower, asian greens and green beans

PREPARATION TIME 20 MINUTES   COOKING TIME 10 MINUTES

You need about half of a bunch of asian greens for this recipe. Try bok choy, choy sum, or gai larn (also known as chinese broccoli).

1 tablespoon peanut oil

2 cloves garlic, crushed in garlic press

1 teaspoon ground turmeric

**1 teaspoon finely chopped cilantro root
    and stem**

4 scallions, sliced thinly

1 pound cauliflower florets

¼ cup water

**7 ounces green beans, trimmed and
    cut into 2-inch pieces**

7 ounces asian greens, chopped coarsely

1 tablespoon fresh lime juice

1 tablespoon soy sauce

1 tablespoon coarsely chopped fresh cilantro

1 Heat oil in wok; stir-fry garlic, turmeric, cilantro mixture and scallion until scallion just softens. Remove from wok; keep warm.

2 Stir-fry cauliflower with the water in same wok until cauliflower is almost tender. Add beans and greens; stir-fry until vegetables are just tender.

3 Add juice, sauce, chopped cilantro and garlic mixture; stir-fry until heated through.

SERVES 4
per serving 4.7g carbohydrate; 5.1g fat; 88 cal; 5.5g protein

roasted mediterranean vegetables with pepper-and-herb baked ricotta salata

PREPARATION TIME 20 MINUTES   COOKING TIME 25 MINUTES

Ricotta that is sold packaged in tubs is not suitable for this recipe.

14-ounce wedge ricotta salata

2 teaspoons plus 2 tablespoons
    extra virgin olive oil

1½ teaspoons freshly ground
    black pepper

½ teaspoon dried red pepper flakes

2 baby eggplants, halved
    lengthwise

2 small zucchini, halved lengthwise

1 small red bell pepper, quartered

olive-oil spray

1 small red onion, quartered

1 stalk celery, trimmed, cut
    into quarters

1 large plum tomato, quartered

4 cloves garlic, unpeeled

2 tablespoons shredded fresh basil

1 tablespoon baby capers, drained

1 tablespoon finely chopped
    fresh oregano

1   Preheat oven to hot. Place ricotta on baking sheet lined with parchment or wax paper. Drizzle with 2 teaspoons oil; sprinkle with ½ teaspoon black pepper and pepper flakes.

2   Place eggplant, zucchini and pepper, in single layer, in large shallow casserole; spray with olive-oil spray. Place onion, celery, tomato and garlic on same baking sheet as ricotta, in single layer; spray with olive-oil spray. Roast baking sheet and casserole, uncovered, together in hot oven about 25 minutes or until vegetables are browned and tender.

3   Sprinkle vegetables with remaining pepper; drizzle with remaining olive oil. Top with basil and capers. Sprinkle cheese with oregano; serve with vegetables.

SERVES 4
per serving 6.6g carbohydrate; 23.9g fat; 289 cal; 12.7g protein

sesame omelet and
crisp mixed vegetable salad

PREPARATION TIME 25 MINUTES   COOKING TIME 10 MINUTES

You need about half a head of a medium napa cabbage for this recipe.

8 eggs

½ cup milk

½ cup coarsely chopped

fresh chives

2 tablespoons toasted

sesame seeds

8 cups finely shredded

napa cabbage

2 fresh thai red chiles, seeded,

sliced thinly

1 large red bell pepper, sliced thinly

1 large green bell pepper,

sliced thinly

1 tablespoon coarsely chopped

fresh mint

1 tablespoon finely chopped

fresh lemongrass

SWEET CHILI DRESSING

2 teaspoons toasted sesame seeds

¼ cup rice vinegar

¼ cup peanut oil

1 teaspoon sesame oil

¼ cup sweet chili sauce

1   Whisk eggs in large measuring cup with milk, chives and seeds until well combined. Pour a quarter of the egg mixture into heated, lightly oiled wok or large skillet; cook over medium heat, tilting skillet, until omelet is just set. Remove from wok; repeat with remaining egg mixture to make three more omelets. Roll cooled omelets tightly; cut into ⅛-inch pinwheels.

2   Make sweet chili dressing.

3   Place three of the sliced omelets in large bowl with cabbage, chile, peppers, mint, lemongrass and dressing; toss gently to combine. Divide salad among serving plates; top with remaining omelet pinwheels.

SWEET CHILI DRESSING   Combine ingredients in screw-top jar; shake well.

SERVES 4

per serving 11.1g carbohydrate; 29.9g fat; 391 cal; 19.7g protein
tip Omelets can be made up to 3 hours ahead and stored, covered, in the refrigerator; roll and slice just before assembling salad.

stir-fried asian greens with grilled tofu

PREPARATION TIME 15 MINUTES (PLUS STANDING TIME)   COOKING TIME 10 MINUTES

Any asian greens can be used in this recipe. Try it with bok choy, choy sum, or gai larn (also known as chinese broccoli).

1 pound firm silken tofu

2 pounds asian greens, trimmed, chopped coarsely

4 tablespoons oyster sauce

1 tablespoon peanut oil

5 scallions, chopped coarsely

2 cloves garlic, crushed in garlic press

2 teaspoons grated fresh ginger

2 tablespoons soy sauce

1 tablespoon fish sauce

2 tablespoons toasted sesame seeds

1 Press tofu between two cutting boards with a weight on top, raise one end to let excess water run out, let stand 25 minutes.

2 Boil, steam or microwave greens until just tender; drain.

3 Cut tofu into 1-inch slices, pat dry with paper towel; place on oiled baking sheet, cook under hot broiler about 3 minutes or until browned lightly. Spread half of the oyster sauce onto tofu pieces. Cook under hot broiler about 2 minutes or until browned lightly.

4 Meanwhile, heat oil in wok or large skillet; stir-fry scallion, garlic and ginger until fragrant. Add greens and remaining sauces; stir until heated through. Toss with sesame seeds. Serve topped with tofu.

SERVES 4
per serving 11g carbohydrate; 16.8g fat; 292 cal; 24g protein

stuffed zucchini flowers and radicchio salad

PREPARATION TIME 20 MINUTES   COOKING TIME 10 MINUTES

Buy zucchini flowers with the tiny young vegetable attached if possible. You need to buy two heads of radicchio; use only the inner leaves and hearts. We used a firm goat cheese; if you use a soft version of this cheese, crumble rather than grate it.

2 tablespoons finely chopped fresh sage

2 teaspoons finely grated lemon peel

1 small red onion, chopped finely

4 ounces firm goat cheese, grated coarsely

4 ounces ricotta

24 tiny zucchini with flowers attached

8 ounces yellow pear tomatoes

1 tablespoon olive oil

1 teaspoon balsamic vinegar

4 ounces radicchio leaves, torn

1 Preheat oven to very hot.

2 Place sage, peel, onion, goat cheese and ricotta in small bowl; beat with wooden spoon until combined.

3 Remove and discard stamens from center of flowers; fill flowers with cheese mixture, twist petal tops to enclose filling. Place filled flowers on lightly oiled baking sheet. Place tomatoes, in single layer, in small shallow casserole; drizzle with combined oil and vinegar. Roast flowers and tomatoes, both uncovered, in very hot oven about 10 minutes or until flowers are browned lightly and heated through, and tomatoes are softened.

4 Toss tomatoes and pan juices in medium bowl with radicchio; serve with zucchini flowers.

SERVES 4
per serving 5.6g carbohydrate; 11.8g fat; 163 cal; 8.6g protein
tip You can use a pastry bag fitted with a large plain tube to pipe filling into the zucchini flowers.

greek salad with taramasalata dressing

PREPARATION TIME 20 MINUTES

Taramasalata is a creamy dip made from carp roe, lemon juice, olive oil, and bread soaked in milk. You can buy it in specialty delicatessens.

1 small red onion

2 medium plum tomatoes, quartered

2 hothouse cucumbers, sliced thickly

1 medium green bell pepper, sliced thickly

½ head romaine lettuce, torn

¼ cup pitted kalamata olives

5 ounces feta cheese, chopped coarsely

1 tablespoon coarsely chopped fresh oregano

1 tablespoon coarsely chopped fresh flat-leaf parsley

1 tablespoon fresh lemon juice

2 tablespoons olive oil

⅓ cup taramasalata

1 Cut onion into thin wedges.

2 Combine onion in large bowl with tomato, cucumber, pepper, lettuce, olives and cheese.

3 Sprinkle herbs over salad then drizzle with combined remaining ingredients; serve without tossing.

SERVES 4
per serving 11.4g carbohydrate; 22.9g fat; 297 cal; 11.8g protein

stir-fried eggplant tofu

PREPARATION TIME 15 MINUTES (PLUS STANDING TIME)   COOKING TIME 15 MINUTES

Any asian greens can be used in this recipe. Try it with bok choy, choy sum, or gai larn (also known as chinese broccoli).

1 large eggplant

salt

10 ounces firm silken tofu

1 medium onion

2 tablespoons peanut oil

1 clove garlic, crushed in garlic press

2 small red serrano chiles, sliced thinly

1 tablespoon light brown sugar

1½ pounds asian greens, chopped coarsely

2 tablespoons fresh lime juice

⅓ cup soy sauce

⅓ cup coarsely chopped fresh basil

1 Cut unpeeled eggplant in half lengthwise; cut each half into thin slices. Place eggplant in colander, sprinkle with salt; let stand 30 minutes.

2 Meanwhile, pat tofu all over with paper towel; cut into 1-inch squares. Spread tofu, in single layer, on paper towel-lined tray; cover tofu with more paper towel, let stand at least 10 minutes.

3 Cut onion in half, then cut each half into thin even-sized wedges. Rinse eggplant under cold water; pat dry with paper towel.

4 Heat oil in wok; stir-fry onion, garlic and chiles until onion softens. Add sugar; stir-fry until dissolved. Add eggplant; stir-fry, 1 minute. Add greens; stir-fry until just wilted. Add tofu, juice and sauce; stir-fry, tossing gently until combined. Remove from heat; toss basil through stir-fry.

SERVES 4
per serving 10.3g carbohydrate; 14.7g fat; 238 cal; 16g protein

japanese omelet salad (see page 307)

PREPARATION TIME 20 MINUTES   COOKING TIME 10 MINUTES

1 medium daikon

2 medium carrots

6 large red radishes, sliced thinly

1½ cups shredded red cabbage

1½ cups (4 ounces) fresh bean sprouts

2 tablespoons pickled ginger, sliced thinly

6 scallions, sliced thinly

4 eggs, beaten lightly

1 tablespoon soy sauce

½ sheet toasted seaweed (yaki-nori), sliced thinly

WASABI DRESSING

1 tablespoon pickled ginger juice

2 tablespoons soy sauce

1 tablespoon mirin

1 teaspoon wasabi paste

1 Make wasabi dressing.

2 Using vegetable peeler, slice daikon and carrots into thin strips. Place in large bowl with radish, cabbage, sprouts, ginger and three-quarters of the scallion; toss salad gently to combine.

3 Combine egg, soy sauce and seaweed in measuring cup. Pour half of the egg mixture into heated, lightly oiled large skillet; cook, uncovered, until just set. Slide omelet onto plate; roll into cigar shape. Repeat with remaining egg mixture. Slice omelet rolls into thin rings.

4 Add dressing to salad; toss gently to combine. Divide salad among serving bowls; top with remaining scallion and omelet rings.

WASABI DRESSING Combine ingredients in screw-top jar; shake well.

SERVES 4
per serving 10.4g carbohydrate; 6.2g fat; 146 cal; 11.7g protein

grilled tuna salad

PREPARATION TIME 10 MINUTES   COOKING TIME 5 MINUTES

1¼-pound fresh tuna fillet

¼ cup rice vinegar

1 teaspoon sugar

1 tablespoon light soy sauce

1 clove garlic, crushed in garlic press

1 red serrano chile, seeded, chopped finely

1 scallion, chopped finely

2 medium red bell peppers, sliced thinly

5½ cups (7 ounces) mesclun

1 Cook tuna on heated oiled grill or grill pan until browned both sides and cooked as desired. Cover, rest 2 minutes; cut into thick slices.

2 Meanwhile, combine vinegar, sugar, soy sauce, garlic, chile and scallion in screw-top jar; shake well.

3 Combine tuna and dressing in large bowl with pepper and mesclun; toss gently to combine.

SERVES 4
per serving 4.1g carbohydrate; 3.6g fat; 184 cal; 32.9g protein
tip Brushing the whole piece of tuna with olive oil 3 hours ahead of cooking will help keep it moist and soft when it's grilled.

crab salad

PREPARATION TIME 15 MINUTES

You need about a quarter of a medium head of napa cabbage for this recipe.

1 pound fresh crab meat

8 ounces napa cabbage, chopped finely

1 hothouse cucumber, seeded, chopped coarsely

1 medium red onion, halved, sliced thinly

6 scallions, cut into 1½-inch lengths

1 cup loosely packed fresh mint leaves

DRESSING

2 cloves garlic, crushed in garlic press

2 tablespoons fresh lime juice

2 tablespoons fish sauce

1 tablespoon light brown sugar

2 small red serrano chiles, chopped finely

1 Drain crab in strainer; remove any shell and if necessary shred the meat to desired texture.

2 Make dressing.

3 Combine crab in large bowl with cabbage, cucumber, onion, scallion and mint; pour in dressing, toss to combine.

DRESSING Combine ingredients in screw-top jar; shake well.

SERVES 4
per serving 9.6g carbohydrate; 1.1g fat; 124 cal; 18.8g protein

fish cakes with herb salad

PREPARATION TIME 15 MINUTES COOKING TIME 10 MINUTES

1 pound red snapper fillets, skinned and boned

2 tablespoons red curry paste

2 scallions, chopped finely

1 tablespoon fish sauce

3 tablespoons fresh lime juice

2 tablespoons finely chopped fresh cilantro

6 green beans, chopped finely

2 small red serrano chiles, chopped finely

1 cup loosely packed fresh basil leaves

1 cup loosely packed fresh mint leaves

1 cup (3½ ounces) fresh bean sprouts

peanut oil, for deep-frying

1 Cut fish into small pieces. Blend or process fish with curry paste, scallion, sauce and 1 tablespoon juice until mixture forms a smooth paste. Combine fish mixture in medium bowl with cilantro, beans and chile.

2 Roll heaped tablespoon of the fish mixture into ball, then flatten into cake shape; repeat with remaining mixture.

3 Just before serving, combine basil, mint, sprouts and remaining lime juice in medium bowl; toss gently to combine.

4 Meanwhile, heat oil in wok or deep skillet; deep-fry fish cakes, in batches, until browned lightly and cooked through. Drain on paper towel; serve topped with herb salad.

SERVES 4
per serving 2.7g carbohydrate; 15.1g fat; 258 cal; 28g protein

salmon and asparagus salad with creamy horseradish dressing

PREPARATION TIME 30 MINUTES   COOKING TIME 20 MINUTES

2 turnips (about 1 pound)

four 8-ounce salmon fillets, skin on

1 cup milk

5 cups water

2 bunches asparagus, trimmed

1 large or 2 small bunches
   watercress, trimmed
   (about 6 ounces)

1 small red onion, sliced thinly

CREAMY HORSERADISH DRESSING

1 egg

2 tablespoons prepared
   white horseradish

1 teaspoon honey

⅔ cup olive oil

1   Boil, steam or microwave turnips until tender; drain. When cool enough to handle, slice thickly.

2   Meanwhile, remove any bones from fish. Place fish in large skillet; cover with milk and the water. Weigh fish down with heavy plate or lid to keep submerged; bring to a boil. Reduce heat; simmer about 5 minutes or until fish is cooked as desired. Discard cooking liquid; when fish is cool enough to handle, remove skin, cut each fillet in half lengthwise.

3   Make creamy horseradish dressing.

4   Boil, steam or microwave asparagus until tender; drain. Rinse under cold water; drain.

5   Divide asparagus, watercress, onion, turnip and fish among serving plates; drizzle with dressing.

CREAMY HORSERADISH DRESSING   Blend or process egg, horseradish and honey until combined. With motor running, add oil in a thin, steady stream until dressing thickens slightly.

SERVES 4
per serving 11.5g carbohydrate; 48.9g fat; 690 cal; 52g protein

shrimp, frisée and pink grapefruit with lime aïoli

PREPARATION TIME 30 MINUTES

You need approximately one head of frisée for this recipe.

2 small pink grapefruits

2 pounds cooked large shrimp

12 ounces frisée or curly endive, torn

¼ cup coarsely chopped fresh chives

2 stalks celery, trimmed, sliced thinly

1 small red onion, sliced thinly

LIME AÏOLI

2 egg yolks

2 teaspoons dijon mustard

½ teaspoon finely grated lime peel

2 tablespoons fresh lime juice

2 cloves garlic, quartered

¾ cup light olive oil

1 tablespoon hot water

1 Peel grapefruits; separate the segments. Shell and devein shrimp, leaving tails intact.

2 Make lime aïoli.

3 Combine grapefruit and shrimp in large serving bowl with remaining ingredients. Serve with lime aïoli.

LIME AÏOLI Blend or process egg yolks, mustard, peel, juice and garlic until combined. With motor running, gradually add oil, blending until aïoli thickens. With motor running, add enough of the water (if any) to achieve desired consistency.

SERVES 4
per serving 7.7g carbohydrate; 45.5g fat; 576 cal; 34.3g protein
tip Lime aïoli can be prepared a day ahead; keep, covered, under refrigeration.

crisp fish salad with chile-lime dressing

PREPARATION TIME 20 MINUTES   COOKING TIME 30 MINUTES

½ pound firm white fish fillets

vegetable oil, for deep-frying

1 medium red onion, sliced thinly

6 scallions, sliced thinly

2 hothouse cucumbers, seeded, sliced thinly

1 cup firmly packed fresh mint leaves

1 cup firmly packed fresh cilantro leaves

2 tablespoons coarsely chopped roasted
    unsalted peanuts

2 teaspoons finely grated lime peel

CHILE-LIME DRESSING

4 small green serrano chiles, seeded,
    chopped finely

2 tablespoons fish sauce

⅓ cup fresh lime juice

1 tablespoon light brown sugar

1   Preheat oven to moderate. Place fish on wire rack over baking sheet; roast, uncovered, 20 minutes. When cool enough to handle, cut fish into pieces, then blend or process, pulsing, until mixture resembles coarse breadcrumbs.

2   Heat oil in wok or deep skillet; deep-fry processed fish, in batches, until lightly browned and crisp. Drain on paper towel.

3   Make chile-lime dressing.

4   Combine onion, scallion, cucumber and herbs in large bowl; add chile-lime dressing, toss to combine. Sprinkle salad with crisp fish, nuts and lime peel; serve immediately.

CHILE-LIME DRESSING   Combine ingredients in screw-top jar; shake well.

SERVES 4
per serving   9.1g carbohydrate; 5.7g fat; 153 cal; 16g protein

smoked salmon and avocado salad

PREPARATION TIME 20 MINUTES

4½ cups (5 ounces) mesclun

1 pound smoked salmon, sliced thinly

2 medium avocados, chopped coarsely

1 medium red onion, sliced thinly

10 ounces baked ricotta, crumbled

2 tablespoons finely chopped fresh dill

⅓ cup fresh lemon juice

1 tablespoon dijon mustard

1 tablespoon honey

2 cloves garlic, crushed in garlic press

1 tablespoon white vinegar

1 tablespoon olive oil

1   Combine mesclun, salmon, avocado, onion and ricotta in large bowl.

2   Whisk remaining ingredients in small bowl then pour over salad; toss gently to combine.

SERVES 4
per serving   10.2g carbohydrate; 38.9g fat; 549 cal; 39.9g protein

fish provençale with herbed fresh tomatoes

PREPARATION TIME 10 MINUTES   COOKING TIME 15 MINUTES

You can use any firm fish, such as perch, snapper or cod.

**2 medium yellow squash,
    quartered lengthwise**

**3 medium green zucchini,
    quartered lengthwise**

¼ cup olive oil

four 5-ounce white fish fillets

**2 medium plum tomatoes, seeded,
    chopped finely**

2 tablespoons fresh lemon juice

1 tablespoon coarsely chopped fresh dill

**1 tablespoon coarsely chopped fresh
    flat-leaf parsley**

**1 tablespoon coarsely chopped
    fresh tarragon**

lemon wedges (optional)

1   Boil, steam or microwave squash and zucchini until just tender; drain.

2   Meanwhile, heat 2 teaspoons of the oil in medium non-stick skillet; cook fish, uncovered, until browned both sides and cooked as desired. Remove from skillet; cover to keep warm.

3   Heat remaining oil in same cleaned skillet; cook tomato and juice, stirring, until just hot. Remove from heat; stir in herbs. Serve vegetables with fish, tomato mixture, and lemon wedges, if desired.

SERVES 4
per serving 3.3g carbohydrate; 17.4g fat; 299 cal; 32.2g protein

salmon with buttered almonds

PREPARATION TIME 10 MINUTES   COOKING TIME 10 MINUTES

¼ cup all-purpose flour

½ teaspoon salt

½ teaspoon ground white pepper

eight 4-ounce salmon fillets

2 tablespoons olive oil

6 tablespoons butter

½ cup sliced almonds

3 cups (4 ounces) baby spinach

2 tablespoons fresh lemon juice

1   Combine flour, salt and pepper in medium bowl; toss fish in flour mixture, shake off excess.

2   Heat oil with a third of the butter in large skillet; cook fish, uncovered, until browned both sides and cooked as desired. Drain on paper towel; cover to keep warm.

3   Heat remaining butter in same cleaned skillet; cook almonds, stirring constantly, until browned lightly. Add spinach; stir until spinach just wilts. Stir in juice; pour almond and spinach mixture over fish.

SERVES 4
per serving 7.3g carbohydrate; 38.8g fat; 545 cal; 42g protein

salade niçoise (see back cover)

PREPARATION TIME 20 MINUTES   COOKING TIME 5 MINUTES

7 ounces green beans, trimmed, chopped coarsely

8 ounces cherry tomatoes, halved

½ cup pitted small black olives

2 hothouse cucumbers, sliced thinly

1 medium red onion, sliced thinly

4½ cups (5 ounces) mesclun

6 hard-boiled eggs, quartered

three 6-ounce cans tuna in water

LIGHT VINAIGRETTE

1 teaspoon olive oil

¼ cup fresh lemon juice

1 clove garlic, crushed in garlic press

2 teaspoons dijon mustard

1 Boil, steam or microwave beans until just tender; drain. Rinse under cold water; drain.

2 Meanwhile, make light vinaigrette.

3 Place tomato, olives, cucumber, onion, mesclun and egg in large bowl with vinaigrette; toss gently to combine. Divide salad among serving plates.

4 Gently flake tuna over salad in large chunks.

LIGHT VINAIGRETTE   Combine ingredients in screw-top jar; shake well.

SERVES 4
per serving 10.9g carbohydrate; 13.8g fat; 358 cal; 46.8g protein

tarragon and lime scallops

PREPARATION TIME 15 MINUTES   COOKING TIME 10 MINUTES

Uncooked scallops and lime wedges can be skewered up to 4 hours ahead. Cover; refrigerate until required.
Soak 24 bamboo skewers in water for at least an hour prior to use to prevent splintering or scorching.

24 sea scallops (about 1 pound)

2 tablespoons coarsely chopped fresh tarragon

¼ cup lime juice

⅓ cup olive oil

2 medium heads belgian endive, shredded coarsely

¼ cup firmly packed fresh flat-leaf parsley leaves

3 limes

1 Rinse scallops under cold water; dry with paper towel. Combine scallops in medium bowl with tarragon, 1 tablespoon juice and 1 tablespoon oil; toss to coat scallops all over.

2 Place endive and parsley in medium bowl; add remaining juice and oil. Toss gently to combine.

3 Cut each lime into eight wedges. Thread one scallop and one lime wedge on each skewer. Cook, in batches, on heated oiled grill or grill pan until scallops are cooked through. Serve on endive salad.

SERVES 4
per serving 1.8g carbohydrate; 19.4g fat; 251 cal; 16.4g protein
tip If using metal skewers, oil them first to prevent the scallops from sticking.

jerusalem artichoke and smoked trout soup

PREPARATION TIME 30 MINUTES   COOKING TIME 1 HOUR 20 MINUTES

Crème fraîche is a commercially soured, mature thick cream; substitute sour cream, if preferred.
Pick over the trout and discard even the most minuscule bone fragments.

¼ cup olive oil

**32 small fresh jerusalem artichokes
   (about 2 pounds), trimmed, peeled**

1 tablespoon butter

3 shallots, chopped coarsely

1 clove garlic, quartered

8 cups chicken broth

2 tablespoons fresh lemon juice

½ cup crème fraîche

**1 medium hot-smoked trout
   (about 13 ounces), flaked**

1 tablespoon finely grated lemon peel

1   Preheat oven to hot.

2   Combine oil and artichokes in large casserole; toss artichokes to coat with oil. Roast in hot oven, uncovered, turning occasionally, about 1 hour or until artichokes are tender.

3   Melt butter in large soup pot; cook shallot and garlic, stirring, until both just soften. Add artichokes, broth and juice; bring to a boil. Simmer, uncovered, 10 minutes; cool 10 minutes.

4   Blend or process soup mixture, in batches, until smooth.

5   Return soup to same cleaned pot; stir over heat until hot. Stir in crème fraîche and trout, then divide soup among serving bowls; sprinkle each bowl with peel.

SERVES 6
per serving 7g carbohydrate; 23g fat; 294 cal; 15.1g protein
tip Jerusalem artichokes can be kept, sealed tightly in a plastic bag in the refrigerator, for about two weeks.

shrimp and scallion skewers

PREPARATION TIME 25 MINUTES (PLUS REFRIGERATION TIME)   COOKING TIME 10 MINUTES

Soak 12 bamboo skewers in water for at least an hour prior to use to prevent splintering or scorching.

**36 uncooked medium shrimp
   (about 3 pounds)**

2 tablespoons fresh lime juice

1 tablespoon olive oil

**2 cloves garlic, crushed in
   garlic press**

12 scallions

36 cherry tomatoes

2 limes, cut into wedges

1   Shell and devein shrimp, leaving tails intact. Combine shrimp in medium bowl with juice, oil and garlic. Cover; refrigerate 1 hour.

2   Cut scallions into 1½-inch lengths. Thread shrimp, scallion and tomato onto skewers. Cook on heated oiled grill or grill pan until shrimp change in color. Serve with lime wedges.

SERVES 4
per serving 4.3g carbohydrate; 6g fat; 267 cal; 40g protein
tip If using metal skewers, oil them first to prevent the shrimp from sticking.

shrimp, scallop and asparagus salad with ginger dressing

PREPARATION TIME 25 MINUTES   COOKING TIME 20 MINUTES

14 ounces uncooked
    medium shrimp

14 ounces sea scallops

1 bunch asparagus,
    trimmed, halved

⅓ cup coarsely chopped chives

2½ cups (4 ounces) baby
    spinach leaves

1 large red bell pepper,
    chopped coarsely

GINGER DRESSING

2-inch piece ginger, grated

1 tablespoon olive oil

2 tablespoons fresh lemon juice

1 teaspoon sugar

1 Peel and devein shrimp.

2 Cook shrimp, scallops and asparagus, in batches, on heated lightly oiled grill or grill pan until browned lightly and cooked as desired.

3 Meanwhile, make ginger dressing.

4 Place shrimp, scallops, asparagus, chives, spinach and pepper in bowl with dressing; toss gently to combine. Divide salad among serving bowls.

GINGER DRESSING Press grated ginger between two spoons over large bowl to extract juice; discard fibers. Whisk oil, lemon juice and sugar with ginger juice until combined.

SERVES 4
per serving 6g carbohydrate; 5.9g fat; 179 cal; 25g protein

shrimp, scallop and asparagus salad with ginger dressing

grilled tuna with cabbage salad

grilled tuna with cabbage salad

PREPARATION TIME 15 MINUTES   COOKING TIME 10 MINUTES

1 tablespoon olive oil

1 medium red onion, sliced thinly

2 cups finely shredded red cabbage

2 cups finely shredded

napa cabbage

¼ cup cider vinegar

1 large granny smith apple,

sliced thinly

1 cup loosely packed fresh flat-leaf

parsley leaves

four 5-ounce tuna steaks

1   Heat oil in wok or large skillet; stir-fry onion and cabbages about 2 minutes or until slightly softened. Add vinegar; boil 1 minute. Remove from heat. Add apple and parsley; toss to combine.

2   Meanwhile, cook tuna on heated lightly oiled grill or grill pan until browned both sides and cooked as desired. Serve tuna on cabbage salad.

SERVES 4
per serving 8.1g carbohydrate; 16.2g fat; 391 cal; 52.5g protein

manhattan clam chowder

PREPARATION TIME 25 MINUTES   COOKING TIME 35 MINUTES

The word "chowder" comes from chaudière, the French name for the huge cauldron used on seaport docks by fishermen to stew their fresh catch.

3 pounds clams

1 cup dry white wine

3 tablespoons butter

1 medium onion, chopped finely

2 slices bacon, chopped finely

2 stalks celery, trimmed,
   chopped finely

¼ cup all-purpose flour

3 cups fish broth

14 ounces canned
   crushed tomatoes

3 cups water

1 tablespoon fresh thyme leaves

2 bay leaves

2 pounds fennel, cut into
   ½-inch cubes

¼ cup coarsely chopped fresh
   flat-leaf parsley

1   Rinse clams under cold water; combine with wine in medium saucepan with a tight-fitting lid. Bring to a boil; steam, covered tightly, about 5 minutes or until clams have opened (discard any that do not). Strain clams over large bowl; reserve ¼ cup cooking liquid.

2   Melt butter in large soup pot; cook onion, stirring, until soft. Add bacon and celery; cook, stirring, 5 minutes. Add flour; cook, stirring, until mixture thickens and bubbles. Gradually stir in broth, then add undrained crushed tomatoes and the water; cook, stirring, until mixture boils and thickens. Stir in thyme, bay leaves and fennel; cook, covered, stirring occasionally, about 15 minutes or until fennel is tender.

3   Just before serving, stir clams, reserved cooking liquid and parsley into chowder.

SERVES 6
per serving 11.1g carbohydrate; 7.8g fat; 203 cal; 14.9g protein

tom yum goong
(spicy thai shrimp soup) (see back cover)

PREPARATION TIME 20 MINUTES   COOKING TIME 20 MINUTES

2 pounds large uncooked shrimp

1 tablespoon peanut oil

1 stalk fresh lemongrass,
    chopped coarsely

2 cloves garlic, quartered

1-inch piece fresh ginger,
    chopped coarsely

12 cups water

2 tablespoons fish sauce

¼ cup lime juice

2 long red chiles, sliced thinly

3 scallions, sliced thinly

⅓ cup loosely packed fresh
    cilantro leaves

¼ cup coarsely chopped fresh mint

1 Peel and devein shrimp; reserve meat and shells separately.

2 Heat oil in soup pot; cook shells and tails, stirring, about 3 minutes or until deep orange in color. Add lemongrass, garlic and ginger, stirring until fragrant.

3 Add the water; cover, bring to a boil. Reduce heat; simmer, uncovered, 10 minutes. Strain broth through cheesecloth into large heatproof bowl; discard solids.

4 Return broth to same cleaned pot; bring to a boil. Reduce heat, add shrimp meat; cook until shrimp meat is changed in color. Remove from heat; stir in sauce and juice. Serve soup topped with chile, scallion, cilantro and mint.

SERVES 4
per serving 2.1g carbohydrate; 5.5g fat; 170 cal; 27.1g protein

salmon teriyaki

PREPARATION TIME 10 MINUTES (PLUS STANDING TIME)   COOKING TIME 10 MINUTES

4 salmon fillets (about 1½ pounds), skinned

½ cup finely shredded daikon

TERIYAKI MARINADE

⅔ cup soy sauce

⅔ cup mirin

2 tablespoons sake

1 tablespoon sugar

1 Make teriyaki marinade.

2 Place salmon in teriyaki marinade for 10 minutes, turning occasionally. Drain salmon over medium bowl; reserve marinade.

3 Stand daikon in small bowl of iced water for 15 minutes; drain well.

4 Cook salmon on heated oiled grill or grill pan, brushing occasionally with a little of the reserved marinade, until cooked as desired. Bring remaining reserved marinade to a boil in small saucepan. Reduce heat; simmer 5 minutes or until sauce thickens slightly.

5 Serve salmon with daikon; drizzle with sauce.

TERIYAKI MARINADE Combine ingredients in medium bowl; stir until sugar dissolves.

SERVES 4
per serving 11.3g carbohydrate; 12.6g fat; 336 cal; 36.6g protein
tip Bought teriyaki sauce may be used, but it's stronger than homemade. Dilute it with mirin, sake or water.

fajitas and guacamole

PREPARATION TIME 15 MINUTES (PLUS REFRIGERATION TIME)   COOKING TIME 20 MINUTES

1¼-pound piece boneless beef rib steak, cut into thin 1-inch-wide slices

2 cloves garlic, crushed in garlic press

¼ cup fresh lemon juice

1½ teaspoons ground cumin

½ teaspoon cayenne

2 tablespoons olive oil

1 small yellow bell pepper

1 small red bell pepper

12 small corn tortillas

13 ounces jarred chunky salsa

GUACAMOLE

2 medium avocados

2 medium tomatoes, seeded, chopped finely

1 small red onion, chopped finely

2 tablespoons fresh lime juice

2 tablespoons coarsely chopped fresh cilantro

1 Place beef in medium bowl with garlic, juice, spices and oil, toss to coat beef in marinade. Cover; refrigerate 3 hours.

2 Quarter peppers; remove seeds and membranes. Roast peppers under broiler, skin-side up, until skin blisters and blackens. Cover with plastic wrap or paper for 5 minutes. Peel away skin; cut peppers into thin strips.

3 Cook beef, in batches, on heated oiled grill or grill pan until browned all over and cooked as desired; cover to keep warm. Reheat pepper strips on same heated grill.

4 Meanwhile, make guacamole.

5 Serve beef and peppers immediately, accompanied by guacamole, tortillas and salsa.

GUACAMOLE Mash avocados roughly in medium bowl; add remaining ingredients, mix to combine.

SERVES 4
per serving 11.9g carbohydrate; 35.9g fat; 522 cal; 37.7g protein

carpaccio with fennel salad

PREPARATION TIME 10 MINUTES (PLUS FREEZING TIME)

14 ounces filet mignon, in one piece

2 medium bulbs fennel

2 stalks celery, trimmed

**2 tablespoons finely chopped fresh
  flat-leaf parsley**

2 tablespoons fresh lemon juice

1 clove garlic, crushed in garlic press

¼ teaspoon sugar

½ teaspoon dijon mustard

⅓ cup olive oil

1   Remove any excess fat from filet mignon, wrap tightly in plastic wrap; freeze about 1 hour or until partially frozen. Using sharp knife, slice filet mignon as thinly as possible.

2   Meanwhile, slice fennel and celery finely. Toss in medium bowl with remaining ingredients.

3   Arrange raw filet mignon slices (carpaccio) in single layer on serving plates; top with fennel salad.

SERVES 4
per serving   4.5g carbohydrate; 22.1g fat; 307 cal; 22.9g protein

teriyaki steak

PREPARATION TIME 10 MINUTES (PLUS REFRIGERATION TIME)   COOKING TIME 10 MINUTES

You need about a quarter of a head of savoy cabbage for this recipe.

1½ pounds london broil

¼ cup rice vinegar

2 tablespoons kecap manis

2 teaspoons light brown sugar

¼ cup lime juice

1 clove garlic, crushed in garlic press

**2 red serrano chiles, seeded,
  chopped finely**

1 teaspoon sesame oil

1 tablespoon peanut oil

1 large carrot, cut into matchsticks

**7 ounces savoy cabbage,
  shredded finely**

japanese pickled cucumber (optional)

1   Combine beef, vinegar, kecap manis, sugar, juice, garlic, chile and sesame oil in large bowl, cover; refrigerate 3 hours or overnight. Drain beef; reserve marinade.

2   Heat peanut oil in wok or large skillet; stir-fry beef, in batches, until browned all over. Cover beef to keep warm.

3   Pour reserved marinade into wok; bring to a boil. Boil, uncovered, until sauce reduces by a third. Divide combined carrot and cabbage among serving plates; top with beef, drizzle with sauce. Serve with japanese pickled cucumber, if desired.

SERVES 4
per serving   11.5g carbohydrate; 18.4g fat; 388 cal; 43g protein
tip   Kecap manis can be found in Asian markets and in the Asian food section of some supermarkets.

sweet and sour grilled beef

PREPARATION TIME 20 MINUTES (PLUS REFRIGERATION TIME)
COOKING TIME 5 MINUTES

This is a loose interpretation of one of our favorite Thai dishes, yum nuah,
and is a good introduction to the flavors of Southeast Asian cuisine.

1¼ pounds london broil

2 teaspoons sesame oil

3 teaspoons sugar

¼ cup soy sauce

1 cup loosely packed fresh
　　mint leaves

1 cup loosely packed fresh
　　cilantro leaves

½ cup loosely packed fresh
　　basil leaves

6 scallions, sliced thinly

5 shallots, sliced thinly

8 ounces cherry tomatoes, halved

1 hothouse cucumber, seeded,
　　sliced thinly

2 cups (3½ ounces) mesclun

SWEET AND SOUR DRESSING

½ cup lime juice

¼ cup fish sauce

1 teaspoon sugar

2 red serrano chiles, sliced thinly

1   Place beef in shallow dish; brush all over with oil, sugar and
     sauce. Cover; refrigerate 30 minutes.

2   Meanwhile, combine herbs, scallion, shallot, tomato and cucumber
     in large bowl; toss gently to combine.

3   Make sweet and sour dressing.

4   Cook beef on heated oiled grill or grill pan until charred lightly and
     cooked as desired. Let stand, covered, 10 minutes; slice thinly.

5   Place beef and mesclun in bowl with herb mixture.
     Add sweet and sour dressing; toss gently to combine.

SWEET AND SOUR DRESSING   Combine ingredients in
screw-top jar; shake well.

SERVES 4
per serving   11.3g carbohydrate; 13.1g fat; 324 cal; 39g protein

souvlaki with greek salad

PREPARATION TIME 30 MINUTES (PLUS REFRIGERATION TIME) COOKING TIME 15 MINUTES

Souvlaki is a Greek specialty: delectably tender meat skewers which have been marinated in an herb, lemon and olive oil mixture. Soak eight bamboo skewers in water for at least an hour prior to use to prevent splintering or scorching.

1½ pounds boneless beef rib steak, cut into 1-inch cubes

1 large onion, cut into wedges

¼ cup olive oil

¼ cup fresh lemon juice

1 tablespoon dried oregano

GREEK SALAD

3 medium plum tomatoes, chopped coarsely

2 hothouse cucumbers, chopped coarsely

1 small red onion, sliced thinly

1 large green bell pepper, chopped coarsely

½ cup pitted kalamata olives

5 ounces feta cheese, chopped coarsely

1 tablespoon olive oil

1 tablespoon fresh lemon juice

2 teaspoons fresh oregano leaves

1   Thread beef and onion alternately on skewers; place souvlaki, in single layer, in large shallow casserole. Combine oil, juice and dried oregano in measuring cup; pour over souvlaki. Cover; refrigerate 3 hours or overnight.

2   Make greek salad.

3   Cook souvlaki, in batches, on heated oiled grill or grill pan until browned all over and cooked as desired. Serve souvlaki with greek salad.

GREEK SALAD Combine tomato, cucumber, onion, pepper, olives and cheese in large bowl. Place remaining ingredients in screw-top jar; shake well. Pour dressing over salad in bowl; toss gently to combine.

SERVES 4
per serving 11.7g carbohydrate; 40g fat; 613 cal; 51.8g protein
tip If using metal skewers, oil them first to prevent meat from sticking.

laila's lamb kofta with spiced yogurt

PREPARATION TIME 30 MINUTES (PLUS REFRIGERATION TIME)   COOKING TIME 20 MINUTES

Kofta is a Middle Eastern specialty: meatballs made from lamb, bulgur, pine nuts and herbs.
Uncooked kofta and spiced yogurt can be made a day ahead. Cover separately; refrigerate until required.

2 tablespoons bulgur

½ pound lean ground lamb

1 egg

1 small onion, chopped finely

2 tablespoons pine nuts, chopped finely

1 tablespoon finely chopped fresh mint

1 tablespoon finely chopped fresh
   flat-leaf parsley

vegetable oil, for shallow-frying

1 head iceberg lettuce, shredded

1 large tomato, chopped coarsely

1 small red onion, sliced thinly

⅓ cup loosely packed fresh flat-leaf
   parsley leaves

SPICED YOGURT

2 red serrano chiles, seeded, chopped finely

1 tablespoon finely chopped fresh mint

1 tablespoon finely chopped fresh
   flat-leaf parsley

1 tablespoon finely chopped fresh cilantro

1 clove garlic, crushed in garlic press

½ teaspoon ground cumin

10 ounces yogurt

1 Cover bulgur with cold water in small bowl; let stand 10 minutes. Drain; pat dry with paper towel to remove as much water as possible.

2 Using one hand, combine bulgur in large bowl with lamb, egg, onion, nuts and herbs. Roll rounded tablespoons of the lamb mixture into kofta balls. Place on tray, cover; refrigerate 30 minutes.

3 Heat oil in large skillet; shallow-fry kofta, in batches, until browned all over and cooked through. Drain on paper towel.

4 Meanwhile, place remaining ingredients in medium bowl; toss to combine.

5 Make spiced yogurt. Serve kofta on salad with spiced yogurt.

SPICED YOGURT Combine ingredients in medium bowl.

SERVES 4
per serving 10.7g carbohydrate; 25.7g fat; 358 cal; 20.6g protein

pork and snow pea stir-fry with sesame seeds

PREPARATION TIME 10 MINUTES COOKING TIME 10 MINUTES

1 tablespoon sesame oil

1¼ pounds snow peas, trimmed

2 scallions, sliced thinly

1 tablespoon toasted sesame seeds

14 ounces chinese barbecued pork, sliced thinly

1 Heat oil in wok or large skillet; stir-fry snow peas and scallion about 5 minutes or until snow peas are just tender.

2 Add seeds and pork to wok; stir-fry briefly to combine.

SERVES 4
per serving 10g carbohydrate; 21.6g fat; 337 cal; 26.2g protein

pork larb

PREPARATION TIME 20 MINUTES   COOKING TIME 20 MINUTES

Larb is a classic Thai salad that can be made with ground beef, chicken or pork, or vegetables.

1 tablespoon peanut oil

2 tablespoons finely chopped
**   fresh lemongrass**

2 red serrano chiles, chopped finely

2 cloves garlic, crushed in
**   garlic press**

3-inch piece fresh ginger, grated

3 pounds lean ground pork

2 tablespoons fish sauce

⅔ cup lime juice

⅔ cup loosely packed fresh
**   mint leaves**

½ cup loosely packed fresh
**   cilantro leaves**

4 scallions, sliced thinly

4 shallots, sliced thinly

8 large leaves iceberg lettuce

1   Heat oil in large non-stick skillet; cook lemongrass, chile, garlic and ginger, stirring, about 2 minutes or until fragrant. Add pork; cook, stirring, about 10 minutes or until cooked through. Add sauce and half of the juice; cook, stirring, 5 minutes. Transfer mixture to large bowl; stir in herbs, scallion, shallot and remaining juice.

2   Place two lettuce leaves together to form a "bowl" on each serving plate; divide larb among leaves.

SERVES 4
per serving 3.5g carbohydrate; 31.3g fat; 612 cal; 77.9g protein

grilled chicken with herbed butter, almonds and gruyère

PREPARATION TIME 15 MINUTES   COOKING TIME 20 MINUTES

5 tablespoons butter, softened

1 tablespoon finely chopped fresh
**   flat-leaf parsley**

2 teaspoons fresh lemon juice

4 skinless, boneless chicken breasts
**   (about 1½ pounds)**

3 medium carrots, cut into thin
**   3-inch matchsticks**

8 ounces baby green beans

¼ cup toasted slivered almonds

¼ cup finely grated gruyère cheese

1   Combine butter, parsley and juice in small bowl, cover; refrigerate.

2   Cook chicken on heated oiled grill or grill pan until browned both sides and cooked through. Cover loosely to keep warm.

3   Meanwhile, boil, steam or microwave carrot and beans, separately, until tender; drain.

4   Serve chicken on vegetables; divide parsley butter among chicken pieces, sprinkle with nuts and cheese.

SERVES 4
per serving 6.1g carbohydrate; 27.5g fat; 447 cal; 44.2g protein

asian chicken broth (see page 344)

PREPARATION TIME 30 MINUTES   COOKING TIME 20 MINUTES

Any asian greens can be used in this recipe. Try it with bok choy, choy sum, or gai larn (also known as chinese broccoli).

4 cups chicken broth

4 cups water

1 stalk lemongrass, finely chopped

1½-inch piece fresh ginger,
sliced thinly

2 red serrano chiles, sliced thinly

2 tablespoons soy sauce

1 tablespoon fresh lime juice

1 tablespoon fish sauce

1 pound asian greens, trimmed,
chopped coarsely

3 scallions, sliced thinly

⅓ cup loosely packed fresh
cilantro leaves

CHICKEN DUMPLINGS

14 ounces lean ground chicken

1 tablespoon finely chopped
fresh cilantro

2 cloves garlic, crushed in
garlic press

1   Combine broth, the water, lemongrass, ginger, chile and soy sauce in soup pot; bring to a boil. Reduce heat; simmer, uncovered, about 5 minutes.

2   Meanwhile, make chicken dumplings.

3   Add chicken dumplings to simmering broth; simmer, covered, about 5 minutes or until dumplings are cooked through.

4   Add juice, fish sauce, greens and scallion to broth; cook, uncovered, about 2 minutes or just until greens wilt. Stir in cilantro just before serving.

CHICKEN DUMPLINGS Combine ground chicken, cilantro and garlic in small bowl. Roll level tablespoons of mixture into balls.

SERVES 4
per serving 4.3g carbohydrate; 9.4g fat; 202 cal; 24.6g protein

mixed satay sticks

PREPARATION TIME 20 MINUTES (PLUS REFRIGERATION TIME)   COOKING TIME 15 MINUTES

Soak 12 bamboo skewers in water for at least an hour prior to use to prevent splintering or scorching.

½ pound skinless, boneless chicken breasts
½ pound beef tenderloin
½ pound boneless pork loin
2 cloves garlic, crushed in garlic press
2 teaspoons light brown sugar
¼ teaspoon hot chili sauce (such as sambal oelek or sriracha)
1 teaspoon ground turmeric
¼ teaspoon curry powder
½ teaspoon ground cumin
½ teaspoon ground coriander
2 tablespoons peanut oil
2 cups (3½ ounces) mesclun

SATAY SAUCE

½ cup roasted unsalted peanuts
2 tablespoons red curry paste
¾ cup unsweetened coconut milk
¼ cup chicken broth
1 tablespoon fresh lime juice
1 tablespoon light brown sugar

1 Cut chicken, beef and pork into long ½-inch-thick strips; thread strips onto skewers. Place skewers, in single layer, on tray or in shallow casserole; brush with combined garlic, sugar, chili sauce, spices and oil. Cover; refrigerate 3 hours or overnight.

2 Make satay sauce.

3 Cook skewers on heated oiled grill or grill pan until browned all over and cooked as desired. Place mesclun in medium bowl; drizzle with ¼ cup satay sauce. Serve skewers on a bed of mesclun with extra satay sauce for dipping.

SATAY SAUCE Blend or process nuts until chopped finely; add paste, process until just combined. Bring coconut milk to a boil in small saucepan; add peanut mixture, whisking until smooth. Reduce heat, add broth; cook, stirring, about 3 minutes or until sauce thickens slightly. Add juice and sugar, stirring, until sugar dissolves.

SERVES 4
per serving 9.9g carbohydrate; 36.5g fat; 561 cal; 49.2g protein
tips Sambal oelek or sriracha can be found in Asian markets and in the Asian food section of some supermarkets.
If using metal skewers, oil them first to prevent the meats from sticking.

mediterranean chicken salad

PREPARATION TIME 30 MINUTES   COOKING TIME 15 MINUTES

Chicken can be poached a day ahead.

1½ cups chicken broth

½ cup dry white wine

4 skinless, boneless chicken breasts
   (about 1½ pounds)

2 medium yellow bell peppers

3½ cups (5½ ounces) baby arugula leaves

8 ounces pear tomatoes, halved

⅓ cup pitted black olives

ANCHOVY DRESSING

½ cup firmly packed fresh basil leaves

½ cup extra virgin olive oil

2 tablespoons finely grated parmesan cheese

2 anchovy fillets, drained

1 tablespoon fresh lemon juice

1   Bring broth and wine to a boil in large skillet. Add chicken, reduce heat; simmer, covered, about 8 minutes or until cooked through, turning once halfway through cooking time. Stand chicken in broth for 10 minutes; slice chicken thinly, reserve broth for another use, if desired.

2   Meanwhile, quarter peppers; remove and discard seeds and membranes. Roast under broiler, skin-side up, until skin blisters and blackens. Cover pepper pieces with plastic wrap or paper for 5 minutes. Peel away skin; slice pepper thinly.

3   Make anchovy dressing.

4   Place chicken and pepper in large bowl with arugula, tomato and olives, add anchovy dressing; toss gently to combine.

ANCHOVY DRESSING Blend or process ingredients until smooth.

SERVES 4
per serving 8.7g carbohydrate; 34.6g fat; 541 cal; 44.1g protein

chicken with salsa verde

PREPARATION TIME 10 MINUTES   COOKING TIME 20 MINUTES

1 tablespoon olive oil

4 skinless, boneless chicken breasts
   (about 1½ pounds), halved lengthwise

2 medium zucchini, quartered lengthwise

SALSA VERDE

½ cup coarsely chopped fresh
   flat-leaf parsley

¼ cup coarsely chopped fresh basil

1 clove garlic, crushed in garlic press

2 teaspoons drained baby capers

1 teaspoon dijon mustard

¼ cup olive oil

2 teaspoons red wine vinegar

1   Heat oil in large skillet; cook chicken, in batches, until browned both sides and cooked through. Cover to keep warm.

2   Boil, steam or microwave zucchini until tender; drain.

3   Make salsa verde.

4   Serve chicken on zucchini topped with salsa verde.

SALSA VERDE Combine parsley, basil, garlic and capers in small bowl; whisk in mustard, oil and vinegar until salsa thickens.

SERVES 4
per serving 2.5g carbohydrate; 23.1g fat; 382 cal; 41.2g protein

smoked chicken and artichoke salad with caper dressing

PREPARATION TIME 30 MINUTES   COOKING TIME 20 MINUTES

2 medium yellow bell peppers

4 baby eggplants, sliced thinly

2 large zucchini, sliced thinly

2 tablespoons olive oil

12 ounces jarred marinated
    artichokes, drained

1½ pounds smoked chicken breast,
    sliced thinly

3 bunches (about 14 ounces)
    watercress, trimmed

CAPER DRESSING

2 hard-boiled eggs, quartered

1 tablespoon drained capers

2 tablespoons white wine vinegar

2 tablespoons coarsely chopped
    fresh oregano

1 clove garlic, quartered

⅓ cup olive oil

1 Quarter peppers; remove and discard seeds and membranes. Roast under broiler, skin-side up, until skin blisters and blackens. Cover pepper pieces with plastic wrap or paper for 5 minutes. Peel away skin; slice pepper thinly.

2 Meanwhile, make caper dressing.

3 Brush eggplant and zucchini with oil; cook, in batches, on heated oiled grill or grill pan until browned lightly and just tender. Cool.

4 Place pepper, eggplant and zucchini in large bowl with artichokes, chicken and dressing; toss gently to combine. Serve salad on watercress.

CAPER DRESSING Blend or process egg, capers, vinegar, oregano and garlic until chopped finely. With motor running, add oil in a thin, steady stream until dressing thickens.

SERVES 4
per serving 5.6g carbohydrate; 40.1g fat; 553 cal; 42.7g protein

lemony chicken with baby spinach salad

PREPARATION TIME 15 MINUTES   COOKING TIME 15 MINUTES

2 pounds skinless, boneless chicken
    breast tenders

2 tablespoons fresh lemon juice

1 tablespoon fresh thyme leaves

½ cup olive oil

2 cups (3½ ounces) baby spinach leaves

1 small red onion, chopped finely

8 ounces cherry tomatoes, halved

1 cup (3 ounces) alfalfa sprouts

⅓ cup red wine vinegar

½ teaspoon dijon mustard

1 Place chicken in large bowl with juice, thyme and 2 tablespoons of the oil; toss to coat chicken in lemon mixture. Cook chicken, in batches, on heated oiled grill or grill pan until browned and cooked through.

2 Meanwhile, combine spinach, onion, tomato and sprouts in large bowl. Combine remaining oil, vinegar and mustard in screw-top jar; shake well. Drizzle dressing over salad; toss gently to combine. Serve salad topped with chicken.

SERVES 4
per serving 7.5g carbohydrate; 33.9g fat; 553 cal; 54g protein

mexican tortilla soup

PREPARATION TIME 25 MINUTES   COOKING TIME 45 MINUTES

The guajillo chile, sometimes called travieso ("impish", because its heat can be deceiving), is the dried form of the fresh mirasol chile. So deep-red in color it is almost black, the medium-hot guajillo chile must be soaked in boiling water before being used.

3 guajillo chiles

¾ cup boiling water

2 teaspoons vegetable oil

1 large onion, chopped coarsely

3 cloves garlic, crushed in
  garlic press

4 medium tomatoes,
  chopped coarsely

6 cups chicken broth

2 tablespoons fresh lime juice

2 cups cold water

12 ounces skinless, boneless
  chicken breast,
  chopped coarsely

4 small corn tortillas

vegetable oil, for shallow-frying,
  extra

1 small red onion, chopped finely

1 small avocado, chopped finely

1 medium tomato, seeded,
  chopped finely, extra

1   Remove stems from chiles. Place chiles in small heatproof bowl; cover with the boiling water, let stand 10 minutes.

2   Meanwhile, heat oil in large soup pot; cook onion and garlic, stirring, until onion is soft. Add coarsely chopped tomatoes and undrained chiles; cook, stirring, about 10 minutes or until tomato is pulpy. Blend or process chile mixture until pureed.

3   Return chile mixture to same cleaned pot; stir in broth, juice and the cold water. Bring to a boil, add chicken; simmer, uncovered, about 25 minutes or until chicken is cooked through.

4   Meanwhile, slice tortillas into ½-inch strips. Heat extra oil in large skillet; shallow-fry tortilla strips, in batches, until browned lightly. Drain on paper towel.

5   Just before serving, divide soup among serving bowls; sprinkle with tortilla strips and combined red onion, avocado and finely chopped tomato.

SERVES 6
per serving 8.8g carbohydrate; 10.3g fat; 205 cal; 18.9g protein
tips Tortilla strips can be fried a day before required and kept in an airtight container. To keep the fat count down, crisp tortilla strips in a hot oven. Other dried Mexican chiles can be substituted for the guajillos but the taste of the soup will be different.

leek and smoked chicken salad with orange-mustard dressing

PREPARATION TIME 35 MINUTES

1 small leek

1 large carrot

1 medium red bell pepper,
   sliced thinly

1 medium yellow bell pepper,
   sliced thinly

1 pound smoked chicken breast,
   sliced thinly

7 ounces snow peas, trimmed,
   sliced thinly

1 head green leaf lettuce,
   trimmed, torn

ORANGE-MUSTARD DRESSING

2 tablespoons fresh orange juice

2 tablespoons apple cider vinegar

2 teaspoons finely grated
   orange peel

1 tablespoon grainy mustard

1 tablespoon sour cream

¼ cup olive oil

1 Make orange-mustard dressing.

2 Cut leek into 3 inch lengths. Cut each in half lengthwise;
   slice into matchstick-sized pieces. Cut carrot into 3-inch
   pieces. Cut each lengthwise into thin slices; cut slices
   into matchstick-sized pieces.

3 Place leek and carrot in large bowl with dressing and
   remaining ingredients; toss gently to combine.

ORANGE-MUSTARD DRESSING Combine ingredients in
screw-top jar; shake well.

SERVES 4
per serving 10.4g carbohydrate; 25g fat; 408 cal; 35.4g protein

chicken and vegetable soup

PREPARATION TIME 25 MINUTES   COOKING TIME 15 MINUTES

2 cups water

6 cups chicken broth

1 medium carrot, cut into
   ½-inch pieces

2 stalks celery, trimmed,
   sliced thinly

½ small cauliflower, cut into florets

12 ounces skinless, boneless
   chicken breast tenders,
   sliced thinly

2 large zucchini, cut into
   ½-inch pieces

5 ounces snow peas, trimmed,
   sliced thinly

3 scallions, sliced thinly

1   Combine the water and broth in soup pot; bring to a boil. Add carrot, celery and cauliflower; return to a boil. Reduce heat; simmer, covered, about 10 minutes or until just tender.

2   Add chicken and zucchini; cook, covered, 5 minutes or until chicken is cooked through.

3   Stir in snow peas and scallion.

SERVES 4
per serving 10.2g carbohydrate; 4g fat; 190 cal; 28.2g protein

chicken and vegetable soup

mixed mushrooms with garlic and chives

mixed mushrooms with garlic and chives

PREPARATION TIME 15 MINUTES   COOKING TIME 40 MINUTES

1¾ pounds portobello mushrooms

4 ounces shiitake mushrooms

4 ounces brown mushrooms

4 ounces medium
   oyster mushrooms

vegetable-oil spray

¼ cup red wine vinegar

1 tablespoon olive oil

2 cloves garlic, crushed in
   garlic press

⅔ cup coarsely chopped
   fresh chives

2 cups loosely packed fresh
   flat-leaf parsley leaves
   1 medium red onion,
   sliced thinly

1 Preheat oven to slow.

2 Cut portobello mushrooms into large pieces; combine with
   remaining mushrooms. Spread mushrooms, in single layer,
   in two shallow casseroles. Spray mushrooms lightly with
   vegetable-oil spray; cook in slow oven, uncovered, about
   40 minutes or until tender.

3 Stir vinegar, oil and garlic in small saucepan over heat 1 minute;
   combine with mushrooms, chives, parsley and onion in large bowl.
   Serve warm or cold.

SERVES 4
per serving 6.7g carbohydrate; 6.3g fat; 132 cal; 11.6g protein

curried eggs with sautéed spinach

PREPARATION TIME 10 MINUTES   COOKING TIME 25 MINUTES

¼ cup peanut oil

8 hard-boiled eggs

1 teaspoon black mustard seeds

1 clove garlic, crushed in garlic press

1 teaspoon grated fresh ginger

1 small onion, sliced thinly

1 teaspoon ground cumin

2 tablespoons mild curry powder

½ teaspoon ground cardamom

14 ounces canned crushed tomatoes

1 teaspoon sugar

½ cup water

1 tablespoon peanut oil, extra

1 clove garlic, crushed in garlic press, extra

7 ounces spinach

1   Heat oil in medium skillet; cook eggs, stirring occasionally, until eggs are well browned all over. Drain on paper towel; at this stage, eggs will have a crusty surface.

2   Discard all but 1 tablespoon of the oil from skillet. Reheat oil in skillet; cook seeds, covered, about 30 seconds or until seeds begin to crack.

3   Stir in garlic, ginger and onion; cook, stirring constantly, until onion is soft. Stir in cumin, curry powder, cardamom, undrained tomatoes, sugar and the water.

4   Bring sauce to a boil. Add eggs; reduce heat. Cover; simmer about 5 minutes or until sauce is thickened slightly.

5   Meanwhile, heat extra oil in medium deep skillet. Add extra garlic; cook until fragrant. Add spinach; cook, stirring, until just wilted. Serve curry with spinach.

SERVES 4
per serving 7.3g carbohydrate; 25.3g fat; 317 cal; 15.6g protein

mixed vegetable and herb frittata

PREPARATION TIME 25 MINUTES   COOKING TIME 20 MINUTES

2 teaspoons olive oil

2 cloves garlic, crushed in garlic press

2 medium zucchini, sliced thinly

3 ounces brown mushrooms, sliced thinly

6 ounces baby spinach leaves

3 eggs

8 egg whites

¼ cup coarsely chopped fresh basil

¼ cup coarsely grated parmesan cheese

TOMATO SALAD

8 ounces yellow pear tomatoes, halved

8 ounces cherry tomatoes, halved

¼ cup loosely packed fresh baby basil leaves

2 tablespoons balsamic vinegar

1   Make tomato salad.

2   Heat oil in large skillet; cook garlic and zucchini until zucchini is just tender. Add mushrooms and spinach; cook, stirring, until spinach is just wilted.

3   Meanwhile, beat eggs and egg whites lightly together in medium bowl; stir in parsley.

4   Preheat broiler.

5   Add egg mixture to pan; cook, uncovered, over medium heat about 10 minutes or until set. Sprinkle with cheese; place under preheated broiler until frittata is browned lightly. Serve with salad.

TOMATO SALAD   Combine tomatoes and parsley in medium serving bowl. Stir in vinegar just before serving.

SERVES 4
per serving 4.6g carbohydrate; 8.5g fat; 166 cal; 17.2g protein

pan-fried tofu with cabbage salad

PREPARATION TIME 20 MINUTES   COOKING TIME 15 MINUTES

You need about half a head of napa cabbage for this recipe.

2 pounds firm tofu

1 tablespoon finely chopped fresh lemongrass

2 red serrano chiles, sliced thinly

1 medium red onion, sliced thinly

1 cup (3½ ounces) fresh bean sprouts

4 cups finely shredded napa cabbage

¾ cup firmly packed fresh cilantro leaves

SWEET AND SOUR DRESSING

⅓ cup fresh lime juice

2 teaspoons light brown sugar

2 tablespoons soy sauce

1 Pat tofu all over with paper towel. Cut tofu into ¼-inch-thick slices. Place tofu slices, in single layer, on paper towel-lined tray; let stand at least 10 minutes.

2 Meanwhile, make sweet and sour dressing.

3 Cook tofu, in batches, in heated, lightly oiled large skillet until browned both sides.

4 Meanwhile, place lemongrass, chile, onion, sprouts, cabbage and cilantro in large bowl; toss to combine.

5 Place cabbage salad on serving platter; top with fried tofu slices, drizzle with dressing.

SWEET AND SOUR DRESSING Combine ingredients in small measuring cup; whisk until sugar dissolves.

SERVES 4
per serving 8.2g carbohydrate; 15.6g fat; 295 cal; 29.9g protein

vegetable and tofu skewers

PREPARATION TIME 20 MINUTES   COOKING TIME 15 MINUTES

Soak 12 bamboo skewers in water for at least an hour prior to use to prevent splintering or scorching.

7 ounces brown mushrooms

2 medium green bell peppers, cut into ¾-inch squares

1 medium red bell pepper, cut into ¾-inch squares

3 baby eggplants, cut into 1-inch pieces

12 ounces firm tofu, diced into 1-inch pieces

7 ounces yellow patty-pan squash, halved

2 cups (3½ ounces) baby arugula leaves

BLUE CHEESE DRESSING

2 ounces blue cheese

2 tablespoons buttermilk

7 ounces low-fat unflavored yogurt

1 small white onion, grated

1 clove garlic, crushed in garlic press

1 tablespoon finely chopped fresh chives

1 tablespoon fresh lemon juice

1 Thread mushrooms, peppers, eggplant, tofu and squash alternately onto skewers.

2 Cook skewers on heated, lightly oiled grill or grill pan until browned all over and cooked through.

3 Meanwhile, make blue cheese dressing.

4 Serve skewers on arugula; drizzle with dressing.

BLUE CHEESE DRESSING Crumble blue cheese into small bowl, add remaining ingredients; stir to combine.

SERVES 4
per serving 11.7g carbohydrate; 12.7g fat; 250 cal; 21.8g protein
tip If using metal skewers, oil them first to prevent the vegetables and tofu from sticking.

goat cheese-stuffed roasted peppers with tapenade

PREPARATION TIME 30 MINUTES   COOKING TIME 20 MINUTES

The name tapenade derives from "tapeno", the Provençal word for capers, a vital ingredient in this tangy condiment that perfectly complements goat cheese.

4 medium red bell peppers

10 ounces firm goat cheese

7 ounces fresh ricotta cheese

2 tablespoons sour cream

2 tablespoons extra virgin olive oil

1 tablespoon fresh basil leaves

cracked black pepper

TAPENADE

1 tablespoon drained capers

3 anchovy fillets, drained

½ cup pitted black olives

1 tablespoon fresh lemon juice

¼ cup extra virgin olive oil

1   Make tapenade.

2   Roast whole peppers under broiler until skin blisters and blackens. Cover peppers with plastic wrap or paper for 5 minutes; peel away skin. Slice off and discard top and bottom of each pepper; carefully remove and discard seeds and membranes from inside peppers. Trim pepper pieces to 3 inches in depth; cut each in half to make two 1½-inch "rings" (you will have eight rings).

3   Blend or process cheeses and sour cream until smooth. Fit one pepper ring inside a 2¼-inch round cutter, place on serving plate, spoon an eighth of the cheese mixture inside pepper ring; carefully remove cutter. Repeat with remaining pepper rings and cheese mixture.

4   Serve stuffed pepper rings with tapenade, drizzle with oil, sprinkle with basil leaves and cracked pepper.

TAPENADE   Blend or process ingredients until smooth.

SERVES 4
per serving   11.5g carbohydrate; 44.8g fat; 519 cal; 18.9g protein

herbed and spiced sashimi with ginger cabbage salad

PREPARATION TIME 45 MINUTES   COOKING TIME 5 MINUTES

Salmon and tuna sold as sashimi have to meet stringent guidelines regarding their handling and treatment after leaving the water; however, it is best to seek local advice from knowledgeable authorities before eating any raw fish. You need half of a medium head of napa cabbage for this recipe.

2 tablespoons sesame seeds

1 tablespoon black sesame seeds

2 teaspoons coriander seeds

1 teaspoon sea salt

½ teaspoon cracked black pepper

2 tablespoons finely chopped fresh chives

10-ounce piece sashimi tuna

10-ounce piece sashimi salmon

7 ounces green beans, trimmed, sliced thinly

6 trimmed red radishes

3 cups finely shredded napa cabbage

6 scallions, sliced thinly

2 cups (6 ounces) fresh bean sprouts

1 cup firmly packed fresh cilantro leaves

GINGER DRESSING

¾-inch piece fresh ginger, grated

2 tablespoons rice vinegar

2 tablespoons vegetable oil

2 teaspoons sesame oil

1 tablespoon mirin

1 tablespoon soy sauce

1   Dry-fry seeds in small skillet, stirring, until fragrant; cool. Using mortar and pestle, crush seeds; combine in large bowl with salt, pepper and chives.

2   Cut each piece of fish into three 2-inch-thick pieces. Roll each piece in seed mixture; enclose tightly, individually, in plastic wrap. Refrigerate until required.

3   Make ginger dressing.

4   Boil, steam or microwave beans until just tender; drain. Rinse beans under cold water; drain. Slice radishes thinly; cut slices into matchstick-sized pieces.

5   Combine beans and radish in large bowl with cabbage, scallion, sprouts, cilantro leaves and half of the dressing; toss gently to combine.

6   Unwrap fish; slice thinly. Divide fish and salad among serving plates; drizzle fish with remaining dressing.

GINGER DRESSING   Combine ingredients in screw-top jar; shake well.

SERVES 4
per serving 3.8g carbohydrate; 26.1g fat; 409 cal; 39.2g protein

lobster tails with avocado and red pepper sauce

PREPARATION TIME 20 MINUTES   COOKING TIME 20 MINUTES

4 uncooked medium lobster tails
   (about 3 pounds)

3 tablespoons butter, melted

2 cloves garlic, crushed in garlic press

AVOCADO PUREE

2 medium avocados

1 tablespoon fresh lime juice

RED PEPPER SAUCE

4 medium red bell peppers

1 tablespoon olive oil

1 medium white onion,
   chopped coarsely

1 clove garlic, crushed in garlic press

½ cup chicken broth

1   Make avocado puree and red pepper sauce.

2   Remove and discard skin from underneath lobster tails to expose flesh. Cut each tail in half lengthwise. Combine butter and garlic in small bowl; brush over lobster flesh. Cook lobster on heated oiled grill or grill pan, uncovered, until browned both sides and changed in color. Serve lobster with avocado puree and red pepper sauce.

AVOCADO PUREE   Blend or process avocados and juice until nearly smooth.

RED PEPPER SAUCE   Quarter peppers; remove and discard seeds and membranes. Cook pepper pieces, skin-side down, on heated oiled grill or grill pan, or skin-side up under a preheated broiler, until skin blisters and blackens. Cover pepper pieces with plastic wrap or paper for 5 minutes; peel away skin. Heat oil in small saucepan; cook onion and garlic, stirring, until onion is soft. Add pepper and broth; bring to a boil. Remove from heat; blend or process pepper mixture until nearly smooth.

SERVES 4
per serving   9.5g carbohydrate; 35.8g fat; 649 cal; 72.2g protein

tuna steaks with olive and feta salsa

PREPARATION TIME 10 MINUTES   COOKING TIME 5 MINUTES

1 tablespoon olive oil

1 tablespoon fresh lemon juice

¼ teaspoon cracked black pepper

four 7-ounce tuna steaks

OLIVE AND FETA SALSA

2 medium tomatoes, seeded, chopped

4 ounces pitted black olives, sliced

5 ounces feta cheese, chopped

¼ cup chopped fresh oregano leaves

1 tablespoon pine nuts, toasted

1   Make olive and feta salsa.

2   Combine oil, juice and pepper in small measuring cup; brush over tuna. Cook tuna on heated oiled grill or grill pan, uncovered, brushing occasionally with oil mixture, until browned both sides and cooked as desired. Serve immediately with olive and feta salsa.

OLIVE AND FETA SALSA   Combine all ingredients in small bowl.

SERVES 4
per serving   7.2g carbohydrate; 27.6g fat; 510 cal; 58.2g protein

salmon with peas and scallions

PREPARATION TIME 15 MINUTES   COOKING TIME 15 MINUTES

4 tablespoons butter

4 salmon fillets (1¾ pounds), skin on

2 cloves garlic, crushed in
   garlic press

2 medium onions, sliced thinly

¾ cup fish broth

2 tablespoons fresh lemon juice

1½ cups frozen peas

8 scallions, trimmed, cut into
   1½-inch pieces

1 tablespoon finely grated lemon peel

1 teaspoon coarse sea salt

1   Melt half of the butter in heated large skillet; cook salmon until browned both sides. Remove from skillet; cover to keep warm.

2   Melt remaining butter in same skillet; cook garlic and onion, stirring, until onion softens. Add broth, juice, peas and scallion; bring to a boil. Reduce heat; simmer, uncovered, 2 minutes.

3   Return salmon to skillet; sprinkle with peel and salt. Cook, uncovered, until salmon is cooked as desired.

SERVES 4
per serving 9.2g carbohydrate; 26.9g fat; 454 cal; 43.7g protein

balsamic-flavored octopus

PREPARATION TIME 20 MINUTES (PLUS REFRIGERATION TIME)   COOKING TIME 5 MINUTES

You need about half of a head of frisée for this recipe.

3 pounds baby octopus,
   thawed if frozen

2 cloves garlic, crushed in
   garlic press

¼ cup olive oil

¼ cup balsamic vinegar

1 tablespoon light brown sugar

2 teaspoons chopped fresh thyme

5 ounces frisée

2 tablespoons olive oil, extra

2 tablespoons balsamic vinegar, extra

1   Remove and discard heads and beaks from octopus; cut each octopus in half, combine in large bowl with garlic, oil, vinegar, sugar and thyme. Cover; refrigerate 3 hours or overnight.

2   Drain octopus over small bowl; reserve marinade. Just before serving, cook octopus, in batches, on heated oiled grill or grill pan, uncovered, until browned all over and just cooked through, brushing occasionally with reserved marinade. Serve with frisée, drizzled with combined extra oil and extra vinegar.

SERVES 4
per serving 8.8g carbohydrate; 26.8g fat; 501 cal; 55.9g protein

roast salmon with mango and lime mayonnaise

PREPARATION TIME 30 MINUTES   COOKING TIME 50 MINUTES

Mayonnaise can be made a day ahead and refrigerated, covered. Salmon can also be roasted a day ahead and served as a cold lunch.

3-pound whole salmon,
   gutted, scaled

1 lime, sliced thinly

2 sprigs fresh dill

vegetable-oil spray

2 tablespoons olive oil

1 tablespoon drained capers

2 cups (3½ ounces) baby arugula

MANGO AND LIME MAYONNAISE

1 egg yolk

¼ teaspoon dry mustard

¼ cup light olive oil

2 tablespoons olive oil

1 tablespoon fresh lime juice

½ teaspoon finely grated lime peel

1 small mango, peeled, quartered

1   Preheat oven to moderate.

2   Wash fish, pat dry inside and out with paper towel; place lime and dill inside cavity. Place two large pieces of foil, overlapping slightly, on baking sheet; spray lightly with vegetable-oil spray. Place fish on foil, fold foil over to enclose fish completely. Roast in moderate oven about 50 minutes or until cooked as desired.

3   Meanwhile, heat oil in small skillet; cook capers, stirring, until crisp. Drain on paper towel.

4   Make mango and lime mayonnaise.

5   Starting behind gills of salmon, peel away and discard skin; scrape away any dark flesh. Flake salmon coarsely; sprinkle with capers. Serve salmon warm or cold on arugula with mango and lime mayonnaise.

MANGO AND LIME MAYONNAISE   Blend or process egg yolk and mustard until smooth. With motor running, add combined oils gradually in thin stream until mixture is thick. Add remaining ingredients; blend until smooth.

SERVES 4
per serving 7.8g carbohydrate; 39.4g fat; 547 cal; 40.9g protein
tip Salmon is best served rare in the center so it remains moist.

shrimp salad with gazpacho salsa

PREPARATION TIME 35 MINUTES   COOKING TIME 2 MINUTES

Saffron is the dried stigma from the crocus. Buy it in small amounts and keep it, sealed
tightly, in the refrigerator to preserve its freshness.

2 pounds cooked
  extra-large shrimp

2 medium avocados

GAZPACHO SALSA

2 medium hothouse cucumbers,
  seeded, chopped finely

2 medium tomatoes, seeded,
  chopped finely

1 clove garlic, crushed in
  garlic press

1 tablespoon olive oil

2 tablespoons tomato juice

1 tablespoon raspberry vinegar

SAFFRON MAYONNAISE

2 tablespoons fresh lemon juice

¼ teaspoon saffron threads

2 egg yolks

1 tablespoon dijon mustard

⅓ cup olive oil

1 tablespoon finely chopped
  fresh dill

1 tablespoon warm water

1 Make salsa and mayonnaise.

2 Shell and devein shrimp, leaving tails intact.

3 Halve avocados; discard pits.

4 Divide three-quarters of the salsa among serving plates. Place
avocado halves on top; fill avocado centers with remaining salsa
and shrimp, spoon mayonnaise over shrimp.

GAZPACHO SALSA Combine ingredients in medium bowl;
mix well.

SAFFRON MAYONNAISE Gently heat juice and saffron in small
saucepan over low heat, about 2 minutes or until juice has
changed color; cool. Strain juice; blend or process juice, egg yolks
and mustard until smooth. With motor running, gradually add oil
in thin stream until combined. Stir in dill; add the water to thin
mayonnaise, if desired.

SERVES 4
per serving 3g carbohydrate; 46.2g fat; 560 cal; 33.6g protein
tip Saffron mayonnaise is even better if made a day ahead; keep,
covered, in refrigerator.

fish and zucchini stacks on tomato salad

PREPARATION TIME 15 MINUTES   COOKING TIME 10 MINUTES

We used sea bass in this recipe, but you can use any firm fish, such as grouper or halibut.

four 7-ounce firm white fish fillets

2 medium green zucchini

2 medium yellow squash

4 medium tomatoes, sliced thinly

⅓ cup dry white wine

coarsely ground black pepper

2 tablespoons balsamic vinegar

2 tablespoons fresh baby basil leaves

1 Preheat oven to very hot.

2 Halve fish pieces lengthwise. Using vegetable peeler, peel zucchini and squash into long thin ribbons.

3 Place four pieces of fish on large individual pieces of lightly oiled foil; top with zucchini and squash ribbons then remaining fish pieces. Cut eight slices of tomato in half; place four half-slices on top of each stack. Drizzle stacks with wine; sprinkle with pepper.

4 Fold foil to enclose fish stacks; place in single layer in casserole. Bake in very hot oven about 10 minutes or until fish is cooked through.

5 Divide remaining tomato slices equally among serving plates; top with unwrapped fish stacks. Drizzle stacks with vinegar; sprinkle with basil.

SERVES 4
per serving 4.6g carbohydrate; 4.9g fat; 253 cal; 43.4g protein
tip Fish stacks can be assembled and wrapped in foil several hours ahead; store in refrigerator.

warm lobster salad with saffron dressing

PREPARATION TIME 30 MINUTES   COOKING TIME 15 MINUTES

12 uncooked lobster tails

**   (about 6 pounds)**

1 pound cherry tomatoes

2 large avocados, sliced thinly

1 medium red onion, sliced thinly

3 cups (3 ounces) trimmed

**   watercress**

½ cup firmly packed fresh purple

**   basil leaves**

SAFFRON DRESSING

8 saffron threads

¼ cup boiling water

1 egg yolk

1 clove garlic, crushed in garlic press

1 teaspoon spicy mustard

2 tablespoons fresh lemon juice

½ cup light olive oil

1 Make saffron dressing.

2 Cut lobster tails lengthwise; remove and discard vein. Remove lobster meat from both tail halves.

3 Cook lobster meat and tomatoes, in batches, on heated oiled grill or grill pan until browned all over.

4 Just before serving, combine tomatoes, avocado, onion, watercress and basil in large bowl with one-third of the saffron dressing. Divide salad mixture among serving plates; top with lobster meat, drizzle with remaining dressing.

SAFFRON DRESSING Combine saffron and the water in small heatproof bowl; let stand 10 minutes. Strain through fine strainer into small bowl; discard threads. Whisk egg yolk, garlic, mustard and juice in small bowl; gradually add oil, in thin stream, whisking continuously. Whisk in saffron liquid.

SERVES 4
per serving 6.7g carboydrate; 60.7g fat; 1128 cal; 138.4g protein
tips Slice the avocado just before assembling the salad.
Tomatoes can be browned on a baking sheet under a broiler or in a hot oven.

seared scallops with mixed cabbage salad

PREPARATION TIME 15 MINUTES   COOKING TIME 10 MINUTES

You need about half of a medium head of red cabbage and a quarter of a medium head of savoy cabbage for this recipe.

32 sea scallops

2 small hothouse cucumbers

3 cups finely shredded red cabbage

2 cups finely shredded savoy cabbage

½ cup coarsely chopped fresh chives

2 tablespoons toasted sesame seeds

HONEY SOY DRESSING

2 tablespoons soy sauce

2 tablespoons fresh lemon juice

2 teaspoons sesame oil

1 tablespoon honey

1 clove garlic, crushed in garlic press

¼ cup peanut oil

1 Make honey soy dressing.

2 Sear scallops in heated oiled large skillet, in batches, until browned both sides and cooked as desired.

3 Using vegetable peeler, slice cucumbers into ribbons. Combine cucumber in large bowl with cabbages, chives, seeds and three-quarters of the dressing.

4 Divide salad among serving plates; top with scallops, drizzle with remaining dressing.

HONEY SOY DRESSING Combine ingredients in screw-top jar; shake well.

SERVES 4
per serving 10.9g carbohydrate; 20.1g fat; 289 cal; 16.3g protein

shrimp and mint salad

PREPARATION TIME 30 MINUTES

This salad makes a good main course for a light meal. You need a quarter of a head of frisée for this recipe.

40 medium cooked shrimp (2 pounds)

1 hothouse cucumber

1 tablespoon fish sauce

¼ cup fresh lime juice

½ cup unsweetened coconut milk

2 tablespoons sugar

1 clove garlic, crushed in garlic press

2 teaspoons grated fresh ginger

1 red serrano chile, sliced thinly

3 ounces frisée

3 cups (3 ounces) trimmed watercress

2 cups (7 ounces) fresh bean sprouts

½ cup thinly sliced fresh mint leaves

1 Shell and devein shrimp, leaving tails intact. Halve cucumber lengthwise, slice thinly on the diagonal.

2 Whisk sauce, juice, milk, sugar, garlic, ginger and chile in large bowl until well mixed; add shrimp, cucumber and remaining ingredients, toss salad gently to combine.

SERVES 4
per serving 10.3g carbohydrate; 7.9g fat; 245 cal; 33g protein
tip If you like, buy uncooked shrimp and marinate them overnight in a little fresh lime juice, then grill and serve on top of the other salad ingredients.

fish with wasabi mayonnaise

PREPARATION TIME 5 MINUTES   COOKING TIME 10 MINUTES

Wasabi (japanese horseradish) is available as a paste in tubes or powdered in cans from Asian food stores and some supermarkets. Any asian greens can be used in this recipe. Try it with bok choy, choy sum, or gai larn (also known as chinese broccoli). You need 1½ bunches of asian greens. We used sea bass, but you can use any firm fish, such as grouper or halibut.

⅓ cup mayonnaise

2 teaspoons wasabi paste

2 scallions, chopped finely

2 tablespoons coarsely chopped
   fresh cilantro

2 tablespoons fresh lime juice

1 tablespoon peanut oil

four 7-ounce firm white fish fillets

1½ pounds asian greens

1 Combine mayonnaise, wasabi, scallion, cilantro and juice in small bowl; cover.

2 Heat oil in large skillet; cook fish, in batches, until browned both sides and cooked as desired. Cover to keep warm.

3 Boil, steam or microwave greens until just tender; drain. Divide among serving plates; top with fish and wasabi mayonnaise.

SERVES 4
per serving 6.8g carbohydrate; 17.1g fat; 353 cal; 42.6g protein
tip For a stronger, more fiery taste, add an extra teaspoon of wasabi to the mayonnaise mixture.

cajun halibut steaks with lime

PREPARATION TIME 15 MINUTES   COOKING TIME 10 MINUTES

2 teaspoons ground cumin

2 teaspoons ground coriander

2 teaspoons sweet paprika

2 teaspoons mustard powder

2 teaspoons onion powder

½ teaspoon garlic powder

¼ teaspoon cayenne

2 teaspoons fennel seeds

four 8-ounce halibut steaks

2 limes, sliced thickly

CUCUMBER SALAD

2 small hothouse cucumbers

2 red serrano chiles, seeded,
  chopped finely

¼ cup peanut oil

2 tablespoons fresh lime juice

1 clove garlic, crushed in
  garlic press

2 teaspoons cumin seeds, toasted

1 tablespoon finely shredded
  mint leaves

1 Combine spices, powders, pepper and seeds with fish in large bowl. Coat fish all over in spice mixture; cook fish steaks, in batches, on heated oiled grill or grill pan until browned both sides and cooked as desired.

2 Meanwhile, make cucumber salad.

3 Cook lime on heated oiled grill or grill pan until browned both sides.

4 Divide fish among serving plates; top with lime slices and serve with cucumber salad.

CUCUMBER SALAD Using a vegetable peeler, peel cucumber into long thin ribbons. Just before serving, gently toss cucumber with remaining ingredients in bowl.

SERVES 4
per serving 1.9g carbohydrate; 19.4g fat; 392 cal; 51.8g protein
tip You can use ⅓ cup bottled cajun spice mix, available from supermarkets, instead of making your own, if preferred.

ceviche

PREPARATION TIME 25 MINUTES (PLUS REFRIGERATION TIME)

Ceviche, also known as seviche or cebiche, is an everyday fish salad eaten throughout the Caribbean and all over Latin America. While marinating the fish in fresh lime juice appears to "cook" it, be aware that the fish is raw. You will need about 10 limes for this recipe.

2 pounds red snapper fillets

1½ cups fresh lime juice

¼ cup sliced jalapeño chile

¼ cup olive oil

1 large tomato, chopped coarsely

¼ cup coarsely chopped
   fresh cilantro

1 small white onion, chopped finely

1 clove garlic, crushed in garlic press

1 cup (1 ounce) trimmed watercress

⅓ cup loosely packed fresh
   basil leaves

¼ cup loosely packed fresh
   cilantro leaves

2 tablespoons fresh lime juice, extra

¼ cup olive oil, extra

1   Remove any remaining skin or bones from fish; cut fish into 1-inch pieces.

2   Combine fish and juice in nonreactive large bowl, cover; refrigerate 4 hours or overnight.

3   Drain fish; discard juice. Return fish to bowl, add chile, oil, tomato, chopped cilantro, onion and garlic; toss gently to combine. Cover; refrigerate 1 hour.

4   Just before serving, place watercress, basil, cilantro leaves, extra lime juice and extra olive oil in medium bowl; toss gently to combine. Serve ceviche topped with herb salad.

SERVES 4
per serving   4.1g carbohydrate; 32.2g fat; 527 cal; 53.3g protein
tip   Fish must be marinated with the fresh lime juice in a nonreactive bowl (one made from glazed porcelain or glass is best) to avoid the metallic taste that can result if marinating takes place in an aluminum bowl. Ensure all of the fish is completely covered with juice.

swordfish with thai dressing

PREPARATION TIME 5 MINUTES   COOKING TIME 10 MINUTES

four 7-ounce swordfish steaks

⅓ cup sweet chili sauce

1 tablespoon fish sauce

½ cup fresh lime juice

2 teaspoons finely chopped
   fresh lemongrass

2 tablespoons finely chopped
   fresh cilantro

½ cup finely chopped fresh mint

1 teaspoon grated fresh ginger

2½ cups (5 ounces) mesclun

1   Cook fish, in batches, on heated oiled grill or grill pan until browned both sides and cooked as desired.

2   Combine sauces, juice, herbs and ginger in screw-top jar; shake well. Drizzle dressing over fish. Serve with mesclun salad.

SERVES 4
per serving   5.3g carbohydrate; 5.1g fat; 242 cal; 42.2g protein
tip   You can substitute tuna steaks or fillets for the swordfish.

cajun seafood kebabs with avocado salsa

PREPARATION TIME 30 MINUTES (PLUS REFRIGERATION TIME)   COOKING TIME 10 MINUTES

Soak 12 bamboo skewers in water for at least an hour prior to use to prevent splintering or scorching.
We used sea bass in this recipe, but you can use any firm fish, such as grouper or halibut.

1¾ pounds uncooked medium shrimp

1¼ pounds firm white fish fillets

2 tablespoons cajun seasoning

2 teaspoons ground cumin

2 tablespoons coarsely chopped
   fresh oregano

2 cloves garlic, crushed in garlic press

¼ cup olive oil

AVOCADO SALSA

1 large avocado, chopped finely

3 medium tomatoes, seeded, chopped finely

1 small red onion, chopped finely

2 tablespoons finely chopped fresh cilantro

2 tablespoons fresh lemon juice

1 tablespoon olive oil

½ teaspoon sugar

1 Peel and devein shrimp, leaving tails intact. Cut fish into 1-inch pieces.

2 Combine shrimp and fish with remaining ingredients in medium bowl. Cover; refrigerate 1 hour.

3 Thread shrimp and fish onto 12 skewers.

4 Cook seafood on heated oiled grill or grill pan, uncovered, until cooked as desired.

5 Make avocado salsa. Serve seafood kebabs with avocado salsa.

   AVOCADO SALSA Combine ingredients in medium bowl.

SERVES 4
per serving 3.8g carbohydrate; 35.1g fat; 543 cal; 53.4g protein
tip If using metal skewers, oil them first to prevent the fish from sticking.

cod and snow pea green curry

PREPARATION TIME 30 MINUTES   COOKING TIME 15 MINUTES

2 teaspoons peanut oil

1 medium onion, chopped finely

3 green serrano chiles, seeded, sliced thinly

¼ cup green curry paste

2 baby eggplants, chopped coarsely

1⅔ cups unsweetened coconut milk

four 7-ounce cod fillets, skinned,
   chopped coarsely

7 ounces snow peas, halved

4 scallions, sliced thinly

¼ cup coarsely chopped fresh cilantro

1 Heat oil in large deep skillet; cook onion, chile and curry paste, stirring, until onion softens. Add eggplant; cook, stirring, until tender.

2 Stir in coconut milk; bring to a boil. Add fish, reduce heat; simmer, uncovered, 5 minutes. Add snow peas and scallion; stir gently until vegetables are just tender. Remove from heat; stir in half of the cilantro. Serve topped with remaining cilantro.

SERVES 4
per serving 10.5g carbohydrate; 33.2g fat; 522 cal; 46.2g protein

red snapper parcels with caper-anchovy salsa

PREPARATION TIME 30 MINUTES   COOKING TIME 15 MINUTES

A modern take on the traditional French method of cooking "en papillote" (in a sealed packet), this recipe uses aluminum foil rather than parchment paper to enclose the ingredients. Cooking this way allows the flavors to mingle and intensify, without added fat.

2 cloves garlic, crushed in garlic press

1 bulb baby fennel, sliced thinly

four 7-ounce red snapper fillets

4 whole fresh large basil leaves

⅓ cup dry white wine

¼ cup coarsely chopped fresh chives

⅓ cup loosely packed fresh
**   tarragon leaves**

½ cup loosely packed fresh basil leaves

1 cup (1 ounce) trimmed watercress

1 tablespoon fresh lemon juice

1 teaspoon olive oil

CAPER-ANCHOVY SALSA

1 small red bell pepper, chopped finely

2 tablespoons finely chopped pitted
**   kalamata olives**

1 tablespoon drained baby capers, rinsed

8 whole anchovy fillets, drained,
**   chopped finely**

¼ cup finely chopped fresh basil

1 tablespoon balsamic vinegar

1 Combine garlic and fennel in small bowl.

2 Place fillets, skin-side down, on four separate squares of lightly oiled foil, large enough to completely enclose fish. Top fillets with equal amounts of fennel mixture; top with one basil leaf each, drizzle each with a quarter of the wine. Gather corners of foil squares together above snapper filling; twist to enclose securely.

3 Place parcels on baking sheet, bake in hot oven about 15 minutes or until fish is cooked as desired.

4 Meanwhile, make caper-anchovy salsa.

5 Place remaining ingredients in medium bowl; toss gently to combine salad.

6 Unwrap parcels just before serving; divide fish, fennel-side up, among serving plates. Top with salsa; accompany with herb salad.

CAPER-ANCHOVY SALSA Place pepper, olive, capers, anchovy, basil and vinegar in small bowl; toss gently to combine.

SERVES 4
per serving 3.6g carbohydrate; 5.3g fat; 255 cal; 43.9g protein

red snapper parcels with caper-anchovy salsa

steamed belgian mussels

steamed belgian mussels

PREPARATION TIME 30 MINUTES   COOKING TIME 10 MINUTES

You need half a head of frisée for this recipe.

2½ pounds mussels

2 teaspoons olive oil

2 cloves garlic, crushed in
garlic press

3 shallots, sliced thinly

2 stalks celery, trimmed,
sliced thinly

2 large plum tomatoes,
chopped finely

½ cup dry white wine

6 ounces frisée

½ cup loosely packed fresh
flat-leaf parsley

¼ cup coarsely chopped
fresh chives

¼ cup fresh lemon juice

1   Scrub mussels; remove beards.

2   Heat oil in wok or large skillet; stir-fry garlic, shallot and celery until shallot softens and mixture is fragrant. Add tomato; stir-fry 30 seconds. Add wine; bring to a boil. Reduce heat; simmer until reduced by half.

3   Add mussels; simmer, covered, about 3 minutes or until mussels open (discard any that do not).

4   Add remaining ingredients to wok; toss gently to combine. Serve mussels in large bowl.

SERVES 4
per serving 6.8g carbohydrate; 3.8g fat; 124 cal; 9.9g protein

grilled swordfish with roasted mediterranean vegetables

PREPARATION TIME 20 MINUTES   COOKING TIME 25 MINUTES

1 medium red bell pepper, sliced thickly

1 medium yellow bell pepper, sliced thickly

1 medium eggplant, sliced thickly

2 large zucchini, sliced thickly

½ cup olive oil

8 ounces cherry tomatoes

¼ cup balsamic vinegar

1 clove garlic, crushed in garlic press

2 teaspoons sugar

2 pounds swordfish steaks

¼ cup coarsely chopped fresh basil

1 Preheat oven to hot.

2 Combine peppers, eggplant and zucchini with 2 tablespoons of the oil in large roasting pan; roast, uncovered, in hot oven 15 minutes. Add tomatoes; roast, uncovered, about 5 minutes or until vegetables are just tender.

3 Meanwhile, combine remaining oil, vinegar, garlic and sugar in screw-top jar; shake well. Brush a third of the dressing over fish; cook fish, in batches, on heated oiled grill or grill pan until browned both sides and cooked as desired.

4 Combine vegetables in large bowl with basil and remaining dressing; toss gently to combine. Divide vegetables among serving plates; top with fish.

SERVES 4
per serving 8.4g carbohydrate; 33.9g fat; 529 cal; 48g protein

seared tuna with salsa verde

PREPARATION TIME 25 MINUTES   COOKING TIME 20 MINUTES

Tuna is at its best if browned both sides but still fairly rare in the middle; overcooking will make it dry.

four 7-ounce tuna steaks

2 cups (3½ ounces) baby arugula leaves

SALSA VERDE

½ cup firmly packed fresh flat-leaf
    parsley leaves

¼ cup loosely packed fresh mint leaves

⅔ cup extra virgin olive oil

¼ cup drained capers, rinsed

2 teaspoons dijon mustard

2 tablespoons fresh lemon juice

8 anchovy fillets, drained

1 clove garlic, quartered

1 Make salsa verde.

2 Cook fish, in batches, on heated oiled grill or grill pan until browned both sides and cooked as desired.

3 Divide arugula among serving plates; top with fish, drizzle with salsa verde.

   SALSA VERDE Blend or process ingredients until just combined. Transfer to medium measuring cup; whisk before pouring over fish.

SERVES 4
per serving 2.2g carbohydrate; 48.5g fat; 656 cal; 53.4g protein

grilled sole with roasted tomatoes

PREPARATION TIME 20 MINUTES   COOKING TIME 30 MINUTES

1 pound cherry tomatoes, halved

1 teaspoon sea salt

1 teaspoon cracked black pepper

four 7-ounce whole sole or flounder

5 tablespoons butter

2 tablespoons fresh lemon juice

1 clove garlic, crushed in garlic press

1 pound broccolini, trimmed

1 Preheat oven to hot.

2 Place tomato, cut-side up, on lightly oiled baking sheet; sprinkle with salt and pepper. Roast, uncovered, in hot oven about 10 minutes or until softened.

3 Cook fish on heated oiled grill or grill pan until browned both sides and cooked as desired.

4 Heat butter, juice and garlic in small saucepan; stir until butter melts.

5 Meanwhile, boil, steam or microwave broccolini until just tender; drain.

6 Divide fish, tomato and broccolini among serving plates; drizzle with butter sauce.

SERVES 4
per serving 3.7g carbohydrate; 21.2g fat; 389 cal; 45.6g protein

pompano, baby leek and fennel parcels with fried cauliflower

PREPARATION TIME 20 MINUTES   COOKING TIME 15 MINUTES

A modern take on the traditional French method of cooking "en papillote" (in a sealed packet), this recipe uses aluminum foil rather than parchment paper to enclose the ingredients. Cooking this way allows the flavors to mingle and intensify, without added fat. We used pompano in this recipe, but you can use any firm fish, such as halibut, sea bass or red snapper.

four 7-ounce pompano fillets,
   with skin

½ medium bulb fennel, trimmed,
   sliced thinly

4 baby leeks, quartered lengthwise

2 tablespoons butter, melted

vegetable oil, for deep-frying

1 medium cauliflower head,
   cut into florets

1 Preheat oven to hot.

2 Place each fish fillet, skin-side down, on a square of lightly oiled foil large enough to completely enclose fish; top each fillet with a quarter of the fennel and a quarter of the leek, drizzle with butter. Gather corners of foil squares together above fish; twist to enclose securely.

3 Place parcels on baking sheet; bake in hot oven about 15 minutes or until fish is cooked as desired.

4 Meanwhile, heat oil in wok or large skillet; deep-fry cauliflower, in batches, until browned and crisp. Drain on paper towels.

5 Discard foil from parcels just before serving on cauliflower.

SERVES 4
per serving 9.5g carbohydrate; 29.4g fat; 498 cal; 49.3g protein
tip When deep-frying the cauliflower, make sure the oil is very hot so the vegetable crisps and browns. If not, the cauliflower will absorb excess oil and become limp and soggy.

mixed seafood with crisp thai basil

PREPARATION TIME 25 MINUTES   COOKING TIME 25 MINUTES

8 ounces cleaned squid (calamari), bodies only

8 ounces firm white fish fillets

12 uncooked extra-large shrimp (1¼ pounds)

8 ounces baby octopus, thawed if frozen

2 tablespoons peanut oil

1 clove garlic, crushed in garlic press

2 red serrano chiles, sliced thinly

1 medium carrot, halved, sliced thinly

1 medium red bell pepper, sliced thinly

4 scallions, sliced thinly

1 tablespoon fish sauce

1 teaspoon oyster sauce

1 tablespoon fresh lime juice

¼ cup peanut oil, extra

⅓ cup loosely packed fresh thai basil leaves

1   Score squid in a diagonal pattern. Cut squid and fish into 1-inch pieces; shell and devein shrimp, leaving tails intact. Remove and discard the head and beak of each octopus; cut each octopus in half. Rinse under cold water; drain.

2   Heat half of the oil in wok or large skillet; stir-fry seafood, in batches, until shrimp is changed in color, fish is cooked as desired, and squid and octopus are tender. Remove and cover to keep warm.

3   Heat remaining oil in same wok; stir-fry garlic, chile and carrot until carrot is just tender. Add pepper; stir-fry until pepper is just tender. Return seafood to wok with scallion, sauces and juice; stir-fry, tossing gently, until hot.

4   Heat extra peanut oil in small skillet until sizzling; fry basil leaves, in batches, until crisp but still green. Drain on paper towel. Top seafood mixture with basil leaves.

SERVES 4
per serving 4.7g carbohydrate; 26.2g fat; 451 cal; 49.4g protein

whole roast snapper in salt crust with gremolata

PREPARATION TIME 10 MINUTES   COOKING TIME 30 MINUTES

2-pound whole red snapper, gutted, scales left on

3 pounds coarse sea salt, approximately

12 cups (12 ounces) trimmed watercress

1 tablespoon fresh lemon juice

GREMOLATA

¼ cup finely chopped fresh flat-leaf parsley

1 clove garlic, crushed in garlic press

2 teaspoons finely grated lemon peel

1 tablespoon extra virgin olive oil

1   Preheat oven to very hot. Make gremolata.

2   Wash fish, pat dry inside and out with paper towel; stuff cavity with half of the gremolata.

3   Sprinkle half of the salt over large baking sheet, place fish on salt. Wet remaining salt with water; drain, press firmly over fish to completely enclose fish.

4   Roast fish, uncovered, in very hot oven about 30 minutes or until cooked through. Let stand 5 minutes.

5   Meanwhile, place watercress and juice in medium bowl; toss gently to combine.

6   Break crust on fish with meat mallet; lift away crust with scales and skin. Sprinkle fish with remaining gremolata; serve topped with watercress.

GREMOLATA   Combine ingredients in small bowl.

SERVES 4
per serving   1g carbohydrate; 7.1g fat; 188 cal; 29.6g protein

grilled snapper fillets with fennel and onion salad

PREPARATION TIME 15 MINUTES   COOKING TIME 10 MINUTES

1 medium red onion, sliced thinly

4 scallions, sliced thinly

1 large bulb fennel, trimmed, sliced thinly

2 stalks celery, trimmed, sliced thinly

½ cup coarsely chopped fresh
    flat-leaf parsley

⅓ cup fresh orange juice

¼ cup olive oil

2 cloves garlic, crushed in garlic press

2 teaspoons hot chili sauce (such as
    sambal oelek or sriracha)

four 8-ounce snapper fillets, with skin

1 Combine onion, scallion, fennel, celery and parsley in medium bowl.

2 Place juice, oil, garlic and chili sauce in screw-top jar; shake well.

3 Cook fish on heated oiled grill or grill pan until browned both sides and cooked as desired.

4 Pour half of the dressing over salad in bowl; toss gently to combine. Serve salad topped with fish; drizzle with remaining dressing.

SERVES 4
per serving 8g carbohydrate; 18.4g fat; 430 cal; 57.9g protein

tuna tartare

PREPARATION TIME 45 MINUTES   COOKING TIME 5 MINUTES

You need one small head of napa cabbage weighing about 14 ounces for this recipe.

7 ounces green beans, halved

1¼-pound piece sashimi tuna

3 cups finely shredded napa cabbage

4 scallions, sliced thinly

½ cup firmly packed fresh cilantro leaves

2 cups (7 ounces) fresh bean sprouts

GINGER DRESSING

2½-inch piece fresh ginger

⅓ cup fresh lime juice

¼ cup olive oil

1 tablespoon soy sauce

3 teaspoons finely chopped fresh cilantro
    leaves and stem

2 cloves garlic, crushed in garlic press

2 teaspoons sesame oil

2 teaspoons sugar

1 Boil, steam or microwave beans until just tender; drain. Rinse under cold water; drain.

2 Make ginger dressing.

3 Cut tuna into ¼-inch cubes. Place in medium bowl with a third of the dressing; toss gently to combine.

4 Place beans in large bowl with cabbage, scallion, cilantro, sprouts and remaining dressing; toss gently to combine.

5 Divide undrained tuna among serving plates, shaping into mound; serve with cabbage salad.

GINGER DRESSING Cut ginger into thin slices; cut slices into thin strips. Combine ginger with remaining ingredients in small bowl.

SERVES 4
per serving 5.8g carbohydrate; 24.8g fat; 414 cal; 41.5g protein
tip Sashimi salmon can be used in place of the tuna.

fish and spinach with olive-basil sauce

PREPARATION TIME 5 MINUTES   COOKING TIME 10 MINUTES

We used grouper in this recipe, but you can use any firm fish, such as halibut or red snapper.

1½ pounds spinach, trimmed, chopped coarsely

⅓ cup extra virgin olive oil

four 7-ounce firm white fish fillets

1 tablespoon fresh lemon juice

¼ teaspoon red pepper flakes

1 clove garlic, crushed in garlic press

⅓ cup pitted kalamata olives

¼ cup finely shredded fresh basil

1   Boil, steam or microwave spinach until just wilted; drain. Cover to keep warm.

2   Meanwhile, heat 1 tablespoon of the oil in large nonstick skillet; cook fish until browned both sides and cooked as desired. Remove from skillet; cover to keep warm.

3   Place remaining oil in same cleaned skillet with remaining ingredients; cook, stirring, until heated through. Divide spinach among serving plates; top with fish and olive-basil sauce.

SERVES 4
per serving   3.1g carbohydrate; 23.4g fat; 395 cal; 43.3g protein

shrimp with garlic

PREPARATION TIME 20 MINUTES (PLUS REFRIGERATION TIME)   COOKING TIME 5 MINUTES

2 pounds uncooked medium shrimp

3 teaspoons coarsely chopped fresh cilantro leaves and stem

2 teaspoons dried coriander seeds

1 teaspoon dried green peppercorns

4 cloves garlic, quartered

2 tablespoons peanut oil

1 cup (3½ ounces) fresh bean sprouts

1 tablespoon finely chopped fresh cilantro

1 tablespoon fresh cilantro leaves, extra

1 tablespoon packaged fried shallot (optional)

1 tablespoon packaged fried garlic (optional)

1   Shell and devein shrimp, leaving tails intact.

2   Crush cilantro mixture, coriander seeds, peppercorns and garlic to a paste using mortar and pestle. Place paste in large bowl with shrimp and half the oil; toss to coat shrimp in marinade. Cover; refrigerate 3 hours or overnight.

3   Heat remaining oil in wok or large skillet; stir-fry shrimp mixture, in batches, until shrimp have changed in color. Remove from heat; toss bean sprouts and chopped cilantro through stir-fry; serve sprinkled with extra cilantro leaves, fried shallot and fried garlic, if desired.

SERVES 4
per serving   0.9g carbohydrate; 10.2g fat; 202 cal; 26.6g protein

fish fillets pan-fried with pancetta and caper-herb butter

PREPARATION TIME 15 MINUTES   COOKING TIME 10 MINUTES

We used red snapper fillets for this recipe, but you can use any firm fish, such as grouper or halibut.

5 tablespoons butter, softened

2 tablespoons coarsely chopped

   fresh flat-leaf parsley

1 tablespoon capers,

   rinsed, drained

2 cloves garlic, quartered

2 scallions, chopped coarsely

8 slices pancetta

four 7-ounce white fish fillets

1 tablespoon olive oil

1 bunch asparagus, trimmed

1   Blend or process butter, parsley, capers, garlic and scallion until mixture forms a smooth paste.

2   Spread 1 heaped tablespoon of the butter mixture and two slices of the pancetta on each fish fillet.

3   Heat oil in large heavy-bottomed skillet; cook fish, pancetta-butter-side down, until pancetta is crisp. Turn fish carefully; cook, uncovered, until cooked as desired.

4   Meanwhile, boil, steam or microwave asparagus until tender; drain.

5   Serve fish and asparagus drizzled with pan juices.

SERVES 4
per serving   1.7g carbohydrate; 28.6g fat; 454 cal; 48.2g protein

swordfish with chermoulla

PREPARATION TIME 10 MINUTES (PLUS REFRIGERATION TIME) COOKING TIME 10 MINUTES

Chermoulla is a spicy Moroccan marinade which can also be served as a sauce. If hot paprika
is unavailable, substitute it with ½ teaspoon of sweet paprika and a hearty pinch of cayenne.

**2 cloves garlic, crushed in
  garlic press**

½ teaspoon ground cumin

¼ teaspoon hot paprika

**1 tablespoon coarsely chopped
  fresh cilantro**

**1 tablespoon coarsely chopped
  fresh flat-leaf parsley**

2 tablespoons olive oil

2 tablespoons fresh lemon juice

1 teaspoon finely grated lemon peel

four 5-ounce swordfish steaks

2½ cups (4 ounces) arugula

1 Combine garlic, spices, herbs, oil, juice and peel in large
   nonreactive bowl; remove and reserve half of the chermoulla
   mixture. Place fish in bowl; toss to coat all over in remaining
   chermoulla. Cover fish mixture and reserved chermoulla,
   separately; refrigerate 3 hours or overnight.

2 Remove fish; discard marinade. Cook fish in heated large nonstick
   skillet until browned both sides and cooked as desired.

3 Serve fish topped with arugula and drizzled with
   reserved chermoulla.

SERVES 4
per serving 1.1g carbohydrate; 12.7g fat; 246 cal; 31.6g protein

mussels with basil and lemongrass

PREPARATION TIME 20 MINUTES   COOKING TIME 10 MINUTES

2 pounds large mussels (about 30)

1 tablespoon peanut oil

1 medium onion, chopped finely

2 cloves garlic, crushed in garlic press

2 tablespoons thinly sliced fresh lemongrass

1 red serrano chile, chopped finely

1 cup dry white wine

2 tablespoons fresh lime juice

2 tablespoons fish sauce

½ cup loosely packed fresh basil leaves

½ cup unsweetened coconut milk

1 red serrano chile, seeded, sliced thinly

2 scallions, sliced thinly

1 Scrub mussels under cold water; remove beards.

2 Heat oil in wok or large skillet; stir-fry onion, garlic, lemongrass and chopped chile until onion softens and mixture is fragrant.

3 Add wine, juice and sauce; bring to a boil. Add mussels; reduce heat, simmer, covered, about 5 minutes or until mussels open (discard any that do not).

4 Meanwhile, shred half of the basil finely. Add shredded basil and coconut milk to wok; stir-fry until heated through. Place mussel mixture in serving bowl; sprinkle with sliced chile, scallion and remaining basil.

SERVES 4
per serving 6.7g carbohydrate; 12.1g fat; 209 cal; 8.2g protein

salmon steaks with fennel salad

PREPARATION TIME 20 MINUTES   COOKING TIME 10 MINUTES

2 tablespoons red wine vinegar

1 tablespoon olive oil

2 teaspoons sugar

2 teaspoons dijon mustard

four 7-ounce salmon steaks

1 tablespoon finely chopped fresh chives

1 tablespoon finely chopped fresh dill

4½ cups (7 ounces) baby spinach leaves

2 medium apples, cored, sliced thinly

2 bulbs baby fennel, trimmed, sliced thinly

1 hothouse cucumber, seeded, sliced thinly

½ cup coarsely chopped fresh chives

¼ cup coarsely chopped fresh dill

1 Combine vinegar, oil, sugar and mustard in screw-top jar; shake well.

2 Combine one tablespoon of the dressing with fish, finely chopped chives and dill in large bowl; toss to coat fish in mixture. Cook fish in heated, lightly oiled skillet about 5 minutes each side or until fish is cooked as desired.

3 Combine spinach, apple, fennel, cucumber, coarsely chopped chives and dill in large bowl with remaining dressing; toss gently to combine. Serve fish with salad.

SERVES 4
per serving 10.7g carbohydrate; 19g fat; 379 cal; 41.1g protein

beef stroganoff with sautéed spinach

PREPARATION TIME 15 MINUTES   COOKING TIME 20 MINUTES

2 tablespoons vegetable oil

1¼ pounds round steak, sliced thinly

1 medium onion, sliced thinly

3 cloves garlic, crushed in garlic press

1 teaspoon sweet paprika

14 ounces brown mushrooms, sliced thickly

10 ounces spinach

2 tablespoons dry red wine

1 tablespoon fresh lemon juice

2 tablespoons tomato paste

1¼ cups sour cream

1 tablespoon coarsely chopped fresh dill

1 tablespoon olive oil

1 teaspoon red pepper flakes

1 Heat half of the oil in large skillet; cook beef, in batches, until browned lightly.

2 Heat remaining oil in same skillet; cook onion and a third of the garlic, stirring, until onion softens. Add paprika and mushrooms; cook, stirring, until mushrooms are just tender.

3 Meanwhile, cook spinach in large saucepan of boiling water, uncovered, until almost tender.

4 Return beef to skillet with wine and juice; bring to a boil. Reduce heat; simmer, covered, about 5 minutes or until beef is tender. Add paste, sour cream and dill; cook, stirring, until heated through.

5 Meanwhile, heat olive oil in medium skillet. Add remaining garlic and pepper flakes. Cook until fragrant; remove from heat. Add spinach; toss to coat. Serve stroganoff with spinach.

SERVES 4
per serving 7.6g carbohydrate; 51.9g fat; 663 cal; 40.6g protein

filet mignon with mushroom sauce and baby carrots

PREPARATION TIME 15 MINUTES   COOKING TIME 15 MINUTES

4 slices bacon

4 filets mignons (1¾ pounds)

2 tablespoons butter

2 tablespoons olive oil

7 ounces baby carrots

1 tablespoon butter, melted

2 medium onions, chopped finely

8 ounces button mushrooms, sliced thinly

4 teaspoons cornstarch

2 cups beef broth

1 teaspoon fresh oregano leaves

1 Wrap one bacon slice around each filet mignon; secure bacon with metal skewer or toothpick.

2 Heat butter and oil in heavy-bottomed skillet; cook filets mignons until browned both sides and cooked as desired. Remove filets mignons from skillet to casserole. Cover; place in slow oven to keep warm while cooking carrots and making mushroom sauce.

3 Boil, steam or microwave baby carrots until almost tender; drain. Place in medium bowl. Add melted butter; toss to coat. Cover; keep warm.

4 Add onion to remaining butter mixture in same skillet in which beef was cooked; stir over medium heat until onion is soft. Add mushrooms; stir over medium heat 2 minutes or until mushrooms are just soft. Blend cornstarch with a tablespoon of the broth; stir in remaining broth. Add to skillet; stir constantly over high heat until sauce boils and thickens. Stir in oregano. Place filets mignons on serving plates; remove skewers. Pour over sauce; serve immediately with baby carrots.

SERVES 4
per serving 9.6g carbohydrate; 32g fat; 546 cal; 55.6g protein

greek-style beef with tzatziki and garlic arugula salad

PREPARATION TIME 25 MINUTES (PLUS REFRIGERATION TIME)   COOKING TIME 10 MINUTES

¼ cup fresh lemon juice

¼ cup olive oil

⅓ cup chopped fresh oregano

2 cloves garlic, crushed in
  garlic press

2 tablespoons dry white wine

four 12-ounce T-bone steaks

TZATZIKI

7 ounces unflavored yogurt

1 clove garlic, crushed in
  garlic press

2 teaspoons fresh lemon juice

1 medium hothouse cucumber,
  chopped finely

½ teaspoon ground cumin

1 tablespoon chopped fresh
  mint leaves

GARLIC ARUGULA SALAD

1 tablespoon dry white wine

1 tablespoon fresh lemon juice

2 teaspoons olive oil

2 cloves garlic, crushed in
  garlic press

5½ cups (8 ounces) torn arugula

2 cups (3½ ounces) baby
  spinach leaves

1   Combine juice, oil, oregano, garlic and wine in large bowl; add beef to marinade. Cover, refrigerate 3 hours or overnight.

2   Make tzatziki.

3   Drain beef; discard marinade. Cook beef on heated oiled grill or grill pan until browned both sides and cooked as desired.

4   Meanwhile, make garlic arugula salad.

5   Serve beef with tzatziki and garlic arugula salad.

TZATZIKI Combine all ingredients in small bowl.

GARLIC ARUGULA SALAD Combine wine, juice, oil and garlic in screw-top jar; shake well. In large bowl gently toss arugula, spinach and dressing.

SERVES 4
per serving 5.7g carbohydrate; 35.4g fat; 510 cal; 54.3g protein

beef, red wine and chile casserole with mesclun salad

PREPARATION TIME 15 MINUTES   COOKING TIME 1 HOUR 45 MINUTES

2 teaspoons butter

3 pounds lean beef chuck steak,
    cut into 1-inch pieces

2 cloves garlic, crushed in
    garlic press

3 red serrano chiles, seeded,
    sliced thinly

2 teaspoons dijon mustard

1 large onion, sliced thickly

2 medium tomatoes,
    chopped coarsely

14 ounces canned tomato puree

¾ cup dry red wine

½ cup beef broth

½ cup water

2½ cups (5 ounces) mesclun

2 tablespoons coarsely chopped
    fresh flat-leaf parsley

TARRAGON DRESSING

⅓ cup olive oil

1½ tablespoons tarragon vinegar

1 teaspoon grainy mustard

1 clove garlic, crushed in
    garlic press

¼ teaspoon sugar

1 Make tarragon dressing.

2 Melt butter in large saucepan; cook beef, in batches, until browned all over. Cook garlic, chile, mustard and onion in same pan, stirring, until onion softens. Return beef to pan with tomato; cook, stirring, 2 minutes.

3 Add puree, wine, broth and the water to pan; bring to a boil. Reduce heat; simmer, covered, about 1 hour 30 minutes or until beef is tender, stirring occasionally.

4 Meanwhile, place mesclun in serving bowl.

5 Just before serving, add enough tarragon dressing to lightly coat leaves; toss gently. Stir parsley into beef casserole; serve with salad.

TARRAGON DRESSING Combine ingredients in screw-top jar; shake well.

SERVES 4
per serving 10.3g carbohydrate; 25.4g fat; 626 cal; 80.7g protein

new york strips in herbed mushroom sauce

PREPARATION TIME 20 MINUTES (PLUS REFRIGERATION TIME)   COOKING TIME 30 MINUTES

1 teaspoon drained prepared
   white horseradish

1 tablespoon heavy cream

four 8-ounce boneless new york strip steaks

⅔ cup dry red wine

2 teaspoons finely chopped fresh
   lemon thyme

1 tablespoon olive oil

1 tablespoon light brown sugar

2 tablespoons butter

1 large white onion, sliced thinly

1 clove garlic, crushed in garlic press

1 pound button mushrooms, sliced thickly

¼ cup beef broth

1 tablespoon chopped fresh parsley

1   Place horseradish and cream in small bowl; stir to combine.

2   Place beef in large shallow roasting pan with ½ cup of the wine, 2 teaspoons of the horseradish mixture, 1 teaspoon of the thyme, and all of the oil and sugar. Cover, refrigerate 3 hours or overnight.

3   Cook beef on heated oiled grill or grill pan until browned both sides and cooked as desired. Meanwhile, melt butter in large pan on grill; cook onion and garlic, stirring, until onion is soft. Add mushrooms; cook until soft. Add remaining horseradish mixture, thyme and wine with broth; simmer, uncovered, about 5 minutes or until most of the liquid has evaporated. Stir in parsley. Serve beef with herbed mushroom sauce.

SERVES 4
per serving 9.2g carbohydrate; 34.5g fat; 603 cal; 57.8g protein

beef and vegetable teppan-yaki

PREPARATION TIME 10 MINUTES (PLUS REFRIGERATION TIME)   COOKING TIME 15 MINUTES

four 5-ounce filets mignons

¼ cup dark soy sauce

2 tablespoons mirin

2 tablespoons sake

1 teaspoon grated fresh ginger

2 teaspoons light brown sugar

1 clove garlic, crushed in garlic press

8 ounces snow peas

1 bunch asparagus, trimmed

1   Place beef in large bowl with combined soy, mirin, sake, ginger, sugar and garlic. Cover, refrigerate 3 hours or overnight.

2   Boil, steam or microwave snow peas and asparagus, separately, until just tender; drain.

3   Drain beef over medium bowl; place vegetables in bowl with reserved marinade. Cook beef on heated oiled grill or grill pan until browned both sides and cooked as desired.

4   Meanwhile, towards end of beef cooking time, drain vegetables; discard marinade. Cook vegetables alongside beef until browned all over.

SERVES 4
per serving 6.0g carbohydrate; 9.2g fat; 261 cal; 35.7g protein

beef with spiced sea salt crust and pepper-cream vegetables

PREPARATION TIME 35 MINUTES (PLUS REFRIGERATION TIME)   COOKING TIME 1 HOUR 20 MINUTES (PLUS STANDING TIME)

2 tablespoons juniper berries, crushed

2 tablespoons grated lemon peel

1 tablespoon coarse sea salt

3 tablespoons cracked black pepper

2 teaspoons ground cumin

3 pounds sirloin roast

1 tablespoon olive oil

1 medium onion, sliced thinly

2 medium carrots, sliced thickly

3 baby eggplants, sliced thickly

8 ounces button mushrooms, halved

2 medium zucchini, sliced thickly

1 medium red bell pepper, sliced thickly

1 clove garlic, crushed in garlic press

½ cup vegetable broth

½ cup heavy cream

1   Combine berries, peel, salt, 2 tablespoons pepper and cumin in small bowl; press onto beef. Cover, refrigerate 3 hours or overnight.

2   Place beef on rack or in disposable roasting pan. Cook in covered barbecue, using indirect heat, following manufacturer's instructions, about 1 hour 20 minutes or until browned all over and cooked as desired. Remove from heat, cover; let stand 15 minutes before slicing.

3   Meanwhile, heat oil in wok or large saucepan. Stir-fry vegetables and garlic, in batches, until just tender; keep warm.

4   Add combined broth, cream and remaining pepper to wok; stir until sauce thickens slightly.

5   Serve beef with vegetables and sauce.

SERVES 4
per serving 10.6g carbohydrate; 43.2g fat; 757 cal; 81.8g protein

moroccan minted beef

PREPARATION TIME 15 MINUTES   COOKING TIME 20 MINUTES

1 tablespoon vegetable oil

1 large onion, sliced thinly

2 teaspoons ground cumin

1 teaspoon finely grated lemon peel

14 ounces canned crushed tomatoes

7 ounces green beans, trimmed

1½ pounds top sirloin steak,
    thinly sliced crosswise

2 tablespoons slivered almonds, toasted

2 teaspoons finely shredded fresh
    mint leaves

1   Heat oil in skillet; cook onion, stirring, until soft. Add cumin and peel to skillet; cook until fragrant. Stir in undrained tomatoes. Bring to boil; simmer, stirring occasionally, about 5 minutes or until mixture thickens slightly.

2   Meanwhile, boil, steam or microwave beans until just tender; drain. Rinse under cold water; drain.

3   Cook beef, in batches, in separate heated oiled large skillet until browned all over and tender; stir in tomato mixture, almonds and mint. Serve with beans.

SERVES 4
per serving 7.5g carbohydrate; 19.1g fat; 373 cal; 43g protein

beef and mushrooms in red wine sauce

PREPARATION TIME 20 MINUTES   COOKING TIME 2 HOURS

7 slices bacon, sliced thinly

1¾-pound brisket, diced into
   ¾-inch pieces

1 cup dry red wine

2 tablespoons tomato paste

1½ cups beef broth

1 cup water

2 cloves garlic, crushed in
   garlic press

1 teaspoon fresh thyme leaves

1 tablespoon vegetable oil

16 shallots

14 ounces button mushrooms

1 head broccoli, trimmed,
   chopped coarsely

½ cup coarsely chopped fresh
   flat-leaf parsley

1   Cook bacon in large heavy-bottomed saucepan, stirring, until browned; drain on paper towel. Cook beef, in batches, in same pan, stirring, until browned all over.

2   Return bacon and beef to pan with wine, paste, broth, the water, garlic and thyme; bring to a boil. Reduce heat; simmer, covered, 1½ hours or until tender.

3   Meanwhile, heat oil in large skillet, cook whole shallots, stirring occasionally, until browned and starting to soften. Add mushrooms; cook, stirring, 10 minutes or until softened.

4   Remove beef from pan; cover to keep warm. Bring sauce in pan to a boil. Reduce heat; simmer, uncovered, until reduced by half.

5   Meanwhile, boil, steam or microwave broccoli until tender; drain.

6   Return beef to pan with red wine sauce, add mushroom mixture; stir gently until heated through. Stir in parsley off the heat. Serve beef and mushrooms in red wine sauce with broccoli.

SERVES 4

per serving 8.7g carbohydrate; 30.8g fat; 626 cal; 67.7g protein

beef and mushrooms in red wine sauce

spicy grilled beef and citrus salad

spicy grilled beef and citrus salad

PREPARATION TIME 25 MINUTES (PLUS REFRIGERATION TIME)   COOKING TIME 10 MINUTES

You need two oranges and four limes for this recipe.

2 cloves garlic, crushed in
   garlic press

⅓ cup fresh orange juice

¼ cup fresh lime juice

1 tablespoon soy sauce

1 teaspoon red pepper flakes

1 tablespoon white wine vinegar

1¾ pounds round steak

1 bunch asparagus, trimmed

1 medium orange

2½ cups (5 ounces) mesclun

8 ounces belgian endive,
   chopped roughly

½ cup coarsely chopped fresh basil

3 shallots, sliced thinly

8 ounces cherry tomatoes, halved

CITRUS DRESSING

⅓ cup fresh lime juice

1 tablespoon fresh orange juice

2 teaspoons olive oil

1 Combine garlic, juices, sauce, pepper flakes and vinegar in large bowl with beef; toss to coat in marinade. Cover; refrigerate 3 hours or overnight.

2 Cook beef on heated oiled grill or grill pan until browned both sides and cooked as desired. Cover; let stand 10 minutes, then slice thinly.

3 Meanwhile, cook asparagus on heated oiled grill or grill pan until browned lightly and just tender; cut each spear into thirds.

4 Make citrus dressing.

5 Peel and segment orange over large bowl. Place beef, asparagus, remaining ingredients and dressing in bowl; toss gently to combine.

CITRUS DRESSING Combine ingredients in screw-top jar; shake well.

SERVES 4
per serving 10.1g carbohydrate; 12.1g fat; 347 cal; 47.6g protein

ginger beef stir-fry

PREPARATION TIME 20 MINUTES   COOKING TIME 10 MINUTES

2½-inch piece fresh ginger

2 tablespoons peanut oil

1¼ pounds beef round steak, sliced thinly

2 cloves garlic, crushed in garlic press

4 ounces green beans, cut into 2-inch lengths

8 scallions, sliced thinly

2 teaspoons light brown sugar

2 teaspoons oyster sauce

1 tablespoon fish sauce

1 tablespoon soy sauce

½ cup loosely packed fresh basil leaves

1   Slice peeled ginger thinly; stack slices, then slice again into thin slivers.

2   Heat half of the oil in wok or large skillet; stir-fry beef, in batches, until browned all over.

3   Heat remaining oil in wok; stir-fry ginger and garlic until fragrant. Add beans; stir-fry until just tender.

4   Return beef to wok with scallion, sugar and sauces; stir-fry until sugar dissolves and beef is cooked as desired. Remove from heat, toss basil leaves through stir-fry.

SERVES 4
per serving 4.7g carbohydrate; 19.4g fat; 334 cal; 35.4g protein

minted veal with baby squash

PREPARATION TIME 15 MINUTES   COOKING TIME 1 HOUR

2 tablespoons olive oil

12 veal loin chops (3 pounds)

2 medium onions, sliced

3 cloves garlic, crushed in garlic press

2 teaspoons ground turmeric

¼ teaspoon cardamom seeds

1 teaspoon ground nutmeg

1 teaspoon grated lemon peel

1 tablespoon tomato paste

2 tablespoons chopped fresh mint

2 cups beef broth

7 ounces baby yellow squash, halved

1 tablespoon cornstarch

2 tablespoons water

1   Heat oil in large saucepan, add veal in batches, cook until browned all over; remove.

2   Add onion, garlic and spices to same pan; cook, stirring, until onion is soft. Add peel, paste, mint, broth and veal; simmer, covered, about 30 minutes or until veal is tender.

3   Add squash; simmer, uncovered, about 10 minutes or until squash is tender. Add blended cornstarch and water; stir over heat until mixture boils and thickens.

SERVES 4
per serving 9.4g carbohydrate; 17g fat; 498 cal; 76g protein

flank steak, cheese and pepper stacks

PREPARATION TIME 20 MINUTES   COOKING TIME 20 MINUTES

1 medium red bell pepper

4 flank steaks (about 1 pound)

4 thick slices gouda cheese

1 cup (1½ ounces) baby
  spinach leaves

14 ounces sugarsnap peas

1   Quarter pepper; remove and discard seeds and membranes. Roast under broiler, skin-side up, until skin blisters and blackens. Cover pepper pieces with plastic wrap or paper for 5 minutes. Peel away skin.

2   Preheat oven to hot.

3   Cut steaks in half horizontally; divide gouda cheese, spinach and pepper among four steak halves, cover with remaining steak halves. Tie stacks with kitchen string; cook, uncovered, in lightly oiled large nonstick skillet until browned both sides. Transfer to roasting pan; cook, uncovered, in hot oven about 10 minutes or until cooked as desired.

4   Meanwhile, boil, steam or microwave peas until just tender; drain.

5   Serve stacks with peas.

SERVES 4
per serving 6.3g carbohydrate; 17.3g fat; 334 cal; 38.4g protein

T-bones with blue-cheese butter and pear salad

PREPARATION TIME 15 MINUTES   COOKING TIME 10 MINUTES

four 14-ounce T-bone steaks

2 tablespoons olive oil

2 ounces soft blue cheese

3 tablespoons butter, softened

2 scallions, chopped finely

1 tablespoon grainy mustard

1 teaspoon honey

¼ cup olive oil, extra

1 tablespoon red wine vinegar

2 cups (3½ ounces) mesclun

1 pear, cored, sliced thinly

½ cup pecans, toasted

1   Brush beef with oil; cook on heated oiled grill or grill pan until browned both sides and cooked as desired.

2   Meanwhile, combine cheese, butter and scallion in small bowl. Combine mustard, honey, extra oil and vinegar in screw-top jar; shake well.

3   Place mesclun, pear and mustard dressing in medium bowl; toss gently to combine. Sprinkle with nuts.

4   Spread blue-cheese butter on hot beef; serve with salad.

SERVES 4
per serving 10g carbohydrate; 63.1g fat; 835 cal; 59g protein

braised vinegared beef with chinese greens

PREPARATION TIME 15 MINUTES (PLUS REFRIGERATION TIME)   COOKING TIME 20 MINUTES

You need one bunch each of bok choy and choy sum for this recipe.

1¾ pounds round steak,
   sliced thinly

1 tablespoon fresh lime juice

1 tablespoon grated fresh ginger

2 cloves garlic, crushed in
   garlic press

1 tablespoon finely shredded fresh
   basil leaves

1 teaspoon sugar

1 tablespoon vegetable oil

2 teaspoons sesame oil

1 medium white onion, sliced thinly

1 small chinese cabbage, shredded
   (about 14 ounces)

14 ounces bok choy, shredded

13 ounces choy sum, shredded

2 tablespoons balsamic vinegar

5 cups (8 ounces) baby
   spinach leaves

5 ounces snow peas

1 tablespoon sesame
   seeds, toasted

1 Combine beef in large bowl with juice, ginger, garlic, basil and sugar. Cover; refrigerate at least 3 hours or overnight.

2 Drain beef; discard marinade. Heat half of the combined oils in wok; stir-fry onion until soft. Add beef; stir-fry, in batches, until browned and cooked as desired. Transfer beef mixture to large bowl.

3 Add cabbage, bok choy, choy sum, half of the vinegar and remaining oils to wok; stir-fry until just wilted, add to bowl with beef. Add spinach, snow peas and remaining vinegar to wok; stir-fry until just wilted.

4 Return beef and vegetables to wok; gently toss over heat until heated through, sprinkle with sesame seeds.

SERVES 4
per serving 9.7g carbohydrate; 22.7g fat; 450 cal; 51.4g protein

beef skewers on lettuce cups

PREPARATION TIME 45 MINUTES (PLUS REFRIGERATION TIME)   COOKING TIME 10 MINUTES

Soak 16 bamboo skewers in water for at least an hour prior to use to prevent splintering or scorching.

1 pound beef round steak, sliced thinly

½ hothouse cucumber, peeled, halved,
   then quartered lengthwise

6 scallions, cut into 2-inch lengths,
   then into thin strips

1 cup (3½ ounces) fresh bean sprouts

1 large carrot cut into 2-inch lengths,
   then into strips

8 large lettuce leaves

MARINADE

2 tablespoons finely chopped
   fresh lemongrass

1 medium white onion, sliced thinly

2 cloves garlic, crushed in garlic press

2 teaspoons sugar

2 red serrano chiles, seeded,
   chopped finely

2 teaspoons sesame oil

2 teaspoons sesame seeds

SAUCE

2 cloves garlic, chopped finely

1 red serrano chile, seeded,
   chopped finely

1 tablespoon sugar

2 tablespoons fresh lime juice

¼ cup rice vinegar

¼ cup fish sauce

¼ cup water

1   Make marinade.

2   Combine beef and marinade in large bowl. Cover; refrigerate 3 hours or overnight.

3   Thread beef onto 16 skewers. Cook beef on heated oiled grill or grill pan, uncovered, until cooked as desired.

4   Meanwhile, make sauce.

5   Divide cucumber, scallion, sprouts and carrot among lettuce leaves. Top with beef; drizzle with sauce.

MARINADE   Combine ingredients in small bowl.

SAUCE   Blend or process ingredients until combined.

SERVES 4
per serving   10.9g carbohydrate; 11.8g fat; 282 cal; 32.3g protein
tip   If using metal skewers, oil them first to prevent the meat from sticking.

veal cutlets with lemon and thyme sauce

PREPARATION TIME 10 MINUTES   COOKING TIME 20 MINUTES

Any asian greens can be used in this recipe. Try it with bok choy, choy sum, or gai larn
(also known as chinese broccoli). You need one bunch of asian greens for this recipe.

10 tablespoons butter

2 tablespoons sweet chili sauce

2 teaspoons grated lemon peel

⅓ cup fresh lemon juice

1 tablespoon chopped fresh thyme

eight 4-ounce boneless veal cutlets

1 pound asian greens

1   Melt butter in small skillet; add sauce, peel and juice. Cook, stirring, over medium heat about 5 minutes or until sauce thickens slightly. Stir in thyme; cool.

2   Spread half of the sauce over both sides of veal; cook veal on heated oiled grill or grill pan until browned both sides and cooked as desired.

3   Just before serving, boil, steam or microwave greens until just wilted; drain. Serve topped with veal and sauce.

SERVES 4
per serving 5g carbohydrate; 38.3g fat; 548 cal; 46g protein

rib roast provençale with pine nut cauliflower

PREPARATION TIME 15 MINUTES (PLUS REFRIGERATION TIME)   COOKING TIME 1 HOUR 25 MINUTES

3-pound standing rib roast

2 cups dry red wine

⅓ cup olive oil

3 cloves garlic, sliced thinly

2 teaspoons chopped fresh thyme

2 teaspoons chopped fresh rosemary

4 bay leaves

3 medium white onions, quartered

1 small cauliflower (about 2 pounds)

2 cloves garlic, extra, crushed in garlic press

2 tablespoons pine nuts

2 teaspoons red pepper flakes

2 tablespoons chopped fresh flat-leaf parsley

1   Place beef in large shallow roasting pan with combined wine, 2 tablespoons oil, sliced garlic, herbs and onions. Cover; refrigerate 3 hours or overnight.

2   Drain beef and onions over small pan; reserve marinade. Bring marinade to boil; simmer, uncovered, until reduced by half.

3   Cook beef on heated oiled grill until browned all over. Place beef and onions on roasting rack or in disposable roasting pan. Cook in covered grill, using indirect heat, following manufacturer's instructions, and brushing occasionally with marinade, about 1 hour or until cooked as desired.

4   Meanwhile, separate cauliflower into florets. Boil, steam or microwave cauliflower until almost tender. Drain; pat dry.

5   Heat remaining oil in medium skillet; cook crushed garlic, pine nuts and pepper flakes, stirring, over low heat until garlic and pepper are fragrant and nuts are browned lightly.

6   Add cauliflower; cook, stirring, until well coated in oil mixture. Add parsley; stir until combined. Serve rib roast with cauliflower.

SERVES 4
per serving 11.9g carbohydrate; 43.5g fat; 823 cal; 76.2g protein

veal with anchovy butter and beans

PREPARATION TIME 10 MINUTES   COOKING TIME 20 MINUTES

5 tablespoons butter, softened

4 anchovy fillets, drained, chopped finely

2 teaspoons fresh lemon juice

1 tablespoon coarsely chopped fresh dill

eight 10-ounce veal chops

10 ounces green beans, trimmed

10 ounces yellow string beans, trimmed

1   Combine butter, anchovy, juice and dill in small bowl.

2   Cook veal, in batches, on heated oiled grill or grill pan until cooked as desired.

3   Meanwhile, boil, steam or microwave beans until just tender; drain.

4   Serve veal with beans; top with anchovy butter.

SERVES 4
per serving 4.1g carbohydrate; 24.4g fat; 398 cal; 40.8g protein

stir-fried beef, bok choy and chinese broccoli

PREPARATION TIME 10 MINUTES   COOKING TIME 25 MINUTES

You need one bunch of chinese broccoli and two bunches of baby bok choy for this recipe.

2 tablespoons peanut oil

1 pound beef round steak, sliced thinly

2 cloves garlic, crushed in garlic press

2 teaspoons grated fresh ginger

1 tablespoon finely chopped
    fresh lemongrass

2 red serrano chiles, seeded, sliced thinly

2 pounds baby bok choy, chopped coarsely

1 pound chinese broccoli, chopped coarsely

4 scallions, sliced thinly

2 tablespoons kecap manis

1 tablespoon fish sauce

¼ cup sweet chili sauce

¼ cup fresh lime juice

¼ cup coarsely chopped fresh mint

¼ cup coarsely chopped fresh cilantro

1   Heat half of the oil in wok or large skillet; stir-fry beef, in batches, until browned all over.

2   Heat remaining oil in same wok; stir-fry garlic, ginger, lemongrass and chile until fragrant. Add vegetables; stir-fry until vegetables just wilt. Return beef to wok with scallion, kecap manis, sauces and juice; stir-fry until heated through. Remove from heat; stir through herbs.

SERVES 4
per serving 8.6g carbohydrate; 17.7g fat; 331 cal; 33.9g protein

corned beef with redcurrant glaze and sautéed red cabbage

PREPARATION TIME 15 MINUTES   COOKING TIME 2 HOURS

You need about half of a head of red cabbage for this recipe.

3-pound piece corned beef brisket

2 bay leaves

¼ cup malt vinegar

8 black peppercorns

8 cloves

1 medium onion, chopped coarsely

1 stalk celery, trimmed,

   chopped coarsely

1½ cups chicken broth

½ cup redcurrant jelly

2 tablespoons port

1 tablespoon fresh rosemary leaves

1 tablespoon olive oil

4½ cups coarsely shredded

   red cabbage

1   Place beef, bay leaves, vinegar, peppercorns, cloves, onion, celery and broth in large saucepan. Cover with cold water; bring to a boil. Reduce heat; simmer, uncovered, 1 hour. Remove beef from broth.

2   Preheat oven to hot. Combine jelly, port and rosemary in small bowl. Place beef in large casserole. Brush beef with half of the redcurrant mixture. Bake, uncovered, in hot oven, about 30 minutes or until browned all over and tender, brushing beef occasionally with remaining redcurrant mixture. Remove beef from casserole; cover to keep warm.

3   Strain broth into same casserole; bring to a boil. Reduce heat; simmer, uncovered, stirring, until sauce thickens slightly.

4   Meanwhile, heat oil in medium skillet. Add cabbage, cook, stirring, for 2 minutes.

5   Top beef with sauce; serve with sautéed cabbage.

SERVES 4

per serving 11.9g carbohydrate; 22.2g fat; 604 cal; 86.1g protein
tip The remaining broth can be used as a base for a soup; refrigerate until cold, then discard the fat from the top before using.

venetian calf's liver and onions

PREPARATION TIME 10 MINUTES   COOKING TIME 25 MINUTES

A traditional Venetian dish, the classic fegato alla veneziana is found on the menus of Italian restaurants around the world yet is easy enough to make at home. The secret to its success is that the calf's liver should be sliced into paper-thin scallops, then quickly seared – overcooking will toughen its delicate texture.

3 tablespoons butter

2 tablespoons olive oil

3 medium onions, sliced thinly

2 teaspoons cornstarch

¾ cup beef broth

2 teaspoons dijon mustard

2 bunches broccoli rabe

1 pound calf's liver, sliced thinly

½ teaspoon balsamic vinegar

1 Heat butter and half of the oil in large skillet; cook onion, stirring, until soft. Stir in blended cornstarch, broth and mustard; cook, stirring, until sauce boils and thickens.

2 Meanwhile, boil, steam or microwave broccoli rabe until just tender; drain.

3 Heat remaining oil in large skillet; cook liver quickly over high heat until browned both sides and cooked as desired. Stir vinegar into sauce just before serving with broccoli rabe and liver.

SERVES 4
per serving 12g carbohydrate; 43.3g fat; 577 cal; 35.8g protein

veal parmigiana

PREPARATION TIME 15 MINUTES   COOKING TIME 25 MINUTES

2 teaspoons olive oil

1 medium onion, chopped finely

2 cloves garlic, crushed in

    garlic press

14 ounces canned crushed tomatoes

¼ cup tomato paste

1 tablespoon balsamic vinegar

1 teaspoon sugar

1 tablespoon shredded fresh

    basil leaves

2 small eggplants, unpeeled, cut into

    ½-inch slices

8 veal cutlets (2 pounds)

1½ cups grated mozzarella cheese

1   Heat oil in small skillet; cook onion and garlic, stirring, until onion is soft. Add undrained tomatoes, paste, vinegar and sugar; simmer, uncovered, about 10 minutes or until sauce thickens, stir in basil.

2   Meanwhile, cook eggplant on heated oiled grill or grill pan until browned both sides.

3   Cook veal on heated oiled grill or grill pan until browned one side. Turn veal, top with sauce, eggplant and cheese; cook until cheese is melted and veal is cooked as desired.

SERVES 4

per serving 10.4g carbohydrate; 11.8g fat; 409 cal; 64.3g protein

asian roast beef

PREPARATION TIME 15 MINUTES   COOKING TIME 55 MINUTES

Any asian greens can be used in this recipe. Try it with bok choy, choy sum, or gai larn (also known as chinese broccoli). You will need one bunch of asian greens for this recipe.

1½ pounds boneless beef rib roast

2 tablespoons kecap manis

1 tablespoon sesame seeds

2 cloves garlic, crushed in garlic press

2 teaspoons sesame oil

1 teaspoon grated fresh ginger

1 small red bell pepper, sliced thinly

1¼ pounds asian greens,

    chopped coarsely

⅓ cup oyster sauce

2 tablespoons water

1 tablespoon fresh lime juice

1   Preheat oven to moderately hot.

2   Cook beef, uncovered, in heated, lightly oiled wok or large skillet about 10 minutes or until browned. Place beef on oiled wire rack in casserole; brush with combined kecap manis, sesame seeds and half of the garlic. Roast beef, uncovered, in moderately hot oven about 45 minutes or until cooked as desired. Cover; let stand 5 minutes, slice thickly.

3   Meanwhile, heat oil in same wok; stir-fry ginger and remaining garlic until fragrant. Add remaining ingredients; stir-fry until greens are just wilted. Serve beef on greens mixture, drizzled with sauce from wok.

SERVES 4

per serving 11.6g carbohydrate; 10.1g fat; 307 cal; 41.5g protein

mustard T-bone with chile-garlic mushrooms

PREPARATION TIME 10 MINUTES   COOKING TIME 20 MINUTES

2 tablespoons olive oil

1 tablespoon butter

3 cloves garlic, crushed in
    garlic press

1 red serrano chile, finely chopped

1 pound button mushrooms

1 tablespoon fresh lemon juice

½ teaspoon cracked black pepper

four 10-ounce T-bone steaks

⅓ cup dijon mustard

½ cup coarsely chopped fresh
    flat-leaf parsley

¼ cup coarsely chopped
    fresh rosemary

1   Heat oil and butter in large skillet, add garlic, chile and mushrooms, cook, stirring, about 5 minutes or until mushrooms are tender. Add juice and pepper. Cover to keep warm.

2   Meanwhile, brush beef all over with mustard; cook on heated oiled grill or grill pan, uncovered, until browned and cooked as desired. Sprinkle beef and mushrooms with combined herbs.

SERVES 4
per serving 2.7g carbohydrate; 24.1g fat; 410 cal; 45.9g protein

veal chops with oregano and vegetables

PREPARATION TIME 30 MINUTES   COOKING TIME 1 HOUR

8 small veal shoulder chops
    (2 pounds)

2 tablespoons all-purpose flour

2 tablespoons vegetable oil

1½ cups chicken broth

⅓ cup dry white wine

10 scallions, trimmed

2 teaspoons finely chopped
    fresh oregano

2 bay leaves

8 baby carrots

3 ounces fresh baby corn

5 ounces baby green beans, halved

1 tablespoon finely chopped
    fresh parsley

1   Toss veal in flour; shake away and reserve excess flour.

2   Heat oil in large deep skillet. Cook veal, in batches, until browned both sides. Remove.

3   Stir reserved flour in skillet over heat until bubbling. Remove from heat; gradually stir in broth and wine. Stir over heat until sauce boils and thickens.

4   Return veal to skillet. Stir in scallion, oregano and bay leaves; simmer, covered, 20 minutes, stirring occasionally.

5   Stir in carrots and corn; simmer, covered, about 10 minutes. Add beans; simmer, covered, about 5 minutes or until veal and vegetables are tender. Discard bay leaves; stir in parsley off the heat.

SERVES 4
per serving 11.9g carbohydrate; 17g fat; 408 cal; 48.2g protein

veal chops with black olive-anchovy butter

PREPARATION TIME 25 MINUTES (PLUS REFRIGERATION TIME)
COOKING TIME 1 HOUR

2 cloves garlic, crushed in garlic press

2 tablespoons olive oil

four 6-ounce veal chops

2 medium eggplants

3 cloves garlic, unpeeled

3 scallions, chopped finely

2 tablespoons fresh lemon juice

2 tablespoons unflavored yogurt

BLACK OLIVE-ANCHOVY BUTTER

¼ cup pitted black olives

2 anchovy fillets, drained

4 ounces butter, softened

1   Combine crushed garlic and half of the oil with veal in large bowl; toss to coat all over. Cover; refrigerate 30 minutes.

2   Preheat oven to moderate.

3   Cut eggplant in half lengthwise; score flesh, brush with half of the remaining oil. Place eggplant on lightly oiled baking sheet with unpeeled garlic cloves; bake, uncovered, in moderate oven about 45 minutes or until eggplant softens. Reserve roasted garlic for black olive-anchovy butter.

4   Meanwhile, make black olive-anchovy butter.

5   Scrape flesh from eggplant; chop coarsely, then push eggplant through fine strainer into medium bowl.

6   Heat remaining oil in small skillet; cook scallion, stirring, until soft. Remove skillet from heat; stir in eggplant, juice and yogurt.

7   Cook veal on heated oiled grill or grill pan until browned all over and cooked as desired. Divide eggplant mixture among serving plates; top each with veal chop then black olive-anchovy butter.

BLACK OLIVE-ANCHOVY BUTTER Remove skin from roasted garlic. Blend or process garlic with remaining ingredients until smooth. Cover; let stand at room temperature until ready to use.

SERVES 4
per serving 6.1g carbohydrate; 34.1g fat; 463 cal; 33g protein

vietnamese beef, chicken and tofu soup

PREPARATION TIME 20 MINUTES   COOKING TIME 1 HOUR 5 MINUTES

Star anise is a dried star-shaped fruit of a tree native to China.
The pods, which have an astringent aniseed or licorice flavor,
are widely used in the Asian kitchen.

12 cups water

1 pound beef brisket

1 star anise

1-inch piece fresh ginger, halved

¼ cup soy sauce

2 tablespoons fish sauce

**12 ounces skinless, boneless
   chicken breasts**

**1½ cups (4 ounces) fresh
   bean sprouts**

**1 cup loosely packed fresh
   cilantro leaves**

4 scallions, sliced thinly

2 red serrano chiles, sliced thinly

⅓ cup fresh lime juice

**10 ounces firm tofu, cut into
   ¾-inch cubes**

1 Combine the water, beef, star anise, ginger and sauces in soup
   pot; bring to a boil. Reduce heat; simmer, covered, 30 minutes.
   Uncover, simmer 20 minutes. Add chicken; simmer, uncovered,
   10 minutes.

2 Combine sprouts, cilantro, scallion, chile and juice in
   medium bowl.

3 Remove beef and chicken from pot; reserve broth. Discard fat and
   sinew from beef, slice thinly. Slice chicken thinly. Return beef and
   chicken to pot; reheat soup.

4 Divide tofu among serving bowls; ladle hot soup over tofu, sprinkle
   with sprout mixture. Serve with lime wedges and extra chile,
   if desired.

SERVES 4
per serving 3.6g carbohydrate; 18.8g fat; 337 cal; 37.6g protein

steak with redcurrant sauce

PREPARATION TIME 5 MINUTES   COOKING TIME 10 MINUTES

¼ cup olive oil

four 7-ounce ribeye steaks

½ cup dry red wine

¾ cup beef broth

2 tablespoons redcurrant jelly

1 bunch broccoli, chopped coarsely

½ cup coarsely grated

    parmesan cheese

1 teaspoon cracked black pepper

1 Heat 1 tablespoon of the oil in large skillet; cook beef, in batches, until cooked as desired. Cover to keep warm.

2 Combine wine, broth and jelly in same skillet; cook, stirring, until mixture boils and thickens slightly.

3 Meanwhile, boil, steam or microwave broccoli until just tender; drain. Place broccoli in large bowl with cheese, pepper and remaining oil; toss gently until cheese melts.

4 Serve beef with redcurrant sauce and cheesy broccoli.

SERVES 4
per serving 9.3g carbohydrate; 29.1g fat; 529 cal; 53g protein
tip If you don't have redcurrant jelly, cranberry sauce is a good substitute.

veal medallions with olive paste and zucchini with chile-basil dressing

PREPARATION TIME 15 MINUTES   COOKING TIME 20 MINUTES (PLUS STANDING TIME)

2 cups firmly packed fresh

    parsley leaves

½ cup pitted black olives

2 tablespoons drained capers

1 tablespoon fresh lemon juice

1 clove garlic, crushed in garlic press

6 medium zucchini, cut lengthwise

    into ½-inch slices

⅓ cup olive oil

2 tablespoons red wine vinegar

2 tablespoons chopped fresh

    basil leaves

2 red serrano chiles, chopped finely

4 veal medallions (1¾ pounds)

8 slices prosciutto

1 Blend or process parsley until finely chopped. With motor running, add olives, capers, juice and garlic; blend until almost smooth.

2 Cook zucchini, in batches, on heated oiled grill or grill pan until charred and tender. Combine hot zucchini with oil, vinegar, basil and chile in large bowl; cover, let stand at room temperature for at least 1 hour before serving.

3 Spread olive mixture around the edge of each medallion; wrap 2 slices prosciutto around each piece to cover olive mixture, secure with toothpicks.

4 Cook veal on heated oiled grill or grill pan until browned both sides and cooked as desired. Just before serving, remove toothpicks. Serve with marinated zucchini.

SERVES 4
per serving 6.1g carbohydrate; 23.5g fat; 449 cal; 52.5g protein

steak with green pepper salsa

PREPARATION TIME 15 MINUTES   COOKING TIME 15 MINUTES

four 6-ounce boneless beef loin steaks

2 cups (3½ ounces) arugula

GREEN PEPPER SALSA

2 small green bell peppers, chopped finely

1 small red onion, chopped finely

1 red serrano chile, seeded, chopped finely

6 scallions, sliced thinly

¼ cup fresh lime juice

2 tablespoons finely chopped fresh mint

1   Make green pepper salsa.

2   Cook beef on heated oiled grill or grill pan until browned both sides and cooked as desired.

3   Divide arugula evenly among four serving plates; top with green pepper salsa. Serve with beef.

GREEN PEPPER SALSA   Combine ingredients in medium bowl.

SERVES 4
per serving   3.9g carbohydrate; 7g fat; 246 cal; 41.3g protein
tip   The salsa can be made several hours ahead and refrigerated, covered.

veal and ratatouille salad with pesto dressing

PREPARATION TIME 35 MINUTES   COOKING TIME 20 MINUTES

5 baby eggplants, sliced thickly

2 medium zucchini, sliced thickly

1 medium red onion, halved, cut into wedges

1 large red bell pepper, cut into 1-inch pieces

**1 medium yellow bell pepper, cut into
   1-inch pieces**

8 ounces pear tomatoes

2 cloves garlic, crushed in garlic press

2 tablespoons olive oil

four 12-ounce veal loin chops

1 cup loosely packed fresh basil leaves

5 ounces firm goat cheese, crumbled

PESTO DRESSING

2 cloves garlic, crushed in garlic press

2 tablespoons finely grated parmesan cheese

1 tablespoon toasted pine nuts

1 tablespoon fresh lemon juice

½ cup firmly packed fresh basil leaves

½ cup olive oil

1   Preheat oven to very hot. Grease two large shallow casseroles.

2   Divide combined eggplant, zucchini, onion, peppers, tomatoes, garlic and oil between casseroles. Roast, uncovered, in very hot oven about 20 minutes or until tender, stirring occasionally.

3   Meanwhile, make pesto dressing.

4   Cook veal in heated large nonstick skillet until browned and cooked as desired. Cover; let stand 5 minutes.

5   Place vegetables in large bowl with basil and cheese; toss gently to combine. Divide vegetables among serving plates; top with veal, drizzle with dressing.

PESTO DRESSING   Blend or process ingredients until smooth.

SERVES 4
per serving   11.6g carbohydrate; 54.8g fat; 852 cal; 78.7g protein

basil and oregano steak with grilled vegetables

PREPARATION TIME 20 MINUTES (PLUS REFRIGERATION TIME)
COOKING TIME 30 MINUTES

2 teaspoons finely chopped
   fresh oregano

¼ cup finely chopped fresh basil

1 tablespoon finely grated
   lemon peel

2 tablespoons fresh lemon juice

4 anchovy fillets, chopped finely

four 8-ounce sirloin steaks

2 bulbs baby fennel, quartered

3 small zucchini, chopped coarsely

1 large red bell pepper,
   sliced thickly

7 ounces portobello mushrooms,
   sliced thickly

4 baby eggplants, chopped coarsely

2 small red onions, sliced thickly

2 teaspoons olive oil

¼ cup fresh lemon juice

2 tablespoons fresh oregano leaves

1   Combine oregano, basil, peel, juice and anchovy in large bowl; add beef, toss to coat in paste. Cover; refrigerate 15 minutes.

2   Meanwhile, combine fennel, zucchini, pepper, mushroom, eggplant, onion and oil in large bowl; cook, in batches, on heated, lightly oiled grill or grill pan until browned all over and just tender. Toss in same cleaned bowl with juice and oregano leaves; cover to keep warm.

3   Cook beef on same grill or grill pan until browned both sides and cooked as desired. Serve beef with vegetables.

SERVES 4
per serving 10.7g carbohydrate; 37.7g fat; 565 cal; 45.2g protein

basil and oregano steak with grilled vegetables

crying tiger

crying tiger

PREPARATION TIME 25 MINUTES (PLUS REFRIGERATION TIME)   COOKING TIME 10 MINUTES

Bangkok's famous crying tiger's spicy flavor is supposed to be hot enough to make even a tiger cry. You need about a quarter of a head of napa cabbage for this recipe.

1¼-pound piece beef tenderloin

1 teaspoon tamarind concentrate

2 cloves garlic, crushed in

  garlic press

2 teaspoons pickled green

  peppercorns, crushed

2 tablespoons fish sauce

2 tablespoons soy sauce

1 stalk fresh lemongrass, trimmed,

  chopped finely

2 red serrano chiles, chopped finely

1 medium red bell pepper,

  sliced thickly

1 cup finely shredded

  napa cabbage

6 trimmed red radishes,

  sliced thickly

4 scallions, cut into 1-inch pieces

CRYING TIGER SAUCE

2 teaspoons tamarind concentrate

¼ cup fish sauce

¼ cup fresh lime juice

2 teaspoons light brown sugar

1 red serrano chile, chopped finely

1 scallion, sliced thinly

2 teaspoons finely chopped

  fresh cilantro

1 Halve beef lengthwise. Combine tamarind, garlic, peppercorns, sauces, lemongrass and chile in large bowl; add beef, toss to coat in marinade. Cover; refrigerate 3 hours or overnight.

2 Cook beef on heated oiled grill or grill pan about 10 minutes or until browned and cooked as desired. Cover beef; let stand 10 minutes, then slice thinly.

3 Meanwhile, make crying tiger sauce.

4 Place beef on serving platter with pepper, cabbage, radish and scallion; serve with crying tiger sauce.

CRYING TIGER SAUCE Combine ingredients in small bowl; whisk until sugar dissolves.

SERVES 4
per serving 6.6g carbohydrate; 7.8g fat; 256 cal; 38.7g protein

stir-fried lamb in black bean sauce

PREPARATION TIME 15 MINUTES   COOKING TIME 15 MINUTES

1¼ pounds trimmed, boneless leg of lamb,
    sliced thinly

1 teaspoon five-spice powder

2 teaspoons sesame oil

2 tablespoons peanut oil

2 cloves garlic, crushed in garlic press

1 teaspoon grated fresh ginger

1 medium onion, sliced thinly

1 small red bell pepper, sliced thinly

1 small yellow bell pepper, sliced thinly

6 scallions, sliced thinly

1 teaspoon cornstarch

½ cup chicken broth

1 tablespoon soy sauce

2 tablespoons black bean sauce

1   Place lamb in medium bowl with combined five-spice and sesame oil; toss lamb to coat in five-spice mixture.

2   Heat half of the peanut oil in wok or large skillet; stir-fry lamb, in batches, until browned lightly.

3   Heat remaining peanut oil in same wok; stir-fry garlic, ginger and onion until onion just softens. Add peppers and scallion; stir-fry until pepper is just tender.

4   Blend cornstarch with broth and sauces in small measuring cup. Add cornstarch mixture to wok with lamb; stir until sauce boils and thickens slightly and lamb is cooked as desired.

SERVES 4
per serving 7.9g carbohydrate; 17.4g fat; 332 cal; 35.8g protein

lamb and artichoke kebabs

PREPARATION TIME 5 MINUTES   COOKING TIME 15 MINUTES

Soak eight bamboo skewers in water for at least an hour prior to use to prevent splintering or scorching.

2 pounds trimmed, boneless leg of lamb,
    cut into 1-inch cubes

1 pound 12 ounces canned artichoke hearts,
    drained, halved

1 large red bell pepper, chopped into
    1-inch pieces

10 ounces button mushrooms, halved

GARLIC BASIL DRESSING

½ cup red wine vinegar

¼ cup olive oil

1 tablespoon shredded fresh basil leaves

1 clove garlic, crushed in garlic press

1 teaspoon sugar

1 teaspoon dijon mustard

1   Make garlic basil dressing.

2   Thread lamb, artichoke hearts, pepper and mushrooms on eight large skewers.

3   Cook kebabs, in batches, on heated oiled grill or grill pan until browned all over and cooked as desired. Serve with garlic basil dressing.

GARLIC BASIL DRESSING   Combine all ingredients in screw-top jar; shake well.

SERVES 4
per serving 6.9g carbohydrate; 19.9g fat; 468 cal; 63.6g protein
tip If using metal skewers, oil them first to prevent the meat from sticking.

tomato and bocconcini lamb stacks

PREPARATION TIME 15 MINUTES   COOKING TIME 15 MINUTES

2 teaspoons olive oil

2 tablespoons balsamic vinegar

2 cloves garlic, crushed in

garlic press

24 french-trimmed lamb rib chops,

bone-in

3 large plum tomatoes, sliced

10 ounces bocconcini cheese, sliced

2 tablespoons coarsely chopped

fresh basil

1 Combine oil, vinegar and garlic in small measuring cup; brush over lamb. Cook lamb, uncovered, on heated oiled grill or grill pan until browned on one side; remove, place on baking sheet, cooked-side up.

2 Layer tomato, bocconcini and basil on cooked side of 12 chops; top with remaining 12 chops, cooked-side down. Tie stacks together with kitchen string; return to grill. Cook until browned both sides and cooked as desired.

SERVES 4
per serving 1.4g carbohydrate; 52.4g fat; 711 cal; 59.2g protein

lamb with garlic and shiitake mushrooms

PREPARATION TIME 10 MINUTES   COOKING TIME 50 MINUTES

12 cloves garlic, peeled

1 tablespoon sugar

¼ cup olive oil

3 boneless lamb loins

(about 2 pounds)

14 ounces stemmed shiitake

mushrooms, halved

3 tablespoons butter, melted

2 tablespoons chopped fresh chives

1 Combine garlic, sugar and 2 tablespoons of the oil in disposable roasting pan. Cook in covered grill, using indirect heat, following manufacturer's instructions, about 15 minutes or until garlic is soft and slightly caramelized. Remove from grill; cover to keep warm.

2 Brush lamb with remaining oil; cook, uncovered, on heated oiled grill about 30 minutes or until cooked as desired.

3 Meanwhile, toss mushrooms, butter and chives together in large bowl. Transfer mushroom mixture to heated oiled grill pan; cook until tender. Serve lamb with roasted garlic and mushrooms.

SERVES 4
per serving 6.1g carbohydrate; 42.1g fat; 601 cal; 50.9g protein

minted lamb chops with mixed fresh beans

PREPARATION TIME 30 MINUTES (PLUS REFRIGERATION TIME)   COOKING TIME 20 MINUTES

12 french-trimmed lamb rib chops (2 pounds)

2 tablespoons olive oil

2 tablespoons fresh lemon juice

2 cloves garlic, crushed in garlic press

2 tablespoons finely chopped fresh mint

2 tablespoons finely grated lemon peel

5 ounces yellow string beans

5 ounces snow peas

5 ounces sugarsnap peas

5 cups (5 ounces) trimmed watercress

1 cup loosely packed fresh mint leaves

1 cup loosely packed fresh basil leaves

BALSAMIC DRESSING

2 tablespoons balsamic vinegar

1 teaspoon dijon mustard

1 teaspoon sugar

¼ cup olive oil

1   Combine lamb, oil, juice, garlic, chopped mint and half of the peel in large bowl; toss to coat lamb. Cover; refrigerate 1 hour.

2   Meanwhile, boil, steam or microwave beans, snow peas and sugarsnap peas, separately, until just tender; drain. Rinse under cold water; drain.

3   Make balsamic dressing.

4   Cook lamb, in batches, on heated oiled grill or grill pan until browned both sides and cooked as desired.

5   Place beans, snow peas and sugarsnap peas in large bowl with watercress and herbs, remaining peel and half of the dressing; toss gently to combine. Divide bean salad and lamb among serving plates, drizzle with remaining dressing.

BALSAMIC DRESSING   Combine ingredients in screw-top jar; shake well.

SERVES 4
per serving 7.8g carbohydrate; 42.5g fat; 520 cal; 27.1g protein

lamb with white wine and mascarpone sauce

PREPARATION TIME 10 MINUTES   COOKING TIME 15 MINUTES

¼ cup olive oil

12 fresh sage leaves

4 ounces sliced prosciutto

8 boned-out leg of lamb steaks (1⅓ pounds)

1 clove garlic, crushed in garlic press

¾ cup dry white wine

½ cup mascarpone

¼ cup heavy cream

**1½ bunches asparagus, trimmed,
    halved crosswise**

1   Heat oil in medium skillet; cook sage until crisp. Drain on paper towel. Cook prosciutto in same skillet, stirring, until crisp; drain on paper towel.

2   Cook lamb in same skillet until browned both sides and cooked as desired. Remove from skillet.

3   Cook garlic in same skillet, stirring, until fragrant. Add wine; bring to a boil. Reduce heat; simmer, uncovered, until liquid reduces by half. Add mascarpone and cream; cook, stirring, over heat until sauce boils and thickens slightly.

4   Meanwhile, boil, steam or microwave asparagus until tender; drain.

5   Divide lamb and asparagus among serving plates; top with prosciutto and sage, drizzle with sauce.

SERVES 4
per serving 2.2g carbohydrate; 51.9g fat; 662 cal; 40.5g protein

herbed lamb steaks with tomatoes and walnut gremolata

PREPARATION TIME 15 MINUTES (PLUS REFRIGERATION TIME)   COOKING TIME 30 MINUTES

2 tablespoons finely chopped fresh oregano

2 tablespoons finely chopped fresh
**   flat-leaf parsley**

1 tablespoon finely chopped fresh rosemary

⅓ cup red wine

¼ cup olive oil

four 7-ounce boned-out lamb steaks

4 medium tomatoes, halved

1 tablespoon balsamic vinegar

1 tablespoon coarsely chopped fresh
**   flat-leaf parsley**

WALNUT GREMOLATA

2 tablespoons toasted walnuts, chopped finely

1 tablespoon finely grated lemon peel

1 clove garlic, crushed in garlic press

½ cup finely chopped fresh flat-leaf parsley

1   Combine oregano, finely chopped parsley, rosemary, wine and oil in shallow dish; add lamb. Cover; refrigerate 3 hours or overnight.

2   Place tomatoes, cut-side up, in lightly oiled disposable roasting pan; drizzle with vinegar.

3   Cook tomatoes in covered grill, using indirect heat, following manufacturer's instructions, about 30 minutes or until soft.

4   Meanwhile, make walnut gremolata.

5   When tomatoes are almost done, cook lamb on heated oiled grill or grill pan, uncovered, until browned and cooked as desired; sprinkle with coarsely chopped parsley. Serve with tomatoes and walnut gremolata.

WALNUT GREMOLATA Combine ingredients in small bowl; mix well.

SERVES 4
per serving 3.2g carbohydrate; 27.8g fat; 462 cal; 46.7g protein

lamb steaks with brussels sprouts

PREPARATION TIME 10 MINUTES   COOKING TIME 10 MINUTES

14 ounces brussels sprouts

3 tablespoons butter

eight 5-ounce boned-out lamb steaks

1 small onion, chopped finely

¼ cup dry white wine

½ cup beef broth

1 teaspoon dijon mustard

1 tablespoon coarsely chopped
**   fresh chives**

1   Boil, steam or microwave sprouts until just tender; drain.

2   Meanwhile, melt half of the butter in large skillet; cook lamb, in batches, about 6 minutes or until browned both sides and cooked as desired. Cover to keep warm.

3   Cook onion in same skillet, stirring, until softened. Stir in wine, broth and mustard; bring to a boil. Reduce heat; simmer, uncovered, 1 minute.

4   Toss brussels sprouts and remaining butter in large bowl with chives. Serve lamb with sauce and sprouts.

SERVES 4
per serving 3.7g carbohydrate; 36g fat; 606 cal; 67.3g protein
tip To cook sprouts evenly, cut a shallow cross in the stem end. Brussels sprouts are far more palatable if they're not overcooked.

lemon and garlic lamb chops with sprout, tomato and feta salad

PREPARATION TIME 15 MINUTES   COOKING TIME 15 MINUTES

1 tablespoon finely grated lemon peel

2 tablespoons fresh lemon juice

2 cloves garlic, crushed in garlic press

12 french-trimmed lamb rib chops (1¼ pounds)

1 cup (3 ounces) alfalfa sprouts

5 ounces pear tomatoes

1 cup coarsely chopped fresh mint

1 cup coarsely chopped fresh basil

6 ounces feta cheese, crumbled

⅓ cup pitted kalamata olives

LEMON DRESSING

¼ cup fresh lemon juice

2 teaspoons extra virgin olive oil

1 teaspoon dijon mustard

1   Combine peel, juice and garlic in large bowl; add lamb, toss to coat in marinade.

2   Make lemon dressing.

3   Cook lamb, in batches, on heated oiled grill or grill pan until browned both sides and cooked as desired.

4   Place sprouts, tomato, herbs, cheese, olives and half of the dressing in medium bowl; toss gently to combine.

5   Serve salad topped with lamb; drizzle with remaining dressing.

LEMON DRESSING Combine ingredients in screw-top jar; shake well.

SERVES 4
per serving 11.5g carbohydrate; 38g fat; 493 cal; 26.4g protein

iskander kebab

PREPARATION TIME 15 MINUTES   COOKING TIME 15 MINUTES

Soak eight bamboo skewers in water for at least an hour prior to use
to prevent splintering or scorching.

2 pounds boneless lamb, cut into
**   1-inch cubes**
1 cup unflavored yogurt
2 tablespoons fresh lemon juice
2 cloves garlic, crushed in
**   garlic press**
2 teaspoons finely chopped
**   fresh thyme**
1½ cups (1½ ounces) mesclun

CHILE TOMATO SAUCE

1 tablespoon olive oil
1 small onion, chopped coarsely
1 clove garlic, crushed in
**   garlic press**
2 long green chiles, seeded,
**   chopped coarsely**
2 medium tomatoes,
**   chopped coarsely**
1 tablespoon tomato paste
⅓ cup dry red wine

1   Thread lamb onto skewers. Combine yogurt, juice, garlic and thyme in small bowl. Place two-thirds of the yogurt mixture into separate bowl; reserve. Use remaining yogurt mixture to brush lamb.

2   Cook lamb skewers, in batches, on heated oiled grill or grill pan until browned all over and cooked as desired.

3   Meanwhile, make chile tomato sauce.

4   Serve kebabs with reserved yogurt mixture, chile tomato sauce and mesclun.

CHILE TOMATO SAUCE   Heat oil in medium skillet; cook onion and garlic, stirring, until onion softens. Add remaining ingredients; bring to a boil. Reduce heat; simmer, uncovered, about 5 minutes or until sauce thickens slightly. Blend or process sauce until smooth.

SERVES 4
per serving 7.1g carbohydrate; 20.6g fat; 472 cal; 60.3g protein
tip You can also use boned-out leg of lamb, cut into cubes. If using metal skewers, oil them first to prevent the meat from sticking.

lamb with caramelized onions and asparagus and watercress salad

PREPARATION TIME 15 MINUTES   COOKING TIME 25 MINUTES

1 tablespoon butter

2 medium red onions, sliced thinly

⅓ cup red wine vinegar

1 tablespoon light brown sugar

¼ cup water

13 ounces lamb loin chops

2 bunches asparagus, trimmed

14 cups (14 ounces) trimmed watercress

1 tablespoon dijon mustard

2 cloves garlic, crushed in garlic press

1 tablespoon fresh lemon juice

2 tablespoons olive oil

1   Melt butter in large skillet; cook onion, stirring, until softened. Add vinegar, sugar and the water; cook, stirring, until sugar dissolves, then bring to a boil. Reduce heat; simmer, uncovered, stirring occasionally, about 10 minutes or until onion caramelizes.

2   Meanwhile, cook lamb, in batches, on heated, lightly oiled grill or grill pan until browned all over and cooked as desired. Let stand 5 minutes.

3   Boil, steam or microwave asparagus until just tender; drain. Combine asparagus in large bowl with watercress. Add combined remaining ingredients; toss gently to combine. Serve salad topped with lamb and caramelized onions.

SERVES 4

per serving 9.8g carbohydrate; 17.2g fat; 354 cal; 39.2g protein

garlic and sage lamb racks with roasted red onion

PREPARATION TIME 10 MINUTES   COOKING TIME 30 MINUTES

3 large red onions

⅓ cup extra virgin olive oil

2 tablespoons coarsely chopped fresh sage

4 cloves garlic, chopped coarsely

4 french-trimmed racks of lamb

   (4 chops each)

1   Preheat oven to hot.

2   Halve onions, then slice into thin wedges; place in large roasting pan with half of the oil.

3   Combine remaining oil in small bowl with sage and garlic. Using hands, press sage mixture all over lamb; place lamb on onion. Roast, uncovered, in hot oven about 25 minutes or until lamb is browned all over and cooked as desired. Cover with foil; let stand 10 minutes.

SERVES 4

per serving 11.5g carbohydrate; 44.2g fat; 572 cal; 33.5g protein

herb and garlic barbecued lamb

PREPARATION TIME 15 MINUTES (PLUS REFRIGERATION TIME)   COOKING TIME 40 MINUTES

2 pounds butterflied leg of lamb

2 tablespoons olive oil

4 cloves garlic, crushed in garlic press

1 tablespoons grainy mustard

½ cup dry white wine

1 tablespoon finely chopped fresh rosemary

1 tablespoon mint jelly

7 ounces green beans

1 tablespoon butter

¼ cup white wine, extra

¼ cup chicken broth

1   Place lamb in large shallow casserole; pour combined oil, half of the garlic, mustard, wine and rosemary over lamb. Cover; refrigerate 3 hours or overnight.

2   Remove lamb from marinade; place marinade in small saucepan, reserve. Place lamb, covered with foil, on heated oiled grill or grill pan; cook about 30 minutes or until cooked as desired, turning halfway through cooking time.

3   Brush lamb all over with jelly; cook, uncovered, until jelly melts and forms a glaze. Stand lamb, covered, 10 minutes before slicing.

4   Meanwhile, boil, steam or microwave beans until just tender; drain. Rinse under cold water; drain. Heat butter in medium skillet; add remaining garlic, cook until fragrant. Add extra wine to skillet, bring to a boil. Reduce heat; simmer, uncovered, until liquid reduces by half. Add beans; toss to warm through and coat.

5   Add broth to reserved marinade; bring to a boil. Reduce heat; simmer, uncovered, 5 minutes. Serve sliced lamb with sauce and beans.

SERVES 4
per serving 3g carbohydrate; 34.2g fat; 569 cal; 55g protein
tip The lamb can also be cooked, covered, in a hot oven for about 25 minutes or until cooked as desired.

teriyaki lamb stir-fry

PREPARATION TIME 15 MINUTES   COOKING TIME 15 MINUTES

You need one bunch of baby bok choy for this recipe.

2 teaspoons olive oil

1¾ pounds trimmed, boneless leg of lamb, sliced thinly

1 teaspoon sesame oil

2 cloves garlic, crushed in garlic press

1 medium onion, sliced thickly

1 long red chile, sliced thinly

⅓ cup bottled teriyaki sauce

¼ cup sweet chili sauce

1 pound baby bok choy, quartered

6 ounces broccolini, trimmed, chopped coarsely

1   Heat olive oil in wok or large skillet; stir-fry lamb, in batches, until browned and cooked as desired.

2   Heat sesame oil in same wok; stir-fry garlic, onion and chile until fragrant. Add sauces; bring to a boil. Add bok choy and broccolini; stir-fry until bok choy just wilts and broccolini is tender.

3   Return lamb to wok; stir-fry until heated through.

SERVES 4
per serving 7.3g carbohydrate; 12.6g fat; 341 cal; 48.4g protein

lamb chops and black-eyed pea salad

PREPARATION TIME 20 MINUTES (PLUS STANDING AND REFRIGERATION TIMES)   COOKING TIME 35 MINUTES

1½ cups dried black-eyed peas

12 french-trimmed lamb rib chops

   (2 pounds)

2 teaspoons ground coriander

½ teaspoon cayenne

2 teaspoons smoked paprika

1 tablespoon vegetable oil

10 baby vine-ripened tomatoes, quartered

2 stalks celery, trimmed, sliced thinly

1 small red boston lettuce, trimmed

2 tablespoons fresh lemon juice

PARSLEY DRESSING

2 tablespoons coarsely chopped fresh

   flat-leaf parsley

1 tablespoon grainy mustard

1 clove garlic, crushed in garlic press

¼ cup extra virgin olive oil

¼ cup white wine vinegar

1 Place peas in large bowl, cover with water; let stand overnight. Rinse under cold water; drain.

2 Combine lamb, coriander, pepper, paprika and oil in large bowl. Cover; refrigerate 3 hours or overnight.

3 Cook peas in medium saucepan of boiling water, uncovered, about 30 minutes or until just tender; drain.

4 Meanwhile, cook lamb, in batches, on heated oiled grill or grill pan until browned both sides and cooked as desired.

5 Make parsley dressing. Place drained peas in large bowl with tomato, celery and dressing; toss gently to combine.

6 Divide lettuce leaves among serving plates; top with black-eyed pea salad then lamb, drizzle with juice.

PARSLEY DRESSING Combine ingredients in screw-top jar; shake well.

SERVES 4
per serving 10.9g carbohydrate; 37.9g fat; 495 cal; 28.6g protein

mint and pistachio pesto kebabs with chermoulla-dressed zucchini

PREPARATION TIME 30 MINUTES   COOKING TIME 25 MINUTES

Soak 12 bamboo skewers in water for at least an hour prior to use to prevent splintering or scorching. Chermoulla, a seasoning often used as a dry marinade or rub, is an integral part of Moroccan cooking. It consists of onion, garlic, herbs and spices. If hot paprika is unavailable, use an extra ½ teaspoon of sweet paprika and a hearty pinch of cayenne.

2 pounds trimmed, boneless leg of lamb, cut into 1-inch cubes

4 medium zucchini, cut in half lengthwise

CHERMOULLA DRESSING

1 small red onion, chopped finely

2 cloves garlic, crushed in garlic press

½ teaspoon hot paprika

1 teaspoon sweet paprika

1 teaspoon ground cumin

⅓ cup olive oil

2 tablespoons fresh lemon juice

¾ cup finely chopped fresh flat-leaf parsley

MINT AND PISTACHIO PESTO

1 cup firmly packed fresh mint leaves

⅓ cup pistachios, toasted

⅓ cup coarsely grated parmesan cheese

2 cloves garlic, crushed in garlic press

1 tablespoon fresh lemon juice

¼ cup olive oil

2 tablespoons water, approximately

1   Thread lamb onto 12 skewers. Cook lamb on heated oiled grill or grill pan, uncovered, until browned and cooked as desired. Cover to keep warm.

2   Meanwhile, cook zucchini on same grill, uncovered, until browned lightly both sides and just tender.

3   Make chermoulla dressing. Make mint and pistachio pesto.

4   Serve zucchini topped with chermoulla and lamb with pesto.

CHERMOULLA DRESSING   Combine ingredients in screw-top jar; shake well.

MINT AND PISTACHIO PESTO   Blend or process mint, nuts, cheese, garlic and juice until well combined. With motor running, gradually pour in oil and just enough of the water to give the desired consistency.

SERVES 4
per serving 6g carbohydrate; 63.4g fat; 827 cal; 59.5g protein
tip If using metal skewers, oil them first to prevent the meat from sticking.

lamb shanks with five-spice, tamarind and ginger (see page 326)

PREPARATION TIME 20 MINUTES   COOKING TIME 2 HOURS 40 MINUTES

Any asian greens can be used in this recipe. Try it with bok choy, choy sum, or gai larn (also known as chinese broccoli). You need one bunch of asian greens for this recipe.

2 teaspoons five-spice powder

1 teaspoon red pepper flakes

1 cinnamon stick

2 star anise

¼ cup soy sauce

½ cup sherry

2 tablespoons tamarind concentrate

2 tablespoons brown sugar

3-inch piece fresh ginger, grated

2 cloves garlic, chopped coarsely

1¼ cups water

4 lamb shanks (about 4 pounds)

1¾ pounds asian greens, chopped into
    3½-inch lengths

1   Preheat oven to moderate.

2   Dry-fry five-spice, pepper flakes, cinnamon and star anise in small skillet, stirring, until fragrant; combine spices with soy, wine, tamarind, sugar, ginger, garlic and the water in medium measuring cup.

3   Place lamb, in single layer, in large shallow casserole; drizzle with spice mixture. Cook, covered, in moderate oven, turning lamb occasionally, about 2½ hours or until meat is almost falling off shanks. Remove lamb from dish; cover to keep warm. Skim away excess fat; strain sauce into small saucepan.

4   Meanwhile, boil, steam or microwave asian greens until tender; drain.

5   Divide greens among serving plates; serve with lamb, drizzle with reheated sauce.

SERVES 4

per serving 10.8g carbohydrate; 20.2g fat; 456 cal; 50.5g protein

lamb shank soup

PREPARATION TIME 30 MINUTES   COOKING TIME 2 HOURS 30 MINUTES (PLUS COOLING AND REFRIGERATION TIMES)

4 lamb shanks (about 4 pounds)

1 medium onion, chopped finely

2 stalks celery, trimmed, sliced thinly

2 medium red bell peppers, chopped coarsely

2 cloves garlic, crushed in garlic press

8 cups water

14 ounces swiss chard, trimmed,
    chopped finely

⅓ cup fresh lemon juice

1   Heat lightly oiled large pot; cook lamb, in batches, until browned. Cook onion, celery, pepper and garlic in same pot, stirring, about 5 minutes or until onion softens. Return lamb to pot with the water; bring to a boil. Reduce heat; simmer, covered, 1 hour 45 minutes.

2   Remove soup from heat; when lamb is cool enough to handle, remove meat from bones, then chop meat coarsely. Refrigerate cooled soup and meat separately, covered, overnight.

3   Discard fat from surface of soup. Place soup and meat in large soup pot; bring to a boil. Reduce heat; simmer, covered, 30 minutes. Add swiss chard and juice; simmer, uncovered, until swiss chard just wilts. Divide soup among serving bowls.

SERVES 4

per serving 7.5g carbohydrate; 20.8g fat; 413 cal; 48.1g protein

grilled lamb steaks with ratatouille

PREPARATION TIME 20 MINUTES   COOKING TIME 25 MINUTES

5 baby eggplants, roughly peeled,

chopped coarsely

2 medium red bell peppers, chopped coarsely

1 medium yellow bell pepper,

chopped coarsely

4 medium plum tomatoes, chopped coarsely

1 medium onion, chopped coarsely

2 cloves garlic, sliced thickly

vegetable-oil spray

4 boned-out 5-ounce lamb steaks

BALSAMIC DRESSING

1 tablespoon olive oil

1 tablespoon fresh lemon juice

1 tablespoon balsamic vinegar

1 clove garlic, crushed in garlic press

¼ cup loosely packed fresh oregano leaves

1   Preheat oven to hot. Make balsamic dressing.

2   Combine vegetables and garlic, in single layer, in two large shallow casseroles; coat vegetables lightly with vegetable-oil spray. Cook, uncovered, in hot oven about 25 minutes or until ratatouille vegetables are just tender, stirring occasionally.

3   Meanwhile, cook lamb on heated oiled grill or grill pan until browned both sides and cooked as desired.

4   Pour half of the dressing into large bowl with ratatouille; toss to combine. Divide ratatouille and lamb among serving plates; drizzle with remaining dressing.

BALSAMIC DRESSING Combine ingredients in screw-top jar; shake well.

SERVES 4
per serving 11g carbohydrate; 13.3g fat; 313 cal; 36.5g protein

omelet spring rolls

PREPARATION TIME 10 MINUTES   COOKING TIME 30 MINUTES

1 pound lean ground pork

2 scallions, chopped coarsely

4 ounces fresh baby corn, sliced thinly

2 ounces button mushrooms, sliced thinly

2 tablespoons oyster sauce

1 tablespoon mild chili sauce

1 tablespoon kecap manis

2 tablespoons dry sherry

6 eggs

2 tablespoons water

1   Cook pork, stirring, in heated oiled large nonstick skillet until browned and cooked through. Stir in scallion, corn, mushroom and combined sauces, kecap manis and sherry until heated through. Remove from skillet; cover to keep warm.

2   Whisk eggs and the water in medium bowl; pour a quarter of the egg mixture into heated oiled nonstick skillet. Cook, tilting skillet, over medium heat until omelet is browned lightly underneath and almost set; turn, cook other side until browned lightly. Remove omelet from skillet; cover to keep warm while making three more omelets with remaining egg mixture.

3   Place a quarter of the pork mixture along one edge of an omelet; roll omelet over filling, fold in sides, roll up. Repeat with remaining pork and omelets.

SERVES 4
per serving 9g carbohydrate; 16.9g fat; 347 cal; 36.9g protein

chili pork with oyster sauce

PREPARATION TIME 15 MINUTES   COOKING TIME 20 MINUTES

1 tablespoon peanut oil

1 pound boneless pork loin,
   sliced thinly

1 medium onion, sliced thinly

1 clove garlic, crushed in garlic press

1 large red bell pepper, sliced thinly

1 small green zucchini, sliced thinly

1 small yellow squash, sliced thinly

¼ cup oyster sauce

1 tablespoon sweet chili sauce

1 tablespoon coarsely chopped
   fresh cilantro

1   Heat oil in large wok or skillet. Stir-fry pork, in batches, until browned.

2   Stir-fry onion and garlic until onion is just soft.

3   Add pepper, zucchini and squash; stir-fry.

4   Return pork to wok. Add sauces; stir-fry until hot. Serve sprinkled
     with cilantro.

SERVES 4
per serving   10g carbohydrate; 7.6g fat; 220 cal; 27.2g protein

pork chops with caraway cabbage

PREPARATION TIME 10 MINUTES   COOKING TIME 20 MINUTES

You need about a quarter of a head of savoy cabbage for this recipe.

four 7-ounce boneless pork
   loin chops

3 slices bacon, chopped finely

1 medium onion, chopped finely

1 tablespoon caraway seeds

3 cups shredded savoy cabbage

2 tablespoons light brown sugar

¼ cup cider vinegar

3 tablespoons butter

2 teaspoons finely chopped
   fresh sage

2 tablespoons sour cream

1   Cook pork on heated oiled grill or grill pan, uncovered, until browned
     both sides and cooked through. Keep warm.

2   Meanwhile, cook bacon, onion and seeds in medium saucepan until
     onion is soft. Add cabbage; cook, stirring, 2 minutes. Stir in sugar,
     vinegar and butter; cook, stirring, about 3 minutes or until cabbage is
     soft. Just before serving, stir in sage. Serve pork topped with cabbage
     and sour cream.

SERVES 4
per serving   10.4g carbohydrate; 25g fat; 519 cal; 62.9g protein

pork and veal sang choy bow (see back cover)

PREPARATION TIME 15 MINUTES   COOKING TIME 10 MINUTES

1 tablespoon sesame oil

1 medium onion, chopped finely

2 cloves garlic, crushed in

   garlic press

10 ounces lean ground pork

10 ounces lean ground veal

¼ cup soy sauce

¼ cup oyster sauce

1 medium red bell pepper,

   chopped finely

2½ cups (8 ounces) fresh

   bean sprouts

3 scallions, chopped coarsely

1 tablespoon toasted sesame seeds

8 large iceberg lettuce leaves

1 Heat oil in wok or medium skillet; cook onion and garlic, stirring, until onion is soft. Add pork and veal; cook, stirring, until pork and veal are browned through.

2 Add sauces and pepper; simmer, uncovered, stirring occasionally, 3 minutes.

3 Just before serving, stir in sprouts, scallion and seeds. Divide mixture among lettuce leaves. Serve immediately.

SERVES 4

per serving 10.1g carbohydrate; 17.2g fat; 350 cal; 37.9g protein

teriyaki pork with wasabi dressing (see front cover)

PREPARATION TIME 10 MINUTES   COOKING TIME 15 MINUTES

1½ pounds boneless pork loin,

   sliced thickly

¼ cup teriyaki marinade

2½ cups (5 ounces) mesclun

3 cups (3 ounces) trimmed

   watercress

1 medium red bell pepper,

   sliced thinly

8 ounces yellow teardrop

   tomatoes, halved

WASABI DRESSING

1½ teaspoons wasabi paste

¼ cup cider vinegar

⅓ cup vegetable oil

1 tablespoon light soy sauce

1 Trim pork; brush with teriyaki marinade. Cook pork, in batches, on heated oiled grill or grill pan, brushing frequently with marinade, until browned both sides and cooked. Cover to keep warm.

2 Meanwhile, combine mesclun, watercress, pepper and tomato in large bowl. Make wasabi dressing.

3 Pour wasabi dressing over salad mixture; toss gently to combine. Slice pork; serve with salad.

WASABI DRESSING Blend wasabi paste with vinegar in small measuring cup; whisk in remaining ingredients.

SERVES 4

per serving 3.9g carbohydrate; 23g fat; 402 cal; 44.1g protein

pork cutlets with beet salad

PREPARATION TIME 20 MINUTES   COOKING TIME 55 MINUTES

10 ounces baby beet

1 tablespoon caraway seeds

2 teaspoons olive oil

four 5-ounce boneless pork chops

5 ounces firm goat cheese,
   crumbled

5 large radishes, sliced thinly

2½ cups (4 ounces) baby
   arugula leaves

DIJON VINAIGRETTE

2 teaspoons dijon mustard

2 teaspoons olive oil

2 tablespoons red wine vinegar

1   Preheat oven to moderately hot.

2   Discard beet stems and leaves; place unpeeled beet in small shallow casserole. Roast, uncovered, in moderately hot oven about 45 minutes or until beet is tender. Cool 10 minutes; peel, cut into quarters.

3   Meanwhile, make dijon vinaigrette.

4   Using mortar and pestle, crush seeds and oil into a paste; rub into pork. Cook pork on heated, lightly oiled grill or grill pan until browned and cooked as desired.

5   Place beet, cheese, radish and arugula in large bowl with vinaigrette; toss gently to combine. Serve salad with pork.

DIJON VINAIGRETTE Combine ingredients in screw-top jar; shake well.

SERVES 4
per serving 7.4g carbohydrate; 23.5g fat; 431 cal; 47.4g protein

pork cutlets with beet salad

pork, lime and peanut salad

pork, lime and peanut salad

PREPARATION TIME 25 MINUTES (PLUS REFRIGERATION TIME) COOKING TIME 15 MINUTES

Any asian greens can be used in this recipe. Try it with bok choy, choy sum, or gai larn (also known as chinese broccoli). You need one bunch of asian greens for this recipe.

1¾-pound pork tenderloin,
   sliced thinly

¼ cup fresh lime juice

1½-inch piece fresh ginger, grated

2 medium carrots, cut into
   2-inch pieces

1 pound asian greens,
   chopped coarsely

2 tablespoons water

½ cup firmly packed fresh
   basil leaves

1 cup firmly packed fresh
   cilantro leaves

4 scallions, sliced thinly

¼ cup coarsely chopped roasted
   unsalted peanuts

SWEET CHILI DRESSING

1 tablespoon fish sauce

1 tablespoon sweet chili sauce

2 tablespoons fresh lime juice

1 red serrano chile, chopped finely

1 Place pork in large bowl with juice and ginger; toss to coat pork in mixture. Cover; refrigerate 3 hours or overnight.

2 Make sweet chili dressing.

3 Slice carrot thinly; stack slices, then slice thinly again into matchsticks.

4 Stir-fry pork, in batches, in heated, lightly oiled wok or large skillet until browned all over and cooked through. Cover to keep warm.

5 Stir-fry asian greens with the water in same wok until just wilted.

6 Place pork, asian greens, carrot, herbs and scallion in large bowl with dressing; toss gently to combine, then sprinkle with nuts.

SWEET CHILI DRESSING Combine ingredients in screw-top jar; shake well.

SERVES 4
per serving 6.8g carbohydrate; 10.4g fat; 321 cal; 48.8g protein

roasted boneless pork with orange

PREPARATION TIME 20 MINUTES (PLUS STANDING TIME)   COOKING TIME 25 MINUTES

1¾ pounds boneless pork loin

2 cloves garlic, slivered

8 small fresh sage leaves

1 teaspoon fennel seeds

2 tablespoons olive oil

1 small onion, sliced thickly

½ cup chicken broth

2 tablespoons fresh orange juice

2 medium oranges

2½ cups (5 ounces) mesclun

ORANGE VINAIGRETTE

2 tablespoons fresh orange juice

1 tablespoon fresh lemon juice

1 clove garlic, crushed in garlic press

⅓ cup olive oil

1   Cut a few small slits along the top of pork; push in garlic and sage. Sprinkle pork with seeds; let stand 30 minutes.

2   Make orange vinaigrette.

3   Preheat oven to hot.

4   Heat half of the oil in large casserole; cook pork until browned all over. Remove from dish.

5   Heat remaining oil in same casserole; cook onion, stirring, until lightly browned. Return pork to casserole. Drizzle with broth and juice. Roast, uncovered, in hot oven about 10 minutes or until pork is cooked through. Cover, let stand 10 minutes.

6   Meanwhile, place mesclun in medium bowl. Segment oranges over salad. Just before serving, add orange vinaigrette; toss to combine. Serve pork sliced, with pan juices and salad.

ORANGE VINAIGRETTE   Combine ingredients in screw-top jar; shake well.

SERVES 4
per serving   10g carbohydrate; 32.2g fat; 512 cal; 45.9g protein

pork with eggplant

PREPARATION TIME 20 MINUTES   COOKING TIME 25 MINUTES

3 red serrano chiles, halved

6 cloves garlic, quartered

1 medium onion, chopped coarsely

1 pound baby eggplants

2 tablespoons peanut oil

1 pound lean ground pork

1 tablespoon fish sauce

1 tablespoon soy sauce

1 tablespoon light brown sugar

4 shallots, sliced thinly

5 ounces green beans, trimmed,
    cut into 2-inch lengths

1 cup loosely packed fresh
    basil leaves

1   Blend or process (or crush using mortar and pestle) chile, garlic and onion until mixture forms a paste.

2   Quarter eggplants lengthwise; slice each piece into 2-inch lengths. Cook eggplant in large pot of boiling water until just tender; drain, pat dry with paper towels.

3   Heat oil in wok; stir-fry eggplant, in batches, until lightly browned. Drain on paper towels.

4   Stir-fry garlic paste in wok about 5 minutes or until lightly browned. Add pork; stir-fry until pork is changed in color and cooked through. Add sauces and sugar; stir-fry until sugar dissolves. Add shallot and beans; stir-fry until beans are just tender. Return eggplant to wok; stir-fry, tossing gently until combined. Remove from heat; toss basil leaves through stir-fry.

SERVES 4
per serving   9.5g carbohydrate; 18.5g fat; 321 cal; 29.3g protein

tarragon chicken with pureed carrots and leek

PREPARATION TIME 20 MINUTES (PLUS REFRIGERATION TIME)   COOKING TIME 25 MINUTES

Soak 12 bamboo skewers in water for at least an hour prior to use to prevent splintering or scorching.

four 6-ounce skinless, boneless
   chicken breasts, sliced thickly
1 tablespoon finely chopped
   fresh tarragon
1 tablespoon grainy mustard
2 tablespoons margarine
2 large leeks, trimmed,
   chopped finely
4 medium carrots, chopped coarsely
1½ cups chicken broth
pinch nutmeg

1 Thread equal amounts of chicken onto each of 12 skewers. Using fingers, press combined tarragon and mustard all over chicken, cover skewers; refrigerate 30 minutes.

2 Meanwhile, melt margarine in large nonstick skillet; cook leek, stirring, until softened. Cover to keep warm.

3 Preheat oven to moderately hot.

4 Boil or microwave carrot in chicken broth until just tender; drain in colander over small bowl. Reserve ½ cup of the cooking liquid; discard the remainder. Blend or process carrot with nutmeg until pureed. Cover to keep warm.

5 Cook chicken and reserved liquid in large shallow casserole, uncovered, in moderately hot oven about 15 minutes or until cooked through.

6 Divide pureed carrot among serving plates; top with chicken and leek.

SERVES 4
per serving 9.4g carbohydrate; 12.6g fat; 319 cal; 40g protein
tip If using metal skewers, oil them first to prevent chicken from sticking.

greek salad with smoked chicken

PREPARATION TIME 20 MINUTES

Smoked chicken breast may be slightly pink, like bacon and ham, but this does not mean it is undercooked.

1 small red onion, sliced thinly
7 ounces feta cheese, crumbled
8 ounces pear tomatoes
14 ounces smoked chicken breast,
   sliced thinly
4½ cups (7 ounces) baby
   spinach leaves
⅔ cup pitted kalamata olives
1 medium red bell pepper,
   sliced thinly
⅓ cup olive oil
¼ cup fresh lemon juice
1 clove garlic, crushed in garlic press

1 Combine onion, cheese, tomatoes, chicken, spinach, olives and pepper in large bowl.

2 Combine remaining ingredients in screw-top jar; shake well. Drizzle dressing over salad; toss gently to combine.

SERVES 4
per serving 10.2g carbohydrate; 38.1g fat; 528 cal; 36.3g protein

roasted whole chicken with caramelized lemon

PREPARATION TIME 10 MINUTES   COOKING TIME 1 HOUR 30 MINUTES

3 tablespoons butter

2 medium lemons, sliced thickly

4 small red onions, chopped coarsely

3¼-pound chicken

¼ cup olive oil

¼ cup fresh lemon juice

2 bunches broccoli rabe

1 Heat half the butter in medium skillet; cook lemon, stirring, until just softened and caramelized slightly. Remove from skillet; cool. Heat remaining butter in same skillet; cook onion, stirring, until soft and browned lightly. Remove from skillet; cool.

2 Push lemon slices between flesh and skin of chicken; spoon onion into body cavity. Tuck trimmed neck flap under body, securing with toothpicks; tie legs together with kitchen string. Place chicken on oiled roasting rack in disposable roasting pan. Brush all over with combined oil and juice. Cook chicken in covered grill, using indirect heat, following manufacturer's instructions, about 1 hour 20 minutes or until browned all over and tender.

3 Just before chicken is done, boil, steam or microwave broccoli rabe; drain. Serve chicken with broccoli rabe, and fresh lemon wedges, if desired.

SERVES 4
per serving 6.3g carbohydrate; 56.6g fat; 776 cal; 59.9g protein

lemongrass and asparagus chicken

PREPARATION TIME 15 MINUTES   COOKING TIME 15 MINUTES

1 pound skinless, boneless chicken breasts, sliced thickly

3 cloves garlic, crushed in garlic press

2 tablespoons finely chopped fresh lemongrass

1 teaspoon sugar

1 teaspoon grated fresh ginger

1 tablespoon peanut oil

1½ bunches asparagus, trimmed

1 large onion, sliced thickly

2 medium tomatoes, seeded, chopped coarsely

2 teaspoons finely chopped fresh cilantro

2 tablespoons roasted sesame seeds

1 Combine chicken, garlic, lemongrass, sugar, ginger and half of the oil in medium bowl.

2 Cut asparagus spears into thirds; boil, steam or microwave until just tender. Rinse immediately under cold water; drain.

3 Heat remaining oil in wok or large skillet. Stir-fry onion until just soft; remove from wok. Stir-fry chicken mixture, in batches, until chicken is browned and cooked through.

4 Return chicken mixture and onion to wok with asparagus and tomato; stir-fry until heated through. Serve sprinkled with cilantro and sesame seeds.

SERVES 4
per serving 5.5g carbohydrate; 10.8g fat; 249 cal; 32.4g protein
tip Chicken can be marinated for up to 3 hours before using.

chicken tagine with olives and preserved lemon

PREPARATION TIME 15 MINUTES   COOKING TIME 50 MINUTES

In Morocco, the word "tagine" refers both to a slowly cooked stew and the special cone-topped pottery casserole dish in which it is served. Preserved lemon is a North African specialty; the citrus peel is preserved in a mixture of salt and lemon juice. It can be rinsed and eaten as is, or added to casseroles and tagines for a rich salty-sour flavor.

1 tablespoon olive oil

1 tablespoon butter

8 skinless, boneless chicken thighs

    (about 2½ pounds)

1 large red onion, chopped finely

½ teaspoon saffron threads, toasted, crushed

1 teaspoon ground cinnamon

1 teaspoon ground ginger

1½ cups chicken broth

16 pitted large green olives

2 tablespoons finely chopped

    preserved lemon

1 Heat oil and butter in large heavy-bottomed saucepan with tight-fitting lid; cook chicken, in batches, until browned all over.

2 Place onion and spices in same pan; cook, stirring, until onion softens. Return chicken to pan with broth; bring to a boil. Reduce heat; simmer, covered, about 30 minutes or until chicken is cooked through.

3 Remove chicken from pan; cover to keep warm. Skim and discard fat from top of sauce; bring to a boil. Reduce heat; cook, stirring, until sauce reduces by half.

4 Return chicken to pan with olives and lemon; stir over medium heat until heated through.

SERVES 4
per serving 10g carbohydrate; 25.4g fat; 444 cal; 44.6g protein

chicken cacciatore

PREPARATION TIME 20 MINUTES   COOKING TIME 55 MINUTES

4 chicken (leg) quarters

all-purpose flour

1 tablespoon olive oil

2 cloves garlic, crushed in garlic press

4 slices pancetta, chopped coarsely

1 large onion, chopped finely

1 medium yellow bell pepper,

    chopped coarsely

3 medium tomatoes, peeled,

    chopped coarsely

½ cup dry white wine

½ cup tomato puree

2 teaspoons finely chopped fresh sage

1 teaspoon finely chopped fresh rosemary

1 bay leaf

1 Cut chicken through joint into two pieces. Toss chicken in flour; shake away excess flour.

2 Heat oil in large, deep skillet; cook chicken, in batches, until browned all over. Drain on paper towels.

3 Drain all but 1 tablespoon of the fat from skillet; cook garlic, pancetta, onion and pepper, stirring, until onion is soft. Add tomato, wine and puree; simmer, uncovered, 2 minutes.

4 Return chicken to skillet. Add herbs and bay leaf; simmer, covered, about 30 minutes or until chicken is tender. Discard bay leaf before serving.

SERVES 4
per serving 11.4g carbohydrate; 39.5g fat; 613 cal; 48.6g protein

chicken, lemon and artichoke skewers (see page 308)

PREPARATION TIME 20 MINUTES   COOKING TIME 15 MINUTES

Soak 12 bamboo skewers in water for at least an hour prior to use to prevent splintering or scorching.

3 medium lemons

3 small red onions

1 pound chicken tenderloins, diced into
    1-inch pieces

14 ounces canned artichoke hearts,
    drained, halved

10 ounces button mushrooms

2 cups (3½ ounces) baby arugula leaves

2 tablespoons drained baby capers, rinsed

LEMON DRESSING

1 tablespoon fresh lemon juice

2 cloves garlic, crushed in garlic press

½ teaspoon dijon mustard

1 tablespoon white wine vinegar

1 tablespoon olive oil

1 Make lemon dressing.

2 Cut each lemon into eight wedges; cut two of the onions into six wedges each. Thread lemon and onion wedges, chicken, artichoke and mushrooms alternately onto skewers.

3 Place skewers in shallow casserole; brush half of the dressing over skewers.

4 Cook skewers on heated, lightly oiled grill or grill pan until browned and cooked through.

5 Meanwhile, slice remaining onion thinly; place in large bowl with arugula, capers and remaining dressing. Serve skewers with salad.

LEMON DRESSING Combine ingredients in screw-top jar; shake well.

SERVES 4
per serving 7.9g carbohydrate; 8.3g fat; 252 cal; 34.3g protein
tip If using metal skewers, oil them first to prevent the chicken from sticking.

lemon-pepper chicken with zucchini salad

PREPARATION TIME 20 MINUTES   COOKING TIME 40 MINUTES

1 tablespoon finely grated lemon peel

2 teaspoons cracked black pepper

⅓ cup fresh lemon juice

2 teaspoons olive oil

four 6-ounce skinless, boneless
    chicken breasts

4 medium green zucchini

4 medium yellow squash

1 clove garlic, crushed in garlic press

4 scallions, chopped finely

1 cup coarsely chopped fresh
    flat-leaf parsley

¼ cup coarsely chopped fresh tarragon

1 Combine peel, pepper, 1 tablespoon of the juice and half of the oil in large bowl, add chicken; toss to coat in mixture. Cover, refrigerate while cooking zucchini and squash.

2 Peel zucchini and squash randomly; slice thinly on an angle. Cook slices, in batches, on heated oiled grill or grill pan until browned lightly and cooked through.

3 Cook chicken on heated, lightly oiled grill or grill pan until browned both sides and cooked through.

4 Meanwhile, whisk remaining juice and oil with garlic in large bowl; place zucchini, squash, scallion and herbs in bowl with dressing, toss gently to combine. Serve chicken with zucchini salad.

SERVES 4
per serving 4.1g carbohydrate; 7.5g fat; 286 cal; 48.9g protein

sumac and paprika-spiced chicken with herb salad

PREPARATION TIME 20 MINUTES   COOKING TIME 15 MINUTES

Soak eight bamboo skewers in water for at least an hour prior to use to prevent splintering or scorching.

1¾ pounds chicken tenderloins

2 cloves garlic, crushed in garlic press

2 teaspoons sweet paprika

2 tablespoons sumac

2 teaspoons finely chopped fresh oregano

2 tablespoons water

1 teaspoon vegetable oil

2½ cups coarsely chopped fresh
   flat-leaf parsley

1 cup coarsely chopped fresh cilantro

½ cup coarsely chopped fresh mint

4 medium tomatoes, chopped coarsely

1 medium red onion, chopped coarsely

⅓ cup fresh lemon juice

1 tablespoon olive oil

1   Thread chicken onto each of eight skewers. Using fingers, rub combined garlic, paprika, sumac, oregano, the water and oil all over chicken. Cook chicken on heated, lightly oiled grill or grill pan until browned and cooked through.

2   Meanwhile, place herbs, tomato and onion in medium bowl with juice and oil; toss to combine. Serve chicken skewers with herb salad.

SERVES 4
per serving 6.6g carbohydrate; 10.7g fat; 327 cal; 48.8g protein
tip If using metal skewers, oil them first to prevent the chicken from sticking.

cajun chicken with chunky salsa (see back cover)

PREPARATION TIME 20 MINUTES (PLUS REFRIGERATION TIME)   COOKING TIME 20 MINUTES

four 6-ounce skinless, boneless
   chicken breasts

1 teaspoon cracked black pepper

2 tablespoons finely chopped fresh oregano

2 teaspoons sweet paprika

1 teaspoon red pepper flakes

2 cloves garlic, crushed in garlic press

2 teaspoons olive oil

SALSA

2 medium tomatoes, chopped coarsely

1 small red onion, chopped coarsely

1 medium green bell pepper, chopped coarsely

2 tablespoons coarsely chopped fresh cilantro

2 teaspoons olive oil

2 tablespoons fresh lime juice

1   Place chicken in large bowl with remaining ingredients; toss to coat chicken in mixture. Cover; refrigerate 15 minutes.

2   Meanwhile, make salsa.

3   Cook chicken in lightly oiled large nonstick skillet until browned both sides and cooked through. Serve chicken with salsa.

SALSA Place ingredients in medium bowl; toss gently to combine.

SERVES 4
per serving 3.9g carbohydrate; 8.7g fat; 259 cal; 40.3g protein

soy chicken and scallion omelet salad

PREPARATION TIME 20 MINUTES (PLUS REFRIGERATION TIME)   COOKING TIME 25 MINUTES

1½ pounds skinless, boneless

   chicken breasts

2 tablespoons soy sauce

1 clove garlic, crushed in garlic press

1 tablespoon peanut oil

6 eggs

4 scallions, sliced thinly

1½ cups (2 ounces) baby spinach leaves

2 cups (2 ounces) trimmed watercress

CHILI DRESSING

1 tablespoon sweet chili sauce

2 tablespoons fresh lime juice

2 red serrano chiles, chopped finely

¼ cup peanut oil

1 tablespoon sugar

1   Combine chicken, soy and garlic in large bowl; cover, refrigerate 3 hours or overnight.

2   Drain chicken; discard marinade. Heat oil in large skillet; cook chicken, in batches, until browned all over and cooked through. Cover chicken; let stand 5 minutes, slice thinly.

3   Meanwhile, whisk eggs in medium bowl with scallion. Pour half of egg mixture into heated large nonstick skillet; cook, tilting skillet, over medium heat until egg mixture is almost set. Turn, cook further 2 minutes. Repeat with remaining mixture.

4   Roll omelets together; cut into thin slices.

5   Make chili dressing.

6   Gently toss chicken and omelet strips in large bowl with greens and three-quarters of the dressing. Serve remaining dressing separately.

CHILI DRESSING   Combine ingredients in screw-top jar; shake well.

SERVES 4
per serving   7.4g carbohydrate; 30g fat; 503 cal; 50.8g protein

chicken breasts in spinach and feta sauce

PREPARATION TIME 10 MINUTES   COOKING TIME 30 MINUTES

2 tablespoons olive oil

four 6-ounce skinless, boneless

   chicken breasts

1 medium onion, chopped finely

2 cloves garlic, crushed in garlic press

¼ cup dry white wine

10 ounces heavy cream

4 ounces firm feta cheese, chopped coarsely

8 ounces spinach, chopped coarsely

1   Heat oil in large skillet; cook chicken, uncovered, until browned both sides and cooked through. Remove from skillet; cover to keep warm.

2   Add onion and garlic to same skillet; cook, stirring, until onion is soft. Stir in wine. Bring to a boil; simmer, uncovered, until liquid is almost evaporated. Add cream and cheese; simmer, uncovered, about 5 minutes or until sauce thickens slightly. Add spinach; stir until spinach just wilts. Top chicken with sauce.

SERVES 4
per serving   4.7g carbohydrate; 48g fat; 644 cal; 46.9g protein

pesto-grilled chicken drumsticks

PREPARATION TIME 5 MINUTES   COOKING TIME 30 MINUTES

We used a sun-dried tomato pesto in this recipe but you might prefer to experiment with a different flavor.

12 chicken drumsticks

1 tablespoon olive oil

2 tablespoons fresh lemon juice

3 cloves garlic, crushed in garlic press

1 stick butter, softened

2 tablespoons bottled pesto

10 ounces broccoli

1   Make deep diagonal cuts across each chicken drumstick. Combine oil, juice and garlic in large bowl; add chicken, coat with oil mixture.

2   Combine butter and pesto in small bowl; press two-thirds of the pesto mixture into cuts and all over chicken.

3   Place chicken under preheated broiler; cook, brushing with remaining pesto mixture occasionally, until browned all over and cooked through.

4   Meanwhile, boil, steam or microwave broccoli until tender; drain. Brush chicken with pan juices just before serving with broccoli.

SERVES 4
per serving 1.1g carbohydrate; 59.6g fat; 756 cal; 55.1g protein

chicken with almond sauce

PREPARATION TIME 15 MINUTES (PLUS REFRIGERATION TIME)   COOKING TIME 25 MINUTES

2 tablespoons olive oil

⅓ cup fresh orange juice

2 cloves garlic, crushed in garlic press

four 6-ounce skinless, boneless

   chicken breasts

1 tablespoon olive oil, extra

1 medium bulb fennel, sliced thinly

14 ounces pearl onions

ALMOND SAUCE

1 tablespoon olive oil

2 tablespoons homemade breadcrumbs

½ cup ground almonds

pinch ground cloves

¾ cup chicken broth

2 tablespoons dry white wine

¼ cup heavy cream

1   Combine oil, juice, garlic and chicken in medium bowl; cover, refrigerate 3 hours or overnight.

2   Heat extra oil in large deep skillet; cook fennel and onions, stirring, until onions are soft and browned lightly. Remove from heat, cover to keep warm.

3   Cook drained chicken on heated, lightly oiled grill or grill pan, in batches, until browned both sides and cooked through.

4   Meanwhile, make almond sauce.

5   Serve chicken with fennel mixture and almond sauce.

ALMOND SAUCE Heat oil in medium saucepan; cook breadcrumbs, stirring, until browned lightly. Add almonds and cloves; cook, stirring, until browned lightly. Gradually add combined broth and wine, stir over heat until mixture is smooth; bring to a boil. Remove from heat, stir in cream.

SERVES 4
per serving 12g carbohydrate; 35.1g fat; 547 cal; 44.7g protein

rosemary-smoked chicken breast

PREPARATION TIME 10 MINUTES (PLUS REFRIGERATION TIME)
COOKING TIME 40 MINUTES (PLUS STANDING TIME)

You need ½ pound smoking chips for this recipe.

1 clove garlic, crushed in
  garlic press
1½ cups dry white wine
1 tablespoon finely chopped
  fresh rosemary
four 6-ounce skinless, boneless
  chicken breasts
2 cups water
1 clove garlic, crushed in
  garlic press, extra
2 tablespoons coarsely chopped
  fresh rosemary
2 tablespoons olive oil
7 ounces oyster mushrooms
7 ounces enoki mushrooms
9 cups (14 ounces) baby
  spinach leaves

1 Combine garlic, ½ cup of the wine and finely chopped rosemary in large shallow casserole; add chicken, mix well. Cover; refrigerate 3 hours or overnight.

2 Combine the water, remaining wine, extra garlic and coarsely chopped rosemary in large bowl; add smoking chips, mix well. Let stand at least 2 hours or overnight.

3 Cook chicken on heated oiled grill for 2 minutes each side. Place chicken on rack or in disposable roasting pan. Place drained smoking chips in smoke box; place alongside chicken on grill. Cook in covered grill, using indirect heat, following manufacturer's instructions, about 35 minutes or until browned all over and tender.

4 Just before serving, heat half the oil in wok or large skillet; stir-fry oyster mushrooms about 3 minutes or until just tender, remove from wok. Heat remaining oil in wok; stir-fry enoki mushrooms and spinach only long enough to heat, not wilt. Serve chicken with spinach and mushrooms.

SERVES 4
per serving 2.2g carbohydrate; 13.6g fat; 372 cal; 44.5g protein

chicken larb

PREPARATION TIME 20 MINUTES   COOKING TIME 20 MINUTES

2 tablespoons peanut oil

1 tablespoon finely chopped
fresh lemongrass

2 red serrano chiles, seeded,
chopped finely

1 clove garlic, crushed in
garlic press

1 tablespoon grated fresh ginger

1½ pounds lean ground chicken

1 tablespoon fish sauce

⅓ cup fresh lime juice

1 medium onion, sliced thinly

1 cup loosely packed fresh
cilantro leaves

1 cup (3½ ounces) fresh
bean sprouts

½ cup loosely packed fresh
basil leaves

½ cup loosely packed fresh
mint leaves

4 cups (4 ounces) trimmed
watercress

1 medium hothouse cucumber,
sliced thinly

1 tablespoon finely chopped
fresh mint

1 Heat half of the oil in large skillet; cook lemongrass, chile, garlic and ginger, stirring, until fragrant. Add chicken; cook, stirring, about 10 minutes or until cooked through.

2 Add half of the fish sauce and half of the lime juice; cook, stirring, 5 minutes.

3 Combine onion, cilantro, sprouts, basil, mint leaves, watercress and cucumber in large bowl; drizzle with combined remaining fish sauce, juice and oil, toss salad mixture gently.

4 Place salad mixture on serving plate, top with chicken mixture; sprinkle with finely chopped mint.

SERVES 4
per serving 4.3g carbohydrate; 24.7g fat; 397 cal; 39.3g protein

barbecued chicken with tomato salad

PREPARATION TIME 15 MINUTES

6 medium plum tomatoes, chopped coarsely

1 tablespoon drained baby capers

1 small red onion, sliced thinly

½ cup coarsely chopped fresh
   flat-leaf parsley

1 tablespoon red wine vinegar

¼ cup extra virgin olive oil

1 barbecued chicken
   (about 2 pounds), quartered

1   Combine tomato, capers, onion, parsley, vinegar and oil in medium bowl.

2   Serve chicken with tomato salad.

SERVES 4
per serving 3.9g carbohydrate; 34.7g fat; 460 cal; 34g protein
tip Purchase the barbecued chicken on the same day you serve it.

chicken with herb sauce

PREPARATION TIME 15 MINUTES   COOKING TIME 15 MINUTES

four 6-ounce skinless, boneless
   chicken breasts

1 tablespoon olive oil

4 scallions, chopped coarsely

2 teaspoons cornstarch

1½ cups chicken broth

4 ounces soft garlic and
   herb cheese, crumbled

1 tablespoon coarsely chopped fresh
   flat-leaf parsley

1 tablespoon coarsely chopped fresh chives

1 tablespoon butter

7 ounces green beans, halved

1 clove garlic, crushed in garlic press

1 medium green bell pepper, sliced thinly

1 medium red bell pepper, sliced thinly

1   Split chicken breasts through center horizontally. Heat oil in large nonstick skillet; cook chicken, in batches, until browned both sides and cooked through. Remove from skillet; cover to keep warm.

2   Place scallion in same skillet; cook, stirring, 2 minutes. Add blended cornstarch and broth; cook, stirring, until mixture boils and thickens. Add cheese; stir until cheese melts. Stir in herbs.

3   Meanwhile, melt butter in medium skillet; cook beans, stirring, until just tender. Add garlic and peppers; cook, stirring, until tender.

4   Serve vegetables topped with chicken and sauce.

SERVES 4
per serving 6.7g carbohydrate; 21.5g fat; 396 cal; 44.1g protein

chicken with tomatoes and green olives

PREPARATION TIME 10 MINUTES   COOKING TIME 30 MINUTES

1 tablespoon olive oil

4 chicken thighs (1¾ pounds)

4 chicken drumsticks (1¼ pounds)

½ cup dry white wine

8 cloves garlic, peeled

1 tablespoon finely chopped fresh
   lemon thyme

3 bay leaves

2 ounces sun-dried tomatoes

1½ cups chicken broth

2 teaspoons cornstarch

1 tablespoon water

⅓ cup pitted green olives

1 bunch asparagus, trimmed

1 Heat oil in large heavy-bottomed skillet; cook chicken until lightly browned all over.

2 Add wine to skillet; bring to a boil. Add garlic, thyme, bay leaves, tomatoes and broth; simmer, covered, about 15 minutes or until chicken is cooked through. Remove chicken from skillet; cover to keep warm.

3 Add blended cornstarch and water to pan; stir until mixture boils and thickens slightly.

4 Meanwhile, boil, steam or microwave asparagus until tender; drain.

5 Return chicken to skillet with olives; simmer until heated through. Discard bay leaves before serving. Serve with steamed asparagus.

SERVES 4
per serving 10.2g carbohydrate; 48.6g fat; 729 cal; 58g protein

chicken and thai basil stir-fry

PREPARATION TIME 20 MINUTES   COOKING TIME 15 MINUTES

2 tablespoons peanut oil

1¼ pounds skinless, boneless chicken
   breasts, sliced thinly

2 cloves garlic, crushed in garlic press

1 teaspoon grated fresh ginger

4 red serrano chiles, sliced thinly

1 medium onion, sliced thinly

4 ounces mushrooms, quartered

1 large carrot, sliced thinly

¼ cup oyster sauce

1 tablespoon soy sauce

1 tablespoon fish sauce

⅓ cup chicken broth

1 cup (3½ ounces) fresh bean sprouts

¾ cup loosely packed fresh thai basil leaves

1 Heat half of the oil in wok or large skillet; stir-fry chicken, in batches, until browned all over and cooked through.

2 Heat remaining oil in wok; stir-fry garlic, ginger, chile and onion until onion softens and mixture is fragrant. Add mushroom and carrot; stir-fry until carrot is just tender. Return chicken to wok with sauces and broth; stir-fry until sauce thickens slightly. Remove from heat; toss bean sprouts and basil leaves through stir-fry.

SERVES 4
per serving 9.4g carbohydrate; 17.9g fat; 344 cal; 36g protein

poached chicken with ruby red grapefruit salad

PREPARATION TIME 40 MINUTES   COOKING TIME 15 MINUTES (PLUS COOLING TIME)

1½ cups chicken broth

1½ cups water

1½ pounds skinless, boneless
   chicken breasts

1 small red onion

4 ruby red grapefruits

4 scallions, sliced thinly

2 red serrano chiles, sliced thinly

1 cup coarsely chopped fresh cilantro

¼ cup roasted unsalted peanuts

2 cups (3½ ounces) baby spinach leaves

2 cloves garlic, crushed in garlic press

1 tablespoon light brown sugar

1 tablespoon fresh lime juice

1 tablespoon soy sauce

1 Combine broth and the water in medium saucepan; bring to a boil. Add chicken; return to boil. Reduce heat; simmer, covered, about 10 minutes or until cooked through. Allow chicken to cool in cooking liquid before draining. Discard liquid; slice chicken thinly.

2 Meanwhile, halve red onion; cut each half into paper-thin wedges.

3 Segment peeled grapefruit over large bowl; add chicken, scallion, chile, cilantro, nuts and spinach, toss gently to combine.

4 Combine remaining ingredients in small measuring cup; whisk until sugar dissolves. Pour dressing over salad; toss to combine.

SERVES 4
per serving 7g carbohydrate; 8g fat; 255 cal; 37.8g protein

clay pot chicken

PREPARATION TIME 10 MINUTES (PLUS REFRIGERATION TIME)   COOKING TIME 1 HOUR

1¾ pounds skinless, boneless chicken thighs

1 large onion, quartered

1 long red chile, seeded, sliced thinly

½ cup chicken broth

4 ounces shiitake mushrooms, halved

4 scallions, cut into 1½-inch pieces

1 small head white cabbage (about 1 pound),
   cut into 2½-inch squares

HOISIN AND CITRUS MARINADE

4 cloves garlic, crushed in garlic press

1 tablespoon fish sauce

1 tablespoon soy sauce

1 tablespoon hoisin sauce

2 tablespoons fresh lime juice

1 stalk fresh lemongrass, chopped finely

1 Make hoisin and citrus marinade.

2 Cut each thigh in half, place in large bowl with marinade; toss to coat chicken in marinade. Cover; refrigerate 3 hours or overnight.

3 Preheat oven to moderate.

4 Place chicken mixture in clay pot or 10-cup casserole with onion, chile and broth; mix gently to combine. Cook, covered, in moderate oven 45 minutes. Add mushroom, scallion and cabbage to dish; cook, covered, 15 minutes, stirring occasionally.

HOISIN AND CITRUS MARINADE   Combine ingredients in large bowl.

SERVES 4
per serving 9.4g carbohydrate; 9.2g fat; 310 cal; 46.6g protein

salt and pepper duck with shallots and cucumber

PREPARATION TIME 10 MINUTES   COOKING TIME 2 HOURS 5 MINUTES

4-pound duck

1 tablespoon finely ground
sichuan peppercorns

2 teaspoons coarse sea salt

1 tablespoon peanut oil

1 tablespoon butter

16 shallots

2 medium hothouse cucumbers,
sliced thickly

1 tablespoon oyster sauce

½ cup chicken broth

¼ cup coarsely chopped fresh cilantro

1 Preheat oven to moderate.

2 Place duck, breast-side up, on wire rack in roasting pan; rub combined pepper and salt into duck breast. Bake, uncovered, in moderate oven 1½ hours. Remove duck from oven; increase oven temperature to very hot.

3 Using metal skewer or fork, prick duck skin all over. Turn duck breast-side down; bake, uncovered, in a very hot oven 15 minutes. Turn duck breast-side up; bake, uncovered, in very hot oven about 20 minutes, or until duck is browned all over and cooked through.

4 Meanwhile, heat oil and butter in large skillet, cook shallots, stirring, until softened. Add cucumber; cook, stirring, 2 minutes. Stir in combined sauce and broth; bring to a boil. Remove from heat; stir in cilantro.

5 Cut duck into pieces, serve on shallot and cucumber mixture.

SERVES 4
per serving 3.8g carbohydrate; 114.1g fat; 1184 cal; 38.5g protein
tip You may prefer to use zucchini instead of cucumber.

anise and ginger braised duck

PREPARATION TIME 30 MINUTES   COOKING TIME 2 HOURS (PLUS REFRIGERATION TIME)

3½-pound duck

¼ cup sweet sherry

1 cup water

2 tablespoons soy sauce

4 cloves garlic, sliced thinly

1-inch piece fresh ginger, sliced thinly

3 star anise

1 teaspoon hot chili sauce (such as
sambal oelek or sriracha)

1 teaspoon cornstarch

2 teaspoons water, extra

1 pound asian greens

1 Using knife or poultry shears, cut down either side of duck backbone; discard. Cut duck in half through breastbone, then cut each half into two pieces. Trim excess fat from duck, leaving skin intact.

2 Place duck pieces in single layer, skin-side down, in large deep skillet; cook over low heat about 10 minutes or until skin is crisp. Drain on paper towels.

3 Place duck in clean deep skillet. Add sherry, the water, sauce, garlic, ginger, star anise and sauce; simmer, covered, about 1½ hours or until duck is very tender. Turn duck halfway through cooking. Refrigerate duck overnight, covered, in cooking liquid.

4 Next day, discard fat layer from surface; place duck mixture in large deep skillet. Cover; cook over low heat until duck is heated through. Remove duck from skillet; keep warm.

5 Strain liquid into small saucepan; stir in blended cornstarch and the extra water. Stir over heat until mixture boils and thickens slightly.

6 Meanwhile, boil, steam or microwave asian greens. Serve sauce over duck with greens.

SERVES 4
per serving 4.3g carbohydrate; 40g fat; 518 cal; 32.2g protein

braised cornish hens
with brussels sprouts and spinach

PREPARATION TIME 30 MINUTES   COOKING TIME 40 MINUTES

three 1-pound cornish hens

1 medium leek, chopped coarsely

2 cloves garlic, crushed in
   garlic press

1 medium onion, chopped coarsely

12 slices bacon, chopped finely

½ cup dry white wine

1 cup chicken broth

2 bay leaves

10 ounces small brussels
   sprouts, halved

1 pound spinach, trimmed,
   chopped coarsely

½ cup coarsely chopped fresh mint

1   Cut along both sides of hens' backbones; discard backbones. Cut each hen into four pieces. Rinse hen pieces under cold water; pat dry.

2   Cook hens, in batches, in lightly oiled large saucepan until browned lightly both sides. Cook leek, garlic, onion and bacon in same pan, stirring, about 5 minutes or until leek softens. Add wine, broth and bay leaves; bring to a boil. Return hens and any pan juices to pan; simmer, uncovered, 20 minutes or until liquid has almost evaporated. Discard bay leaves. Remove hens from pan; keep warm.

3   Add sprouts; simmer, uncovered, about 3 minutes or until tender. Stir in spinach and mint; cook until spinach just wilts. Serve hens with sprout and spinach mixture.

SERVES 4
per serving 7.4g carbohydrate; 30.1g fat; 551 cal; 57.6g protein

braised cornish hens with brussels sprouts and spinach

minted lemongrass and ginger iced tea

minted lemongrass and ginger iced tea

PREPARATION TIME 10 MINUTES (PLUS REFRIGERATION TIME)

6 lemongrass and ginger tea bags

4 cups boiling water

2 tablespoons sugar

**4-inch stalk finely chopped
  fresh lemongrass**

½ small orange, sliced thinly

½ small lemon, sliced thinly

**¼ cup firmly packed fresh
  mint leaves, torn**

1 Place tea bags and the boiling water in large heatproof pitcher; let stand 5 minutes.

2 Discard tea bags. Add sugar, lemongrass, and orange and lemon slices to pitcher; stir to combine. Refrigerate, covered, until cold.

3 Stir mint into cold tea; serve over ice.

SERVES 4
per serving 8g carbohydrate; 0.1g fat; 35 cal; 0.4g protein

japanese chicken skewers

PREPARATION TIME 20 MINUTES   COOKING TIME 10 MINUTES

The uncooked chicken can be skewered and sauce made a day ahead.
Cover separately; refrigerate until required. Soak 16 bamboo skewers in
water for at least an hour prior to use to prevent splintering or scorching.

1 pound chicken tenderloins

2 tablespoons light soy sauce

1 tablespoon mirin

1 teaspoon sugar

½ teaspoon sesame oil

1 teaspoon sesame seeds

1   Cut chicken into 16 long thin slices; thread each slice on a skewer.
    Cook, in batches, on heated oiled grill or grill pan until chicken is
    browned all over and cooked through.

2   Meanwhile, combine remaining ingredients in small bowl.

3   Serve chicken hot with sauce.

SERVES 4
per serving 1.7g carbohydrate; 3.8g fat; 161 cal; 29g protein

turkish spinach dip

PREPARATION TIME 10 MINUTES (PLUS COOLING AND REFRIGERATION TIMES)   COOKING TIME 10 MINUTES

Dip can be made a day ahead. Cover; refrigerate until required.
You need one bag of spinach weighing about 10 ounces for this recipe.

1 tablespoon olive oil

1 small onion, chopped finely

1 clove garlic, crushed in garlic press

1 teaspoon ground cumin

½ teaspoon curry powder

¼ teaspoon ground turmeric

2 cups (3½ ounces) spinach leaves,
    shredded finely

2 cups unflavored yogurt

1   Heat oil in medium skillet; cook onion and garlic, stirring, until onion
    softens. Add spices; cook, stirring, until fragrant. Add spinach; cook,
    stirring, until spinach wilts. Transfer mixture to serving bowl; cool.

2   Stir yogurt through mixture, cover; refrigerate 1 hour.

3   Serve cold with assorted crudités.

SERVES 4
per serving 6.8g carbohydrate; 8.9g fat; 139 cal; 6.8g protein

peking duck wraps

PREPARATION TIME 25 MINUTES

Buy a whole barbecued duck from a Chinese restaurant the day before
serving this recipe. Remove and discard skin and bones; slice the meat thinly.
Cover; refrigerate until required.

8 scallions, trimmed

¼ cup hoisin sauce

1 tablespoon plum sauce

2 cups thinly sliced barbecued
  duck meat

16 small boston lettuce leaves

1 Cut white section of each scallion from green section. Discard green
section; thinly slice white section lengthwise.

2 Divide combined sauces, duck and scallion among lettuce leaves.
Roll lettuce to enclose filling.

3 Serve peking duck wraps cold or at room temperature.

SERVES 4
per serving 10.6g carbohydrate; 17.3g fat; 249 cal; 13.5g protein

bocconcini, olives and cherry tomatoes with pesto

PREPARATION TIME 25 MINUTES

Pesto can be made up to 2 days ahead. Cover; refrigerate until required.

½ cup finely grated parmesan cheese

½ cup toasted pine nuts

2 cloves garlic, crushed in
  garlic press

1 cup extra virgin olive oil

2 cups firmly packed fresh
  basil leaves

16 cherry tomatoes, halved

32 baby bocconcini

32 medium pitted green olives

1 Blend or process cheese, nuts, garlic and half of the oil until combined.
Add basil and remaining oil; process until almost smooth. Transfer pesto
to serving bowl.

2 Serve tomato, bocconcini and olives with cold pesto.

SERVES 4
per serving 8.5g carbohydrate; 91.7g fat; 952 cal; 26.6g protein
tip Serve with toothpicks.

chili con queso

PREPARATION TIME 10 MINUTES   COOKING TIME 10 MINUTES

2 teaspoons vegetable oil

½ small green bell pepper,
   chopped finely

½ small onion, chopped finely

1 tablespoon drained pickled
   jalapeño chiles, chopped finely

1 clove garlic, crushed in garlic press

7 ounces canned chopped
   tomatoes, undrained

one 8-ounce package cream
   cheese, softened

1   Heat oil in medium saucepan; cook pepper, onion, chile and garlic, stirring, until onion softens. Add tomato; cook, stirring, 2 minutes.

2   Add cheese; whisk until cheese melts and dip is smooth.

3   Serve hot with assorted crudités.

SERVES 4
per serving   3.8g carbohydrate; 23.1g fat; 243 cal; 5.9g protein

smoked salmon cones

PREPARATION TIME 40 MINUTES (PLUS REFRIGERATION TIME)

Cheese mixture can be made up to a day ahead. Cover; refrigerate until required.

14 ounces smoked salmon, sliced

⅔ cup heavy cream

2 ounces cream cheese, softened

2 tablespoons toasted pistachios,
   chopped finely

2 tablespoons finely chopped
   fresh chives

24 baby spinach leaves

1   Blend or process 3 ounces of the salmon until chopped finely. Add cream and cheese; process until smooth. Transfer mixture to medium bowl; stir in nuts and chives. Refrigerate until firm.

2   Halve remaining salmon slices widthwise; place one spinach leaf on each salmon slice, top with 1 teaspoon of the cheese mixture. Roll each into small cone to enclose filling. Refrigerate to set; serve cold.

SERVES 4
per serving   3g carbohydrate; 27.3g fat; 364 cal; 27.1g protein

BLT open sandwich

PREPARATION TIME 20 MINUTES   COOKING TIME 5 MINUTES

2 slices thick-cut bacon

2 boston lettuce leaves

2 tablespoons mayonnaise

20 mini toasts

10 pear or grape tomatoes, halved

1   Cut bacon into 20 pieces. Heat large skillet; cook bacon, stirring, until browned and crisp. Drain on paper towel.

2   Cut lettuce into pieces slightly larger than mini toasts.

3   Divide mayonnaise among mini toasts; top each mini toast with lettuce, bacon and tomato.

4   Serve at room temperature.

SERVES 4
per serving 3.7g carbohydrate; 11.6g fat; 129 cal; 2.8g protein

fried chorizo with garlic

PREPARATION TIME 5 MINUTES   COOKING TIME 10 MINUTES

Chorizo is a sausage made traditionally of coarsely ground pork and seasoned with garlic and chiles. If you cannot find fresh chorizo, substitute with any spicy sausage.

2 chorizo sausages, cut into
¼-inch slices

2 teaspoons olive oil

1 clove garlic, crushed in garlic press

2 tablespoons finely chopped fresh
flat-leaf parsley

1   Cook sausage slices in heated large skillet, stirring, until crisp; drain on paper towel.

2   Discard fat from skillet. Heat oil in same skillet; cook sausage slices, garlic and parsley until heated through.

SERVES 4
per serving 2.8g carbohydrate; 21.1g fat; 240 cal; 10.3g protein

denver omelet

PREPARATION TIME 10 MINUTES   COOKING TIME 15 MINUTES

10 eggs

⅓ cup sour cream

2 red serrano chiles, chopped finely

2 teaspoons vegetable oil

3 scallions, sliced thinly

1 medium green bell pepper,
    chopped finely

4 ounces deli ham, chopped finely

2 small tomatoes, seeded,
    chopped finely

½ cup coarsely grated
    cheddar cheese

1   Break eggs into large bowl, whisk lightly; whisk in sour cream and chile.

2   Heat oil in large nonstick skillet; cook scallion and pepper, stirring, until scallion softens. Place scallion mixture in medium bowl with ham, tomato and cheese; toss to combine.

3   Pour ½ cup of the egg mixture into same lightly oiled skillet; cook, tilting skillet, over low heat until almost set. Sprinkle about ⅓ cup of the filling over half of the omelet; using spatula, fold omelet over to completely cover the filling.

4   Pour ¼ cup of the egg mixture into empty half of skillet; cook over low heat until almost set. Sprinkle about ⅓ cup of the filling over folded omelet, fold second omelet over top of first omelet to cover filling. Repeat twice more, using ¼ cup of the egg mixture each time, to form one large layered omelet. Carefully slide omelet onto plate; cover to keep warm.

5   Repeat steps 3 and 4 to make second omelet, using remaining egg and filling. Cut each denver omelet in half.

SERVES 4
per serving 3.4g carbohydrate; 29.5g fat; 383 cal; 26.9g protein

herbed olive, white bean and anchovy dip

PREPARATION TIME 15 MINUTES   COOKING TIME 5 MINUTES

8 anchovy fillets in oil, drained

¼ cup milk

2 tablespoons olive oil

1 small red onion, chopped finely

1 clove garlic, crushed in
   garlic press

2 tablespoons finely chopped fresh
   flat-leaf parsley

2 teaspoons finely chopped
   fresh marjoram

1 teaspoon finely chopped
   fresh thyme

10 ounces canned small
   white beans, rinsed, drained

¼ cup pitted black olives,
   chopped finely

1½ tablespoons capers,
   rinsed, drained

2 teaspoons red wine vinegar

1 tablespoon fresh lemon juice

2 tablespoons olive oil, extra

1 Combine anchovies and milk in small bowl; let stand 10 minutes, drain well.

2 Heat oil in large skillet; cook onion, garlic and herbs, stirring, until onion is soft.

3 Blend or process anchovies, onion mixture, beans, olives, capers, vinegar and juice until combined; with motor running, add extra oil in thin stream, process until almost smooth. Serve with assorted crudités.

SERVES 4
per serving 9.8g carbohydrate; 13.3g fat; 174 cal; 4.4g protein

chile-garlic mushrooms

PREPARATION TIME 10 MINUTES   COOKING TIME 5 MINUTES

¼ cup olive oil

3 tablespoons butter

5 cloves garlic, crushed in
   garlic press

1 red serrano chile, chopped finely

1¾ pounds button mushrooms

1 tablespoon fresh lemon juice

½ teaspoon cracked black pepper

2 tablespoons finely chopped fresh
   flat-leaf parsley

1   Heat oil and butter in large skillet; cook garlic, chile and mushrooms, stirring, about 5 minutes or until mushrooms are tender.

2   Add remaining ingredients. Serve immediately.

SERVES 4
per serving 1.6g carbohydrate; 9.6g fat; 104 cal; 3.2g protein

prosciutto-wrapped melon with vinaigrette

PREPARATION TIME 10 MINUTES

½ medium cantaloupe

12 slices prosciutto

1 tablespoon red wine vinegar

¼ cup olive oil

½ clove garlic, crushed in
   garlic press

¼ teaspoon sugar

1 teaspoon finely chopped fresh
   flat-leaf parsley

1 teaspoon finely chopped
   fresh oregano

1   Peel and seed cantaloupe; cut into 12 slices. Wrap a slice of prosciutto around each cantaloupe slice.

2   Combine remaining ingredients in screw-top jar; shake well. Drizzle vinaigrette over cantaloupe.

SERVES 4
per serving 8.4g carbohydrate; 16.4g fat; 216 cal; 9g protein

eggplant salad caprese

PREPARATION TIME 20 MINUTES (PLUS STANDING AND REFRIGERATION TIMES)   COOKING TIME 15 MINUTES

3 small eggplants, cut into
   ½-inch slices

kosher salt

2 medium tomatoes, sliced thinly

13 ounces bocconcini cheese,
   sliced thinly

¼ cup firmly packed fresh
   basil leaves

CLASSIC ITALIAN DRESSING

¼ cup olive oil

1 clove garlic, crushed in garlic press

1 teaspoon grainy mustard

1 teaspoon sugar

2 tablespoons red wine vinegar

1 Place eggplant slices on wire racks, sprinkle with salt; let stand 30 minutes. Rinse eggplant; drain on paper towel. Cook eggplant, in batches, on heated oiled grill or grill pan until browned both sides.

2 Meanwhile, make classic italian dressing.

3 Layer eggplant with remaining ingredients on serving platter; drizzle with three-quarters of the dressing. Cover; refrigerate at least 15 minutes or up to 3 hours. Just before serving, drizzle with remaining dressing.

CLASSIC ITALIAN DRESSING Combine ingredients in screw-top jar; shake well.

SERVES 4
per serving 5.7g carbohydrate; 27.4g fat; 337 cal; 17.2g protein

tomato, basil and red onion salad

PREPARATION TIME 15 MINUTES

4 large plum tomatoes, sliced thinly

1 small red onion, sliced thinly

2 tablespoons small fresh
   basil leaves

pinch salt

pinch cracked black pepper

pinch sugar

2 teaspoons balsamic vinegar

2 teaspoons extra virgin olive oil

1 Alternate layers of tomato, onion and basil on serving plate; sprinkle with salt, pepper and sugar. Drizzle with vinegar and oil.

SERVES 4
per serving 2.7g carbohydrate; 2.3g fat; 36 cal; 1.1g protein

arugula and prosciutto frittata

PREPARATION TIME 15 MINUTES   COOKING TIME 25 MINUTES

4 slices prosciutto

¾ cup (1 ounce) arugula

1 tablespoon finely grated
   parmesan cheese

5 eggs, beaten lightly

1 tablespoon heavy cream

1   Preheat oven to moderate.

2   Grease deep 8-inch square cake pan; line base and two opposite sides with parchment or wax paper.

3   Cook prosciutto, in batches, in medium nonstick skillet until browned all over and crisp; drain on paper towel.

4   Place half of the prosciutto in prepared pan; cover with half of the arugula then half of the cheese. Repeat with remaining prosciutto, arugula and cheese.

5   Pour combined egg and cream into pan, pressing down on prosciutto mixture to completely cover with egg mixture; bake, uncovered, in moderate oven about 20 minutes or until firm. Let stand 5 minutes; turn out of pan, cut into eight pieces.

SERVES 4
per serving   0.5g carbohydrate; 9.9g fat; 137 cal; 11.9g protein
tip   Serve frittata hot or cold.

marinated olives

PREPARATION TIME 10 MINUTES (PLUS MARINATING TIME)

4 ounces green olives

4 ounces kalamata olives

1 lime wedge

1 cup (approximately) olive oil

1 clove garlic, sliced thinly

¼ cup fresh lime juice

3 sprigs fresh thyme

2 sprigs fresh rosemary

1   Combine ingredients in large sterilized jar, ensuring olives are covered with oil; seal jar.

SERVES 4
per serving   8.7g carbohydrate; 58.4g fat; 558 cal; 1.2g protein
tip   Olives are best prepared at least two weeks before you serve them; store, covered, in a cool dark place.

grilled radicchio parcels with buffalo mozzarella and sun-dried tomatoes

PREPARATION TIME 15 MINUTES   COOKING TIME 10 MINUTES

While mozzarella is traditionally made from buffalo milk, you could use a fresh variety made from cow milk.

4 large radicchio leaves

2 balls buffalo mozzarella, sliced into 8 pieces

8 sun-dried tomato pieces

8 basil leaves

1 Boil, steam or microwave radicchio until wilted slightly; rinse under cold water, pat dry with paper towel.

2 Center one piece mozzarella on each leaf; top with one piece tomato and one basil leaf. Repeat with one piece each mozzarella, tomato and basil; roll radicchio to enclose filling.

3 Grill radicchio parcels on heated oiled grill or grill pan until browned all over and heated through.

SERVES 4
per serving 3.5g carbohydrate; 8.4g fat; 132 cal; 10.6g protein

citrus crush

PREPARATION TIME 10 MINUTES

2 medium limes, cut into wedges

2 medium lemons, cut into wedges

1 tablespoon light brown sugar

½ cup firmly packed fresh mint leaves

4 cups crushed ice

2 cups diet lemon-lime soda

1 Using mortar and pestle, crush lime, lemon, sugar and mint until mixture is pulpy and sugar is dissolved.

2 Combine citrus mixture in large pitcher with crushed ice. Stir soda into pitcher; serve immediately.

SERVES 4
per serving 4.4g carbohydrate; 0.2g fat; 30 cal; 0.6g protein

spicy lamb and garlic skewers

PREPARATION TIME 10 MINUTES (PLUS REFRIGERATION TIME)   COOKING TIME 10 MINUTES

Soak eight bamboo skewers in water for at least an hour prior to use to prevent splintering or scorching.

1 pound boneless leg of lamb in
  one piece
½ large onion, grated coarsely
1 clove garlic, crushed in
  garlic press
1 teaspoon finely grated lemon peel
2 teaspoons finely chopped
  fresh rosemary
¼ teaspoon cayenne
½ teaspoon ground coriander
1 teaspoon ground cumin
2 tablespoons red wine vinegar
¼ cup olive oil

1   Cut lamb into 1-inch pieces. Thread lamb onto eight skewers. Place skewers in large shallow casserole; pour over combined remaining ingredients. Cover; refrigerate 3 hours or overnight. Drain skewers; reserve marinade.

2   Cook skewers, in batches, on heated oiled grill or grill pan, brushing occasionally with reserved marinade, until browned all over and cooked as desired.

SERVES 4
per serving 0.9g carbohydrate; 18.2g fat; 279 cal; 27.7g protein

pesto fish kebabs

PREPARATION TIME 10 MINUTES   COOKING TIME 15 MINUTES

You can use any large firm fish fillets or steaks – such as halibut, monkfish or mahi-mahi – for this recipe. Soak eight bamboo skewers in water for at least an hour prior to use to prevent splintering or scorching. You need half of a small head of savoy cabbage.

1¼ pounds firm fish fillets

1 tablespoon bottled pesto

½ cup loosely packed, finely
chopped fresh flat-leaf parsley

1¼ pounds savoy cabbage,
shredded finely

⅓ cup drained baby capers

1 teaspoon finely grated lemon peel

½ cup loosely packed, finely
chopped fresh mint leaves

1   Cut fish into 1-inch cubes; combine with pesto and 1 tablespoon of the parsley in medium bowl. Thread onto eight skewers.

2   Cook kebabs, in batches, in heated, lightly oiled large skillet until browned and cooked as desired. Cover to keep warm.

3   Add cabbage to same skillet; cook, stirring, until just tender. Stir in remaining parsley, capers, peel and mint.

4   Serve fish kebabs on stir-fried cabbage.

SERVES 4
per serving 5g carbohydrate; 5.5g fat; 204 cal; 33.4g protein
tip Fish can be marinated and threaded onto skewers a day ahead; store, covered, in refrigerator.

Losing Weight Slower (no more than 25g carbs per serving)

baked apples with berries and honey yogurt

PREPARATION TIME 10 MINUTES (PLUS REFRIGERATION TIME)   COOKING TIME 45 MINUTES

10 ounces frozen mixed berries

4 large granny smith apples

¼ teaspoon cardamom seeds

½ cup whole milk yogurt

1 teaspoon honey

1   Place berries in fine strainer set over small bowl, cover; thaw in refrigerator overnight.

2   Preheat oven to moderately slow.

3   Core unpeeled apples about three-quarters of the way in from the stem end, making hole 1½ inches in diameter. Use small sharp knife to score around circumference of each apple. Make small deep cut in base of each apple; divide seeds evenly between apples, inserting into each cut.

4   Pack berries firmly into apples; reserve remaining berries. Place apples in small casserole; bake, uncovered, in moderately slow oven about 45 minutes or until just tender.

5   Meanwhile, push remaining berries through strainer into bowl; stir in yogurt and honey. Divide apples among serving plates; top with yogurt mixture.

SERVES 4
per serving 24.2g carbohydrate; 1.2g fat; 121 cal; 3.5g protein

citrus compôte

PREPARATION TIME 20 MINUTES

2 large limes

3 large oranges

2 medium pink grapefruit

2 teaspoons sugar

½ vanilla bean, split

1 tablespoon small fresh mint leaves

1   Grate the peel of 1 lime and 1 orange finely; reserve grated peel. Peel remaining lime, remaining oranges, and grapefruit.

2   Segment all citrus over a large bowl to save juice, removing and discarding membrane from each segment. Add segments to bowl with sugar, vanilla bean and reserved peel; stir gently to combine.

3   Let stand, covered, at room temperature 5 minutes; sprinkle with mint leaves.

SERVES 4
per serving 21.6g carbohydrate; 0.5g fat; 110 cal; 3g protein

banana-passionfruit-soy smoothie

PREPARATION TIME 10 MINUTES (PLUS REFRIGERATION TIME)

⅔ cup frozen concentrated
**   passionfruit juice cocktail**

2 cups nonfat soy milk

2 medium ripe bananas,
**   chopped coarsely**

1   Blend or process passionfruit liquid, soy milk and banana, in batches, until smooth.

2   Pour smoothie into large pitcher. Refrigerate, covered, until cold.

MAKES 4 CUPS
per 1 cup serving   19.9g carbohydrate; 0.6g fat; 106 cal; 5.3g protein

peach galette

PREPARATION TIME 15 MINUTES   COOKING TIME 20 MINUTES

2 medium peaches

6 sheets phyllo pastry

4 tablespoons butter, melted

3 teaspoons sugar

1 tablespoon apricot jelly,
**   warmed, strained**

1   Preheat oven to moderately hot. Line baking sheet with parchment or waxed paper.

2   Halve peaches, discard pits; slice peach halves thinly.

3   Place two phyllo sheets on cutting board; brush lightly with a third of the butter. Top with two more phyllo sheets; brush lightly with half of the remaining butter. Repeat layering with remaining phyllo and butter.

4   Fold phyllo in half to form a square; cut 10-inch diameter circle from phyllo square. Arrange peach slices on phyllo circle; sprinkle with sugar. Bake in moderately hot oven about 20 minutes or until galette browns.

5   Serve warm galette brushed with jelly

SERVES 4
per serving   23.1g carbohydrate; 12.8g fat; 217 cal; 2.7g protein
tips   Cover the phyllo with wax paper then a damp towel when you're working with it, to prevent it drying out.
Nectarines, apricots, apples, plums and pears are all suitable to use in place of the peaches.

mixed berry smoothie

PREPARATION TIME 5 MINUTES

8 ounces low-fat strawberry frozen
   yogurt, softened slightly

8 ounces frozen mixed berries

3 cups low-fat milk

1   Blend or process ingredients, in batches, until smooth.
Serve immediately.

MAKES 4 CUPS
per 1 cup serving 23.7g carbohydrate; 3.4g fat; 163 cal;
10.3g protein

mixed berry smoothie

crisp prosciutto with mango and avocado salsa

crisp prosciutto with mango and avocado salsa

PREPARATION TIME 15 MINUTES   COOKING TIME 5 MINUTES

1 medium mango,
   chopped coarsely

1 large avocado, chopped coarsely

1 small red onion, chopped finely

1 small red bell pepper,
   chopped finely

1 red serrano chile, chopped finely

2 tablespoons fresh lime juice

8 slices prosciutto,
   halved lengthwise

1   Place mango, avocado, onion, pepper, chile and juice in medium bowl, toss salsa to combine.

2   Cook prosciutto in lightly oiled medium skillet until crisp. Serve prosciutto with salsa.

SERVES 4
per serving 12.2g carbohydrate; 14.7g fat; 213 cal; 8.2g protein

saffron scrambled eggs on corn cakes

PREPARATION TIME 15 MINUTES COOKING TIME 20 MINUTES

1 fresh ear corn, shucked

½ cup all-purpose flour

1 teaspoon sweet paprika

1 tablespoon finely chopped
   fresh cilantro

¼ cup milk

3 egg whites

3 eggs

3 egg whites, extra

pinch saffron threads

1 Cut corn kernels from cob. Combine corn, flour, paprika and cilantro in medium bowl; stir in milk, mix until combined.

2 Beat egg whites in small bowl with electric mixer until soft peaks form; fold egg whites into corn mixture.

3 Drop corn mixture, 2 tablespoons per cake, into heated oiled large nonstick skillet; cook until browned both sides and cooked through.

4 Combine eggs, extra egg whites and saffron in medium bowl; beat lightly with a fork. Cook egg mixture in lightly oiled nonstick skillet, stirring gently, until creamy and just set. Serve scrambled eggs with corn cakes.

SERVES 4
per serving 22g carbohydrate; 5.2g fat; 195 cal; 14.7g protein

pancetta and eggs

PREPARATION TIME 10 MINUTES COOKING TIME 10 MINUTES

8 slices pancetta

2 scallions, chopped coarsely

4 eggs

4 thick slices white bread

1 Preheat oven to moderately hot. Grease four cups of a regular muffin pan.

2 Line each of the prepared cups with two slices of the pancetta, overlapping to form cup shape. Divide scallion among pancetta cups; break one egg into each pancetta cup.

3 Bake, uncovered, in moderately hot oven about 10 minutes or until eggs are just cooked and pancetta is crisp around edges. Remove from pan carefully. Serve on toasted bread.

SERVES 4
per serving 18.4g carbohydrate; 10.2g fat; 228 cal; 15.6g protein

poached eggs with browned sage butter and asparagus

PREPARATION TIME 10 MINUTES   COOKING TIME 10 MINUTES

5 tablespoons butter

12 fresh sage leaves

4 eggs

1 bunch asparagus, trimmed

2 multi-grain english muffins

1½ ounces shaved parmesan cheese

1   Melt butter in small saucepan; cook sage, stirring, about 3 minutes or until butter changes color to deep brown. Remove from heat; cover to keep warm.

2   Half-fill a shallow skillet with water; bring to a boil. One at a time, break eggs into cup or saucer, then slide into skillet. When all eggs are in skillet, allow water to return to a boil. Cover skillet, turn off heat; let stand about 4 minutes or until a light film of egg white sets over yolks. One at a time, remove eggs, using spatula, and place on paper towel-lined saucer to blot up poaching liquid.

3   Meanwhile, boil, steam or microwave asparagus until tender. Drain; cover to keep warm. Split muffins; toast cut-side.

4   Place muffin halves on serving plates; top each with a quarter of the asparagus, one egg, 1 tablespoon of sage butter, and a quarter of the cheese.

SERVES 4
per serving 12.6g carbohydrate; 26.1g fat; 347 cal; 16.2g protein

spiced iced coffee milkshake

PREPARATION TIME 10 MINUTES

¼ cup ground espresso coffee

¾ cup boiling water

pinch of cardamom seeds

¼ teaspoon ground cinnamon

1 tablespoon light brown sugar

3 scoops low-fat vanilla ice-cream

2½ cups low-fat milk

1   Place coffee, then the boiling water in coffee press pot; let stand 2 minutes before plunging. Pour coffee into small heatproof bowl with cardamom, cinnamon and sugar; stir to dissolve sugar, then cool 10 minutes.

2   Strain coffee mixture through fine strainer into blender or processor; process with ice-cream and milk until smooth. Serve immediately.

MAKES 4 CUPS
per 1 cup serving 19.9g carbohydrate; 1.6g fat; 122 cal; 7.9g protein

soufflé with berry compôte

PREPARATION TIME 10 MINUTES   COOKING TIME 15 MINUTES

1 tablespoon sugar

2 egg yolks

⅓ cup confectioners' sugar, sifted

4 egg whites

2 teaspoons confectioners' sugar, sifted, extra

BERRY COMPÔTE

½ cup frozen mixed berries

2 tablespoons fresh orange juice

1 teaspoon sugar

1 Make berry compôte.

2 Preheat oven to moderate. Lightly grease four 1-cup ovenproof dishes.

3 Sprinkle insides of dishes evenly with sugar; shake away excess. Place dishes on baking sheet.

4 Whisk yolks and 2 tablespoons of the confectioners' sugar in large bowl until mixture is combined.

5 Beat egg whites in small bowl with electric mixer until soft peaks form. Gradually add remaining confectioners' sugar; beat until firm peaks form.

6 Gently fold egg white mixture, in two batches, into egg mixture; divide mixture between prepared dishes.

7 Bake, uncovered, in moderate oven about 12 minutes or until soufflés are puffed and browned lightly. Dust tops with extra confectioners' sugar.

8 Serve soufflés with berry compôte.

BERRY COMPÔTE Combine berries, juice and sugar in small saucepan; bring to a boil. Reduce heat; simmer, uncovered, 2 minutes.

SERVES 4
per serving 24g carbohydrate; 2.9g fat; 140 cal; 5.5g protein

ham, avocado and roasted tomato toast

PREPARATION TIME 10 MINUTES   COOKING TIME 30 MINUTES

4 large plum tomatoes

1 tablespoon light brown sugar

1 small red onion, sliced thinly

5 ounces shaved deli ham

4 thick slices crusty white bread

½ small avocado, sliced thinly

1 tablespoon shredded fresh basil leaves

1 Cut tomatoes in half lengthwise; place cut-side up on oiled baking sheet, sprinkle with sugar. Bake tomato, uncovered, in very hot oven 15 minutes. Add onion; bake further 15 minutes or until tomato is soft.

2 Cook ham in heated small skillet until browned lightly and almost crisp.

3 Toast bread; top with ham, onion, tomato, avocado and basil.

SERVES 4
per serving 24.8g carbohydrate; 7.5g fat; 217 cal; 12.3g protein

red pepper and cheese soufflés

PREPARATION TIME 15 MINUTES   COOKING TIME 45 MINUTES

1 medium red bell pepper

4 tablespoons butter

1 medium leek, sliced thinly

2 tablespoons all-purpose flour

1 cup milk

½ cup heavy cream

1 tablespoon grainy mustard

⅓ cup grated parmesan cheese

4 eggs, separated

1 Lightly grease four 1-cup ovenproof dishes.

2 Quarter peppers; remove and discard seeds and membranes. Roast under broiler, skin-side up, until skin blisters and blackens. Cover pepper pieces with plastic wrap or paper for 5 minutes. Peel away skin; chop pepper finely.

3 Heat butter in large skillet; cook leek, stirring, until soft. Stir in flour, stir over heat until bubbling. Remove skillet from heat, gradually stir in milk, cream, mustard and red pepper. Return to heat and stir until mixture boils and thickens; cool 5 minutes.

4 Stir in cheese and egg yolks. Beat egg whites in small bowl until soft peaks form; gently fold egg whites into pepper mixture in two batches. Spoon mixture into prepared dishes. Place dishes on baking sheet; bake in moderately hot oven about 20 minutes or until soufflés are puffed and browned lightly.

SERVES 4
per serving 12.3g carbohydrate; 33.3g fat; 401 cal; 14.2g protein

haloumi and vegetable salad (see page 182)

(see page 182)

PREPARATION TIME 25 MINUTES   COOKING TIME 30 MINUTES

2 medium red bell peppers

2 medium yellow bell peppers

1 medium eggplant, sliced thickly

vegetable-oil spray

2 cloves garlic, crushed in
   garlic press

12 ounces haloumi or white frying
   cheese, sliced thinly

1 tablespoon fresh lemon juice

1 small red onion, sliced thinly

2 cups (3½ ounces) baby
   arugula leaves

¼ cup loosely packed fresh basil

½ cup drained caperberries, rinsed

1 lemon, cut into wedges

LEMON DRESSING

⅓ cup fresh lemon juice

2 teaspoon olive oil

1 teaspoon sugar

1 Quarter peppers; remove and discard seeds and membranes. Roast under broiler, skin-side up, until skin blisters and blackens. Cover pepper pieces in plastic wrap or paper for 5 minutes. Peel away skin; slice pepper thinly.

2 Place eggplant slices on oiled baking sheets; spray with oil, sprinkle with half the garlic. Roast under broiler, turning occasionally, 15 minutes or until softened. Cool 10 minutes. Slice into thick strips.

3 Meanwhile, make lemon dressing.

4 Place haloumi in small bowl with lemon juice and remaining garlic; toss gently to combine.

5 Cook undrained cheese in heated oiled large skillet, turning occasionally, about 5 minutes or until browned and soft in middle.

6 Meanwhile, combine pepper, eggplant, onion, arugula, basil, caperberries and dressing in large bowl; toss gently to combine.

7 Divide salad among serving plates, top with haloumi and lemon wedges.

LEMON DRESSING Combine ingredients in screw-top jar; shake well.

SERVES 4
per serving 14.5g carbohydrate; 26g fat; 389 cal; 23.9g protein

sesame tofu salad

PREPARATION TIME 25 MINUTES   COOKING TIME 10 MINUTES

24 ounces firm silken tofu

2 tablespoons toasted
  sesame seeds

2 teaspoons red pepper flakes

2 tablespoons cornstarch

vegetable oil, for deep-frying

5 scallions, sliced thinly

1 large avocado, chopped coarsely

4 ounces red-leaf lettuce
  leaves, torn

2 cups (3½ ounces) mizuna or
  baby arugula leaves

1 long red chile, seeded,
  sliced thinly

SESAME DRESSING

2 shallots, chopped finely

2 tablespoons toasted
  sesame seeds

1 tablespoon sesame oil

1 tablespoon kecap manis

½-inch piece fresh ginger, grated

¼ cup fresh lemon juice

1 Make sesame dressing.

2 Cut each tofu block lengthwise into four slices; dry gently
with paper towel. Combine sesame seeds, red pepper flakes
and cornstarch in large shallow bowl; press seed mixture onto
both sides of tofu slices.

3 Heat oil in wok or large nonstick skillet; deep-fry tofu, in batches,
until browned lightly. Drain on paper towel.

4 Place remaining ingredients in large bowl; toss gently to combine.
Divide salad among serving plates; top with tofu, drizzle
with dressing.

SESAME DRESSING Combine ingredients in screw-top jar;
shake well.

SERVES 4
per serving 12.5g carbohydrate; 44g fat; 546 cal; 25.7g protein
tip Kecap manis can be found in Asian markets and in the Asian food
section of some supermarkets.

beet soup

PREPARATION TIME 10 MINUTES (PLUS REFRIGERATION TIME)   COOKING TIME 35 MINUTES

1 teaspoon olive oil

1 small brown onion, chopped coarsely

1 clove garlic, crushed in garlic press

3 medium beets, trimmed, chopped coarsely

1 medium apple, cored, chopped coarsely

4 cups vegetable broth

½ cup water

¼ cup fresh lemon juice

¼ teaspoon Tabasco sauce

½ hothouse cucumber, seeded,
   chopped finely

½ small red onion, chopped finely

1 tablespoon sour cream

1   Heat oil in soup pot; cook onion and garlic, stirring, until onion softens. Add beet, apple, broth and the water; bring to a boil. Reduce heat; simmer, covered, about 20 minutes or until beet is tender, stirring occasionally.

2   Blend or process soup, in batches, until smooth. Stir in juice and Tabasco; refrigerate, covered, until cold.

3   Serve chilled soup topped with combined remaining ingredients.

SERVES 4
per serving   17.4g carbohydrate 3.4g fat; 124 cal; 5.8g protein

butternut squash, basil and chile stir-fry

PREPARATION TIME 10 MINUTES   COOKING TIME 15 MINUTES

⅓ cup peanut oil

1 large onion, sliced thinly

2 cloves garlic, sliced thinly

4 red serrano chiles, sliced thinly

2 pounds butternut squash, chopped coarsely

7 ounces sugarsnap peas

1 teaspoon light brown sugar

¼ cup vegetable broth

2 tablespoons soy sauce

¾ cup loosely packed fresh basil leaves

4 scallions, sliced thinly

½ cup roasted unsalted peanuts

1   Heat oil in wok; cook onion, in batches, until browned and crisp. Drain on paper towel.

2   Stir-fry garlic and chile in wok until fragrant. Add squash; stir-fry until browned all over and just tender. Add peas, sugar, broth and sauce; stir-fry until sauce thickens slightly.

3   Remove from heat; toss basil, scallion and nuts through stir-fry until well combined. Serve topped with fried onion.

SERVES 4
per serving   21.1g carbohydrate; 28.2g fat; 384 cal; 12.2g protein

brown mushroom and barley soup

PREPARATION TIME 10 MINUTES   COOKING TIME 55 MINUTES

10 ounces brown mushrooms, quartered

1 clove garlic, crushed in garlic press

2 teaspoons soy sauce

2 teaspoons water

1 small onion, chopped finely

4 cups chicken broth

4 cups water, extra

½ cup pearl barley

1 stalk celery, untrimmed, chopped coarsely

2 small carrots, chopped coarsely

½ teaspoon freshly ground black pepper

1 Cook mushrooms, garlic, soy sauce and the water in heated large nonstick skillet until mushrooms soften.

2 Cook onion in heated lightly oiled large soup pot, stirring, until softened. Add broth and the extra water; bring to a boil. Add barley, reduce heat; simmer, covered, 30 minutes.

3 Add mushroom mixture to pot with remaining ingredients; cook, uncovered, about 20 minutes or until barley and vegetables are tender.

SERVES 4
per serving 21.8g carbohydrate; 1.9g fat; 139 cal; 8.5g protein

eggplant, spinach and squash stacks

PREPARATION TIME 15 MINUTES   COOKING TIME 15 MINUTES

1 large eggplant

kosher salt

7 ounces butternut squash, sliced thinly

1 pound 10 ounces bottled pasta sauce

2 cups (3½ ounces) baby spinach leaves

4 green onions, sliced thinly lengthwise

1 cup coarsely shredded mozzarella cheese

¼ cup toasted pine nuts

1 Discard top and bottom of eggplant; cut eggplant lengthwise into ten ¼-inch slices. Discard rounded-skin-side slices; place remaining eight slices in colander, sprinkle all over with salt; let stand 10 minutes.

2 Rinse eggplant well under cold water; pat dry with paper towel. Cook eggplant and squash, in batches, on heated grill or grill pan until tender.

3 Meanwhile, place pasta sauce in medium saucepan; bring to a boil. Reduce heat; simmer, uncovered, 2 minutes.

4 Place four slices of the eggplant, in single layer, on baking sheet; top with half of the spinach, half of the squash, and half of the onion. Spoon 2 tablespoons of the sauce over each stack, then repeat layering process, using remaining spinach, squash, onion and another 2 tablespoons of the sauce for each stack. Top stacks with remaining eggplant slices; pour over remaining sauce, sprinkle stacks with cheese and nuts. Place under hot broiler until cheese browns lightly.

SERVES 4
per serving 17.4g carbohydrate; 13.2g fat; 242 cal; 13.3g protein
tip Weight the eggplant when draining to extract as much water as possible; otherwise, the liquid causes the eggplant to soften and lose its shape when cooked. This process is called degorging.

five-colored salad

PREPARATION TIME 20 MINUTES (PLUS STANDING TIME)   COOKING TIME 10 MINUTES

Daikon is a large white radish with a sweet, fresh taste. In Japan it is often served, grated raw, as an accompaniment. If you cannot find daikon, substitute jicama.

6 dried shiitake mushrooms

2½-inch long, 2-inch diameter
   piece daikon, peeled, sliced
   thinly lengthwise

1 medium carrot, sliced
   thinly lengthwise

4 ounces green beans, quartered
   lengthwise, cut into
   1½-inch lengths

10 dried apricots, sliced thinly

1 teaspoon finely shredded
   lemon peel

DRESSING

8 ounces firm tofu

2 tablespoons tahini

2 teaspoons sugar

2 teaspoons soy sauce

1 tablespoon rice vinegar

1 tablespoon mirin

1   Make dressing.

2   Meanwhile, place mushrooms in small heatproof bowl, cover with boiling water, let stand 20 minutes or until just tender; drain. Remove and discard stems, slice caps thinly.

3   Boil, steam or microwave daikon, carrot and beans, separately, until just tender; drain. Rinse under cold water to cool; drain.

4   Combine apricot and vegetables in medium bowl, toss gently to combine.

5   Just before serving, pour dressing over salad and mix through. Divide salad among individual serving bowls, shape into mounds, sprinkle with peel.

DRESSING Press tofu between two cutting boards with a weight on top, raise one end to drain; let stand 25 minutes. Blend or process tofu until smooth, place in small bowl; stir in tahini. Add remaining ingredients; stir until sugar dissolves.

SERVES 4
per serving 12.3g carbohydrate; 10.7g fat; 187 cal; 10.4g protein
tip The salad and dressing can be prepared ahead and refrigerated separately. Combine just before serving.

gazpacho

PREPARATION TIME 30 MINUTES (PLUS REFRIGERATION TIME)

A chilled soup originating in the southern province of Andalusia in Spain, gazpacho,
like other peasant soups, makes clever use of the garden's overripe vegetables.

4 cups tomato juice

10 medium plum tomatoes,
 chopped coarsely

2 medium red onions,
 chopped coarsely

1 red serrano chile, chopped finely

2 cloves garlic, quartered

1 small hothouse cucumber,
 chopped coarsely

2 tablespoons sherry vinegar

1 medium red bell pepper,
 chopped coarsely

1 small red onion,
 chopped finely

1 small hothouse cucumber,
 chopped finely

1 small red bell pepper,
 chopped finely

1 tablespoon finely chopped
 fresh dill

1   Blend or process juice, tomato, coarsely chopped onion, chile, garlic, coarsely chopped cucumber, vinegar and coarsely chopped pepper, in batches, until pureed. Cover; refrigerate 3 hours or overnight.

2   Just before serving, divide soup among serving bowls; stir equal amounts of finely chopped onion, finely chopped cucumber, finely chopped pepper, and dill into each bowl.

SERVES 6
per serving 17.3g carbohydrate; 0.3g fat; 95 cal; 4.6g protein
tip Red wine vinegar can be used instead of sherry vinegar.
serving suggestion To make this soup a complete meal, add ½ cup of both finely chopped raw celery and finely chopped green pepper to the soup, then top each serving with 1 tablespoon of finely diced hard-boiled egg.

braised leek and belgian endive salad with poached eggs

PREPARATION TIME 20 MINUTES   COOKING TIME 40 MINUTES

1 tablespoon olive oil

9 leeks, trimmed to 6 inches in length

6 heads belgian endive,
   halved lengthwise

⅔ cup dry white wine

1 cup vegetable broth

1 teaspoon sugar

8 eggs

CREAMY BASIL DRESSING

2 tablespoons fresh lemon juice

1 tablespoon grainy mustard

⅔ cup heavy cream

¼ cup loosely packed fresh basil
   leaves, chopped coarsely

1 Preheat oven to moderately hot. Make creamy basil dressing.

2 Heat oil in large casserole; cook leeks and endive, cut-side down, in single layer, for 1 minute. Add wine, broth and sugar; bring to a boil. Reduce heat; simmer, uncovered, 2 minutes. Cover tightly; transfer dish to oven for 20 minutes more.

3 With 10 minutes left of braising time, half-fill a large shallow saucepan with water; bring to a boil. One at a time, break eggs into cup and slide into pan. When all eggs are in pan, allow water to return to a boil. Cover pan, turn off heat; let stand about 4 minutes or until a light film of egg white sets over yolks. One at a time, remove eggs, using slotted spoon, and place on paper towel-lined saucer to blot poaching liquid.

4 Divide endive among serving plates; top with leeks and 2 eggs each, drizzle with dressing.

CREAMY BASIL DRESSING Combine ingredients in screw-top jar; shake well.

SERVES 4
per serving 12.3g carbohydrate; 31.2g fat; 439 cal; 21.3g protein

roast baby turnip soup

PREPARATION TIME 25 MINUTES   COOKING TIME 1 HOUR 10 MINUTES

4 bunches baby turnips (approximately
   6 pounds)

2 tablespoons olive oil

1 large onion, chopped coarsely

1 clove garlic, quartered

8 cups chicken broth

½ cup heavy cream

¼ cup loosely packed, finely chopped
   fresh flat-leaf parsley

1 Preheat oven to hot. Trim and discard turnip leaves; leave 1 inch of stem attached to 24 of the smallest turnips, remove and discard stems on remainder. Scrub turnips thoroughly; peel the 24 small turnips, retaining the 1-inch stem. Chop remaining unpeeled turnips coarsely.

2 Combine all turnips with half of the oil in large casserole; toss to coat thoroughly. Roast, uncovered, in hot oven about 45 minutes or until turnips are tender and browned all over.

3 Heat remaining oil in soup pot; cook onion and garlic, stirring, until onion softens. Add chopped turnip and broth; bring to a boil. Simmer, uncovered, 10 minutes.

4 Blend or process soup mixture, in batches, until pureed.

5 Return soup to same cleaned pot with whole turnips and cream; stir over heat until hot. Just before serving, stir in parsley.

SERVES 6
per serving 16.6g carbohydrate; 15.1g fat; 238 cal; 9.2g protein
tip Choose 24 of the smallest turnips you have, matching them as closely as possible in size. Spoon four of these tiny roasted turnips into each portion of soup when serving.

squid, chorizo and tomato salad

PREPARATION TIME 30 MINUTES   COOKING TIME 15 MINUTES

Chorizo is a sausage made traditionally of coarsely ground pork and seasoned with garlic and chiles.
If you cannot find fresh chorizo, substitute any spicy sausage.

2 pounds squid (calamari),
   bodies only, cleaned

2 fresh chorizo sausages (12 ounces),
   sliced thinly

1 tablespoon olive oil

4 medium tomatoes, seeded,
   sliced thickly

three 14-ounce cans white beans,
   rinsed, drained

2 cups loosely packed fresh flat-leaf
   parsley leaves

1 teaspoon finely grated lemon peel

¼ cup fresh lemon juice

1 Cut squid down center to open out; score the inside in diagonal pattern then cut into ¾-inch strips.

2 Cook chorizo in heated large skillet, stirring occasionally, until browned.

3 Cook squid, in batches, in same reheated skillet until tender.

4 Place chorizo and squid in large bowl with remaining ingredients; toss gently to combine.

SERVES 4
per serving 24.4g carbohydrate; 25.1g fat; 472 cal; 38.2g protein

radicchio with thai crab salad

PREPARATION TIME 20 MINUTES (PLUS REFRIGERATION TIME)   COOKING TIME 5 MINUTES

Dressing can be made a day ahead. Cover; refrigerate until required.
Crab salad can be assembled up to 4 hours ahead. Cover; refrigerate until required.

¼ cup water

¼ cup fresh lime juice

2 tablespoons sugar

2 red serrano chiles, seeded,
   chopped finely

1 pound fresh crab meat

1 small hothouse cucumber, seeded,
   chopped finely

1 small red bell pepper,
   chopped finely

2 scallions, sliced thinly

4 small heads of radicchio

1 Combine the water, juice, sugar and chiles in small saucepan; stir over heat, without boiling, until sugar dissolves. Bring to a boil; remove from heat, cool. Cover; refrigerate dressing until cold.

2 Combine crab, cucumber, pepper, scallion and dressing in medium bowl.

3 Trim ends and cores from radicchio; separate leaves. Serve radicchio topped with crab salad.

SERVES 4
per serving 19.1g carbohydrate; 1.5g fat; 175 cal; 21g protein
tip We used radicchio, but you can use red or white belgian endive, if you prefer.

grilled cuttlefish, arugula and parmesan salad

PREPARATION TIME 20 MINUTES   COOKING TIME 10 MINUTES

2 pounds cuttlefish or squid
  (calamari), bodies only, cleaned

2 tablespoons olive oil

1 tablespoon finely grated
  lemon peel

⅓ cup fresh lemon juice

1 clove garlic, crushed in
  garlic press

4 cups (6 ounces) arugula

5 ounces sun-dried tomatoes,
  drained, chopped coarsely

1 small red onion, sliced thinly

1 tablespoon drained
  baby capers, rinsed

3 ounces parmesan cheese, shaved

2 tablespoons balsamic vinegar

⅓ cup olive oil, extra

1   Halve cuttlefish lengthwise, score insides in crosshatch pattern, then cut into 2-inch strips. Combine cuttlefish in medium bowl with oil, peel, juice and garlic. Cover; refrigerate 10 minutes.

2   Meanwhile, combine arugula, tomato, onion, capers and cheese in large bowl.

3   Drain cuttlefish; discard marinade. Cook cuttlefish, in batches, on heated oiled grill or grill pan until browned and cooked through.

4   Add cuttlefish to salad with combined vinegar and extra oil; toss gently to combine.

SERVES 4
per serving 15.6g carbohydrate; 40.1g fat; 646 cal; 55g protein

deep-fried shrimp balls

PREPARATION TIME 25 MINUTES (PLUS REFRIGERATION TIME)   COOKING TIME 10 MINUTES

2 pounds extra-large

   cooked shrimp

5 scallions, chopped finely

2 cloves garlic, crushed in

   garlic press

4 red serrano chiles, seeded,

   chopped finely

1 teaspoon grated fresh ginger

1 tablespoon cornstarch

2 teaspoons fish sauce

¼ cup coarsely chopped

   fresh cilantro

¼ cup packaged breadcrumbs

½ cup homemade

   soft breadcrumbs

vegetable oil, for deep-frying

⅓ cup sweet chili sauce

1 Shell and devein shrimp; cut in half. Blend or process shrimp, pulsing, until chopped coarsely. Place in large bowl with scallion, garlic, chile, ginger, cornstarch, sauce and cilantro; mix well.

2 Using hands, roll rounded tablespoons of shrimp mixture into balls. Roll shrimp balls in combined breadcrumbs; place, in single layer, on plastic wrap-lined tray. Cover, refrigerate 30 minutes.

3 Heat oil in wok or large skillet; deep-fry shrimp balls, in batches, until lightly browned and cooked through. Serve with sweet chili sauce.

SERVES 4
per serving 17.2g carbohydrate; 11.83g fat; 302 cal; 32.4g protein

grilled squid and octopus salad

PREPARATION TIME 30 MINUTES (PLUS REFRIGERATION TIME)   COOKING TIME 10 MINUTES

1 pound squid (calamari), bodies
   only, cleaned

1 pound cleaned whole baby
   octopus, thawed if frozen

2 long green chiles, chopped finely

6 cloves garlic, crushed in
   garlic press

2 bunches asparagus, trimmed
   and halved

1 pound yellow
   pear tomatoes, halved

7 ounces cornichons,
   rinsed, drained

1 orange, peeled, sliced thickly

2 cups (3½ ounces) baby
   arugula leaves

ORANGE VINAIGRETTE

1 tablespoon olive oil

¼ cup fresh orange juice

½-inch piece fresh ginger,
   grated finely

1 teaspoon finely grated
   orange peel

2 tablespoons malt vinegar

1   Cut squid down the center to open out; score inside in diagonal pattern then cut into thick strips. Quarter octopus lengthwise.

2   Combine squid and octopus in a large bowl with chile and garlic; toss to coat seafood in marinade. Cover; refrigerate 3 hours or overnight.

3   Meanwhile, make orange vinaigrette.

4   Boil, steam or microwave asparagus until just tender; drain. Rinse under cold water; drain. Combine in large bowl with remaining ingredients.

5   Cook seafood, in batches, on heated lightly oiled grill or grill pan until browned lightly and cooked through.

6   Place seafood in bowl with salad, add vinaigrette; toss gently to combine.

ORANGE VINAIGRETTE Combine ingredients in screw-top jar; shake well.

SERVES 4
per serving 16.8g carbohydrate; 7g fat; 259 cal; 31.3g protein

grilled squid and octopus salad

haloumi and vegetable salad (see page 170)

crab and apple salad

PREPARATION TIME 20 MINUTES   COOKING TIME 5 MINUTES

8 ounces sugarsnap peas

1 large apple, cored

1 pound cooked crab meat

1 medium red onion, halved,
    sliced thinly

2 long red chiles, seeded,
    sliced thinly lengthwise

2 medium avocados,
    sliced thickly

2½ cups (5 ounces) mesclun

⅓ cup olive oil

¼ cup fresh lemon juice

1 tablespoon dijon mustard

1 clove garlic, crushed in garlic press

1   Boil, steam or microwave peas until just tender; drain. Rinse under cold
    water; drain.

2   Slice apple thinly; cut slices into thin strips. Combine peas and apple in
    large bowl with crab, onion, chile, avocado and mesclun.

3   Place remaining ingredients in screw-top jar; shake well. Drizzle dressing
    over salad; toss gently to combine.

SERVES 4
per serving   12.6g carbohydrate; 39.1g fat; 480 cal; 20.4g protein

grilled scallops with papaya salsa

PREPARATION TIME 15 MINUTES   COOKING TIME 10 MINUTES

1 medium firm papaya,
    chopped coarsely

2 medium tomatoes, seeded,
    chopped coarsely

1 medium red onion,
    chopped coarsely

¼ cup fresh lime juice

1 red serrano chile, seeded,
    chopped finely

2 tablespoons coarsely chopped
    fresh cilantro

1 tablespoon vegetable oil

36 sea scallops

1   Combine papaya, tomato, onion, juice, chile, cilantro and oil in
    large bowl.

2   Cook scallops on heated oiled grill pan, in batches, until browned
    both sides.

3   Serve papaya salsa topped with scallops.

SERVES 4
per serving   13.8g carbohydrate; 5.6g fat; 169 cal; 15.3g protein

beef and corn soup

PREPARATION TIME 10 MINUTES   COOKING TIME 10 MINUTES

6 cups water

14 ounces canned beef consomme

2 teaspoons grated fresh ginger

2 tablespoons soy sauce

1 teaspoon sesame oil

2 ounces bean thread (cellophane) noodles

1 pound beef sirloin, trimmed, sliced thinly

1 small red bell pepper, sliced thinly

7 ounces fresh baby corn

1 scallion, sliced thinly

1 bunch baby bok choy, chopped coarsely

2 cups (6 ounces) fresh bean sprouts

1 small long red chile, sliced thinly

1 Combine the water, consomme, ginger, sauce and oil in large soup pot; bring to a boil. Add noodles; using fork, separate noodles. Reduce heat; simmer, uncovered, until noodles are just tender.

2 Add remaining ingredients; stir until mixture is heated through and beef is cooked as desired.

SERVES 4
per serving 20.4g carbohydrate; 5.7g fat; 284 cal; 36.9g protein

beef salad with blue-cheese dressing

PREPARATION TIME 10 MINUTES   COOKING TIME 20 MINUTES

1 pound butternut squash, chopped coarsely

2 medium red bell peppers, chopped coarsely

1 tablespoon olive oil

4 minute steaks (1 pound)

10 ounces green beans, trimmed,
**   halved crosswise**

8 ounces pear tomatoes, halved

2½ cups (4 ounces) baby arugula leaves

BLUE-CHEESE DRESSING

¼ cup olive oil

2 cloves garlic, crushed in garlic press

¼ cup fresh orange juice

2 ounces blue cheese, crumbled

1 Preheat oven to very hot.

2 Place squash and pepper, in single layer, in large shallow casserole; drizzle with oil. Roast, uncovered, in very hot oven about 20 minutes or until lightly browned and tender.

3 Meanwhile, make blue-cheese dressing.

4 Cook steaks on heated oiled grill or grill pan until browned both sides and cooked as desired. Cover; let stand 5 minutes.

5 Meanwhile, boil, steam or microwave beans until just tender; drain.

6 Slice steaks thinly. Combine steak, beans, squash and pepper in large bowl with tomato and arugula, drizzle with blue-cheese dressing; toss gently to combine.

BLUE-CHEESE DRESSING Combine ingredients in screw-top jar; shake well.

SERVES 4
per serving 15.3g carbohydrate; 29.3g fat; 468 cal; 36g protein

reuben salad

PREPARATION TIME 15 MINUTES   COOKING TIME 10 MINUTES

2 tablespoons mayonnaise

1 tablespoon chili sauce

¼ teaspoon drained prepared
  white horseradish

¾ teaspoon heavy cream

2 scallions, chopped finely

14 ounces sauerkraut, drained

1 tablespoon finely chopped fresh chives

4 slices rye bread

8 slices corned beef (about ¾ pound)

6 ounces swiss cheese, sliced thinly

4 large dill pickles, sliced thinly

1 Combine mayonnaise, chili sauce, horseradish, cream and scallion in small bowl. Combine sauerkraut and chives in another bowl.

2 Divide bread, corned beef, cheese, mayonnaise mixture and pickle among serving plates; serve with sauerkraut mixture.

SERVES 4
per serving 22.6g carbohydrate; 18.9g fat; 409 cal; 36g protein

italian fennel and steak salad with balsamic vinaigrette

PREPARATION TIME 15 MINUTES   COOKING TIME 15 MINUTES

3 ounces bean thread (cellophane) noodles

4 filet mignon steaks (about 1¾ pounds)

2 medium bulbs fennel, sliced thinly

1 medium red onion, sliced thinly

3 cups (5 ounces) baby arugula leaves

1¼ cups shaved parmesan cheese

BALSAMIC VINAIGRETTE

¼ cup fresh lemon juice

2 cloves garlic, crushed in garlic press

¼ cup olive oil

2 tablespoons balsamic vinegar

1 tablespoon coarsely chopped fresh thyme

1 Place noodles in medium heatproof bowl; cover with boiling water, let stand until noodles are just tender, drain.

2 Make balsamic vinaigrette.

3 Cook beef on heated oiled grill or grill pan until browned both sides and cooked as desired. Cover; let stand 5 minutes.

4 Cut noodles into 2-inch lengths; place in large bowl with fennel, onion and arugula. Slice beef thinly, add to noodles with balsamic vinaigrette; toss gently to combine. Serve salad topped with cheese.

BALSAMIC VINAIGRETTE Combine ingredients in screw-top jar; shake well.

SERVES 4
per serving 19.2g carbohydrate; 32g fat; 590 cal; 55.1g protein

beef and bean tacos

PREPARATION TIME 15 MINUTES   COOKING TIME 20 MINUTES

1 clove garlic, crushed in
    garlic press

3 ounces lean ground beef

½ teaspoon chili powder

¼ teaspoon ground cumin

10 ounces canned kidney beans,
    rinsed, drained

2 tablespoons tomato paste

½ cup water

1 medium tomato,
    chopped coarsely

4 taco shells

¼ small head iceberg lettuce,
    shredded finely

SALSA CRUDA

½ hothouse cucumber, seeded,
    chopped finely

½ small red onion, chopped finely

1 small tomato, seeded,
    chopped finely

1 teaspoon medium salsa

1   Preheat oven to moderate.

2   Heat large lightly oiled nonstick skillet; cook garlic and beef, stirring, until beef is browned all over. Add chili powder, cumin, beans, tomato paste, water and tomato; cook, covered, over low heat about 15 minutes or until mixture thickens slightly.

3   Meanwhile, toast taco shells, upside-down and uncovered, on baking sheet in moderate oven for 5 minutes.

4   Make salsa cruda.

5   Just before serving, fill taco shells with beef mixture, lettuce and salsa cruda.

SALSA CRUDA Combine ingredients in small bowl.

SERVES 4
per serving 17.5g carbohydrate; 4.8g fat; 154 cal; 9.7g protein

beet and pastrami salad with horseradish mayonnaise

PREPARATION TIME 30 MINUTES   COOKING TIME 10 MINUTES

7 red radishes, trimmed

8 ounces red-leaf lettuce, trimmed and torn

10 ounces pastrami, torn into large pieces

12 cornichons, drained, halved lengthwise

2 tablespoons coarsely chopped fresh dill

1 tablespoon olive oil

1 tablespoon red wine vinegar

3 medium fresh beets, peeled, grated coarsely

HORSERADISH MAYONNAISE

1 egg

1 teaspoon drained prepared white horseradish

1 tablespoon heavy cream

1 tablespoon fresh lemon juice

½ cup olive oil

1   Make horseradish mayonnaise.

2   Slice radishes thinly; cut slices into thin strips. Place radishes in large bowl with lettuce, pastrami, cornichons and dill. Combine oil, vinegar and beets in medium bowl.

3   Divide pastrami salad among serving plates; top with beet salad, drizzle with horseradish mayonnaise.

HORSERADISH MAYONNAISE   Blend or process egg, horseradish, cream and juice until combined. With motor running, add oil in a thin, steady stream until mayonnaise thickens slightly.

SERVES 4
per serving   16.5g carbohydrate; 38.4g fat; 506 cal; 24.5g protein

harira

PREPARATION TIME 20 MINUTES (PLUS STANDING TIME)   COOKING TIME 2 HOURS 15 MINUTES

This hearty lamb and vegetable soup from Morocco is traditionally eaten during the four weeks of Ramadan, after sundown, to break the day's fast.

½ cup dried garbanzo beans (chickpeas)

1 pound boned shoulder of lamb

2 tablespoons olive oil

1 large onion, chopped coarsely

2 teaspoons ground ginger

1 tablespoon ground cumin

1 teaspoon ground cinnamon

2 teaspoons ground coriander

6 saffron threads

3 stalks celery, trimmed, chopped coarsely

7 medium tomatoes, seeded,
   chopped coarsely

10 cups water

½ cup brown lentils

¼ cup loosely packed, coarsely chopped
   fresh cilantro

1 Place garbanzos in small bowl, cover with water; let stand overnight, drain.

2 Trim lamb of excess fat; cut into ¾-inch cubes.

3 Heat oil in soup pot; cook onion, stirring, until soft. Add spices; cook, stirring, about 2 minutes or until fragrant. Add lamb and celery; cook, stirring, about 2 minutes or until lamb is coated in spice mixture. Add tomato; cook, stirring, about 10 minutes or until tomato slightly softens. Stir in the water and drained garbanzos; bring to a boil. Simmer, covered, about 1½ hours or until lamb is tender, stirring occasionally.

4 Stir in lentils; cook, covered, about 30 minutes or until lentils are just tender.

5 Just before serving, stir fresh cilantro into soup.

SERVES 6
per serving 16.4g carbohydrate; 12.2g fat; 276 cal; 25.1g protein
tip One 28-ounce can of tomatoes can be substituted for fresh tomatoes.
serving suggestion Serve with lemon wedges.

rosemary lamb open sandwich

PREPARATION TIME 5 MINUTES (PLUS REFRIGERATION TIME)   COOKING TIME 15 MINUTES

four 12-ounce boneless lamb leg steaks

2 cloves garlic, crushed in garlic press

¼ cup fresh lemon juice

2 tablespoons fresh rosemary leaves

1 tablespoon grainy mustard

2 small tomatoes

1 bunch asparagus, trimmed, halved

4 slices dark rye bread

4 ounces boston lettuce, chopped coarsely

1 In a small bowl, combine lamb, garlic, juice, rosemary and mustard, cover; refrigerate 3 hours or overnight.

2 Cut each tomato into six wedges. Cook tomato and asparagus, in batches, on heated oiled grill or grill pan until browned lightly and just tender. Toast bread both sides.

3 Drain lamb; discard marinade. Cook lamb on same heated grill until browned and cooked as desired. Cover; let stand 5 minutes before slicing thickly.

4 Place one slice of the toast on each serving plate; top each slice with equal amounts of lettuce, tomato, asparagus and lamb.

SERVES 4
per serving 20.7g carbohydrate; 8.9g fat; 263 cal; 24.3g protein

roasted butternut squash, bacon and feta frittata

PREPARATION TIME 20 MINUTES   COOKING TIME 1 HOUR 15 MINUTES

1¼-pound butternut squash, chopped coarsely

1 tablespoon olive oil

1 medium red bell pepper, chopped coarsely

6 scallions, cut into 2-inch pieces

7 slices bacon, chopped coarsely

1 clove garlic, crushed in garlic press

½ cup finely grated parmesan cheese

6 eggs

2 teaspoons cornstarch

½ cup heavy cream

4 ounces feta cheese, crumbled

1   Preheat oven to hot.

2   Combine squash and oil in large casserole; bake, uncovered, in hot oven 15 minutes. Add pepper, scallion, bacon and garlic; bake, uncovered, about 15 minutes or until squash and bacon are browned lightly.

3   Meanwhile, grease deep 8-inch square cake pan; sprinkle base and sides with half of the parmesan.

4   Reduce oven temperature to moderate. Spoon butternut squash mixture into prepared pan. Whisk eggs in medium bowl with remaining parmesan and blended cornstarch and cream. Pour egg mixture over butternut squash mixture; sprinkle with feta. Bake, uncovered, in moderate oven about 45 minutes or until frittata sets. Let stand 10 minutes; turn out. Cut into quarters; serve with a fresh green salad, if desired.

SERVES 4
per serving 12.8g carbohydrate; 38.8g fat; 516 cal; 309g protein
tip A frittata can be served hot or at room temperature.

pork and peach salad

PREPARATION TIME 20 MINUTES (PLUS STANDING TIME)   COOKING TIME 10 MINUTES

1 tablespoon peanut oil

¾ pound boneless pork loin

1 pound peaches, peeled, chopped coarsely

1 medium red bell pepper, sliced thinly

1 stalk fresh lemongrass, sliced thinly

1 large bunch (about 4 ounces)
   watercress, trimmed

2 tablespoons coarsely chopped fresh mint

2 tablespoons drained, thinly sliced pickled
   ginger, optional

2 tablespoons fried shallots, optional

LIME AND GARLIC DRESSING

1 clove garlic, chopped finely

2 red serrano chiles, seeded, sliced thinly

1 tablespoon rice vinegar

1 tablespoon fresh lime juice

1 tablespoon fish sauce

1 tablespoon light brown sugar

1   Make lime and garlic dressing.

2   Heat oil in wok; cook pork, turning, until browned all over and cooked as desired. Cover, let stand 10 minutes; slice thinly. Place pork in medium bowl with lime and garlic dressing; toss to coat pork all over. Let stand 10 minutes.

3   Meanwhile, combine peaches, pepper, lemongrass, watercress and mint in large bowl.

4   Add pork mixture to peach mixture; toss gently to combine. Serve sprinkled with pickled ginger and fried shallot, if desired.

LIME AND GARLIC DRESSING   Combine all ingredients in screw-top jar; shake well.

SERVES 4
per serving 12.4g carbohydrate; 6.8g fat; 191 cal; 19.3g protein

mixed cabbage slaw with chinese barbecued pork

PREPARATION TIME 30 MINUTES

Napa cabbage, also known as chinese cabbage, is elongated in shape with pale-green crinkly leaves. The most common cabbage in Southeast Asia, it is the basis of the pickled Korean national condiment, kim chi. It can be shredded or chopped and eaten raw or braised, steamed or stir-fried. You need about a quarter of a head of savoy cabbage, a quarter of a head of red cabbage and half a small head of napa cabbage for this recipe.

3 cups finely shredded

   savoy cabbage

3 cups finely shredded red cabbage

3 cups finely shredded

   napa cabbage

2 medium carrots, grated coarsely

1 small red bell pepper,

   sliced thinly

⅓ cup coarsely chopped

   fresh cilantro

1 long red chile, sliced thinly

1 pound chinese barbecued pork,

   sliced thinly

SWEET SOY DRESSING

1 tablespoon sesame oil

1 tablespoon fish sauce

2 tablespoons soy sauce

1 tablespoon light brown sugar

1 Make sweet soy dressing.

2 Place ingredients and dressing in large bowl; toss gently to combine.

SWEET SOY DRESSING Combine ingredients in screw-top jar; shake well.

SERVES 4
per serving 16g carbohydrate; 24.1g fat; 406 cal; 31.7g protein

smoked ham salad
with mustard vinaigrette

PREPARATION TIME 20 MINUTES   COOKING TIME 2 MINUTES

10 ounces snow peas

2 medium avocados,
    sliced thickly

1 cup drained sun-dried tomatoes
    in oil, chopped coarsely

4½ cups (7 ounces) baby
    spinach leaves

¾ pound smoked ham, torn into
    large pieces

MUSTARD VINAIGRETTE

2 cloves garlic, crushed in
    garlic press

2 tablespoons white wine vinegar

2 tablespoons finely chopped fresh
    flat-leaf parsley

½-inch piece fresh ginger, grated

1 tablespoon grainy mustard

1 tablespoon warm water

¼ cup extra light olive oil

1 Boil, steam or microwave snow peas until tender; drain. Rinse under cold water; drain.

2 Meanwhile, make mustard vinaigrette.

3 Place snow peas in large bowl with remaining ingredients; toss gently to combine. Divide salad among serving plates; drizzle with vinaigrette.

MUSTARD VINAIGRETTE Place ingredients in screw-top jar; shake well.

SERVES 4
per serving 21.5g carbohydrate; 40.8g fat; 558 cal; 25.8g protein

grilled pork loin chops with baby beet salad

PREPARATION TIME 20 MINUTES   COOKING TIME 10 MINUTES

four 1-inch-thick pork loin chops
   (about 6 ounces each)
1½ pounds canned baby beets, rinsed,
   drained, quartered
1 cup (3½ ounces) fresh bean sprouts
1 small red bell pepper, sliced thinly
1 stalk celery, trimmed, sliced thinly
1 small red onion, sliced thinly
½ cup loosely packed fresh mint leaves
1 tablespoon finely grated lime peel
¼ cup fresh lime juice
2 tablespoons olive oil

1 Cook pork on heated oiled grill or grill pan until browned on both sides and cooked as desired. Let stand 5 minutes.

2 Meanwhile, place beets, sprouts, pepper, celery, onion and mint in large serving bowl.

3 Combine remaining ingredients in screw-top jar; shake well.

4 Drizzle three-quarters of the dressing over salad; toss gently to combine. Top with pork; drizzle with remaining dressing.

SERVES 4
per serving 15.5g carbohydrate; 23.9g fat; 444 cal; 41.9g protein

grilled turkey kebabs with belgian endive and grapefruit salad

PREPARATION TIME 40 MINUTES   COOKING TIME 15 MINUTES

1¾ pounds turkey breast cutlets, diced into
   ¾-inch pieces
2 tablespoons olive oil
1 clove garlic, crushed in garlic press
3 small pink grapefruit
4 heads belgian endive
2 stalks celery, trimmed, sliced thinly
2 cups loosely packed fresh flat-leaf
   parsley leaves
1 medium red onion, sliced thinly
2 tablespoons dried cranberries
¼ cup toasted shelled pistachios,
   chopped coarsely

CITRUS DRESSING

¼ cup olive oil
1 tablespoon fresh lime juice
2 teaspoons sugar

1 Thread turkey onto skewers; brush with combined oil and garlic. Cover; refrigerate until required.

2 Peel and segment grapefruit over small bowl to save juice; reserve segments and juice separately.

3 Separate endive leaves; combine in large bowl with grapefruit segments, celery, parsley, onion and cranberries. Make citrus dressing.

4 Cook turkey skewers on heated oiled grill or grill pan until browned and cooked through.

5 Add dressing and nuts to salad; toss gently to combine. Serve salad with turkey skewers.

CITRUS DRESSING Strain reserved grapefruit juice into screw-top jar with oil, lime juice and sugar; shake well.

SERVES 4
per serving 16.9g carbohydrate; 34.3g fat; 577 cal; 49.7g protein
tip Soak 12 small bamboo skewers in water for at least an hour prior to use to prevent splintering or scorching.

yakitori (seasoned chicken on skewers)

PREPARATION TIME 20 MINUTES   COOKING TIME 15 MINUTES (PLUS COOLING TIME)

Chicken wings, chicken liver or vegetables of your choice can be used in this dish, but remember to cut even-sized pieces and use ingredients that take about the same time to cook. Soak eight bamboo skewers in water for at least an hour prior to use to prevent splintering or scorching.

1 pound skinless, boneless chicken thighs or
breasts, cut into 1-inch pieces

1 medium red bell pepper, chopped coarsely

4 fresh shiitake mushrooms,
stems removed, halved

6 thick scallions, trimmed,
cut into 1-inch lengths

¼ teaspoon freshly ground pepper

SAUCE

½ cup soy sauce

½ cup sake

¼ cup mirin

2 tablespoons sugar

1 Make sauce.

2 Thread chicken and vegetables onto eight bamboo skewers, leaving space between pieces to allow even cooking.

3 Cook, in batches, on heated oiled grill or grill pan, turning and brushing with sauce occasionally, until browned all over and cooked through.

4 Serve yakitori sprinkled with pepper.

SAUCE Combine ingredients in small saucepan; bring to a boil. Reduce heat; simmer, uncovered, over medium heat until sauce reduces by a third, cool.

SERVES 4
per serving 12.7g carbohydrate; 3.1g fat; 243 cal; 32.3g protein
tips Bottled yakitori sauce is readily available from Asian grocery stores. The sauce can be used as a marinade for the chicken before cooking, but cook chicken on medium heat so marinade does not burn before meat cooks through.

chicken, lemon and green bean salad

PREPARATION TIME 15 MINUTES   COOKING TIME 5 MINUTES

You need to purchase a 2-pound barbecued chicken for this recipe.

½ cup golden raisins

1 cup warm water

¼ cup fresh lemon juice

1 barbecued chicken (about 2 pounds)

6 ounces baby green beans

2 tablespoons finely chopped lemon peel

12 ounces jarred marinated
artichokes, drained

2 cups firmly packed fresh flat-leaf
parsley leaves

2 tablespoons olive oil

2 tablespoons white wine vinegar

1 Combine raisins, the warm water and lemon juice in medium bowl, cover; let stand 5 minutes. Drain; discard liquid.

2 Meanwhile, discard skin and bones from chicken; slice meat thickly.

3 Boil, steam or microwave beans until tender; drain. Rinse under cold water; drain.

4 Place raisins, chicken and beans in large bowl with lemon peel, artichokes, parsley, oil and vinegar; toss gently to combine.

SERVES 4
per serving 16.5g carbohydrate; 20g fat; 406 cal; 39.4g protein

chicken, belgian endive and cashew salad

PREPARATION TIME 20 MINUTES

Like mushrooms, belgian endive is grown in the dark to retain its pale color and bittersweet taste.
This versatile vegetable is as good eaten cooked as it is raw. You need to purchase a barbecued chicken
weighing approximately 2 pounds for this recipe.

1 medium head belgian endive

**2 small heads romaine lettuce or the inner
    leaves of 2 large heads romaine lettuce**

1 medium yellow bell pepper, sliced thinly

1 small red onion, sliced thinly

1 cup roasted unsalted cashews

4 cups shredded chicken

DRESSING

1 cup yogurt

2 cloves garlic, crushed in garlic press

2 teaspoons finely grated lemon peel

¼ cup fresh lemon juice

**¼ cup loosely packed, coarsely chopped
    fresh cilantro**

1 Make dressing.

2 Trim and discard ½ inch from endive base; separate leaves. Trim core from lettuce; separate leaves.

3 Place endive and lettuce in large bowl with pepper, onion, cashews, chicken and dressing; toss gently to combine.

DRESSING   Combine ingredients in screw-top jar; shake well.

SERVES 4
per serving 18.6g carbohydrate; 26g fat; 475 cal; 40.8g protein
tips Belgian endive is also delicious braised, grilled or baked. It is particularly compatible with asparagus, ham and dairy products such as cream and cheese. Roast cashews briefly in a dry small heavy-bottomed skillet, stirring, over medium heat to bring out their flavor.

grilled chili drumettes with coleslaw

PREPARATION TIME 25 MINUTES (PLUS REFRIGERATION TIME)   COOKING TIME 20 MINUTES

You need about a quarter of both a large head of red cabbage and a large head of savoy cabbage for this recipe.

16 chicken wing drumettes (1½ pounds)

½ cup mexican chili sauce

5 cups finely shredded red cabbage

5 cups finely shredded savoy cabbage

1 cup coarsely chopped fresh mint

CHILI DRESSING

1 tablespoon mexican chili sauce

½ cup peanut oil

¼ cup fresh lemon juice

1 Combine chicken and sauce in large bowl, cover; refrigerate 3 hours or overnight.

2 Make chili dressing.

3 Cook undrained chicken on heated oiled grill or grill pan until browned and cooked through.

4 Place cabbages and mint in large bowl with dressing; toss gently to combine. Serve coleslaw with chicken.

CHILI DRESSING Place ingredients in screw-top jar; shake well.

SERVES 4
per serving 14.3g carbohydrate; 48.3g fat; 655 cal; 41.5g protein

chicken and chorizo gumbo

PREPARATION TIME 30 MINUTES   COOKING TIME 2 HOURS 15 MINUTES

Traditionally made with andouille, a spicy smoked sausage of French descent, gumbo is just as delicious made with chorizo. If you cannot find fresh chorizo, substitute any spicy sausage.

one 3-pound chicken

1 medium onion, chopped coarsely

2 medium carrots, chopped coarsely

2 stalks celery, trimmed,
      chopped coarsely

1 bay lcaf

12 black peppercorns

12 cups water

3 tablespoons butter

2 cloves garlic, crushed in
      garlic press

1 small onion, chopped finely

1 medium green bell pepper,
      chopped finely

1 teaspoon sweet paprika

¼ teaspoon cayenne

¼ teaspoon ground cloves

2 tablespoons finely chopped
      fresh oregano

¼ cup tomato paste

2 tablespoons worcestershire sauce

14 ounces canned
      crushed tomatoes

7 ounces fresh small okra, or frozen
      whole okra, thawed

½ cup basmati rice

7 ounces chorizo sausage,
      sliced thinly

1 Rinse chicken under cold water, pat dry with paper towel.

2 Combine chicken, coarsely chopped onion, carrot, celery, bay leaf, peppercorns and water in soup pot; bring to a boil. Simmer, covered, 1½ hours, skimming occasionally; strain through cheesecloth-lined strainer into large bowl. Reserve broth and chicken; discard vegetables.

3 When chicken is cool enough to handle, remove and discard skin. Remove chicken meat from carcass; shred meat, discard bones.

4 Melt butter in another soup pot; cook garlic and finely chopped onion, stirring, until onion is soft. Add pepper, paprika, cayenne, cloves and oregano; cook, stirring, about 2 minutes or until fragrant.

5 Stir in reserved broth, tomato paste, Worcestershire and undrained crushed tomatoes; stir until mixture boils. Stir in halved okra and rice; simmer, uncovered, stirring occasionally, about 15 minutes or until both okra and rice are tender.

6 Meanwhile, heat large nonstick skillet; cook sausage, in batches, until browned, drain on paper towels.

7 Add reserved chicken and sausage; stir gumbo over heat until heated through.

SERVES 6
per serving 22.8g carbohydrate; 19.9g fat; 420 cal; 37.6g protein
tip If using fresh okra, choose bright green, small, firm okra pods; large okra are generally tough and stringy. And take great pains not to overcook okra or it will break down to an unpleasantly pulpy state.

honey-chile chicken salad

PREPARATION TIME 15 MINUTES   COOKING TIME 10 MINUTES

1 pound skinless, boneless chicken
     breasts, sliced thinly

¼ cup honey

4 red serrano chiles, seeded,
     sliced thinly

1 tablespoon grated fresh ginger

2 bunches asparagus, trimmed

2 tablespoons peanut oil

4 scallions, sliced thinly

1 medium green bell pepper,
     sliced thinly

1 medium yellow bell pepper,
     sliced thinly

1 medium carrot, sliced thinly

¼ medium napa cabbage,
     shredded finely

⅓ cup fresh lime juice

1   Combine chicken, honey, chile and ginger in medium bowl.

2   Cut aparagus spears in half; boil, steam or microwave until just tender; drain. Rinse under cold water; drain.

3   Meanwhile, heat half of the oil in large wok or skillet; stir-fry chicken, in batches, until browned all over and cooked through.

4   Place chicken and asparagus in large bowl with onion, peppers, carrot, cabbage, juice and remaining oil; toss gently to combine.

SERVES 4
per serving 24.1g carbohydrate; 12.3g fat; 338 cal; 32.6g protein
tip A small barbecued chicken can also be used; remove and discard bones and skin, then shred meat coarsely before tossing with remaining salad ingredients.

curried chicken and zucchini soup

PREPARATION TIME 10 MINUTES   COOKING TIME 25 MINUTES

1 tablespoon butter

1 small onion, chopped finely

1 clove garlic, crushed in garlic press

1 teaspoon curry powder

½ cup basmati rice

¾ pound skinless, boneless chicken
     breasts, sliced thinly

2 cups water

4 cups chicken broth

4 medium zucchini, grated coarsely

1   Melt butter in soup pot; cook onion and garlic, stirring, until onion softens. Add curry powder; cook, stirring, until mixture is fragrant.

2   Add rice and chicken; cook, stirring, 2 minutes. Add the water and broth; bring to a boil. Reduce heat; simmer, covered, 10 minutes. Add zucchini; cook, stirring, about 5 minutes or until chicken is cooked through.

SERVES 4
per serving 24.7g carbohydrate; 7.4g fat; 271 cal; 25.4g protein

chicken and almonds

PREPARATION TIME 15 MINUTES   COOKING TIME 15 MINUTES

1 cup blanched whole almonds

1 tablespoon peanut oil

1½ pounds skinless, boneless
   chicken breasts, sliced thinly

1 medium red onion,
   chopped coarsely

1 small leek, sliced thickly

2 cloves garlic, crushed in
   garlic press

2 tablespoons hoisin sauce

7 ounces green beans, halved

2 stalks celery, trimmed, sliced thinly

1 tablespoon soy sauce

1 tablespoon plum sauce

1 Heat wok or large skillet. Stir-fry almonds until lightly browned; remove from wok. Heat half of the oil in same wok; stir-fry chicken, in batches, until browned all over and cooked through.

2 Heat remaining oil in wok; stir-fry onion, leek and garlic until fragrant. Add hoisin sauce, beans and celery; stir-fry until beans are just tender. Return chicken to wok with remaining sauces; stir-fry until heated through. Toss almonds through chicken mixture.

SERVES 4
per serving 14.6g carbohydrate; 34g fat; 574 cal; 52.9g protein
tip You can use cashews instead of almonds, if preferred.

chicken and haloumi salad

PREPARATION TIME 10 MINUTES   COOKING TIME 15 MINUTES

Assemble this salad just before serving.

10 ounces prepared mixed vegetable
   salad in oil

1 pound skinless, boneless chicken
   breasts, chopped coarsely

¼ cup pine nuts

8 ounces haloumi or white
   frying cheese

5 cups (8 ounces) baby
   arugula leaves

6 ounces jarred marinated
   artichoke hearts, drained

8 ounces cherry tomatoes

¼ cup balsamic vinegar

1 Drain vegetable salad in strainer over small bowl; reserve ⅓ cup of the oil. Chop salad finely.

2 Heat 1 tablespoon of the reserved oil in wok or large skillet; stir-fry chicken, in batches, until browned all over and cooked through. Cover to keep warm. Stir-fry pine nuts in same wok until lightly browned.

3 Cut haloumi crosswise into 16 slices. Heat 1 tablespoon of the reserved oil in same wok; cook haloumi, in batches, until browned both sides.

4 Toss antipasto, chicken and haloumi in large bowl with arugula, artichokes and tomatoes. Drizzle with combined remaining oil and vinegar; sprinkle with pine nuts.

SERVES 4
per serving 12.2g carbohydrate; 34g fat; 572 cal; 42.6g protein
tips Haloumi is a firm salty cheese, available from most delicatessens and some supermarkets.
If there is not enough oil in the mixed vegetable salad to make ⅓ cup, add olive oil to make up the required amount.

vegetable curry with yogurt

PREPARATION TIME 25 MINUTES   COOKING TIME 15 MINUTES

2 teaspoons olive oil

1½-inch piece fresh ginger,
    grated coarsely

3 scallions, sliced thinly

2 cloves garlic, crushed in
    garlic press

1 long green chile, chopped finely

¼ teaspoon ground cardamom

1 teaspoon garam masala

1 tablespoon curry powder

1 teaspoon turmeric

2 medium granny smith apples,
    grated coarsely

1 tablespoon fresh lemon juice

2 cups vegetable broth

⅓ small head of cauliflower,
    separated into florets

4 yellow patty pan squash, halved

1 large zucchini, sliced thickly

3 cups (5 ounces) baby
    spinach leaves

7 ounces unflavored low-fat yogurt

1   Heat oil in large saucepan; cook ginger, scallion, garlic, chile,
    cardamom, garam masala, curry powder and turmeric about
    2 minutes or until fragrant.

2   Add apple, juice, broth and cauliflower; cook, uncovered,
    5 minutes, stirring occasionally.

3   Add squash and zucchini; cook until just tender. Remove from
    heat; stir spinach and yogurt into curry just before serving.

SERVES 4
per serving 14.5g carbohydrate; 3.6g fat; 128 cal; 8.5g protein

vegetable curry with yogurt

roasted vegetables with eggplant

roasted vegetables with eggplant

PREPARATION TIME 20 MINUTES   COOKING TIME 50 MINUTES

We used fresh okra in this recipe. If fresh is unavailable, substitute frozen okra.

1 large green bell pepper

2 large red bell peppers

2 large yellow bell peppers

2 medium eggplants

vegetable-oil spray

2 cloves garlic, unpeeled

¼ cup fresh lemon juice

2 teaspoons tahini

**1½ pounds portobello mushrooms,
    sliced thickly**

8 ounces cherry tomatoes

12 yellow patty pan squash, halved

14 ounces okra

**¾ cup loosely packed fresh
    basil leaves**

1 teaspoon sumac

1   Preheat oven to hot.

2   Quarter peppers; remove and discard seeds and membranes. Using fork prick eggplants all over; divide among two lightly oiled baking dishes with garlic and pepper, skin-side up. Roast vegetables, uncovered, in hot oven about 30 minutes or until skins blister. Cover pepper pieces with plastic wrap or paper for 5 minutes; peel away skin, slice thickly. Cover to keep warm.

3   When cool enough to handle, peel eggplants and garlic. Coarsely chop eggplants; combine with finely chopped garlic in medium bowl with juice and tahini; cover to keep warm.

4   Meanwhile, cook mushrooms in lightly oiled large skillet until browned lightly. Add tomatoes and squash, cook, covered, until tomatoes are just soft.

5   Spread okra onto flat baking sheet, spray with oil, roast, uncovered, in hot oven about 20 minutes or until just tender.

6   Combine peppers, mushroom, tomato, squash, okra and basil in large bowl; divide among serving plates, top with eggplant mixture. Sprinkle with sumac and serve immediately.

SERVES 4
per serving 21.8g carbohydrate; 3.1g fat; 181 cal; 15.8g protein

italian-style stuffed mushrooms

PREPARATION TIME 15 MINUTES   COOKING TIME 15 MINUTES

Marsala is a sweet fortified wine originally from Sicily; it can be found in liquor stores.

8 medium portabello mushrooms

6 tablespoons butter

½ medium red bell pepper,
   chopped finely

1 clove garlic, crushed in garlic press

¼ cup marsala

1 tablespoon fresh lemon juice

1¼ cups homemade breadcrumbs

2 tablespoons coarsely chopped
   fresh flat-leaf parsley

1 cup coarsely grated
   pecorino cheese

1 Preheat oven to moderately hot.

2 Carefully remove stems from mushrooms; chop stems finely.

3 Melt butter in small skillet. Brush mushroom caps with about half of the butter; place on oiled baking sheet.

4 Cook pepper and garlic, stirring, in remaining butter until pepper is just tender. Add chopped mushroom stems, marsala, juice and breadcrumbs; cook, stirring, 3 minutes. Remove from heat; stir in parsley and cheese. Spoon filling into mushroom caps; bake, uncovered, in moderately hot oven about 10 minutes or until browned lightly.

SERVES 4
per serving 21.5g carbohydrate; 27.8g fat; 416 cal; 16.7g protein
tip Vegetable broth can be substituted for marsala, if desired.

cauliflower and broccoli curry

PREPARATION TIME 20 MINUTES   COOKING TIME 15 MINUTES

Any asian greens can be used in this recipe. Try it with bok choy, choy sum, or gai larn
(also known as chinese broccoli). You need one bunch of asian greens for this recipe.

1 tablespoon peanut oil

2 tablespoons red curry paste

1 large red bell pepper, sliced thinly

2 teaspoons honey

3⅓ cups unsweetened
   coconut cream

1 cup water

1 pound broccoli, chopped coarsely

½ small head cauliflower,
   chopped coarsely

14 ounces canned whole baby
   corn spears, drained

1 pound asian greens,
   chopped coarsely

1 Heat oil in large saucepan; cook paste, stirring, until fragrant. Add pepper; cook, stirring, until almost tender.

2 Stir in honey, coconut cream and the water; bring to a boil. Add broccoli and cauliflower, reduce heat; simmer, uncovered, 2 minutes. Add corn and asian greens; cook, stirring, until greens just wilt.

SERVES 4
per serving 20.8g carbohydrate; 52.3g fat; 613 cal; 16.9g protein
tip Different brands of commercially prepared curry pastes vary in strength and flavor, so you may want to adjust the amount of paste to suit your taste.

tofu and sugarsnap pea stir-fry

PREPARATION TIME 25 MINUTES (PLUS STANDING TIME)   COOKING TIME 15 MINUTES

Mirin is a sweetened rice wine used in Japanese cooking; it is sometimes referred to in cookbooks simply as rice wine. You can substitute sweet white wine, or even sweet sherry, if mirin is unavailable.

1¼ pounds firm tofu

1 tablespoon sesame oil

1 large red onion, sliced thickly

2 cloves garlic, crushed in garlic press

2 teaspoons grated fresh ginger

1 teaspoon cornstarch

⅓ cup soy sauce

14 ounces sugarsnap peas

1 tablespoon light brown sugar

⅓ cup oyster sauce

2 tablespoons mirin

¼ cup coarsely chopped fresh cilantro

1   Preheat oven to moderately hot.

2   Press tofu between two cutting boards with a weight on top, raise one end to drain excess liquid, let stand 25 minutes. Cut tofu into ¾-inch cubes; pat tofu dry between layers of paper towel. Place tofu on parchment paper-lined baking sheet. Bake, uncovered, in moderately hot oven about 10 minutes or until browned lightly.

3   Heat oil in wok or large skillet; stir-fry onion, garlic and ginger until onion softens. Add blended cornstarch and soy sauce to wok with tofu, peas, sugar, oyster sauce and mirin; stir-fry until sauce boils and thickens slightly. Remove from heat; stir in chopped cilantro.

SERVES 4
per serving 24.7g carbohydrate; 15.6g fat; 353 cal; 26.7g protein

eggplant stuffed with squash and feta

PREPARATION TIME 20 MINUTES (PLUS STANDING TIME)   COOKING TIME 1 HOUR 25 MINUTES

You will need to cook ⅓ cup rice for this recipe.

4 medium eggplants, halved

kosher salt

¼ cup olive oil

7-ounce piece butternut squash,
    finely chopped

1 small onion, finely chopped

2 cloves garlic, crushed in
    garlic press

1 teaspoon ground cumin

2 tablespoons light brown sugar

1 cup cooked long-grain rice

2 tablespoons chopped fresh
    cilantro leaves

⅓ cup hazelnuts, toasted, chopped

4 ounces feta cheese, crumbled

1   Preheat oven to moderate. Sprinkle cut surface of eggplants with salt, place on wire rack over baking sheet, cut-side down; let stand 30 minutes. Rinse eggplants, pat dry with paper towel. Brush cut surface of eggplants with half the oil, place on wire rack over baking sheet. Bake, uncovered, in moderate oven about 40 minutes or until eggplants are tender; cool 10 minutes.

2   Scoop flesh from eggplants, leaving ⅛-inch shells. Chop eggplant flesh.

3   Heat remaining oil in deep skillet, add squash, onion, garlic and cumin; cook, stirring, until squash is just tender. Stir in eggplant flesh, sugar, rice, cilantro and nuts.

4   Divide squash mixture between eggplant shells, place on baking sheet; top with cheese. Bake, uncovered, in moderate oven about 30 minutes or until cheese is lightly browned.

SERVES 4
per serving 22.7g carbohydrate; 28.3g fat; 386 cal; 11.1g protein

triple mushroom omelet

PREPARATION TIME 15 MINUTES (PLUS STANDING TIME)   COOKING TIME 35 MINUTES

12 dried shiitake mushrooms

3 dried cloud ear mushrooms

2 teaspoons peanut oil

6 scallions, sliced thinly

2 teaspoons grated fresh ginger

2 cloves garlic, crushed in
garlic press

½ medium red bell pepper,
chopped finely

4 ounces button mushrooms,
sliced thinly

¾ cup (2½ ounces) fresh
bean sprouts

¼ cup pine nuts, toasted

3 ounces snow peas, sliced thinly

1 tablespoon reduced-sodium
soy sauce

1 tablespoon oyster sauce

1 tablespoon water

10 eggs, beaten lightly

⅓ cup water, extra

SPICY SAUCE

2 red serrano chiles, sliced thinly

¼ cup chinese barbecue sauce

⅓ cup water

1   Place dried mushrooms in large heatproof bowl; cover with boiling water. Let stand 20 minutes; drain. Discard stems; slice caps thinly.

2   Heat oil in wok or large skillet; stir-fry scallion, ginger, garlic, pepper and mushrooms until pepper is just soft. Add sprouts, pine nuts, snow peas and combined sauces and water, stirring until peas are just tender; keep warm.

3   Meanwhile, whisk eggs with the extra water in large bowl. Lightly oil a 10-inch heavy-bottomed skillet; heat skillet. Add ⅓ cup of the egg mixture to skillet; swirl skillet to form a thin omelet over base. Cook until set; remove. Repeat with remaining egg mixture; cover omelets with foil to keep warm. You will need eight omelets.

4   Make spicy sauce.

5   Place ¼ cup of the mushroom mixture on each omelet. Fold omelet over filling; fold over again. Serve omelets topped with spicy sauce.

SPICY SAUCE   Combine ingredients in small saucepan; stir over heat until mixture boils. Reduce heat; simmer, uncovered, about 3 minutes or until thickened slightly.

SERVES 4
per serving   16g carbohydrate; 22.9g fat; 354 cal; 22.2g protein

vegetable and cottage cheese terrine

PREPARATION TIME 40 MINUTES (PLUS REFRIGERATION TIME)   COOKING TIME 5 MINUTES

Buy zucchini and squash just large enough to make 5-inch-long strips once trimmed and sliced.

2½ cups low-fat cottage cheese

1 small yellow squash,
grated coarsely

4 scallions, chopped finely

1 tablespoon finely shredded
fresh basil

1 tablespoon finely chopped
fresh thyme

1 clove garlic, crushed in
garlic press

1 teaspoon fresh lemon juice

1 large green zucchini

1 large yellow squash

½ cup (½ ounce) of baby spinach
leaves, shredded coarsely

5 ounces snow peas

2 teaspoons olive oil

PEPPER AND TOMATO SALSA

2 medium tomatoes, chopped finely

1 small yellow bell pepper,
chopped finely

1 small red bell pepper,
chopped finely

1 tablespoon finely shredded
fresh basil

1 clove garlic, crushed in
garlic press

2 teaspoons sugar

2 teaspoons olive oil

2 teaspoons fresh lemon juice

1 Place cheese in cheesecloth-lined strainer or colander set over large bowl. Cover cheese; weight with an upright saucer topped with a heavy can. Drain overnight in refrigerator; discard liquid.

2 Line base and two long sides of 8- x 4-inch loaf pan with parchment paper or plastic wrap, extending paper 2 to 3 inches above sides of pan.

3 Combine drained cheese in medium bowl with grated squash, scallion, herbs, garlic and juice.

4 Discard ends of large zucchini and squash; using vegetable peeler, slice into thin strips (discard skin-only outer strips).

5 Overlap alternate-colored zucchini and squash strips in prepared pan, starting from center of base and extending over both long sides. Cover both short sides of pan with alternate-colored zucchini and squash strips, ensuring slices overlap to cover corners and extend over both short sides.

6 Spread half of the cheese mixture into zucchini and squash-lined pan; cover with spinach, carefully spread remaining cheese mixture over spinach. Fold zucchini and squash strips at short sides over filling then repeat with strips over long sides to completely enclose filling (mixture may be slightly higher than pan). Fold over paper, then cover terrine tightly with foil; refrigerate 1 hour.

7 Meanwhile, make pepper and tomato salsa.

8 Boil, steam or microwave snow peas; drain.

9 Uncover terrine and turn onto serving plate; remove paper. Drizzle with oil. Using fine serrated knife, cut terrine into thick slices; serve with salsa and snow peas.

PEPPER AND TOMATO SALSA Combine ingredients in small bowl.

SERVES 4
per serving 12.1g carbohydrate; 4.4g fat; 198 cal; 27g protein
tip Do not add any salt to the cottage-cheese mixture as this will cause the filling to become too wet.

thyme and tofu stir-fry

PREPARATION TIME 25 MINUTES   COOKING TIME 15 MINUTES

⅓ small head cauliflower,
    chopped coarsely

½ small head broccoli, chopped coarsely

1 bunch asparagus, sliced thickly

12 ounces green beans, sliced thickly

3 medium carrots, sliced thickly

¼ cup olive oil

2 cloves garlic, crushed in garlic press

1 tablespoon finely chopped fresh thyme

1 teaspoon cracked black pepper

13 ounces firm tofu, drained, cubed

2 medium onions, sliced thickly

8 ounces button mushrooms, sliced thickly

½ cup dry white wine

3 teaspoons cornstarch

1 cup vegetable broth

1   Cook cauliflower, broccoli, asparagus, beans and carrot in large saucepan of boiling water, uncovered, 2 minutes; drain. Rinse in cold water; drain.

2   Heat oil in wok or large skillet. Stir-fry garlic, thyme, pepper and tofu until tofu is browned lightly; remove from wok.

3   Add onion and mushroom to wok; stir-fry until onion is soft.

4   Add cauliflower mixture to wok with wine and blended cornstarch and broth; stir-fry until sauce boils and thickens.

5   Add tofu mixture; stir gently until heated through.

SERVES 4
per serving 15.3g carbohydrate; 21.1g fat; 362 cal; 22.6g protein

turnip ratatouille

PREPARATION TIME 20 MINUTES   COOKING TIME 35 MINUTES

2 medium eggplants

¼ cup olive oil

2 cloves garlic, crushed in garlic press

2 pounds turnips, chopped coarsely

2 small red bell peppers, chopped coarsely

2 medium green zucchini, chopped coarsely

2 large yellow squash, chopped coarsely

28 ounces canned crushed
    tomatoes, undrained

2 tablespoons tomato paste

1 tablespoon capers, rinsed,
    drained, chopped

2 tablespoons dry red wine

¼ cup firmly packed basil leaves, shredded

1   Cut eggplants into ½-inch slices; quarter slices.

2   Heat oil in large heavy-bottomed saucepan; cook eggplant and garlic, stirring, about 5 minutes or until just tender and browned lightly. Add turnip, pepper, zucchini, squash, tomato, paste, capers and wine; simmer, covered, about 30 minutes or until vegetables are tender. Stir in half the basil; sprinkle remaining half over top of ratatouille just before serving.

SERVES 4
per serving 19.1g carbohydrate; 14.7g fat; 249 cal; 8.2g protein

triple cheese-crusted red snapper with roasted turnips

PREPARATION TIME 20 MINUTES   COOKING TIME 45 MINUTES

We used red snapper in this recipe, but you can use any firm fish, such as grouper or halibut.

2 pounds turnips, chopped coarsely

8 cloves garlic, unpeeled

1 tablespoon light brown sugar

2 tablespoons olive oil

1 teaspoon cumin seeds

1 tablespoon dijon mustard

1 cup homemade breadcrumbs

⅓ cup coarsely grated mozzarella cheese

⅓ cup coarsely grated cheddar cheese

⅓ cup coarsely grated parmesan cheese

2 tablespoons finely chopped fresh
    flat-leaf parsley

2 cloves garlic, crushed in garlic press

2 teaspoons lemon-pepper seasoning

four 7-ounce red snapper fillets

vegetable-oil spray

1   Toss turnips and garlic cloves with combined sugar, oil and seeds in large bowl. Place in casserole; bake, uncovered, stirring occasionally, in moderately hot oven for about 30 minutes or until browned lightly. Remove from oven, cover to keep warm. Increase oven temperature to hot.

2   Combine mustard, breadcrumbs, cheeses, parsley, garlic and seasoning in large bowl.

3   Place fish, skin-side down, on oiled baking sheet; press cheese mixture onto fish, spray with oil. Bake fish, uncovered, in hot oven about 15 minutes or until cheese browns and fish is cooked as desired.

4   Serve fish with turnips and garlic.

SERVES 4
per serving 22.4g carbohydrate; 21.3g fat; 497 cal; 53.5g protein

coco-lime fish with papaya and raspberry salsa

PREPARATION TIME 10 MINUTES (PLUS REFRIGERATION TIME)   COOKING TIME 20 MINUTES

We used red snapper in this recipe, but you can use any firm fish, such as halibut or grouper.

2 tablespoons light brown sugar

14 ounces unsweetened coconut cream

2 tablespoons finely grated lime peel

2 red serrano chiles, chopped finely

4 thick 7-ounce red snapper fillets

PAPAYA AND RASPBERRY SALSA

2 tablespoons raspberry vinegar

8 ounces fresh raspberries

1¼ pounds papaya, chopped roughly

1 tablespoon chopped fresh mint leaves

1   Combine sugar, coconut cream, peel and chile in small saucepan. Simmer, stirring occasionally, for 10 minutes; cool. Pour coconut mixture over fish in large bowl. Cover fish; refrigerate 3 hours or overnight.

2   Make papaya and raspberry salsa.

3   Drain fish over small pan; reserve marinade. Cook fish, uncovered, on heated oiled grill or grill pan until browned both sides and just cooked through.

4   Meanwhile, place reserved marinade on grill or stove, bring to boil; simmer, uncovered, until thickened slightly. Drizzle marinade over fish and serve with the papaya and raspberry salsa.

PAPAYA AND RASPBERRY SALSA Combine all ingredients in medium bowl; cover, refrigerate 30 minutes.

SERVES 4
per serving 21.1g carbohydrate; 24.3g fat; 478 cal; 43.8g protein

swordfish with olive paste and carrot and dill fritters

PREPARATION TIME 20 MINUTES   COOKING TIME 25 MINUTES

7 ounces black olives, pitted

¼ cup drained capers

⅓ cup finely chopped fresh dill

⅓ cup finely chopped fresh flat-leaf parsley

2 cloves garlic, crushed in garlic press

2 tablespoons fresh lemon juice

4 medium carrots, grated

2 eggs, beaten lightly

1 tablespoon chopped fresh dill, extra

¼ cup all-purpose flour

four 7-ounce swordfish steaks

1   Blend or process olives, capers, dill, parsley, garlic and juice until almost a smooth paste.

2   Combine carrot, eggs, extra dill, and flour in large bowl. Cook ¼ cup measures of carrot mixture, in batches, on heated oiled grill pan, until fritters are browned both sides.

3   Meanwhile, cook swordfish steaks on heated oiled grill or grill pan, uncovered, until browned both sides and just cooked through; spread tops with olive paste. Serve with carrot and dill fritters.

SERVES 4
per serving 24.3g carbohydrate 7.9g fat; 357 cal; 46.5g protein

sweet and spicy mussels with stir-fried asian greens

PREPARATION TIME 20 MINUTES   COOKING TIME 15 MINUTES

You will need about one bunch each of baby bok choy and chinese broccoli.

2 pounds large black mussels

1 tablespoon peanut oil

1 clove garlic, crushed in garlic press

3-inch piece fresh ginger, chopped finely

⅓ cup maple syrup

2 tablespoons soy sauce

1 tablespoon oyster sauce

¼ cup fish broth

1 tablespoon fresh lemon juice

4 scallions, sliced thinly

12 ounces baby bok choy, chopped coarsely

14 ounces chinese broccoli, chopped coarsely

2 cups (6 ounces) fresh bean sprouts

1   Scrub mussels; remove beards.

2   Heat oil in wok or large skillet; stir-fry garlic and ginger until fragrant. Add syrup, sauces, broth and juice; bring to a boil. Add mussels; return to a boil. Reduce heat; simmer, covered, about 5 minutes or until mussels open (discard any that do not). Remove mussels; cover to keep warm.

3   Return broth mixture to a boil. Add remaining ingredients to wok; stir-fry until greens are just wilted. Return mussels to wok; stir-fry until heated through.

SERVES 4
per serving 21.1g carbohydrate; 6g fat; 184 cal; 11.6g protein
tip Use a stiff brush to scrub the mussels under cold water.

moroccan cod fillets
with orange-and-maple baby carrots

PREPARATION TIME 20 MINUTES (PLUS REFRIGERATION TIME)   COOKING TIME 20 MINUTES

1 clove garlic, crushed in garlic press

½-inch piece fresh ginger,
    grated finely

1 teaspoon ground cumin

½ teaspoon ground turmeric

½ teaspoon hot paprika

½ teaspoon ground coriander

four 7-ounce cod fillets, skinned

1¾ pounds baby carrots, halved

1 tablespoon butter

1 teaspoon finely grated orange peel

1 tablespoon orange juice

1 tablespoon maple syrup

1 tablespoon olive oil

1   Combine garlic, ginger and spices in large bowl. Add fish; toss to coat fish in spice mixture. Cover; refrigerate for 15 minutes.

2   Meanwhile, boil, steam or microwave carrots until just tender; drain.

3   Heat butter in large skillet, cook peel, juice and syrup, stirring; bring to a boil. Reduce heat; simmer, uncovered, until mixture thickens slightly. Add carrots; stir gently to coat carrots in mixture.

4   Heat oil in large skillet; cook fish, in batches, until browned both sides and cooked as desired.

SERVES 4
per serving 14.7g carbohydrate; 12.2g fat; 337 cal; 42.1g protein

baby octopus and eggplant in tomato and caper sauce

PREPARATION TIME 10 MINUTES   COOKING TIME 25 MINUTES

1 tablespoon olive oil

2 pounds 7 ounces whole cleaned
    baby octopus, thawed if frozen

1 clove garlic, sliced thinly

3 shallots, sliced thinly

4 baby eggplants, sliced thinly

1 medium red bell pepper,
    sliced thinly

½ cup dry red wine

2¾ cups bottled pasta sauce

⅓ cup water

¼ cup drained baby capers, rinsed

2 tablespoons coarsely chopped
    fresh oregano

whole fresh oregano leaves

1   Heat half of the oil in large deep skillet; cook octopus, in batches, until just changed in color and tender. Remove octopus from skillet; cover to keep warm.

2   Heat remaining oil in same skillet; cook garlic and shallot, stirring, until shallot softens. Add eggplant and pepper; cook, stirring, about 5 minutes or until vegetables are just tender.

3   Add wine, sauce, the water and octopus; bring to a boil. Reduce heat; simmer, covered, about 10 minutes or until sauce thickens slightly. Stir in capers and chopped oregano. Top with oregano leaves.

SERVES 4
per serving 18.4g carbohydrate; 10.5g fat; 517 cal; 80.7g protein

salt and pepper salmon with radish and snow pea salad

PREPARATION TIME 25 MINUTES   COOKING TIME 10 MINUTES

2 teaspoons coarse sea salt

1 teaspoon freshly ground black pepper

four 8-ounce salmon steaks

1 tablespoon peanut oil

7 ounces radish

2 cups (6 ounces) fresh bean sprouts

7 ounces snow peas, sliced thinly

1 long red chile, seeded, sliced thinly

½ cup loosely packed fresh basil leaves

½ cup loosely packed fresh mint leaves

2 small pink grapefruit

CHILI-LIME VINAIGRETTE

2 tablespoons sweet chili sauce

2 tablespoons fresh lime juice

1 tablespoon rice vinegar

1 tablespoon finely chopped
   fresh lemongrass

1 clove garlic, crushed in garlic press

2 teaspoons light brown sugar

1 Make chili-lime vinaigrette.

2 Combine salt and pepper in large bowl, add fish; toss gently to coat in mixture. Heat oil in large skillet; cook fish, in batches, until browned both sides and cooked as desired.

3 Meanwhile, slice radish thinly lengthwise; cut slices into thin sticks. Combine radish in large bowl with sprouts, snow peas, chile and herbs.

4 Segment grapefruit over salad to save juice; discard membranes from segments. Add segments and half of the vinaigrette to salad; toss gently to combine. Divide salad among serving plates; top with fish, drizzle with remaining vinaigrette.

CHILI-LIME VINAIGRETTE Place ingredients in screw-top jar; shake well.

SERVES 4
per serving 13.2g carbohydrate; 24.2g fat; 497 cal; 56g protein

sweet and sour grilled cod (see back cover)

PREPARATION TIME 20 MINUTES   COOKING TIME 25 MINUTES

½ small pineapple, chopped coarsely

1 large red bell pepper, chopped coarsely

1 medium green bell pepper, chopped coarsely

1 medium red onion, sliced thickly

four 7-ounce skinless cod fillets

2 tablespoons sugar

½ cup white vinegar

2 tablespoons soy sauce

1 long red chile, seeded, sliced thinly

1½-inch piece fresh ginger, grated

3 scallions, sliced thinly

1 Cook pineapple, peppers and red onion on heated oiled grill or grill pan until browned all over and tender. Remove; cover to keep warm.

2 Cook fish on heated oiled grill pan until browned both sides and cooked as desired.

3 Combine sugar, vinegar, soy, chile and ginger in large bowl with pineapple, peppers and red onion; toss gently to combine sweet-and-sour mixture. Divide among serving plates, top with fish then scallion.

SERVES 4
per serving 16.2g carbohydrate; 1.7g fat; 243 cal; 38.9g protein

chili-plum crabs

PREPARATION TIME 20 MINUTES (PLUS REFRIGERATION TIME)   COOKING TIME 15 MINUTES

4 uncooked blue crabs

⅓ cup plum sauce

⅓ cup sweet chili sauce

2 tablespoons oyster sauce

2 tablespoons peanut oil

1 tablespoon soy sauce

1 clove garlic, crushed

1 tablespoon grated fresh ginger

½ teaspoon sesame oil

HERB SALAD

½ cup firmly packed fresh flat-leaf
    parsley leaves

½ cup firmly packed fresh basil leaves

¼ cup firmly packed fresh mint leaves

1 cup (3½ ounces) fresh bean sprouts

2 tablespoons fresh lime juice

2 teaspoons sesame oil

1 Remove triangular flap from underside of each crab. Remove top shell and grey fibrous tissue; wash and dry crabs. Crack claws slightly; cut crabs in half.

2 Combine remaining ingredients in large bowl; add crab. Cover; refrigerate 3 hours or overnight.

3 Cook crab on heated oiled grill, uncovered, until cooked through.

4 Make herb salad. Serve crab with salad.

HERB SALAD Place all ingredients in medium bowl; toss to combine.

SERVES 4
per serving 23.9g carbohydrate; 13.5g fat; 265 cal; 12.3g protein

stir-fried octopus with basil

PREPARATION TIME 20 MINUTES   COOKING TIME 10 MINUTES

2 pounds whole cleaned baby octopus,
    thawed if frozen

2 teaspoons peanut oil

2 teaspoons sesame oil

2 cloves garlic, crushed in garlic press

2 red serrano chiles, sliced thinly

2 large red bell peppers, sliced thinly

6 scallions, cut into 1-inch lengths

¼ cup firmly packed fresh basil leaves

14 cups (14 ounces) trimmed watercress,
    chopped coarsely

¼ cup fish sauce

2 tablespoons light brown sugar

1 tablespoon kecap manis

¾ cup loosely packed fresh cilantro leaves

1 Remove and discard head and beak of each octopus; cut each octopus in half. Rinse under cold water; drain.

2 Heat peanut oil in wok or deep skillet; stir-fry octopus, in batches, until browned all over and tender. Remove octopus from wok; cover to keep warm.

3 Heat sesame oil in same wok; stir-fry garlic, chile and pepper until pepper is just tender. Return octopus to wok with scallion, basil, watercress, sauce, sugar and kecap manis; stir-fry until greens wilt and sugar dissolves. Stir in cilantro off the heat.

SERVES 4
per serving 14.5g carbohydrate; 7.7g fat; 294 cal; 41.3g protein

cioppino (see page 1)

PREPARATION TIME 30 MINUTES   COOKING TIME 40 MINUTES

2 teaspoons olive oil

1 medium onion, chopped coarsely

1 bulb baby fennel, chopped coarsely

3 cloves garlic, crushed in garlic press

6 medium tomatoes, chopped coarsely

14 ounces canned crushed tomatoes

½ cup dry white wine

1½ cups fish broth

2 cooked blue crabs (about 1½ pounds)

1 pound uncooked large shrimp

1 pound swordfish steaks

14 ounces clams, rinsed

5 ounces scallops

¼ cup coarsely chopped fresh basil

½ cup coarsely chopped fresh flat-leaf parsley

1   Heat oil in large heavy-bottomed saucepan; cook onion, fennel and garlic, stirring, until onion is soft. Add fresh tomato; cook, stirring, 5 minutes or until pulpy. Stir in crushed tomato, wine and broth; simmer, covered, 20 minutes.

2   Meanwhile, remove back shells from crabs; discard grey gills and rinse. Chop each crab into quarters with cleaver. Shell and devein shrimp, leaving tails intact. Cut swordfish into 1-inch cubes.

3   Add clams to saucepan; simmer, covered, 5 minutes. Discard any clams that do not open. Add remaining seafood; cook, stirring occasionally, about 5 minutes, or until seafood has changed in color and is cooked through. Stir in herbs off the heat.

SERVES 4
per serving   13.1g carbohydrate; 6.4g fat; 352 cal; 54.2g protein

vineleaf-wrapped salmon with braised fennel

PREPARATION TIME 20 MINUTES   COOKING TIME 50 MINUTES

We used fresh grapevine leaves in this recipe. If fresh ones are not available, substitute vineleaves packed in brine, rinsed.

2 medium bulbs fennel

1 large onion, sliced thinly

2 cloves garlic, sliced thinly

1 tablespoon olive oil

¼ cup fresh orange juice

½ cup chicken broth

¼ cup dry white wine

8 large fresh grapevine leaves

four 7-ounce skinless salmon fillets

1 tablespoon finely grated orange peel

1 cup seedless white grapes

1   Preheat oven to moderate.

2   Trim fennel; reserve enough frond tips to make ¼ cup. Slice fennel thinly; place in large shallow casserole with onion, garlic, oil, juice, broth and wine. Cook, covered, in moderate oven 30 minutes. Uncover. Stir; cook about 20 minutes, stirring occasionally, or until vegetables soften and cooking liquid has almost evaporated.

3   Dip vineleaves in boiling water for 10 seconds. Transfer immediately to bowl of iced water to cool. Drain on paper towels.

4   Meanwhile, slightly overlap two vineleaves, vein-side up, on cutting board; center one fish fillet on leaves, top with quarter of the peel and a quarter of the reserved frond tips. Fold leaves over to enclose fish. Repeat with remaining leaves, fish, peel and frond tips. Place vine leaf parcels on lightly oiled baking sheet; cook in moderate oven about 15 minutes or until fish is cooked as desired.

5   Stir grapes into hot fennel mixture; let stand, covered, for 2 minutes before serving with fish. Scatter with extra fennel fronds, if desired.

SERVES 4
per serving   13.6g carbohydrate; 12.5g fat; 342 cal; 41g protein

grilled kingfish with tamarind stir-fried vegetables

PREPARATION TIME 20 MINUTES   COOKING TIME 10 MINUTES

You will need about half a bunch each of baby bok choy and chinese broccoli for this recipe.

2-inch piece fresh ginger, sliced thinly

2 teaspoons peanut oil

2 cloves garlic, crushed in garlic press

2 long red chiles, chopped finely

1 medium red bell pepper, sliced thinly

¼ cup chicken broth

2 tablespoons oyster sauce

1 tablespoon fish sauce

2 tablespoons light brown sugar

1 tablespoon tamarind nectar

8 ounces baby bok choy, chopped coarsely

8 ounces chinese broccoli, trimmed,
    chopped coarsely

8 scallions, cut into 1-inch lengths

½ cup firmly packed fresh cilantro leaves

four 7-ounce kingfish steaks

1 Stack slices of ginger and slice again into matchsticks.

2 Heat oil in wok or deep skillet; stir-fry ginger, garlic and chile until fragrant. Add pepper; stir-fry until pepper is tender.

3 Add broth, sauces, sugar and tamarind, bring to a boil; boil 1 minute. Add bok choy, chinese broccoli and scallion; stir-fry until greens are just wilted. Remove from heat; toss cilantro leaves through stir-fry.

4 Meanwhile, cook fish on heated oiled grill or grill pan about 8 minutes or until browned both sides and cooked as desired.

5 Serve fish with vegetables.

SERVES 4
per serving 17.2g carbohydrate; 16g fat; 421 cal; 52.1g protein

singapore chili crab

PREPARATION TIME 45 MINUTES (PLUS STANDING TIME)   COOKING TIME 35 MINUTES

2 uncooked dungeness crabs (3 pounds)

2 tablespoons peanut oil

1 long red chile, chopped finely

2 cloves garlic, crushed in garlic press

1-inch piece fresh ginger, grated

⅓ cup sweet sherry

14 ounces canned crushed tomatoes

1 cup water

1 tablespoon light brown sugar

3 hothouse cucumbers, halved lengthwise,
    sliced thinly

3½-inch piece fresh ginger, sliced thinly

3 scallions, sliced thinly

¼ cup loosely packed fresh cilantro leaves

2 long red chiles, seeded, sliced thinly

1 Place crabs in large container filled with ice and water; let stand about 1 hour. Clean crabs, leaving flesh in claws and legs. Using cleaver or heavy knife, chop each body into sixths.

2 Heat oil in wok or large saucepan; stir-fry chopped chile, garlic and grated ginger until fragrant. Add sherry; cook until liquid has reduced by half. Add undrained tomatoes, the water and sugar; bring to a boil. Reserve half of the sauce in small bowl.

3 Add half of the crab to wok, reduce heat; simmer, covered, about 15 minutes or until crab has changed in color. Stir in half of the cucumber. Transfer to large serving bowl; cover to keep warm. Repeat with reserved sauce, remaining crab and cucumber.

4 Cut sliced ginger into thin strips. Combine with scallion, cilantro and sliced chile; sprinkle over crab.

SERVES 4
per serving 12.3g carbohydrate; 10.5g fat; 255 cal; 23.6g protein
tip Provide finger bowls filled with warm water and lemon slices – and plenty of large napkins – with this dish.

salt-baked whole salmon in saffron cream sauce with lemon-roasted onions and carrots

PREPARATION TIME 30 MINUTES   COOKING TIME 1 HOUR

Kosher salt is coarser than table salt but not as large-grained as sea salt.

2 large onions

2 medium lemons

7 small carrots, halved

4 cloves garlic, unpeeled

6 sprigs fresh rosemary

2 tablespoons olive oil

4 pounds kosher salt

3 egg whites

3-pound whole salmon

12 cups (12 ounces)

trimmed watercress

SAFFRON CREAM SAUCE

⅓ cup dry white wine

2 tablespoons white wine vinegar

1 tablespoon fresh lemon juice

pinch saffron threads

⅓ cup heavy cream

6 tablespoons butter, chilled,

chopped finely

1   Preheat oven to moderately hot.

2   Cut onions and lemons into eight wedges. Combine onion, lemon, carrot, garlic and rosemary in casserole. Drizzle with oil; stir gently. Bake, uncovered, in moderately hot oven about 1 hour, or until tender.

3   Meanwhile, mix salt with egg whites in medium bowl (mixture will have the consistency of wet sand). Spread about half of the salt mixture evenly over the base of a large casserole; place fish on salt mixture then cover completely (except for tail) with remaining salt mixture. Bake fish in moderately hot oven 50 minutes.

4   Make saffron cream sauce.

5   Remove fish, vegetables and lemons from oven; break salt crust on fish with heavy knife, taking care not to cut into fish. Discard salt crust; transfer fish to large serving plate. Carefully remove skin from fish; flake meat into large pieces.

6   Divide watercress and garlic among serving plates; top with fish, drizzle sauce over fish. Serve with vegetables and lemons.

SAFFRON CREAM SAUCE Combine wine, vinegar, juice and saffron in medium saucepan; bring to a boil. Boil until mixture is reduced to about a third. Add cream; return to boil, then whisk in butter, one piece at a time, until mixture thickens slightly. Pour into medium measuring cup; cover to keep warm.

SERVES 4
per serving 12.2g carbohydrate; 43.2g fat; 646 cal; 47.1g protein

cold seafood platter with dipping sauces

PREPARATION TIME 1 HOUR

2 cooked medium lobsters (4 pounds)

2 cooked blue crabs (1¼ pounds)

16 cooked extra large shrimp (2¼ pounds)

12 oysters, on the half shell

3 lemons, cut into wedges

1   Prepare lobsters. Pat dry with paper towel.

2   Prepare crabs. Rinse well under cold water; cut crab bodies into halves.

3   Shell and devein shrimp, leaving tails intact.

4   Arrange seafood on large serving platter with lemon. Serve with dipping sauces.

SERVES 4
per serving (with dipping sauces) 24.7g carbohydrate; 25.3g fat; 682 cal; 86.3g protein

dipping sauces

chili mayonnaise

PREPARATION TIME 5 MINUTES

½ cup mayonnaise

1 tablespoon water

2 tablespoons ketchup

1 teaspoon worcestershire sauce

1 teaspoon chili sauce (such as sambal oelek or sriracha)

Combine ingredients in small bowl.

MAKES ¾ CUP

soy and mirin

PREPARATION TIME 5 MINUTES

2 tablespoons water

1 tablespoon soy sauce

2 tablespoons mirin

2 teaspoons rice vinegar

½ teaspoon chili sauce (such as sambal oelek or sriracha)

Combine ingredients in small bowl.

MAKES ½ CUP

mustard and dill

PREPARATION TIME 5 MINUTES

½ cup mayonnaise

1 tablespoon water

1 tablespoon drained baby capers, rinsed

1 teaspoon grainy mustard

1 tablespoon coarsely chopped fresh dill

Combine ingredients in small bowl.

MAKES ⅔ CUP

chili and lime

PREPARATION TIME 5 MINUTES

¼ cup sweet chili sauce

2 tablespoons fresh lime juice

1 tablespoon water

1 teaspoon fish sauce

2 teaspoons finely chopped fresh mint

Combine ingredients in small bowl.

MAKES ½ CUP

grilled shrimp and tropical fruits

PREPARATION TIME 15 MINUTES   COOKING TIME 15 MINUTES

24 large uncooked shrimp
   (3½ pounds)
¼ medium pineapple,
   chopped coarsely
1 slightly firm large mango,
   chopped coarsely
1 slightly firm large banana,
   chopped coarsely
¼ cup loosely packed fresh
   mint leaves
2 tablespoons fresh lime juice

MINT AND PARSLEY SAUCE
½ cup loosely packed fresh
   mint leaves
½ cup loosely packed fresh
   flat-leaf parsley
1 clove garlic, crushed in
   garlic press
2 tablespoons fresh lime juice
1 tablespoon olive oil

1   Make mint and parsley sauce.

2   Cook shrimp on heated oiled grill or grill pan until changed in color and cooked through.

3   Meanwhile, grill pineapple, mango and banana on grill pan until browned lightly.

4   Combine fruit with mint and juice in large bowl. Divide fruit among serving plates. Serve with shrimp and sauce.

MINT AND PARSLEY SAUCE Blend or process ingredients until combined.

SERVES 4
per serving 25g carbohydrate; 6.2g fat; 335 cal; 43.7g protein

grilled shrimp and tropical fruits

poached halibut with nam jim and herb salad

poached halibut
with nam jim and herb salad

PREPARATION TIME 30 MINUTES   COOKING TIME 10 MINUTES

eight 4-ounce halibut fillets

4 cups water

1 tablespoon fish sauce

1 tablespoon fresh lime juice

NAM JIM

2 cloves garlic

3 long green chiles, seeded, chopped coarsely

¼ cup coarsely chopped cilantro leaves and stem

2 tablespoons fish sauce

2 tablespoons light brown sugar

3 shallots, chopped coarsely

⅓ cup fresh lime juice

1 tablespoon peanut oil

HERB SALAD

1½ cups loosely packed fresh mint leaves

1 cup loosely packed fresh cilantro leaves

1 cup loosely packed fresh basil leaves, torn

1 medium red onion, sliced thinly

2 hothouse cucumbers, seeded, sliced thinly

1 Make nam jim.

2 Cut each fillet into half. Combine the water, sauce and juice in large skillet; bring to a boil. Reduce heat, add fish; simmer, uncovered, about 5 minutes or until cooked through. Remove fish from skillet with slotted spoon; cover to keep warm.

3 Meanwhile, make herb salad.

4 Serve fish on salad; top with remaining nam jim.

NAM JIM Blend or process ingredients until mixture is smooth.

HERB SALAD Combine ingredients in medium bowl with a third of the nam jim.

SERVES 4
per serving 12.2g carbohydrate; 7.6g fat; 348 cal; 56.7g protein

seafood casserole

PREPARATION TIME 30 MINUTES   COOKING TIME 45 MINUTES

1 tablespoon olive oil

1 medium leek, sliced thinly

4 cloves garlic, crushed in garlic press

14 ounces canned crushed
tomatoes, undrained

¾ cup dry white wine

¼ cup sweet sherry

2 cups fish broth

pinch saffron threads

2 medium carrots, chopped finely

⅓ cup finely chopped fresh flat-leaf parsley

1 tablespoon finely chopped fresh thyme

2 pounds small mussels

2 pounds uncooked large shrimp

1 pound squid (calamari), bodies only

1 pound uncooked lobster tails

12 ounces scallops

1 Heat oil in large saucepan; cook leek and garlic, stirring, until leek is soft.

2 Add tomato, wine, sherry, broth, saffron, carrot and herbs; simmer, covered, 30 minutes.

3 Meanwhile, scrub mussels; remove beards. Shell and devein shrimp, leaving tails intact. Cut squid open, score inside surface; cut into 2½-inch pieces. Shell lobster tails; cut lobster meat into 2-inch pieces.

4 Add mussels to pan; simmer, covered, 2 minutes. Add shrimp, squid and lobster pieces; simmer, covered, about 2 minutes. Add the scallops; simmer, uncovered, about 2 minutes or until seafood is just cooked. Discard any unopened mussels.

SERVES 4
per serving 12.2g carbohydrate; 9.9g fat; 540 cal; 88.5g protein

grilled lobster-tail salad

PREPARATION TIME 15 MINUTES   COOKING TIME 20 MINUTES

4 uncooked small lobster tails in shell
(about 1¾ pounds)

2 heads radicchio, trimmed, leaves separated

1 medium avocado, chopped coarsely

4 radishes, trimmed, sliced thinly

⅓ cup toasted pine nuts

4 scallions, sliced thinly

5 ounces drained sun-dried tomatoes,
chopped coarsely

ROSEMARY VINAIGRETTE

⅓ cup vegetable oil

¼ cup red wine vinegar

1 tablespoon coarsely chopped
fresh rosemary

1 tablespoon dijon mustard

1 Make rosemary vinaigrette.

2 Using kitchen scissors, discard soft shell from underneath lobster tails to expose meat; cook, in batches, on heated oiled grill or grill pan until browned and cooked through, brushing with a third of the vinaigrette. Cut lobster tails in half lengthwise.

3 Meanwhile, place remaining ingredients in large bowl with remaining vinaigrette; toss gently to combine. Serve lobster on salad.

ROSEMARY VINAIGRETTE Place ingredients in screw-top jar; shake well.

SERVES 4
per serving 15.8g carbohydrate; 41.7g fat; 613 cal; 43.5g protein

salmon in sesame crust

PREPARATION TIME 10 MINUTES   COOKING TIME 10 MINUTES

You need one and a half bunches of baby bok choy for this recipe.

2 tablespoons sesame seeds

1 teaspoon coriander seeds

1 teaspoon black peppercorns

four 8-ounce skinless salmon fillets

1 tablespoon vegetable oil

1 tablespoon sesame oil

1 clove garlic, crushed in garlic press

1 teaspoon grated fresh ginger

1 red serrano chile, seeded,
**   sliced thinly lengthwise**

1½ pounds baby bok choy,
**   quartered lengthwise**

¼ cup reduced-sodium soy sauce

2 tablespoons mirin

2 tablespoons honey

2 tablespoons fresh lime juice

1 Place seeds and peppercorns in strong plastic bag; crush with rolling pin or meat mallet. Coat one side of each fish fillet with seed mixture.

2 Heat vegetable oil in large skillet; cook fish, seeded-side down, uncovered, for 1 minute. Turn; cook, uncovered, until fish is cooked as desired.

3 Meanwhile, heat sesame oil in wok or large skillet; stir-fry garlic, ginger and chile until fragrant. Add remaining ingredients; stir-fry until bok choy just wilts.

4 Serve fish with bok choy.

SERVES 4
per serving 15.5g carbohydrate; 28.4g fat; 507 cal; 47.4g protein

salt cod with chile and tomatoes

PREPARATION TIME 15 MINUTES (PLUS REFRIGERATION TIME)   COOKING TIME 15 MINUTES

1 pound skinless, boneless salt cod

1 large red onion

1 tablespoon olive oil

2 cloves garlic, sliced

1 red serrano chile, sliced

4 medium tomatoes, peeled, chopped

½ cup pitted black olives

¼ cup tomato paste

¼ cup dry white wine

1 tablespoon fresh lemon juice

1 tablespoon drained capers, rinsed, chopped

3 teaspoons sugar

¼ cup chopped fresh flat-leaf parsley

1 Place cod in large bowl, cover with cold water. Cover bowl with plastic wrap, refrigerate 24 hours, changing water several times. Drain cod, add to large pot of boiling water, simmer, uncovered, 1 minute. Drain, rinse under cold water; drain well. Flake cod using fork.

2 Cut onion into wedges. Heat oil in large skillet, cook onion, garlic and chile, stirring, until onion is almost soft. Add tomatoes, olives, paste, wine, juice, capers and sugar. Simmer, covered, 5 minutes, then simmer, uncovered, 5 minutes or until slightly thickened. Stir in cod and parsley.

SERVES 4
per serving 14.8g carbohydrate; 5.8g fat; 216 cal; 23.2g protein

hot and sour steamed fish with thai salad (see back cover)

PREPARATION TIME 35 MINUTES (PLUS REFRIGERATION TIME)   COOKING TIME 10 MINUTES

We used red snapper in this recipe, but you can use any firm fish, such as grouper or halibut.

four 7-ounce fish fillets

**3 red serrano chiles, seeded,
    sliced thinly**

**1 stalk fresh lemongrass,
    chopped finely**

**½ cup loosely packed fresh
    cilantro leaves**

**½ cup loosely packed fresh
    mint leaves**

**½ cup loosely packed fresh
    basil leaves**

5 ounces snow peas, sliced thinly

**2 long red chiles, seeded,
    sliced thinly**

2 scallions, sliced thinly

⅓ cup (1 ounce) alfalfa sprouts

1 large mango, sliced thinly

LIME AND SWEET CHILI DRESSING

2 teaspoons sweet chili sauce

⅓ cup fish sauce

⅓ cup fresh lime juice

2 teaspoons peanut oil

**1 clove garlic, crushed in
    garlic press**

½-inch piece fresh ginger, grated

1 teaspoon light brown sugar

1   Make lime and sweet chili dressing.

2   Combine fish, serrano chile and lemongrass in large bowl with half of the dressing, cover; refrigerate 30 minutes.

3   Place fish mixture, in single layer, in parchment paper-lined steamer; steam, covered, over wok or large skillet of simmering water about 10 minutes or until fish is just cooked through.

4   Meanwhile, place remaining ingredients in large bowl with remaining dressing; toss salad gently to combine. Divide fish among serving plates; accompany with salad.

LIME AND SWEET CHILI DRESSING   Combine ingredients in screw-top jar; shake until sugar dissolves.

SERVES 4
per serving   19.8g carbohydrate; 8.7g fat; 347 cal; 46.5g protein

seafood skewers
with radicchio and fennel salad

PREPARATION TIME 25 MINUTES (PLUS REFRIGERATION TIME)   COOKING TIME 10 MINUTES

Soak eight bamboo skewers in water for at least an hour prior to use to prevent splintering or scorching. We used mahi mahi in this recipe, but you can use any firm fish, such as red snapper or halibut.

8 uncooked extra-large shrimp

8 whole cleaned baby octopus, thawed if frozen

14 ounces skinless firm white fish fillets

8 sea scallops

2 teaspoons fennel seeds

2 teaspoons dried green peppercorns

2 tablespoons white wine vinegar

2 cloves garlic, crushed in garlic press

1 tablespoon olive oil

2 medium heads radicchio

2 small bulbs fennel, trimmed, sliced thinly

1 cup firmly packed fresh flat-leaf parsley leaves

5 ounces sugarsnap peas

MUSTARD DRESSING

⅓ cup white wine vinegar

1 teaspoon dijon mustard

2 tablespoons olive oil

1 tablespoon honey

4 scallions, chopped coarsely

1   Shell and devein shrimp, leaving tails intact. Remove and discard heads and beaks from octopus. Cut fish into 1-inch cubes. Combine seafood in large bowl.

2   Using mortar and pestle, crush seeds and peppercorns coarsely, add to seafood with vinegar, garlic and oil; toss gently to combine. Cover; refrigerate 3 hours or overnight.

3   Make mustard dressing

4   Thread seafood, alternating varieties, on skewers; cook on heated, lightly oiled grill or grill pan until seafood is just changed in color and cooked as desired.

5   Meanwhile, discard dark outer leaves of radicchio, tear inner leaves roughly. Combine radicchio in medium bowl with fennel, parsley and dressing; toss gently to combine. Serve seafood skewers on salad.

MUSTARD DRESSING   Place ingredients in screw-top jar; shake well.

SERVES 4
per serving   12.5g carbohydrate; 20.1g fat; 584 cal; 86.9g protein
tips   Use green peppercorns in brine if you can't find the dried variety; rinse then drain them thoroughly before using.
If using metal skewers, oil them first to prevent seafood from sticking.

beef and haloumi kebabs with caper butter

PREPARATION TIME 10 MINUTES (PLUS REFRIGERATION TIME)   COOKING TIME 15 MINUTES

Soak eight bamboo skewers in water for at least an hour prior to use to prevent splintering or scorching.

2 pounds round steak,
**   cut into 2-inch cubes**

2 tablespoons olive oil

1 tablespoon grated lemon peel

2 tablespoons fresh lemon juice

1 tablespoon grated fresh horseradish

14 ounces haloumi or white frying
**   cheese, cut into 2-inch cubes**

8 medium corn tortillas

CAPER BUTTER

2 tablespoons drained capers,
**   chopped finely**

6 tablespoons (¾ stick) butter, melted

1 Place beef in large casserole with combined oil, peel, juice and horseradish. Cover beef; refrigerate 3 hours or overnight.

2 Make caper butter.

3 Thread beef and cheese on 8 skewers; cook on heated oiled grill or grill pan until browned all over and cooked as desired.

4 Meanwhile, wrap tortillas in foil in parcels of 4 and heat on grill. Remove tortillas from foil, wrap each skewer in a tortilla. To serve, remove skewers, leaving beef and cheese enclosed; accompany with caper butter.

CAPER BUTTER Combine capers and butter in small bowl.

SERVES 4
per serving 19.2g carbohydrate; 64.4g fat; 972 cal; 79.9g protein
tip If using metal skewers, oil them first to prevent beef and cheese from sticking.

balsamic and ginger beef with red cabbage slaw

PREPARATION TIME 15 MINUTES (PLUS REFRIGERATION TIME)   COOKING TIME 15 MINUTES

This slaw, of German origin, can be served either warm or cold.

½ cup olive oil

¼ cup balsamic vinegar

1 tablespoon grated fresh ginger

1 teaspoon light brown sugar

1 teaspoon soy sauce

four 1-pound T-bone steaks

1 medium green apple

½ medium red cabbage, shredded finely

2 tablespoons caraway seeds, toasted

2 teaspoons dijon mustard

⅓ cup olive oil

2 tablespoons raspberry vinegar

1 Combine oil, balsamic vinegar, ginger, sugar and sauce in screw-top jar; shake well. Reserve ¼ cup of the vinegar mixture; brush steaks all over using about half of the remaining mixture. Cover steaks; refrigerate 3 hours or overnight.

2 Cook steaks on heated oiled grill or grill pan until browned both sides and cooked as desired, brushing steaks occasionally with remaining vinegar mixture. Remove steaks from heat, cover; let stand for about 10 minutes.

3 Meanwhile, core unpeeled apple; cut into matchstick-sized pieces. Combine apple in large bowl with cabbage and seeds; drizzle with combined mustard, extra oil, and raspberry vinegar, toss to combine.

4 Just before serving, pour reserved vinegar mixture over beef. Serve with slaw.

SERVES 4
per serving 13.9g carbohydrate; 73.6g fat; 990 cal; 69.4g protein
tip If your supermarket doesn't stock raspberry vinegar, use any fruit-flavored vinegar in this recipe.

saltimbocca
with brussels sprouts and sun-dried tomatoes

PREPARATION TIME 25 MINUTES   COOKING TIME 20 MINUTES

Saltimbocca is a classic Italian veal dish that literally means "jump in the mouth" – just the sensation the wonderful flavors will produce with your first bite.

eight 6-ounce slices veal scallopine,

    pounded thin

4 slices prosciutto, halved crosswise

8 fresh sage leaves

¹/₂ cup finely grated pecorino cheese

3 tablespoons butter

1 cup dry white wine

1 tablespoon coarsely chopped fresh sage

2 tablespoons olive oil

2 pounds brussels sprouts, sliced thickly

1 clove garlic, crushed in garlic press

¹/₂ cup drained sun-dried tomatoes,

    sliced thinly

¼ cup toasted pine nuts

2 tablespoons fresh lemon juice

1 Place scallopine on flat surface. Place one piece prosciutto, one sage leaf and one-eighth of the cheese on each scallopine; fold in half to enclose filling, secure with a toothpick or small skewer.

2 Melt half of the butter in medium nonstick skillet; cook saltimbocca, in batches, about 5 minutes or until browned both sides and cooked through. Remove meat from skillet; cover to keep warm.

3 Pour wine into same skillet; bring to a boil. Boil, uncovered, until wine reduces by half. Stir in remaining butter then chopped sage.

4 Meanwhile, heat half of the oil in wok or large skillet; stir-fry sprouts and garlic until sprouts are just tender. Add tomato, nuts, juice and remaining oil; toss gently until heated through.

5 Serve veal drizzled with sauce, accompanied by brussels sprouts.

SERVES 4
per serving 12.9g carbohydrate; 34.8g fat; 631 cal; 55.8g protein

red beef curry

PREPARATION TIME 10 MINUTES   COOKING TIME 20 MINUTES

2 tablespoons peanut oil

1 pound beef round, cut into ¾-inch cubes

1 large onion, sliced thinly

¼ cup red curry paste

1 large red bell pepper, sliced thinly

5 ounces green beans, chopped coarsely

1²/₃ cups (14-ounce can) unsweetened

    coconut milk

14 ounces canned crushed

    tomatoes, undrained

¼ cup coarsely chopped fresh cilantro

1 Heat half of the oil in wok or large skillet; stir-fry beef, in batches, until browned all over.

2 Heat remaining oil in same wok; stir-fry onion until soft. Add paste; stir-fry until fragrant. Add pepper and beans; stir-fry until vegetables just soften.

3 Return beef to wok with remaining ingredients; stir-fry until sauce thickens slightly.

SERVES 4
per serving 12.4g carbohydrate; 44.5g fat; 583 cal; 34.6g protein

corned beef with steamed cauliflower and mustard sauce

PREPARATION TIME 15 MINUTES   COOKING TIME 2 HOURS 20 MINUTES

2½-pound piece uncooked corned
    beef brisket

2 bay leaves

1 teaspoon black peppercorns

2 whole cloves

2 tablespoons light brown sugar

2 tablespoons malt vinegar

1 medium head cauliflower,
    cut into florets

¾ cup coarsely grated
    cheddar cheese

½ cup water

½ cup dry white wine

½ cup chicken broth

2 teaspoons cornstarch

1 tablespoon grainy mustard

½ cup heavy cream

1   Preheat oven to hot.

2   Place beef in large saucepan with bay leaves, peppercorns,
    cloves, sugar and vinegar. Cover with cold water; bring to a boil.
    Reduce heat; simmer, covered, about 2 hours or until beef is
    tender. Remove from heat; cool 10 minutes in liquid.

3   Meanwhile, boil, steam or microwave cauliflower until just tender;
    drain. Place cauliflower in medium shallow casserole; sprinkle
    with cheese. Bake cauliflower, uncovered, in hot oven about
    5 minutes or until cheese is melted. Cover to keep warm.

4   Bring the water, wine and broth to a boil in small saucepan.
    Reduce heat; simmer, uncovered, about 5 minutes or until mixture
    reduces by a third. Stir in blended cornstarch, mustard and
    cream; cook, stirring, until sauce boils and thickens.

5   Remove beef from liquid; slice thinly. Serve beef with cheesy
    cauliflower and mustard sauce.

SERVES 4
per serving   16.8g carbohydrate; 42g fat; 717 cal; 63.2g protein

beef and vegetable rolls

PREPARATION TIME 15 MINUTES   COOKING TIME 15 MINUTES

2 medium carrots

6 asparagus spears,
   halved lengthwise

3 scallions, trimmed,
   halved lengthwise

12 thin slices top round steak
   (about 12 ounces)

1 tablespoon cornstarch

2 teaspoons vegetable oil

1 tablespoon sugar

¼ cup mirin or sweet rice wine

2 tablespoons sake

¼ cup soy sauce

1 Using a vegetable peeler, slice carrots lengthwise into thin strips. Cut carrot strips to width of beef. Place asparagus in heatproof bowl, cover with boiling water, let stand 2 minutes; drain, rinse under cold water, drain. Cut asparagus and scallions to width of beef.

2 Lay beef slices flat and sift 2 teaspoons of the cornstarch lightly over top. Lay two pieces each of carrot and scallion and one piece of asparagus across the dusted side of each slice of beef and roll up. Tie rolls with kitchen string or secure ends with toothpicks. Dust rolls lightly with remaining cornstarch.

3 Heat oil in medium skillet and cook rolls until lightly browned all over. Remove rolls from skillet, wipe oil from skillet with paper towel; return rolls to skillet. Add combined sugar, mirin, sake and sauce; bring to a boil. Reduce heat; simmer, turning occasionally, until rolls are cooked through. (If a thicker sauce is preferred, remove rolls and boil sauce to reduce; return rolls to skillet and coat with sauce.)

4 Remove rolls from skillet, cool 2 minutes. Remove and discard toothpicks; cut rolls in half. Arrange on serving plate and serve with remaining sauce.

SERVES 4
per serving 12.9g carbohydrate; 7.9g fat; 228 cal; 18.3g protein

indian spiced beef with dhal

PREPARATION TIME 15 MINUTES (PLUS REFRIGERATION TIME)   COOKING TIME 1 HOUR 20 MINUTES

2 tablespoons cumin seeds

1 tablespoon coriander seeds

2 teaspoons sweet paprika

2 teaspoons ground cinnamon

1 teaspoon ground cardamom

1 teaspoon chili powder

5 cloves garlic, crushed in garlic press

2 teaspoons grated fresh ginger

¼ cup peanut oil

2½ pounds top or bottom round, in 1 piece

DHAL

1 cup red lentils

¼ cup shredded fresh mint leaves

3 cups vegetable broth

1   Cook cumin and coriander seeds, paprika, cinnamon, cardamom and chili powder in dry medium skillet, stirring, until fragrant. Place seed mixture in small bowl with garlic, ginger and oil; mix to a paste. Trim as much fat from beef as possible; spread paste all over beef. Cover beef; refrigerate 3 hours or overnight.

2   Place beef on roasting rack or in disposable roasting pan. Cook in covered grill, using indirect heat, following manufacturer's instructions, about 1 hour 20 minutes or until browned all over and cooked as desired. Remove from heat, cover; let stand 10 minutes before slicing.

3   Meanwhile, make dhal. Serve with thickly sliced beef.

DHAL   Combine lentils, mint and broth in medium saucepan. Bring to a boil; simmer, uncovered, stirring occasionally, about 15 minutes or until lentils are tender.

SERVES 4
per serving   20.9g carbohydrate; 36.5g fat; 745 cal; 84.5g protein

sweet chili ribs with pamela's cole slaw

PREPARATION TIME 20 MINUTES (PLUS REFRIGERATION TIME)   COOKING TIME 30 MINUTES

3 pounds pork spareribs

⅓ cup sweet chili sauce

1 tablespoon soy sauce

¼ cup rice wine

2 cloves garlic, crushed in garlic press

1 teaspoon grated fresh ginger

2 tablespoons finely chopped fresh cilantro

½ medium savoy cabbage, shredded finely

6 scallions, chopped finely

1 red serrano chile, chopped finely

½ cup coarsely chopped fresh flat-leaf parsley

¼ cup coarsely chopped fresh cilantro

LEMON DRESSING

2 tablespoons fresh lemon juice

2 teaspoons dijon mustard

⅓ cup peanut oil

1   Place spareribs in large shallow casserole with combined sauces, wine, garlic, ginger and finely chopped cilantro. Cover spareribs; refrigerate 3 hours or overnight.

2   Cook ribs in covered grill, using indirect heat, following manufacturer's instructions, about 30 minutes or until browned all over and cooked as desired.

3   Meanwhile, combine cabbage in large bowl with scallion, chile and herbs. Make lemon dressing.

4   Pour lemon dressing over salad; toss gently to combine. Serve with spareribs.

LEMON DRESSING   Combine all ingredients in screw-top jar; shake well.

SERVES 4
per serving   15.1g carbohydrate; 31.2g fat; 491 cal; 35.9g protein

veal steaks with italian white bean salad

PREPARATION TIME 15 MINUTES   COOKING TIME 10 MINUTES

1 tablespoon olive oil

eight 8-ounce veal steaks

½ cup beef broth

4 tablespoons butter

ITALIAN WHITE BEAN SALAD

2 cups (3½ ounces) baby arugula leaves

1 large tomato, chopped coarsely

½ cup firmly packed fresh basil leaves, torn

28 ounces (2 cans) white beans,

   rinsed, drained

1 tablespoon finely chopped fresh chives

¼ cup fresh lemon juice

2 cloves garlic, crushed in garlic press

¼ cup olive oil

1 Make italian white bean salad.

2 Heat oil in large nonstick skillet; cook veal, in batches, until browned both sides and cooked as desired. Cover to keep warm.

3 Pour broth into same skillet; bring to a boil, stirring. Add butter, stir until butter melts. Reduce heat; simmer, stirring, 2 minutes.

4 Serve veal, drizzled with sauce, with italian white bean salad.

ITALIAN WHITE BEAN SALAD Combine arugula, tomato, basil and beans in large bowl. Combine chives, juice, garlic and oil in screw-top jar; shake well. Pour dressing over salad; toss gently to combine.

SERVES 4
per serving 20.1g carbohydrate; 35.1g fat; 583 cal; 44.3g protein
tip Many varieties of already cooked white beans are available canned, among them cannellini, butter and great northern; any of these are suitable here.

satay beef and stir-fried vegetables

PREPARATION TIME 20 MINUTES   COOKING TIME 20 MINUTES

1 teaspoon peanut oil

1 pound london broil, sliced thinly

1 large onion, sliced thinly

1 clove garlic, crushed in garlic press

2 teaspoons grated fresh ginger

2 red serrano chiles, seeded, chopped finely

1 medium red bell pepper, chopped coarsely

1 medium green bell pepper, chopped coarsely

4 ounces button mushrooms, halved

8 ounces canned sliced

   bamboo shoots, drained

1 teaspoon curry powder

2 teaspoons cornstarch

½ cup chicken broth

¼ cup reduced-fat creamy peanut butter

2 tablespoons oyster sauce

1 tablespoon unsalted, roasted, coarsely

   chopped peanuts

1 Heat oil in wok or large nonstick skillet; stir-fry beef, in batches, until browned all over.

2 Stir-fry onion and garlic in same wok until onion softens. Add ginger, chile, peppers, mushroom, bamboo shoots and curry powder; stir-fry until vegetables are just tender.

3 Blend cornstarch with broth in small measuring cup; pour into wok, stir to combine with vegetable mixture. Return beef to wok with peanut butter and oyster sauce; bring to a boil, stirring, until sauce boils and thickens slightly and beef is cooked as desired. Stir in peanuts.

SERVES 4
per serving 16g carbohydrate; 14g fat; 350 cal; 39.8g protein

herb and mustard-seasoned beef fillet with lima bean and corn succotash

PREPARATION TIME 40 MINUTES   COOKING TIME 30 MINUTES

3 tablespoons butter, softened

2 cloves garlic, crushed in

garlic press

2 teaspoons finely chopped

fresh rosemary

1 tablespoon finely chopped fresh

flat-leaf parsley

1 tablespoon finely chopped pitted

black olives

1 tablespoon coarsely chopped

toasted pine nuts

¼ cup grainy mustard

1½ pounds beef

tenderloin, trimmed

1 tablespoon extra virgin olive oil

2 teaspoons drained prepared

white horseradish

2 tablespoons heavy cream

LIMA BEAN AND CORN SUCCOTASH

2 fresh ears corn, shucked

7 ounces frozen lima

beans, thawed

1 small red bell pepper,

chopped finely

1 tablespoon butter

1   Combine butter, garlic, herbs, olives, nuts and 2 tablespoons of the mustard in small bowl. Transfer to small pastry bag fitted with medium plain tube.

2   Preheat oven to moderately hot.

3   Tie beef firmly with kitchen string at 1-inch intervals. Using knife-sharpening steel or thick butcher's skewer, pierce beef through center, lengthwise. Pipe butter mixture into cavity.

4   Heat oil in medium casserole; cook beef over high heat about 5 minutes or until browned all over. Transfer casserole to oven; roast, uncovered, in moderately hot oven about 20 minutes or until cooked as desired. Cover with foil; let stand 5 minutes.

5   Meanwhile, make lima bean and corn succotash.

6   Serve beef, sliced, with combined remaining mustard, horseradish and cream, accompanied by succotash.

LIMA BEAN AND CORN SUCCOTASH   Cook corn on heated oiled grill or grill pan until just tender; cool 10 minutes. Using sharp knife, remove kernels from cob. Boil, steam or microwave lima beans until tender; drain. Place corn and beans in large bowl with pepper and butter; toss gently to combine

SERVES 4

per serving 24.2g carbohydrate; 31.4g fat; 575 cal; 49.3g protein

mustard-crusted rack of veal
with mashed butternut squash

PREPARATION TIME 25 MINUTES   COOKING TIME 45 MINUTES

2 tablespoons grainy mustard

3 scallions, chopped finely

2 cloves garlic, crushed in
    garlic press

1 tablespoon finely chopped
    fresh rosemary

2 tablespoons olive oil

2-pound veal rack
    (8 chops), trimmed

1½ pounds butternut squash,
    chopped coarsely

1 tablespoon butter

⅓ cup heavy cream

1 large onion, sliced thinly

14 ounces button mushrooms,
    sliced thinly

1 tablespoon all-purpose flour

¼ cup dry white wine

¾ cup chicken broth

¼ cup coarsely chopped fresh
    flat-leaf parsley

1 Preheat oven to moderately hot.

2 Combine mustard, scallion, half of the garlic, rosemary and half of the oil in small measuring cup. Place veal on wire rack over large shallow casserole; coat veal all over with mustard mixture. Roast, uncovered, in moderately hot oven, about 30 minutes or until browned all over and cooked as desired. Cover to keep warm.

3 Meanwhile, boil, steam or microwave squash until tender; drain. Mash squash in large bowl with butter and half of the cream until smooth.

4 Heat remaining oil in same casserole; cook onion and remaining garlic, stirring, until onion softens. Add mushroom; cook, stirring, about 5 minutes or until just tender. Add flour; cook, stirring, until mixture thickens and bubbles. Gradually stir in wine and broth; stir until sauce boils and thickens. Add remaining cream and parsley; stir until heated through.

5 Serve veal with mashed squash and mushroom sauce.

SERVES 4
per serving 16.9g carbohydrate; 26.8g fat; 526 cal; 52.3g protein

hearty beef stew with red wine and mushrooms

PREPARATION TIME 10 MINUTES　COOKING TIME 2 HOURS 50 MINUTES

The rich combination of broth and wine, plus the long, slow cooking time, gives this stew its robust intensity.
Top round steak is also suitable for this recipe.

2 tablespoons olive oil

3 pounds boneless beef chuck,

   cut into ¾-inch cubes

1 large onion, sliced thickly

2 cloves garlic, crushed in garlic press

8 ounces button mushrooms, quartered

2 stalks celery, trimmed, sliced thickly

28 ounces canned crushed tomatoes

½ cup dry red wine

1½ cups beef broth

2 teaspoons coarsely chopped fresh thyme

12 ounces green beans, trimmed

12 ounces yellow beans, trimmed

1 tablespoons butter

¼ cup slivered almonds, toasted

¼ cup loosely packed fresh flat-leaf

   parsley leaves

1　Heat half of the oil in large heavy-bottomed saucepan; cook beef, in batches, over high heat until browned all over.

2　Heat remaining oil in same saucepan; cook onion and garlic, stirring, until onion softens. Add mushroom and celery; cook, stirring, 3 minutes. Return beef to saucepan with undrained tomatoes, wine and broth; bring to a boil. Reduce heat; simmer, covered, 2½ hours or until steak is tender. Stir in thyme.

3　Meanwhile, boil, steam or microwave beans until just tender; drain. While still hot, place beans in medium bowl; add butter, almonds and parsley. Toss to coat and combine.

4　Serve stew with beans.

SERVES 4
per serving　12.4g carbohydrate; 43.6g fat; 823 cal; 89.8g protein

chili con carne

PREPARATION TIME 25 MINUTES　COOKING TIME 1 HOUR 30 MINUTES

1 pound boneless beef chuck

2 tablespoons olive oil

2 medium onions, chopped finely

3 cloves garlic, crushed in garlic press

3 teaspoons ground cumin

1 teaspoon ground coriander

1 teaspoon chili powder

1 tablespoon finely chopped fresh oregano

28 ounces canned crushed tomatoes

1 cup beef broth

2 teaspoons light brown sugar

15 ounces canned red kidney beans,

   rinsed, drained

1　Cut beef into ¾-inch cubes. Heat half of the oil in large saucepan; cook beef, in batches, until browned. Drain on paper towels.

2　Heat remaining oil in saucepan; cook onion, garlic, spices and oregano, stirring, until onion is soft.

3　Add undrained tomatoes, broth, sugar and beef; simmer, covered, about 1 hour or until beef is tender.

4　Stir beans into beef mixture; simmer 5 minutes or until heated through.

SERVES 4
per serving　18.5g carbohydrate; 21.2g fat; 498 cal; 58g protein

barbecue glazed meatloaf

PREPARATION TIME 20 MINUTES   COOKING TIME 50 MINUTES

1 small red bell pepper

14 ounces lean ground beef

5 ounces sweet italian sausage,
   casings discarded

1 medium onion, chopped finely

2 cloves garlic, crushed in garlic press

¼ cup, packaged breadcrumbs

1 egg, beaten lightly

½ cup coarsely chopped pitted green olives

¼ cup coarsely chopped fresh basil

1 tablespoon coarsely chopped fresh oregano

8 slices bacon, sliced lengthwise

7 ounces green beans

BARBECUE GLAZE

¼ cup water

1 tablespoon tomato paste

1 tablespoon red wine vinegar

2 tablespoons brown sugar

1 Quarter pepper; remove and discard seeds and membranes. Roast pepper, skin-side-up, under broiler until skin blisters and blackens. Cover pepper pieces in plastic wrap or paper 5 minutes. Peel away skin; cut pepper into thin strips.

2 Preheat oven to moderate. Lightly oil 10 x 15-inch jelly roll pan.

3 Combine meat, onion, garlic, breadcrumbs, egg, olives, basil and oregano in large bowl. Place a sheet of plastic wrap on a flat surface. Press half of the meatloaf mixture into a 3 x 10-inch rectangle. Lay pepper strips over top, leaving ½-inch border; press remaining meatloaf mixture over pepper.

4 Turn plastic wrap onto prepared jelly roll pan; remove plastic wrap from meatloaf. Cover top and sides of meatloaf with bacon, overlapping bacon.

5 Bake, uncovered, in moderate oven 15 minutes. Make barbecue glaze.

6 Pour off any excess fat from meatloaf, brush with glaze; bake, uncovered, about 25 minutes or until meatloaf is cooked through. Let stand 10 minutes before slicing.

7 Meanwhile, boil, steam or microwave green beans; drain. Serve with meatloaf.

BARBECUE GLAZE Combine ingredients in small saucepan; bring to a boil. Reduce heat; simmer, uncovered, 5 minutes.

SERVES 4
per serving 20.8g carbohydrate; 27.2g fat; 478 cal; 38.2g protein

cajun steaks with mango salsa

PREPARATION TIME 15 MINUTES   COOKING TIME 5 MINUTES

1½ teaspoons cajun seasoning

4 thin 6-ounce top round steaks

2 cups (3½ ounces) mesclun

MANGO SALSA

1 large mango, chopped coarsely

2 medium tomatoes, seeded, chopped coarsely

1 small red onion, chopped finely

1 clove garlic, crushed in garlic press

2 tablespoons finely shredded fresh basil

1 tablespoon balsamic vinegar

1 Make mango salsa.

2 Sprinkle seasoning over beef; cook on heated oiled grill or grill pan until browned both sides and cooked as desired.

3 Divide steaks among serving plates; top with mesclun and mango salsa.

MANGO SALSA Combine ingredients in medium bowl.

SERVES 4
per serving 16.2g carbohydrate; 8.8g fat; 304 cal; 39.1g protein

eggplant bolognese

PREPARATION TIME 30 MINUTES   COOKING TIME 1 HOUR 10 MINUTES

2 medium eggplants

4½ cups (7 ounces) baby
  spinach leaves

5 ounces ricotta

1 egg white

½ cup grated mozzarella

⅓ cup grated parmesan

BOLOGNESE SAUCE

2 teaspoons olive oil

1 large onion, chopped coarsely

1 small red bell pepper,
  chopped coarsely

1 small green bell pepper,
  chopped coarsely

2 cloves garlic, crushed in
  garlic press

8 ounces lean ground beef

1 large plum tomato,
  chopped coarsely

1 tablespoon tomato paste

½ cup red wine

14 ounces canned whole tomatoes

2 tablespoons coarsely chopped
  fresh basil

1 tablespoon coarsely chopped
  fresh oregano

ARUGULA SALAD

2 cups (3½ ounces) arugula

½ cup loosely packed fresh
  basil leaves

1 tablespoon balsamic vinegar

1 teaspoon olive oil

1   Preheat oven to moderate. Make bolognese sauce.

2   Meanwhile, cut eggplants into ⅛-inch-thick slices; cook on heated oiled grill pan until just tender.

3   Boil, steam or microwave spinach until wilted; drain. Press as much liquid as possible from spinach; cool. Combine spinach, ricotta and egg white in medium bowl; mix well.

4   Spread 1 cup of the sauce over base of shallow 8-cup casserole. Top with half of the eggplant, then half of the spinach mixture, then another cup of sauce, remaining eggplant and remaining spinach mixture. Spread remaining sauce over the top then sprinkle with combined cheeses. Bake, uncovered, in moderate oven about 20 minutes or until golden brown. Remove from oven, let stand 10 minutes.

5   Meanwhile make arugula salad.

6   Divide bolognese bake among serving plates, serve with arugula salad.

BOLOGNESE SAUCE   Heat oil in medium skillet; cook onion, peppers and garlic until onion is soft. Add beef to skillet; cook, stirring, until beef changes color. Add chopped tomato and tomato paste; cook 3 minutes. Add wine and undrained canned tomatoes; bring to a boil. Reduce heat; simmer, uncovered, about 25 minutes or until sauce thickens. Stir in herbs off the heat.

ARUGULA SALAD   Combine ingredients in medium bowl; toss gently.

SERVES 4
per serving 13.4g carbohydrate; 20.3g fat; 373 cal; 29.1g protein

eggplant bolognese

osso buco

osso buco

PREPARATION TIME 30 MINUTES   COOKING TIME 2 HOURS 30 MINUTES

Ask your butcher to cut the veal into fairly thick (2- to 2½-inch) pieces for you.

1 tablespoon olive oil

8 veal shanks (4 pounds)

1 medium onion, chopped coarsely

2 cloves garlic, crushed in
   garlic press

1 stalk celery, trimmed,
   chopped coarsely

1 large carrot, chopped coarsely

2 tablespoons tomato paste

½ cup dry white wine

1 cup beef broth

1 cup water

14 ounces canned
   crushed tomatoes

1 teaspoon fresh rosemary leaves

1 medium eggplant,
   chopped coarsely

1 medium green bell pepper,
   chopped coarsely

1 medium yellow bell pepper,
   chopped coarsely

GREMOLATA

2 teaspoons finely grated
   lemon peel

¼ cup finely chopped fresh
   flat-leaf parsley

1 tablespoon finely chopped
   fresh rosemary

1 clove garlic, chopped finely

1 Heat half of the oil in large saucepan; cook veal, in batches, until browned all over.

2 Heat remaining oil in same saucepan; cook onion, garlic, celery and carrot, stirring, until vegetables soften. Add paste, wine, broth, the water, undrained tomatoes and rosemary; bring to a boil.

3 Return veal to casserole, fitting pieces upright and tightly together in single layer; return to a boil. Cover, reduce heat; simmer 1½ hours. Add eggplant, cook, uncovered, 15 minutes, stirring occasionally. Add peppers; cook, uncovered, about 15 minutes or until vegetables are tender.

4 Meanwhile, make gremolata.

5 Remove veal and vegetables from casserole; cover to keep warm. Bring sauce to a boil; boil, uncovered, about 10 minutes or until sauce thickens slightly.

6 Divide veal and vegetables among serving plates; top with sauce, sprinkle with gremolata.

GREMOLATA Combine ingredients in small bowl.

SERVES 4
per serving 12.6g carbohydrate; 6.6g fat; 433 cal; 74.4g protein

tuscan beef stew

PREPARATION TIME 15 MINUTES   COOKING TIME 2 HOURS 40 MINUTES

Top round steak and skirt steak are also suitable for this recipe.

1 tablespoon olive oil

14 ounces spring onions, trimmed

2 pounds boneless beef chuck,

cut into 2-inch cubes

2 tablespoons butter

2 tablespoons all-purpose flour

2 cups dry red wine

1 cup beef broth

1 cup water

2 cloves garlic, crushed in garlic press

6 sprigs thyme

2 bay leaves

1 stalk celery, trimmed, chopped coarsely

14 ounces baby carrots, halved

2 cups frozen peas

⅓ cup coarsely chopped fresh

flat-leaf parsley

1   Heat oil in large heavy-bottomed saucepan; cook onions, stirring occasionally, about 10 minutes or until browned lightly, remove from saucepan. Cook beef, in batches, over high heat in same saucepan, until browned all over.

2   Melt butter in same saucepan, add flour; cook, stirring, until mixture bubbles and thickens. Gradually stir in wine, broth and the water; stir until mixture boils and thickens. Return beef to saucepan with garlic, thyme and bay leaves; bring to a boil. Reduce heat; simmer, covered, 1½ hours.

3   Add onions to saucepan with celery and carrot; simmer, covered, 30 minutes. Add peas; simmer, uncovered, until peas are just tender. Remove bay leaves; stir in parsley just before serving.

SERVES 4
per serving   19g carbohydrate; 22.7g fat; 597 cal; 58.2g protein

tandoori beef with grilled limes

PREPARATION TIME 10 MINUTES (PLUS REFRIGERATION TIME)   COOKING TIME 10 MINUTES

four 5-ounce ribeye steaks

1 clove garlic, crushed in garlic press

¼ cup tandoori paste

4 limes, halved

14 ounces green beans

½ cup mango chutney

¾ cup unflavored yogurt

1   Combine beef, garlic and paste in large bowl. Cover; refrigerate 3 hours or overnight.

2   Cook beef on heated oiled grill or grill pan, uncovered, until browned and cooked as desired.

3   Meanwhile, cook lime, cut-side down, on heated oiled grill pan; cook about 2 minutes or until browned.

4   Boil, steam or microwave beans until just tender; drain.

5   Serve beef with lime, chutney, yogurt and beans.

SERVES 4
per serving   24.6g carbohydrate; 16.8g fat; 385 cal; 31.4g protein

veal and mushroom casserole

PREPARATION TIME 15 MINUTES   COOKING TIME 1 HOUR 10 MINUTES

1½ pounds boneless veal, cut into
    ¾-inch pieces

2 medium onions, chopped coarsely

1 clove garlic, crushed in garlic press

½ teaspoon hot paprika

4 medium tomatoes, chopped coarsely

¼ cup tomato paste

1½ cups beef broth

2 cups water

7 ounces button mushrooms, halved

1 tablespoon fresh oregano leaves

10 ounces baby carrots

2 tablespoons butter

1 Heat oiled large nonstick saucepan; cook veal, in batches, until browned all over. Cook onion and garlic in same saucepan, stirring, until onion softens. Add paprika; cook, stirring, until fragrant.

2 Return veal to saucepan with tomato, paste, broth and the water; bring to a boil. Reduce heat; simmer, uncovered, about 45 minutes or until veal is tender. Add mushroom; bring to a boil. Reduce heat; simmer, uncovered, about 10 minutes or until mushroom is tender. Stir in oregano.

3 Meanwhile, boil, steam or microwave baby carrots; drain. Place carrots in medium bowl. While still hot, add butter; toss to coat.

4 Serve carrots with casserole.

SERVES 4
per serving 13.3g carbohydrate; 13.4g fat; 370 cal; 48.3g protein
tip This recipe becomes more flavorsome if made a day or two ahead and refrigerated, covered; reheat slowly to serve. If holding stew for later, do not cook carrots until just before serving.

thai-style steaks with cucumber salad

PREPARATION TIME 25 MINUTES (PLUS REFRIGERATION TIME)   COOKING TIME 15 MINUTES

four 7-ounce ribeye steaks

2 tablespoons sweet chili sauce

1 clove garlic, crushed in garlic press

1 teaspoon fish sauce

2 tablespoons fresh lime juice

1 tablespoon coarsely chopped fresh cilantro

CUCUMBER SALAD

2 small hothouse cucumbers

2 tablespoons sugar

½ cup white vinegar

1 red serrano chile, seeded, sliced thinly

¼ cup chopped, unsalted, roasted peanuts

1 tablespoon coarsely chopped fresh cilantro

1 Combine beef with remaining ingredients in shallow casserole. Cover; refrigerate 3 hours or overnight.

2 Meanwhile, make cucumber salad.

3 Drain beef; discard marinade.

4 Cook beef on heated oiled grill or grill pan, uncovered, until browned and cooked as desired.

5 Serve beef with drained cucumber salad.

CUCUMBER SALAD Halve cucumbers lengthwise. Scoop out and discard seeds; slice cucumber thinly. Combine sugar and vinegar in medium saucepan; stir over heat, without boiling, until sugar dissolves. Simmer, uncovered, about 5 minutes or until reduced by half. Combine hot vinegar mixture with cucumber and remaining ingredients in heatproof bowl; mix well. Cover; refrigerate 3 hours or overnight.

SERVES 4
per serving 14.6g carbohydrate; 18g fat; 417 cal; 48.1g protein

hoisin beef stir-fry (see page 325)

PREPARATION TIME 20 MINUTES (PLUS REFRIGERATION TIME)   COOKING TIME 15 MINUTES

1 teaspoon sesame oil

1 teaspoon cracked black pepper

⅓ cup unsweetened rice wine

⅓ cup soy sauce

2 scallions, chopped finely

1 red serrano chile, chopped finely

2 cloves garlic, crushed in garlic press

2½-inch piece fresh ginger, grated finely

1¾ pounds beef strips

1 tablespoon peanut oil

1 medium onion, sliced thinly

1 medium red bell pepper, sliced thinly

4 ounces shiitake mushrooms, trimmed,
    sliced thinly

1 pound asian greens, halved crosswise

¼ cup water

¼ cup hoisin sauce

4 scallions, sliced thinly

1   Combine sesame oil, pepper, half of the wine, half of the soy sauce, finely chopped scallion, chile, garlic and ginger in large bowl with beef, toss to coat in marinade. Cover; refrigerate 3 hours or overnight.

2   Heat half of the peanut oil in wok or large skillet; cook undrained beef, in batches, until beef is browned and just cooked through.

3   Heat remaining peanut oil in same wok; stir-fry onion and pepper until almost tender. Add mushroom, stalks of asian greens, the water, remaining wine, remaining soy sauce and hoisin; cook, covered, 5 minutes or until vegetables are tender.

4   Return beef to wok with leaves of asian greens; stir-fry until leaves just wilt.

5   Divide stir-fry among serving bowls, top with scallion.

SERVES 4
per serving 13.7g carbohydrate 16.6g fat; 413 cal; 46.8g protein
tip Any asian greens can be used in this recipe. Try it with bok choy, choy sum, or gai larn (also known as chinese broccoli). You will need one bunch of asian greens.

grilled sausages and ratatouille

PREPARATION TIME 15 MINUTES   COOKING TIME 20 MINUTES

You can use any sausages you like in this recipe; beef and fennel sausages also suit the Italian qualities of this meal.

2 tablespoons olive oil

1 medium red onion, chopped coarsely

2 medium red bell peppers, chopped coarsely

3 medium green zucchini, chopped coarsely

3 baby eggplants, chopped coarsely

3 medium tomatoes, chopped coarsely

3 teaspoons chili sauce (such as sambal
    oelek or sriracha)

3 tablespoons tomato paste

¾ cup beef broth

2 tablespoons coarsely chopped fresh chives

12 veal and mushroom sausages

1   Heat oil in medium saucepan; cook onion and pepper, stirring, until onion softens. Add zucchini and eggplant; cook, stirring, 3 minutes. Stir in tomato, chili sauce, paste and broth; bring to a boil. Reduce heat; simmer, uncovered, about 8 minutes or until mixture thickens. Stir in chives off the heat.

2   Meanwhile, cook sausages on heated oiled grill or grill pan until cooked through.

3   Serve sausages on ratatouille.

SERVES 4
per serving 15.6g carbohydrate; 50.7g fat; 609 cal; 23.9g protein

green chile stew

PREPARATION TIME 15 MINUTES   COOKING TIME 2 HOURS

2 tablespoons olive oil

2 pounds beef chuck, cut into 1-inch cubes

1 large onion, sliced thinly

2 cloves garlic, sliced thinly

2 teaspoons ground cumin

2 long green chiles, seeded, sliced thinly

2 cups beef broth

1 tablespoon tomato paste

3 large plum tomatoes, chopped coarsely

2 small turnips, chopped coarsely

2 medium carrots, chopped coarsely

¼ cup coarsely chopped fresh cilantro

2 fresh ears corn, shucked, halved
   crosswise and grilled

1 Heat half of the oil in large casserole; cook beef, in batches, stirring, until browned all over.

2 Preheat oven to moderate.

3 Heat remaining oil in same dish; cook onion, garlic, cumin and chile, stirring, until onion softens. Add broth and tomato paste; bring to a boil, stirring. Return beef to casserole; cook, covered, in moderate oven 45 minutes.

4 Add tomato and turnip; cook, covered, in moderate oven 35 minutes. Uncover; add carrot, cook 20 minutes.

5 Stir cilantro into stew just before serving with grilled corn.

SERVES 4
per serving 18.6g carbohydrate; 21.5g fat; 498 cal; 57.2g protein

roast beef and arugula salad

PREPARATION TIME 10 MINUTES   COOKING TIME 20 MINUTES

1 tablespoon olive oil

1¼-pound piece beef tenderloin

1 medium hothouse cucumber,
   chopped coarsely

1 medium tomato, chopped coarsely

4 ounces sun-dried tomatoes

2 cups (3½ ounces) baby arugula leaves

1 small red onion, sliced thinly

4 scallions, sliced thinly

½ cup buttermilk

⅓ cup mayonnaise

1 tablespoon dijon mustard

1 clove garlic, crushed in garlic press

1 teaspoon freshly ground black pepper

1 Preheat oven to moderately hot.

2 Heat oil in medium casserole; cook beef, turning, until browned. Roast, uncovered, in moderately hot oven about 15 minutes or until cooked as desired. Remove from oven. Cover; let stand 5 minutes, slice beef thinly.

3 Combine beef, cucumber, tomato, sun-dried tomato, arugula, onion, and scallions in large bowl. Combine remaining ingredients in screw-top jar; shake well. Drizzle dressing over salad; toss gently to combine.

SERVES 4
per serving 21.1g carbohydrate; 21.6g fat; 448 cal; 41.4g protein
tip Beef can be cooked up to 2 hours ahead; cover, refrigerate until required.

marjoram and lemon grilled veal chops with greek salad

PREPARATION TIME 25 MINUTES (PLUS REFRIGERATION TIME)   COOKING TIME 10 MINUTES

1 teaspoon finely grated lemon peel

¼ cup fresh lemon juice

1 tablespoon finely

chopped marjoram

2 teaspoons olive oil

four 7-ounce veal chops

GREEK SALAD

¾ cup pitted kalamata olives

7 ounces feta cheese,

chopped coarsely

6 large plum tomatoes, seeded,

chopped coarsely

1 medium red bell pepper,

chopped coarsely

2 medium hothouse cucumbers,

seeded, sliced thinly

2 stalks celery, trimmed,

sliced thinly

1 tablespoon whole

marjoram leaves

LEMON DRESSING

1 clove garlic, crushed in

garlic press

⅓ cup fresh lemon juice

2 teaspoons olive oil

1 Combine peel, juice, marjoram and oil in large bowl; add veal, toss to coat veal in mixture. Cover; refrigerate 1 hour.

2 Meanwhile, make greek salad. Make lemon dressing.

3 Cook veal on heated, lightly oiled grill or grill pan until browned both sides and cooked as desired.

4 Pour dressing over salad; toss gently to combine. Serve veal with salad.

GREEK SALAD Combine ingredients in large bowl.

LEMON DRESSING Combine ingredients in screw-top jar, shake well.

SERVES 4
per serving 12.9g carbohydrate; 20.7g fat; 405 cal; 40.6g protein

raan with green beans and spiced yogurt (see page 253)

PREPARATION TIME 35 MINUTES (PLUS REFRIGERATION TIME)   COOKING TIME 30 MINUTES

Raan is a leg of lamb usually butterflied, then either marinated in spicy yogurt and roasted in a tandoor or pot-roasted.

2 teaspoons coriander seeds

1 teaspoon cumin seeds

¼ teaspoon cardamom seeds

1 teaspoon chili powder

1 teaspoon ground turmeric

1 cinnamon stick

2 whole cloves

2 star anise

1 medium onion, chopped coarsely

4 cloves garlic, quartered

1-inch piece fresh ginger,
   chopped coarsely

¼ cup blanched almonds

½ cup low-fat yogurt

2 tablespoons fresh lemon juice

2½-pound butterflied
   leg of lamb, trimmed

GREEN BEAN SALAD

1 pound green beans, halved

3 shallots, sliced thinly

⅓ cup sliced almonds, toasted

¼ cup white raisins

⅓ cup loosely packed fresh
   mint leaves

1 teaspoon extra virgin olive oil

⅓ cup fresh lemon juice

SPICED YOGURT

1 cup low-fat yogurt

¼ cup finely chopped fresh mint

1 clove garlic, crushed in garlic press

¼ teaspoon ground cumin

¼ teaspoon ground coriander

1 Dry-fry seeds, cardamom, chili, turmeric, cinnamon, cloves and star anise in heated small skillet, stirring, about 2 minutes or until fragrant. Blend or process spices with onion, garlic, ginger, nuts, yogurt and juice until mixture forms a paste.

2 Pierce lamb all over with sharp knife; place on metal rack in large shallow roasting pan. Spread paste over lamb, pressing firmly into cuts. Cover; refrigerate 3 hours or overnight.

3 Cook lamb on heated oiled grill or grill pan, covered, about 30 minutes or until browned both sides and cooked as desired. Cover; let stand 10 minutes then slice thickly.

4 Meanwhile, make green bean salad. Make spiced yogurt.

5 Serve lamb with salad and yogurt.

GREEN BEAN SALAD Boil, steam or microwave beans until just tender; drain. Place warm beans in medium bowl with remaining ingredients; toss gently to combine.

SPICED YOGURT Combine ingredients in small bowl.

SERVES 4
per serving 21.5g carbohydrate; 18.8g fat; 529 cal; 66.2g protein
tip Buy baby green beans if available.

minted lamb with baby beet and arugula salad

PREPARATION TIME 10 MINUTES (PLUS REFRIGERATION TIME)   COOKING TIME 35 MINUTES

¼ cup olive oil

2 cloves garlic, crushed in garlic press

½ cup chopped fresh mint

2 french-trimmed racks of lamb
   with 8 chops each

2-pound bunch baby beets

1 tablespoon olive oil, extra

¼ cup chopped fresh mint, extra

1 medium lemon

5½ cups (8 ounces) arugula

2 tablespoons olive oil

2 tablespoons raspberry vinegar

¼ cup shaved parmesan cheese

1   Combine oil, garlic and mint in large shallow casserole; add lamb, mix well. Cover lamb; refrigerate 3 hours or overnight.

2   Drain lamb; discard marinade. Place lamb on roasting rack or in disposable baking dish. Cook in covered grill, using indirect heat, following manufacturer's instructions, 25 minutes.

3   Meanwhile, cut beet stems 3 inches from top of beets; remove and discard roots. Wrap beets in foil, cook next to lamb on heated grill 10 minutes or until tender; remove from foil. Remove skin from beets.

4   Brush top of lamb with extra oil, sprinkle with extra mint; cook, covered, about 10 minutes or until cooked as desired. Remove from heat, cover; let stand 10 minutes.

5   Cut peel thinly from lemon, avoiding any white pith; cut peel into thin strips. Place arugula and beets in medium bowl, drizzle with combined oil and vinegar, sprinkle with lemon peel. Scatter parmesan over salad; serve with minted lamb.

SERVES 4
per serving 21.1g carbohydrate; 41g fat; 535 cal; 21.5g protein

herb-crusted lamb racks with butternut squash and leek

PREPARATION TIME 25 MINUTES   COOKING TIME 55 MINUTES

4 french-trimmed 3-chop racks
   of lamb (2 pounds)

¼ cup homemade white breadcrumbs

1 tablespoon finely chopped fresh rosemary

1 tablespoon finely chopped fresh
   flat-leaf parsley

2 teaspoons finely chopped fresh thyme

3 cloves garlic, crushed in garlic press

3 teaspoons bottled pesto

1¾ pounds butternut squash, chopped coarsely

vegetable-oil spray

1 teaspoon sea salt

2 medium leeks

2 teaspoons margarine

¼ cup chicken broth

¼ cup dry white wine

1   Preheat oven to moderately hot.

2   Remove any excess fat from lamb. Combine breadcrumbs, herbs, garlic and pesto in small bowl. Using hands, press breadcrumb mixture onto lamb racks, cover; refrigerate until required.

3   Place squash in large shallow casserole; spray with oil, sprinkle with sea salt. Roast, uncovered, in moderately hot oven 15 minutes.

4   Place lamb on top of the squash; roast, uncovered, in moderately hot oven 10 minutes. Reduce heat to slow; cook about 20 minutes or until squash is tender and lamb is cooked as desired.

5   Meanwhile, cut leeks into 4-inch lengths; slice thinly lengthwise. Melt margarine in large skillet; cook leek, stirring, until leek softens. Stir in broth and wine; bring to a boil. Reduce heat; simmer, uncovered, until liquid reduces by half.

6   Stand lamb 5 minutes before cutting racks into chops; serve chops with squash and leek.

SERVES 4
per serving 17.9g carbohydrate; 14.9g fat; 344 cal; 32g protein

olive-citrus lamb shanks

PREPARATION TIME 20 MINUTES   COOKING TIME 2 HOURS 15 MINUTES

4 lamb shanks (about 4 pounds)

1 tablespoon all-purpose flour

½ teaspoon cracked black pepper

2 tablespoons olive oil

1 large red onion

4 cloves garlic, crushed in garlic press

2 teaspoons sweet paprika

6 medium tomatoes, peeled, seeded, quartered

1 medium fennel bulb, sliced thinly

3 large carrots, chopped coarsely

2 tablespoons tomato paste

2 teaspoons sugar

1 cup dry red wine

½ cup water

1 beef bouillon cube

2 sprigs fresh rosemary

three 2-inch strips lemon peel

1 cinnamon stick

¾ cup pitted black olives

2 tablespoons fresh lemon juice

2 tablespoons chopped fresh mint

1 Toss lamb in combined flour and pepper. Heat oil in large skillet, cook lamb, in batches, until browned all over; drain on paper towels.

2 Cut onion in half lengthwise, slice into thick wedges. Cook onion, garlic and paprika in same skillet, stirring, until onion is just soft.

3 Return lamb to skillet; add tomato, fennel, carrot, paste, sugar, wine, the water, bouillon, rosemary, peel and cinnamon. Simmer, covered, 1½ hours, stirring occasionally. Stir in olives; simmer, uncovered, about 30 minutes, or until lamb shanks are tender. Just before serving, remove cinnamon and stir in juice and mint.

SERVES 4
per serving 30.3g carbohydrate; 34.6g fat; 729 cal; 62.9g protein

lamb chops with olive salsa, polenta and fennel

PREPARATION TIME 10 MINUTES   COOKING TIME 10 MINUTES

12 lamb rib chops (about 1½ pounds), trimmed

¾ cup water

1 cup chicken broth

½ cup instant polenta

⅓ cup finely grated parmesan cheese

½ cup heavy cream

2 tablespoons olive oil

1¼ pounds baby fennel, sliced thinly

4 ounces pitted black olives, chopped coarsely

2 tablespoons fresh lemon juice

1 clove garlic, crushed in garlic press

1 tablespoon coarsely chopped fresh flat-leaf parsley

1 Cook lamb on heated oiled grill or grill pan until browned both sides and cooked as desired.

2 Meanwhile, combine the water and broth in medium saucepan; bring to a boil. Stir in polenta gradually; cook, stirring, over low heat until mixture thickens. Stir in cheese and cream. Keep warm.

3 Heat half of the oil in medium skillet; cook fennel, stirring, until tender.

4 Combine remaining oil with olives, juice, garlic and parsley in small bowl. Serve lamb with olive salsa, polenta and fennel.

SERVES 4
per serving 24.7g carbohydrate; 30.8g fat; 490 cal; 28.8g protein

greek lamb salad

PREPARATION TIME 40 MINUTES (PLUS REFRIGERATION TIME)   COOKING TIME 30 MINUTES

Skordalia is a pungent Greek sauce or dip made with bread (or sometimes potato), garlic, lemon juice and olive oil. It can be served with almost any kind of dish – from grilled meats and poultry to fish and raw vegetables.

1¼-pound boneless leg of lamb,
    trimmed, butterflied

2 tablespoons olive oil

2 teaspoons finely grated lemon peel

1 teaspoon finely chopped
    fresh marjoram

1 clove garlic, crushed in garlic press

1 large green bell pepper, sliced thinly

1 small hothouse cucumber, diced into
    ¾-inch pieces

14 ounces pear tomatoes, halved

2 stalks celery, trimmed, sliced thinly

4 scallions, sliced thinly

2 small heads romaine lettuce or inner
    leaves of 2 large heads romaine
    lettuce, chopped coarsely

1 cup pitted kalamata olives

7 ounces feta, crumbled

SKORDALIA

2 slices stale white bread

2 cloves garlic, crushed in garlic press

2 tablespoons olive oil

2 teaspoons white wine vinegar

1 tablespoon fresh lemon juice

⅓ cup water

MARJORAM DRESSING

2 tablespoons olive oil

2 tablespoons white wine vinegar

1 tablespoon finely chopped
    fresh marjoram

pinch cayenne

1   Place lamb, oil, peel, marjoram and garlic in large bowl; toss to coat lamb. Cover; refrigerate 3 hours or overnight.

2   Cook lamb on a heated oiled grill or grill pan until browned on all sides and cooked as desired. Let stand 5 minutes; slice lamb thickly.

3   Meanwhile, make skordalia. Make marjoram dressing.

4   Place lamb in large bowl with remaining ingredients and marjoram dressing; toss gently to combine. Divide salad among serving plates; drizzle with skordalia.

SKORDALIA Discard crusts from bread, soak in small bowl of cold water; drain. Squeeze out excess water; blend or process bread and remaining ingredients until mixture is smooth.

MARJORAM DRESSING Combine ingredients in screw-top jar; shake well.

SERVES 4
per serving 23.9g carbohydrate; 45.9g fat; 700 cal; 47.6g protein

roast lamb with scallions, garlic and baby onions

PREPARATION TIME 40 MINUTES (PLUS REFRIGERATION TIME)
COOKING TIME 1 HOUR 15 MINUTES

12 scallions

1 clove garlic, crushed in

   garlic press

8 sprigs thyme, chopped coarsely

1 bay leaf

3 black peppercorns, crushed

1 boned leg of lamb (1¾ pounds)

⅓ cup extra virgin olive oil

20 whole garlic cloves, peeled

2 tablespoons balsamic vinegar

¾ cup pitted black olives

BABY ONIONS

1 tablespoon balsamic vinegar

2 tablespoons honey

1 tablespoon grainy mustard

2 tablespoons vegetable oil

14 ounces boiling onions, halved

1 Trim scallions to 4-inch lengths. Slice green end of each scallion, lengthwise, to halfway. Stand scallions, cut-end down, in small pitcher of cold water; refrigerate 1 hour or until scallions separate and curl slightly.

2 Preheat oven to slow.

3 Combine crushed garlic, thyme, bay leaf and peppercorns in small bowl. Place lamb on cutting board, cut-side up; cover with plastic wrap, pound with meat mallet to flatten to uniform thickness, then rub cut-side of lamb with garlic mixture.

4 Roll leg of lamb tightly; tie with kitchen string at 1-inch intervals. Place lamb in large deep roasting pan, brush with 1 tablespoon of the oil; roast, uncovered, in slow oven about 40 minutes.

5 Meanwhile, place whole garlic cloves in small casserole, sprinkle with 1 tablespoon of the oil; bake, uncovered, alongside lamb in slow oven, about 20 minutes.

6 Make baby onions.

7 Dry scallions with paper towel. Combine remaining oil and vinegar in small measuring cup. Place scallions, cut-end down, in vinegar mixture; reserve.

8 When lamb is cooked as desired and garlic just tender, remove from oven. Cover lamb with foil to keep warm. Increase oven temperature to moderately hot.

9 Add olives to garlic in small casserole; heat, uncovered, in moderately hot oven 5 minutes.

10 Cut lamb into eight rounds. Divide baby onions among serving plates; add lamb rounds, topped with garlic and olive mixture and scallions. Drizzle with remaining vinegar mixture.

BABY ONIONS Combine vinegar, honey and mustard in small saucepan; bring to a boil. Reduce heat; simmer, uncovered, about 5 minutes or until glaze thickens slightly. Heat oil in large skillet; cook onion, stirring, until soft. Brush frequently with glaze while cooking.

SERVES 4
per serving 24.8g carbohydrate; 44.9g fat; 684 cal; 46.3g protein

garlic and rosemary smoked lamb with parsnip and carrot ribbons

PREPARATION TIME 15 MINUTES (PLUS REFRIGERATION TIME)   COOKING TIME 50 MINUTES

2 pounds boneless leg of lamb

4 cloves garlic, halved

8 fresh rosemary sprigs

1 teaspoon red pepper flakes

1 tablespoon olive oil

2 large parsnips

2 large carrots

vegetable oil, for deep-frying

1 Place lamb in large bowl. Pierce lamb in eight places with sharp knife; push garlic halves and rosemary sprigs into cuts. Sprinkle lamb with pepper flakes; rub with oil. Cover lamb; refrigerate 3 hours or overnight.

2 Cook lamb, uncovered, on heated oiled grill until browned all over. Place drained smoking chips (see tip) in smoke box on grill next to lamb. Cook lamb in covered grill, using indirect heat, following manufacturer's instructions, for about 40 minutes or until cooked as desired.

3 Meanwhile, using a vegetable peeler, peel thin strips from parsnips and carrots. Heat oil in large deep skillet; deep-fry parsnip and carrot strips, separately, in batches, until browned and crisp. Drain on paper towels; serve immediately with lamb.

SERVES 4
per serving 12.6g carbohydrate; 51.1g fat; 708 cal; 50.8g protein
tip You need 8 ounces of smoking chips. Soak in large bowl of water for 2 hours.

lamb, bulgur and grilled zucchini salad

PREPARATION TIME 45 MINUTES (PLUS REFRIGERATION AND STANDING TIMES)   COOKING TIME 30 MINUTES

1¼-pound butterflied leg of lamb, trimmed

2 tablespoons olive oil

1 clove garlic, crushed in garlic press

1 tablespoon coarsely chopped fresh sage

2 tablespoons coarsely chopped fresh oregano

¾ cup bulgur

2 teaspoons finely grated lemon peel

¼ cup loosely packed fresh oregano leaves

2 medium yellow squash

2 medium green zucchini

8 ounces yellow pear tomatoes, halved

8 ounces cherry tomatoes, halved

1 cup firmly packed fresh flat-leaf parsley leaves

LEMON-GARLIC DRESSING

2 tablespoons fresh lemon juice

1 clove garlic, crushed in garlic press

¼ cup olive oil

1 Combine lamb, oil, garlic, sage and chopped oregano in large bowl, cover; refrigerate 3 hours or overnight.

2 Place bulgur in medium bowl; cover with cold water. Let stand 10 minutes; drain. Using hands, squeeze out as much excess water as possible. Spread bulgur in a thin, even layer on tray; let stand 15 minutes. Return bulgur to same bowl with peel and oregano leaves; toss gently to combine.

3 Meanwhile, make lemon-garlic dressing.

4 Cook lamb on heated oiled grill or grill pan until browned and cooked as desired. Cover; let stand 10 minutes. Slice lamb thickly.

5 Meanwhile, using sharp knife, V-slicer or mandoline, cut squash and zucchini into ribbons; cook, in batches, on same cleaned heated oiled grill pan until just tender. Combine squash and zucchini in medium bowl with tomatoes, parsley and half of the dressing.

6 Add remaining dressing to bulgur mixture; toss gently to combine. Divide bulgur mixture among serving plates; top with squash mixture then lamb.

LEMON-GARLIC DRESSING Combine ingredients in screw-top jar; shake well.

SERVES 4
per serving 14g carbohydrate; 30.8g fat; 528 cal; 48.2g protein
tips Drain away any juice from the meat platter before slicing the lamb. This helps prevent the bulgur from becoming soggy. This salad can be served warm or cold.

spicy pork with caramelized onions

PREPARATION TIME 20 MINUTES   COOKING TIME 30 MINUTES

1 tablespoon olive oil

2 large onions, chopped finely

1 small red bell pepper, chopped finely

4 slices prosciutto, chopped finely

four 8-ounce pork tenderloins

2 tablespoons olive oil, extra

1 teaspoon red pepper flakes

1 tablespoon sweet paprika

2 teaspoons ground cumin

2½ cups (5 ounces) mesclun

CARAMELIZED ONIONS

2 tablespoons olive oil

3 large onions, sliced thinly

¼ cup red wine vinegar

4 ounces guava paste, chopped coarsely

1 tablespoon coarsely chopped fresh cilantro

1 tablespoon light brown sugar

1 Heat oil in large skillet, add onion, pepper and prosciutto; cook, stirring, until onion is soft. Remove from skillet.

2 Slice tenderloins lengthwise down the center, almost all the way through. Open each tenderloin flat, pound gently with a meat mallet until an even thickness. Spoon the onion mixture along center of pork, roll up from long side; secure with toothpicks. Heat extra oil in skillet, add pepper flakes and spices; cook, stirring, until fragrant. Add pork, cook, uncovered, turning occasionally, about 20 minutes or until just tender.

3 Meanwhile, make caramelized onions. Serve with pork, top with mesclun.

CARAMELIZED ONIONS: Heat oil in large skillet; cook onion, stirring, about 15 minutes or until onion is very soft and a rich caramel color. Add remaining ingredients; cook, stirring, until guava paste and sugar are dissolved.

SERVES 4
per serving 17.8g carbohydrate; 29.8g fat; 586 cal; 61.6g protein

pork loin with wilted cabbage

PREPARATION TIME 15 MINUTES   COOKING TIME 35 MINUTES

You need a small head of savoy cabbage for this recipe.

1 tablespoon olive oil

1½ pounds boneless pork loin, sliced thickly

1 cup chicken broth

¾ cup port

¼ cup cranberry sauce

3 tablespoons butter

1½ pounds savoy cabbage, sliced thickly

1 teaspoon caraway seeds

1 Heat oil in large skillet; cook pork, in batches, until browned both sides. Cover to keep warm.

2 Place broth and port in same skillet; bring to a boil. Reduce heat; simmer, uncovered, until mixture reduces by half. Add cranberry sauce. Return pork to skillet; heat, uncovered, until cooked through.

3 Heat butter in separate large skillet; cook cabbage, stirring, until just wilted. Stir in caraway seeds.

4 Serve pork and sauce with cabbage.

SERVES 4
per serving 18.8g carbohydrate; 18.5g fat; 461 cal; 44.6g protein

pork, coconut, lime and tofu salad

PREPARATION TIME 40 MINUTES   COOKING TIME 15 MINUTES

You need about one and a quarter bunches of baby bok choy for this recipe.

2 pounds boneless pork loin

1 tablespoon vegetable oil

2 tablespoons fresh lime juice

1¼ pounds baby bok choy, quartered

1 large carrot

8 ounces fried tofu pieces

½ cup coarsely chopped fresh basil

½ cup coarsely chopped fresh cilantro

1 cup (3½ ounces) fresh bean sprouts

4 scallions, sliced thinly

¼ cup shredded unsweetened coconut

COCONUT DRESSING

2 tablespoons fresh lime juice

1 tablespoon fish sauce

1 tablespoon sweet chili sauce

1 red serrano chile, seeded, sliced thinly

¾ cup unsweetened coconut milk

1   Make coconut dressing.

2   Place pork, oil and juice in medium bowl; toss to coat pork. Cook pork on heated oiled grill or grill pan until browned and cooked as desired. Cover; let stand 5 minutes. Slice pork thinly.

3   Meanwhile, boil, steam or microwave bok choy until just wilted; drain.

4   Cut carrot into 3-inch pieces. Using sharp knife, mandoline or V-slicer, cut pieces lengthwise into thin slices; cut slices into matchstick-sized pieces.

5   Place pork, bok choy and carrot in large bowl with dressing and remaining ingredients; toss gently to combine.

COCONUT DRESSING   Combine ingredients in screw-top jar; shake well.

SERVES 4
per serving   13.2g carbohydrate; 29.7g fat; 582 cal; 65.3g protein

pork with beans and beer

PREPARATION TIME 20 MINUTES (PLUS STANDING TIME)   COOKING TIME 2 HOURS 20 MINUTES

We used a dish with a base measuring 10½ inches, so the pork was covered with liquid during cooking. Any small white dried bean can be used. You need about a quarter of a small head of savoy cabbage for this recipe.

½ cup dried white beans

2 cloves garlic, crushed in garlic press

½ teaspoon freshly ground black pepper

1 pound boneless pork shoulder

1 tablespoon olive oil

6 slices bacon, chopped finely

1 medium onion, sliced thinly

1 teaspoon caraway seeds

7 fluid ounces beer

¾ cup chicken broth

5 ounces savoy cabbage, shredded finely

1   Place beans in large bowl; cover completely with cold water. Cover; let stand overnight.

2   Rub combined garlic and pepper all over pork. Tie pork with kitchen string at 1-inch intervals to make an even shape. Heat oil in medium casserole. Cook pork, turning, until browned all over. Remove from dish. Cook bacon, onion and seeds in casserole, stirring, until onion is soft and bacon browned lightly.

3   Drain beans. Return pork to casserole. Add beer, beans and broth; simmer, covered, about 2 hours or until beans and pork are tender. Remove pork from casserole. Add cabbage; cook, stirring, until just wilted. Remove from heat. Slice pork; return to casserole.

SERVES 4
per serving   13.6g carbohydrate; 25.9g fat; 531 cal; 58.5g protein

pork with apple and leek

PREPARATION TIME 20 MINUTES   COOKING TIME 40 MINUTES

1¾ pounds boneless pork loin

¾ cup chicken broth

2 medium leeks, sliced thickly

1 clove garlic, crushed in garlic press

2 tablespoons light brown sugar

2 tablespoons red wine vinegar

2 medium granny smith apples

1 tablespoon butter

3 teaspoons light brown sugar, extra

10 ounces baby carrots, halved

8 medium patty-pan squash, quartered

1 bunch asparagus, coarsely chopped

1　Preheat oven to very hot. Place pork, in single layer, in large baking dish; bake, uncovered, in very hot oven about 25 minutes or until pork is browned and cooked as desired. Cover; let stand 5 minutes before slicing thickly.

2　Meanwhile, heat half of the broth in medium skillet; cook leek and garlic, stirring, until leek softens and browns slightly. Add sugar and vinegar; cook, stirring, about 5 minutes or until leek caramelizes. Add remaining broth; bring to a boil. Reduce heat; simmer, uncovered, about 5 minutes or until liquid reduces by half. Place leek mixture in medium bowl; cover to keep warm.

3　Peel, core and halve apples; cut into thick slices. Melt butter in same skillet; cook apple and extra sugar, stirring, until apple is browned and tender.

4　Boil, steam or microwave carrot, squash and asparagus, separately, until just tender; drain.

5　Serve pork, topped with caramelized apple and sweet and sour leek, on top of the mixed vegetables.

SERVES 4
per serving 24.9g carbohydrate; 7.4g fat; 360 cal; 48.6g protein
tip You can make the sweet and sour leek several hours ahead; reheat before serving.

pork vindaloo

PREPARATION TIME 15 MINUTES (PLUS REFRIGERATION TIME)   COOKING TIME 50 MINUTES

2 medium onions, chopped coarsely

5 cloves garlic, quartered

1 teaspoon ground cardamom

½ teaspoon ground clove

1 teaspoon ground cinnamon

2 teaspoons ground cumin

2 teaspoons ground turmeric

2 teaspoons cracked black pepper

2 teaspoons black mustard seeds

3 red serrano chiles, quartered

1 tablespoon grated fresh ginger

⅓ cup white vinegar

2 pounds pork tenderloin, trimmed

1 tablespoon vegetable oil

1 medium onion, sliced thinly

1 tablespoon tamarind nectar

2 medium tomatoes, chopped coarsely

1½ cups cooked basmati rice

1　Blend or process chopped onion, garlic, spices, chile, ginger and vinegar to a smooth paste.

2　Trim any excess fat from pork; cut into 1-inch pieces. Combine pork with a quarter of the curry paste in medium bowl; stir to coat pork all over. Cover; refrigerate 3 hours or overnight. Reserve remaining curry paste.

3　Heat oil in large saucepan; cook sliced onion, stirring, until just soft. Add reserved curry paste; cook, stirring, over low heat 5 minutes. Add pork; cook, stirring, about 5 minutes or until pork changes color. Stir in tamarind nectar and tomato; bring to a boil. Reduce heat; simmer, covered, about 40 minutes or until pork is tender and cooked through.

4　Serve curry on rice.

SERVES 4
per serving 24.6g carbohydrate; 11.8g fat; 449 cal; 59.5g protein
tip You need to cook ½ cup rice for this recipe.

pork and broccolini stir-fry

PREPARATION TIME 15 MINUTES   COOKING TIME 20 MINUTES

2 tablespoons peanut oil

**1 pound thin-sliced boneless pork chops,
     cut into narrow strips**

2 medium red onions, sliced thinly

2 medium red bell peppers, sliced thinly

1 clove garlic, crushed in garlic press

1 teaspoon grated fresh ginger

2 bunches broccolini

1 teaspoon cornstarch

2 tablespoons fresh lemon juice

¼ cup water

¼ cup sweet chili sauce

1 teaspoon fish sauce

1 tablespoon light soy sauce

1 teaspoon sesame oil

1 tablespoon coarsely chopped fresh cilantro

1 tablespoon coarsely chopped fresh mint

1 Heat half of the peanut oil in wok or large skillet; stir-fry pork, in batches, until browned.

2 Heat remaining peanut oil in wok; stir-fry onion, pepper, garlic and ginger until vegetables are just tender.

3 Meanwhile, trim and halve broccolini. Blend cornstarch with juice in small bowl; add the water, sauces and sesame oil. Stir mixture to combine.

4 Return pork to wok with broccolini and cornstarch mixture; stir-fry about 2 minutes or until mixture boils and thickens slightly. Remove from heat; stir in cilantro and mint just before serving.

SERVES 4
per serving 12.9g carbohydrate; 14.3g fat; 311 cal; 31.9g protein

warm pork and tangerine salad

PREPARATION TIME 20 MINUTES (PLUS REFRIGERATION TIME)   COOKING TIME 15 MINUTES

1 pound boneless pork loin, sliced thinly

2 cloves garlic, crushed in garlic press

1 teaspoon grated fresh ginger

1 tablespoon sweet chili sauce

2 teaspoons soy sauce

3 small tangerines, segmented

5 ounces sugarsnap peas

2 tablespoons peanut oil

12 ounces frisée

¼ cup firmly packed fresh cilantro leaves

1 small red onion, sliced thinly

CHILI DRESSING

1 tablespoon white wine vinegar

1 tablespoon peanut oil

1 tablespoon sweet chili sauce

2 teaspoons soy sauce

1 Combine pork, garlic, ginger and sauces in small bowl, cover; refrigerate 3 hours or overnight.

2 Halve tangerine segments lengthwise; discard seeds.

3 Make chili dressing.

4 Boil, steam or microwave peas until just tender; drain.

5 Heat oil in wok or large skillet; stir-fry pork, in batches, until browned and cooked as desired.

6 Gently toss pork, tangerine and peas in large bowl with frisée, cilantro, onion and dressing.

CHILI DRESSING Combine ingredients in screw-top jar; shake well.

SERVES 4
per serving 12.4g carbohydrate; 17.4g fat; 335 cal; 31.9g protein
tip Pork has a particular affinity with citrus flavors. If tangerines are out of season, you can substitute a drained can of mandarin orange segments. You will need one head of frisée for this recipe.

raan with baby beans and spiced yogurt (see page 243)

chicken tikka with raita

wilted chinese greens, pork and tofu with macadamia dressing

PREPARATION TIME 30 MINUTES   COOKING TIME 10 MINUTES

1 pound choy sum

12 ounces chinese broccoli

1 pound baby bok choy

4 scallions

2 tablespoons peanut oil

7 ounces fresh shiitake mushrooms, quartered

1 pound chinese barbecued pork, sliced thinly

10 ounces fresh tofu, cut into 1-inch cubes

1 cup (3½ ounces) mung bean sprouts

MACADAMIA DRESSING

½ cup macadamias, toasted, chopped finely

½ cup peanut oil

¼ cup mirin

1 tablespoon soy sauce

⅓ cup rice vinegar

1   Trim green vegetables; chop coarsely. Cut scallions into 2-inch lengths. Make macadamia dressing.

2   Heat half of the oil in wok or large skillet; stir-fry scallion and mushroom until mushroom is just tender. Add pork, stir-fry 1 minute; remove mixture from wok.

3   Heat remaining oil in same wok; stir-fry choy sum, broccoli and bok choy until just wilted.

4   Gently toss pork mixture, vegetable mixture, tofu and sprouts in large bowl with dressing.

MACADAMIA DRESSING   Combine ingredients in screw-top jar; shake well.

SERVES 4
per serving   19.2g carbohydrate; 75.9g fat; 938 cal; 44.6g protein
tip   Ready-to-eat barbecued pork can be purchased from specialty Asian food stores or Asian restaurants. You will need one bunch each of choy sum, gai larn (also known as chinese broccoli) and bok choy.

chicken tikka with raita

PREPARATION TIME 20 MINUTES   COOKING TIME 15 MINUTES

1¾ pounds skinless, boneless chicken thighs, sliced thickly

1 medium onion, cut into wedges

1 large red bell pepper, chopped coarsely

2 long green chiles, sliced thinly

⅓ cup tikka curry paste

10 fluid ounces light cream

8 ounces cherry tomatoes, halved

¾ cup loosely packed fresh cilantro leaves

2½ cups (8 ounces) fresh bean sprouts

RAITA

7 ounces unflavored low-fat yogurt

1 small hothouse cucumber, seeded, chopped finely

1 tablespoon finely chopped fresh mint

1   Cook chicken, in batches, in lightly oiled large deep skillet until browned all over.

2   Cook onion and pepper in same skillet, stirring, until onion softens. Add chile and paste; cook, stirring, until fragrant. Return chicken to skillet with cream; bring to a boil. Reduce heat; simmer, uncovered, about 5 minutes or until chicken is cooked through. Remove from heat; stir in tomato and cilantro.

3   Meanwhile, make raita.

4   Serve chicken on sprouts, topped with raita.

RAITA   Combine ingredients in small bowl.

SERVES 4
per serving   16g carbohydrate; 38.8g fat; 605 cal; 48.3g protein

barbecue-flavored chicken and onions with creamed spinach

PREPARATION TIME 15 MINUTES   COOKING TIME 20 MINUTES

We used crème fraîche in our creamed spinach, but light sour cream can be substituted.

2 tablespoons fresh lemon juice

2 tablespoons light brown sugar

1 tablespoon honey

1 clove garlic, crushed in garlic press

¼ cup soy sauce

2 medium onions

1 medium rotisserie chicken, quartered

1 tablespoon butter

2 bunches (2 pounds) spinach

1 tablespoon olive oil

1 large onion, chopped coarsely

5 slices prosciutto, chopped coarsely

2 cloves garlic, crushed in garlic press, extra

7 ounces crème fraîche

¼ cup chopped fresh chives

¼ teaspoon ground nutmeg

1   Preheat oven to moderately hot.

2   Combine juice, sugar, honey, garlic and sauce in small measuring cup. Cut onions into wedges. Place chicken and onion in shallow casserole; pour over half of the glaze mixture.

3   Bake, uncovered, in moderately hot oven about 20 minutes or until chicken is crisp and heated through, brushing with remaining glaze mixture frequently.

4   Meanwhile, heat butter in large deep saucepan; cook spinach, covered, stirring occasionally, until just wilted. Drain; gently squeeze spinach to remove excess liquid.

5   Heat oil in same saucepan; cook onion, prosciutto and garlic, stirring, until the prosciutto is browned and crisp. Add spinach and remaining ingredients; cook, stirring, until heated through.

SERVES 4
per serving 19.2g carbohydrate; 53.4g fat; 740 cal; 47.4g protein

mexican wings with cherry tomato salsa

PREPARATION TIME 10 MINUTES   COOKING TIME 25 MINUTES

8 large chicken wings (about 2 pounds)

2 packets taco seasoning mix

2 tablespoons ketchup

1 tablespoon vegetable oil

⅓ cup fresh lime juice

1 pound cherry tomatoes

2 medium avocados, chopped coarsely

10 ounces canned corn kernels, drained

1 medium red onion, chopped finely

¼ cup firmly packed fresh cilantro leaves

1   Preheat oven to moderately hot.

2   Combine chicken, seasoning, ketchup, oil and 1 tablespoon of the juice in large bowl; toss to coat chicken all over.

3   Place chicken, in single layer, in large shallow oiled casserole; roast, uncovered, in moderately hot oven about 25 minutes or until chicken is browned all over and cooked through.

4   Meanwhile, quarter tomatoes; combine in medium bowl with avocado, corn, onion, cilantro and remaining juice.

5   Serve salsa topped with wings.

SERVES 4
per serving 18.8g carbohydrate; 34.7g fat; 553 cal; 41.1g protein

chicken with bok choy and portobello mushrooms

PREPARATION TIME 10 MINUTES   COOKING TIME 25 MINUTES

2 tablespoons honey

⅓ cup soy sauce

2 tablespoons dry sherry

1 teaspoon five-spice powder

1½-inch piece fresh ginger, grated

1 tablespoon peanut oil

four 6-ounce skinless, boneless

   chicken breasts

4 large portobello mushrooms

1 pound baby bok choy, quartered lengthwise

1 cup chicken broth

2 teaspoons cornstarch

2 tablespoons water

1 Combine honey, sauce, sherry, five-spice, ginger and oil in small measuring cup. Place chicken in medium bowl with half of the honey mixture; toss to coat chicken in marinade. Cover; refrigerate 10 minutes.

2 Meanwhile, cook mushrooms and bok choy, in batches, on heated lightly oiled grill or grill pan until just tender; cover to keep warm.

3 Cook drained chicken on same lightly oiled grill or grill pan until browned both sides and cooked through. Cover; let stand 5 minutes, then slice thickly.

4 Meanwhile, combine remaining honey mixture in small saucepan with broth; bring to a boil. Stir in blended cornstarch and water; cook, stirring, until sauce boils and thickens slightly.

5 Divide mushrooms and bok choy among serving plates; top with chicken, drizzle with sauce.

SERVES 4
per serving 16.8g carbohydrate; 9.5g fat; 352 cal; 47.2g protein

good old-fashioned chicken salad

PREPARATION TIME 40 MINUTES   COOKING TIME 15 MINUTES

4 cups boiling water

4 cups chicken broth

1¾ pounds skinless, boneless

   chicken breasts

4 ounces fresh or frozen peas

½ cup mayonnaise

½ cup sour cream

2 tablespoons fresh lemon juice

4 stalks celery, trimmed, sliced thinly

1 medium white onion, chopped finely

3 dill pickles, sliced thinly

2 tablespoons finely chopped fresh

   flat-leaf parsley

1 tablespoon finely chopped fresh tarragon

1 large head boston lettuce, leaves separated

1 Bring the water and broth to a boil in large skillet; poach chicken, covered, about 10 minutes or until cooked through. Cool chicken in liquid 10 minutes; slice thinly. Discard liquid.

2 Meanwhile, boil, steam or microwave peas until just tender; drain.

3 Whisk mayonnaise, cream and juice in small bowl. Combine chicken with peas, celery, onion, pickle and herbs in large bowl; toss gently to combine. Place lettuce leaves on serving platter; top with chicken salad, drizzle with mayonnaise mixture.

SERVES 4
per serving 16.6g carbohydrate; 29.9g fat; 547 cal; 52.3g protein
tip Cooling chicken in liquid prevents the chicken from drying out.

mixed pea, lima bean and turkey salad with lemon-mustard dressing

PREPARATION TIME 1 HOUR 15 MINUTES   COOKING TIME 50 MINUTES

You need about 1½ pounds unshelled fresh peas and 1½ pounds unshelled fresh lima beans for this recipe.

3-pound single turkey breast

1 tablespoon olive oil

1 tablespoon sea salt

½ teaspoon freshly ground
   black pepper

2 teaspoons finely grated
   lemon peel

1½ cups shelled fresh
   lima beans

1¾ cups shelled fresh peas

10 ounces sugarsnap
   peas, trimmed

7 ounces snow peas, trimmed

¼ cup coarsely chopped fresh mint

3 cups (3 ounces)
   trimmed watercress

½ cup (2 ounces) baby
   arugula leaves

LEMON-MUSTARD DRESSING

2 tablespoons fresh lemon juice

2 teaspoons grainy mustard

2 tablespoons white wine vinegar

1 teaspoon sugar

⅓ cup olive oil

1   Preheat oven to moderately hot.

2   Tie turkey breast at 3-inch intervals with kitchen string. Place in oiled roasting pan; rub with combined oil, salt, pepper and peel. Cover with foil; bake in moderately hot oven 40 minutes. Remove foil; bake in moderately hot oven about 10 minutes or until cooked through.

3   Meanwhile, make lemon-mustard dressing.

4   Boil, steam or microwave beans until just tender; drain. Rinse under cold water; drain.

5   Meanwhile, boil, steam or microwave all peas, together, until just tender; drain. Rinse under cold water; drain.

6   Place beans and pea mixture in large bowl with mint, watercress, arugula and dressing; toss gently to combine. Slice turkey thinly; top salad with turkey to serve.

LEMON-MUSTARD DRESSING Combine ingredients in screw-top jar; shake well.

SERVES 4
per serving 24.7g carbohydrate; 37.1g fat; 859 cal; 105g protein
tip You can use a 10-ounce package of frozen baby lima beans for this recipe; after thawing, boil, steam or microwave until just tender.

chicken chermoulla

PREPARATION TIME 15 MINUTES   COOKING TIME 20 MINUTES

Chermoulla is a Moroccan blend of herbs and spices traditionally used for preserving
or seasoning meat and fish. We used our chermoulla blend here as a quick baste for
chicken, but you can also make it for use as a sauce or marinade.

1½ pounds skinless, boneless
   chicken thighs, sliced thinly

½ cup loosely packed, coarsely
   chopped fresh flat-leaf parsley

1 tablespoon finely grated
   lemon peel

1 tablespoon fresh lemon juice

2 teaspoons ground turmeric

1 teaspoon cayenne

1 tablespoon ground coriander

1 medium red onion, chopped finely

2 tablespoons olive oil

1 cup red lentils

2½ cups chicken broth

4½ cups (7 ounces) baby
   spinach leaves

½ cup loosely packed, coarsely
   chopped fresh cilantro

½ cup loosely packed, coarsely
   chopped fresh mint

1 tablespoon red wine vinegar

⅓ cup unflavored yogurt

1   Combine chicken, parsley, peel, juice, spices, onion and half of the
    oil in large bowl. Heat wok or large skillet; stir-fry chicken mixture,
    in batches, until chicken is browned and cooked through.

2   Meanwhile, combine lentils and broth in large saucepan. Bring to
    a boil; reduce heat. Simmer, uncovered, about 8 minutes or until
    just tender; drain. Place lentils in large bowl with spinach, cilantro,
    mint and combined vinegar and remaining oil; toss gently
    to combine.

3   Serve chicken mixture on lentil mixture; drizzle with yogurt.

SERVES 4
per serving 24g carbohydrate; 24.5g fat; 512 cal; 49.9g protein

chicken marengo

PREPARATION TIME 20 MINUTES   COOKING TIME 1 HOUR 30 MINUTES

2 tablespoons olive oil

6 skinless, boneless chicken thighs
   (about 2 pounds)

6 skinless chicken drumsticks
   (about 2 pounds)

8 ounces button mushrooms

8 ounces portobello mushrooms, sliced thickly

2 large onions, sliced thickly

2 cloves garlic, crushed in garlic press

2 tablespoons all-purpose flour

½ cup chicken broth

½ cup dry white wine

1 tablespoon tomato paste

14 ounces canned crushed tomatoes

1 tablespoon coarsely chopped fresh
   flat-leaf parsley

1   Preheat oven to moderate.

2   Heat oil in medium casserole; cook chicken, in batches, until browned. Drain on paper towels.

3   Drain all but 1 tablespoon of the fat from casserole; cook mushrooms, onion and garlic in casserole, stirring, until onion is soft.

4   Add blended flour and broth, wine, paste and undrained tomatoes; stir over heat until mixture boils and thickens. Return chicken to casserole; cook, covered, in moderate oven about 1 hour or until chicken is tender.

5   Serve sprinkled with parsley.

serves 4
per serving   12.5g carbohydrate; 31.5g fat; 620 cal; 66.8g protein

chicken cassoulet

PREPARATION TIME 25 MINUTES (PLUS STANDING TIME)   COOKING TIME 2 HOURS 30 MINUTES

½ cup dried white beans

8 ounces spicy italian sausages

4 ounces pork sausages

2 chicken thighs on the bone (about 1 pound)

2 chicken breasts on the bone (about 1 pound)

2 teaspoons vegetable oil

6 slices bacon, sliced thinly

1 clove garlic, crushed in garlic press

1 bay leaf

2 whole cloves

6 black peppercorns

1 stalk celery, trimmed, cut into 2-inch lengths

2 medium carrots, sliced thinly

3 boiling onions, halved

½ cup dry white wine

3 cups water

1 tablespoon tomato paste

1   Place beans in large bowl; cover well with cold water. Cover; let stand overnight.

2   Bring a large saucepan of water to a boil; add sausages and boil, uncovered, 2 minutes, drain.

3   Remove and discard skin from chicken; cut breasts in half.

4   Heat oil in 5-quart casserole; cook chicken and sausages, in batches, until browned. Drain on paper towels; slice sausages thickly.

5   Add bacon to casserole; cook, stirring, until crisp. Drain on paper towels.

6   Drain beans. Return chicken to casserole with beans, garlic, bay leaf, cloves, peppercorns, celery, carrot, onion, wine, the water and paste. Cook, covered, in moderate oven 1 hour 45 minutes.

7   Add sausage slices; cover. Cook about 15 minutes or until sausages are cooked. Serve sprinkled with bacon.

SERVES 4
per serving   17.2g carbohydrate; 37.4g fat; 664 cal; 63.7g protein

african-style gumbo

PREPARATION TIME 30 MINUTES   COOKING TIME 50 MINUTES

We used fresh okra in this recipe. However, if fresh is not available, substitute frozen okra.

2 tablespoons peanut oil

1¾ pounds skinless, boneless chicken thighs,
   chopped coarsely

2 large onions, sliced thickly

3 cloves garlic, crushed in garlic press

1 teaspoon chili sauce (such as sambal oelek
   or sriracha)

10 ounces okra

5 medium tomatoes, peeled, seeded,
   chopped finely

¼ cup tomato paste

⅓ cup crunchy peanut butter

1 large potato, chopped coarsely

2 cups water

1 Heat half of the oil in large saucepan; cook chicken, in batches, stirring, until browned. Drain on paper towels.

2 Heat remaining oil in saucepan; cook onion, garlic and chili sauce, stirring, until onion is soft.

3 Meanwhile, trim stems from okra and add to saucepan. Return chicken to saucepan. Add remaining ingredients; simmer, covered, about 30 minutes or until potato is tender.

SERVES 4
per serving 20.4g carbohydrate; 34.6g fat; 593 cal; 50.2g protein

green chicken curry

PREPARATION TIME 20 MINUTES   COOKING TIME 20 MINUTES

¼ cup green curry paste

2 cans (28 fluid ounces) unsweetened
   coconut milk

2 pounds skinless, boneless chicken thighs

2 tablespoons peanut oil

2 tablespoons fish sauce

2 tablespoons fresh lime juice

1 tablespoon light brown sugar

2 baby eggplants, quartered

1 small zucchini, cut into 2-inch pieces

⅓ cup loosely packed fresh basil leaves

¼ cup coarsely chopped fresh cilantro

1 tablespoon fresh cilantro leaves

1 long green chile, sliced thinly

2 scallions, sliced thinly

1 Place curry paste in large saucepan; stir over heat until fragrant. Add coconut milk; bring to a boil. Reduce heat; simmer, stirring, 5 minutes.

2 Meanwhile, quarter chicken pieces. Heat oil in large skillet; cook chicken, in batches, until just browned. Drain on paper towels.

3 Add chicken to curry mixture with sauce, juice, sugar and eggplant; simmer, covered, about 5 minutes or until eggplant is tender and chicken is cooked through. Add zucchini, basil and chopped cilantro; cook, stirring, until zucchini is just tender.

4 Place curry in serving bowl; sprinkle with cilantro leaves, chile and scallion.

SERVES 4
per serving 14.5g carbohydrate; 74.7g fat; 932 cal; 53.2g protein

roasted duck and stir-fried greens salad with hoisin dressing

PREPARATION TIME 25 MINUTES   COOKING TIME 20 MINUTES

For this recipe, we deboned a whole chinese barbecued duck, available from
Asian barbecue takeaway stores. You need one bunch of asian greens for this recipe.

2 pounds chinese barbecued duck

1 tablespoon sesame oil

6 scallions, sliced thinly

1 pound asian greens,
 chopped coarsely

1 pound watercress, trimmed,
 chopped coarsely

7 ounces fresh shiitake
 mushrooms, quartered

¼ cup water

7 ounces snow peas

2 cups (6 ounces) fresh
 bean sprouts

2 tablespoons toasted
 sesame seeds

HOISIN DRESSING

1-inch piece fresh ginger, grated

2 tablespoons soy sauce

1 tablespoon sesame oil

1 clove garlic, crushed in
 garlic press

1 red serrano chile, chopped finely

¼ cup hoisin sauce

1   Preheat oven to hot.

2   Quarter duck; discard all bones. Slice duck meat thickly, keeping
    skin intact; place in roasting pan. Roast, uncovered, in hot oven
    about 10 minutes or until skin crisps; discard duck fat.

3   Meanwhile, make hoisin dressing.

4   Heat oil in wok or large skillet; stir-fry scallion, asian greens and
    watercress, in batches, until greens just wilt. Remove. Place
    mushroom in same wok; stir-fry 2 minutes. Add the water; bring
    to a boil. Reduce heat; simmer, uncovered, about 2 minutes or
    until mushroom softens.

5   Place duck, vegetable mixture and mushroom in large bowl with
    dressing and snow peas; toss gently to combine. Divide sprouts
    among serving plates; top with salad, sprinkle with sesame seeds.

HOISIN DRESSING   Combine ingredients in small saucepan;
bring to a boil. Reduce heat; simmer, uncovered, 2 minutes.
Cool 10 minutes.

SERVES 4
per serving   18.5g carbohydrate; 46.4g fat; 615 cal; 32.8g protein

prosciutto and herb-butter cornish hens with rosemary roasted squash and potato

PREPARATION TIME **30 MINUTES**   COOKING TIME **1 HOUR**

1½ pounds butternut squash, chopped coarsely

2 medium russet potatoes, chopped coarsely

3 tablespoons olive oil

2 cloves garlic, sliced thinly

3 tablespoons butter, softened

2 cloves garlic, crushed in garlic press

2 tablespoons finely chopped fresh flat-leaf parsley

2 tablespoons finely chopped fresh basil

four 1-pound cornish hens

12 sprigs fresh thyme

4 slices prosciutto

2 tablespoons fresh lemon juice

2 tablespoons fresh rosemary

2 teaspoons coarse sea salt

1 Preheat oven to hot.

2 Combine squash, potato, 1 tablespoon of oil and sliced garlic in large casserole. Roast, uncovered, in hot oven about 1 hour or until vegetables are just tender and browned lightly.

3 Meanwhile, combine butter, crushed garlic, parsley and basil in small bowl.

4 Wash cornish hens under cold water; pat dry with paper towels. Loosen skin of one hen by sliding fingers between skin and meat at neck joint; push an eighth of the herb butter under skin on hen's breast and spread evenly. Place one thyme sprig inside cavity; tie legs together with kitchen string. Wrap prosciutto around hen; secure with toothpick. Repeat with remaining hens.

5 Place hens in large deep roasting pan; drizzle with combined remaining oil and juice. Roast, uncovered, next to vegetables, in hot oven 30 minutes. Brush hens with pan juices; top hens with remaining thyme sprigs. Roast, uncovered, in hot oven about 20 minutes more or until hens are browned and cooked through.

6 Serve hens topped with remaining herb butter, accompanied by vegetables sprinkled with rosemary and sea salt.

SERVES 4
per serving 24.6g carbohydrate; 63.5g fat; 910 cal; 61.2g protein

portuguese-style chicken thighs

PREPARATION TIME 15 MINUTES   COOKING TIME 15 MINUTES

2 teaspoons cracked black pepper

2 red serrano chiles, seeded, chopped finely

½ teaspoon hot paprika

1 clove garlic, crushed in garlic press

1 teaspoon finely grated orange peel

¼ cup fresh orange juice

2 tablespoons red wine vinegar

¼ cup olive oil

6 skinless, boneless chicken thighs

(about 1¼ pounds), halved

3 medium oranges, peeled, segmented

7 cups (10½ ounces) baby spinach leaves

1 medium red onion, sliced thinly

1 Combine pepper, chile, paprika, garlic, peel, juice, vinegar and oil in medium bowl. Reserve about a quarter of the spicy dressing in small measuring cup; use hands to rub remaining spicy dressing into chicken pieces.

2 Cook chicken, in batches, on heated oiled grill or grill pan until browned both sides and cooked through.

3 Toss orange segments, spinach and onion in large bowl. Divide among serving plates; top with chicken. Drizzle with reserved spicy dressing.

SERVES 4
per serving 13.8g carbohydrate; 26g fat; 426 cal; 34.6g protein

stir-fried chicken and asian greens

PREPARATION TIME 10 MINUTES   COOKING TIME 15 MINUTES

Any asian greens can be used in this recipe. Try it with bok choy, choy sum, or gai larn
(also known as chinese broccoli). You need one bunch of asian greens for this recipe.

2 tablespoons sesame oil

1 pound skinless, boneless chicken thighs,

sliced thinly

2 teaspoons chili sauce (such as

sambal oelek or sriracha)

6 ounces canned sliced

water chestnuts, drained

7 ounces canned bamboo

shoot strips, drained

1 large red bell pepper, sliced thinly

⅓ cup kecap manis

1 pound asian greens, chopped coarsely

2 cups (6 ounces) fresh bean sprouts

1 Heat half of the oil in wok or large skillet; stir-fry chicken, in batches, until browned lightly.

2 Heat remaining oil in same wok; stir-fry chili sauce, water chestnuts, bamboo shoots and pepper for 2 minutes.

3 Return chicken to wok with kecap manis and greens; stir-fry until greens are just wilted and chicken is cooked through. Remove from heat; stir in sprouts.

serves 4
per serving 21.7g carbohydrate; 18.9g fat; 374 cal; 29.6g protein

quail with pancetta and sun-dried tomatoes

PREPARATION TIME 5 MINUTES (PLUS REFRIGERATION TIME)   COOKING TIME 40 MINUTES

⅔ cup peanut oil

2 tablespoons balsamic vinegar

2 tablespoons fresh lemon juice

2 tablespoons soy sauce

1 tablespoon light brown sugar

6 quail

12 slices pancetta

2½ cups (5 ounces) mesclun

1 cup sun-dried tomatoes in oil, drained

1   Combine oil, vinegar, juice, sauce and sugar in large bowl; add quail, mix well. Cover quail; refrigerate 3 hours or overnight.

2   Drain quail over small saucepan; reserve marinade. Tie legs together with kitchen string; place quail in oiled disposable roasting pan. Cook in covered grill, using indirect heat, following manufacturer's instructions, for 30 minutes or until browned and tender.

3   Meanwhile, cook pancetta on heated oiled grill or in skillet until browned and crisp. Bring reserved marinade to a boil; simmer, whisking, 2 minutes. Divide mesclun among serving plates. Serve quail with tomatoes, pancetta, mesclun and hot marinade.

SERVES 4
per serving 21g carbohydrate; 58g fat; 799 cal; 48.2g protein

cornish hens with fennel and okra

PREPARATION TIME 15 MINUTES   COOKING TIME 1 HOUR

We used fresh okra in this recipe. However, if fresh is not available, substitute frozen okra.

¼ cup olive oil

12 boiling onions, halved

1½ pounds okra

2 cloves garlic, crushed in garlic press

2 teaspoons ground cumin

1 teaspoon ground cinnamon

½ teaspoon ground allspice

14 ounces canned crushed tomatoes

2 cups chicken broth

four 1-pound cornish hens

6 tablespoons butter

2 medium bulbs fennel, sliced

¼ cup Pernod

1   Heat half of the oil in large deep skillet; cook onion, stirring occasionally, about 15 minutes or until browned. Remove from skillet.

2   Heat remaining oil in same skillet; cook okra, garlic and spices, stirring, about 5 minutes or until okra is fragrant and lightly browned. Remove okra from skillet.

3   Return onion to skillet with undrained tomatoes and broth; simmer, uncovered, about 30 minutes, stirring occasionally. Return okra to skillet; cook about 10 minutes or until okra is tender and tomato mixture thickens.

4   Meanwhile, wash cornish hens under cold water; pat dry with paper towels. Cut hens along both sides of backbone; discard backbones. Place hens, breast-side up, on cutting board; press breastbone to flatten each hen.

5   Heat butter in large skillet; cook fennel, stirring, until soft and browned lightly, add Pernod. Transfer fennel mixture to disposable roasting pan.

6   Cook hens on heated oiled grill until browned both sides; place on top of fennel mixture in roasting pan. Cook hens in covered grill, using indirect heat, following manufacturer's instructions, about 30 minutes or until browned all over and tender.

7   Serve hens and fennel with okra and baby onions.

SERVES 4
per serving 21.8g carbohydrate; 66.3g fat; 943 cal; 57.9g protein

crisp-skinned soy chicken with spiced salt

PREPARATION TIME 25 MINUTES (PLUS STANDING AND REFRIGERATION TIMES)   COOKING TIME 40 MINUTES

16 cups water

1 cup light soy sauce

2-inch piece ginger, peeled,
    sliced thickly

2 cloves garlic, crushed in
    garlic press

2 teaspoons five-spice powder

3-pound whole chicken

20 yellow pattypan squash

14 ounces sugarsnap peas

2 teaspoons sesame oil

1 tablespoon soy sauce

1 tablespoon sesame seeds

vegetable oil, for deep-frying

SOY MARINADE

1 tablespoon honey

1 tablespoon light soy sauce

1 tablespoon dry sherry

½ teaspoon five-spice powder

½ teaspoon sesame oil

SPICED SALT

¼ cup coarse sea salt

½ teaspoon cracked black pepper

1 teaspoon five-spice powder

1   Combine the water, sauce, ginger, garlic and five-spice in large saucepan; bring to a boil. Boil, uncovered, 2 minutes. Add chicken; return to a boil. Reduce heat; simmer, uncovered, about 10 minutes, turning once during cooking. Remove from heat, cover; let stand 30 minutes. Remove chicken from broth; pat dry with paper towels.

2   Meanwhile, make soy marinade. Make spiced salt.

3   Using kitchen scissors, cut chicken in half through breastbone and along side of backbone; cut legs and wings from chicken halves. Place chicken pieces on tray; coat skin in soy marinade. Cover; refrigerate 2 hours.

4   Boil, steam or microwave squash and peas, separately, until tender; drain. Combine vegetables in serving bowl with sesame oil and soy. Sprinkle with seeds; cover to keep warm.

5   Heat vegetable oil in wok or large deep skillet; deep-fry chicken, in batches, until browned all over, drain on paper towel.

6   Cut chicken into serving-sized pieces; serve with vegetables and spiced salt.

SOY MARINADE   Combine ingredients in small bowl.

SPICED SALT   Heat small nonstick skillet; cook salt and pepper, stirring, 2 minutes. Add five-spice; cook, stirring, about 1 minute or until fragrant.

SERVES 4

per serving 15.8g carbohydrate; 51.6g fat; 788 cal; 64.9g protein

tips When deep-frying the chicken, have the pan no more than one-third filled with oil.

The broth can be used as a base for an Asian soup; refrigerate until cold, then discard the fat from the top before using.

spanish-style seared cornish hens with olive, tomato and chile salad

PREPARATION TIME 20 MINUTES   COOKING TIME 40 MINUTES

four 1-pound cornish hens

1 tablespoon cracked black pepper

1 tablespoon ground cumin

1 tablespoon fresh lemon juice

1 tablespoon olive oil

½ teaspoon chili powder

½ teaspoon hot paprika

¼ teaspoon cayenne

1 clove garlic, crushed in

garlic press

4 medium plum tomatoes, cut into

6 wedges each

1 small red onion, sliced thinly

into rounds

2½ cups pitted black olives

3 cups (3 ounces)

trimmed watercress

1 bunch arugula

1 red serrano chile, sliced thinly

1 tablespoon chopped

fresh cilantro

LEMON DRESSING

2 tablespoons olive oil

1 tablespoon fresh lemon juice

½ teaspoon chopped

fresh rosemary

1 teaspoon cumin seeds

2 cloves garlic, crushed in

garlic press

1   Wash cornish hens under cold water; pat dry with paper towels. Cut hens along both sides of backbone; discard backbones. For each hen, insert metal skewer through thigh and opposite wing. Repeat with other thigh and wing. Combine pepper, cumin, juice, oil, chili powder, paprika, cayenne and garlic in small bowl; mix to a smooth paste. Using hands, rub paste all over hens.

2   Cook in covered grill, using indirect heat, following manufacturer's instructions, 20 minutes. Turn hens; cook about 20 minutes or until browned all over and tender.

3   Meanwhile, make lemon dressing.

4   Combine tomato, onion, olives, watercress, arugula and chile in large bowl; mix well. Drizzle with dressing; top with cilantro. Serve with cornish hens.

LEMON DRESSING: Combine all ingredients in screw-top jar; shake well.

SERVES 4
per serving 15.7g carbohydrate; 50.9g fat; 738 cal; 54.5g protein

chicken with lentil salsa

PREPARATION TIME 10 MINUTES   COOKING TIME 20 MINUTES

The spices of North Africa give the chicken a flavor-packed jolt in this recipe.
And, as it can be served hot or cold, this is a good make-ahead dish.

2 teaspoons ground cumin

2 teaspoons ground coriander

1 teaspoon ground turmeric

12 chicken tenderloins
   (about 1 pound)

1 cup red lentils

1 clove garlic, crushed in
   garlic press

1 red serrano chile, seeded,
   chopped finely

1 hothouse cucumber, seeded,
   chopped finely

1 medium red bell pepper,
   chopped finely

¼ cup fresh lemon juice

2 teaspoons peanut oil

2 tablespoons coarsely chopped
   fresh cilantro

2 limes, cut into wedges

1   Combine spices in medium bowl with chicken; toss to coat chicken with spices.

2   Cook lentils in large saucepan of boiling water, uncovered, until just tender; drain. Rinse under cold water; drain. Place lentils in large bowl with garlic, chile, cucumber, pepper, juice, oil and fresh cilantro; toss gently.

3   Meanwhile, cook chicken on heated, lightly oiled grill or grill pan until browned both sides and cooked through. Add limes to pan; cook until browned both sides. Serve chicken with lentil salsa and lime wedges.

SERVES 4
per serving 21.9g carbohydrate; 8.7g fat; 424 cal; 64.1g protein
tip You could add 1 teaspoon of harissa to the salsa instead of the chile.

mexican chicken with pepper and barley salad

PREPARATION TIME 10 MINUTES   COOKING TIME 45 MINUTES

⅔ cup pearl barley

1⅓ cups chicken broth

2 cups water

1 packet (1¼ ounces) taco
    seasoning mix

four 6-ounce skinless, boneless
    chicken breasts

1 medium red bell pepper,
    chopped finely

1 medium green bell pepper,
    chopped finely

1 medium tomato, chopped finely

1 clove garlic, crushed in
    garlic press

¼ cup fresh lime juice

2 teaspoons olive oil

½ cup loosely packed fresh
    cilantro leaves

1   Preheat oven to moderately hot.

2   Combine barley with 1 cup of the broth and the water in medium
    saucepan; bring to a boil. Reduce heat; simmer, uncovered, until
    just tender; drain. Rinse under cold water; drain.

3   Blend seasoning with remaining broth in medium bowl, add
    chicken; toss to coat chicken in mixture. Drain chicken; reserve
    marinade. Place chicken, in single layer, on metal rack in large
    shallow casserole; bake, uncovered, in moderately hot oven
    about 30 minutes or until cooked through, brushing with reserved
    marinade halfway through cooking time. Cover; let stand
    5 minutes, then slice thickly.

4   Place barley in large bowl with remaining ingredients; toss gently
    to combine. Divide salad among serving plates; top with chicken.

SERVES 4
per serving 24.7g carbohydrate; 14.6g fat; 420 cal; 46.7g protein

pepper-roasted garlic and lemon chicken

PREPARATION TIME 35 MINUTES   COOKING TIME 1 HOUR 50 MINUTES

2 bulbs garlic

4-pound whole chicken

vegetable-oil spray

2 teaspoons salt

2 tablespoons cracked
   black pepper

1 medium lemon, cut into 8 wedges

1 cup water

3 medium globe artichokes

2 tablespoons fresh lemon juice

2 medium red onions, quartered

3 bulbs baby fennel,
   trimmed, halved

2 medium leeks, halved,
   cut into 4 pieces

8 ounces cherry tomatoes

⅓ cup dry white wine

¼ cup fresh lemon juice, extra

1   Preheat oven to moderately hot.

2   Separate cloves from garlic bulbs, leaving skin intact. Coat chicken with vegetable-oil spray. Press combined salt and pepper onto skin and inside cavity. Place garlic and lemon inside cavity; tie legs together with kitchen string. Place chicken, breast-side down, on small wire rack in large roasting pan, pour the water in pan; roast, uncovered, in moderately hot oven 50 minutes.

3   Meanwhile, discard outer leaves from artichokes; cut tips from remaining leaves. Trim then peel stalks. Quarter artichokes lengthwise; using teaspoon, remove chokes. Place artichokes in medium bowl, cover with water, add lemon juice.

4   Add drained artichokes, onion, fennel and leek to roasting pan, coat with vegetable-oil spray. Roast, uncovered, 40 minutes or until vegetables are just tender.

5   Add tomatoes, roast 20 minutes or until tomatoes soften and chicken is cooked through. Place chicken on serving dish and vegetables in large bowl; cover to keep warm.

6   Meanwhile, add wine and juice to same roasting pan with pan juices, bring to a boil. Boil mixture for 2 minutes, then strain over bowl containing vegetables; toss to combine.

7   Cut chicken into pieces; discard garlic and lemon from cavity. Divide vegetables among serving plates, top with chicken pieces.

SERVES 4
per serving 19.3g carbohydrate; 42.3g fat; 732 cal; 60.4g protein

pepper-roasted garlic and lemon chicken

neapolitan chicken parcels with arugula and red onion salad

neapolitan chicken parcels with arugula and red onion salad

PREPARATION TIME 20 MINUTES   COOKING TIME 30 MINUTES

four 6-ounce skinless, boneless
   chicken breasts

8 large fresh basil leaves

8 drained marinated artichoke
   heart quarters

⅔ cup sun-dried tomatoes

5 ounces bocconcini, sliced thinly

ARUGULA AND RED ONION SALAD

1 tablespoon olive oil

2 tablespoons fresh lemon juice

1 teaspoon dijon mustard

2 cups (3½ ounces) baby
   arugula leaves

½ cup loosely packed fresh
   basil leaves

1 medium red onion, sliced thinly

1 tablespoon drained
   baby capers, rinsed

1. Using meat mallet, gently pound one chicken breast between sheets of plastic wrap until ½-inch thick. Place two of the large basil leaves toward one side of chicken breast, then top with two artichoke quarters, a quarter of the tomatoes, and a quarter of the cheese. Fold chicken over filling; tie with kitchen string to enclose securely. Repeat process with remaining chicken breasts, basil, artichoke, tomatoes and cheese.

2. Cook chicken parcels, uncovered, on heated oiled grill or grill pan until browned both sides. Cover parcels with a flameproof lid or foil; cook about 15 minutes or until chicken is cooked through.

3. Meanwhile, make arugula and red onion salad. Serve chicken parcels with salad.

ARUGULA AND RED ONION SALAD Whisk oil, juice and mustard in large bowl. Add remaining ingredients to dressing; toss salad gently to combine.

SERVES 4
per serving 12.4g carbohydrate; 16.3g fat; 427 cal; 56.3g protein;

red fruit salad with lemon mascarpone

PREPARATION TIME 20 MINUTES

1¾ pounds seedless watermelon

8 ounces fresh strawberries,

   hulled, quartered

5 ounces fresh raspberries

2 medium plums, sliced thinly

2 teaspoons sugar

¼ cup kirsch

LEMON MASCARPONE

8 ounces mascarpone

2 teaspoons finely grated lemon peel

2 teaspoons sugar

1 tablespoon fresh lemon juice

1   Using melon baller, scoop watermelon into balls. Place watermelon in large serving bowl with strawberry, raspberries, plum, sugar and liqueur; toss gently to combine.

2   Make lemon mascarpone.

3   Serve fruit salad accompanied by lemon mascarpone.

LEMON MASCARPONE   Combine ingredients in small bowl.

SERVES 4
per serving   25g carbohydrate; 21.2g fat; 342 cal; 7.5g protein

guacamole

PREPARATION TIME 20 MINUTES

2 medium avocados

1 medium white onion,

   chopped finely

2 small tomatoes, chopped finely

1 tablespoon fresh lime juice

2 tablespoons coarsely chopped

   fresh cilantro

7 ounces corn chips

1   Using a fork, mash avocados in medium bowl until almost smooth. Add onion, tomato, juice and cilantro; mix well.

2   Serve with corn chips.

SERVES 6
per serving   19.3g carbohydrate; 22.9g fat; 300 cal; 4.2g protein

tahini dip with pita

PREPARATION TIME 10 MINUTES

Tahini, a paste made from sesame seeds, is available from selected supermarkets and gourmet food shops.

¾ cup tahini

2 cloves garlic, crushed in
   garlic press

¼ cup fresh lemon juice

¼ cup water

¼ teaspoon ground cumin

1 tablespoon finely chopped fresh
   flat-leaf parsley

3 pitas, cut into 8 wedges each

1   Combine tahini and garlic in small bowl.

2   Gradually beat in juice, water, cumin and parsley, beating well until mixture thickens. Warm pita wedges according to manufacturer's instructions. Serve with dip.

SERVES 6
per serving 20.9g carbohydrate; 19.2g fat; 295 cal; 9.9g protein

eggplant dip

PREPARATION TIME 10 MINUTES (PLUS REFRIGERATION TIME)   COOKING TIME 1 HOUR (PLUS STANDING TIME)

1 large eggplant

2 tablespoons pine nuts, toasted

1 medium onion, chopped finely

1 cup packaged breadcrumbs

2 tablespoons unflavored yogurt

3 cloves garlic, crushed in
   garlic press

½ cup finely chopped fresh
   flat-leaf parsley

1 tablespoon cider vinegar

1½ tablespoons fresh lemon juice

½ cup olive oil

1   Preheat oven to hot. Pierce eggplant all over with fork or skewer; place whole eggplant on oiled baking sheet. Bake, uncovered, in hot oven about 1 hour or until soft. Let stand 15 minutes. Peel eggplant, discard skin; chop flesh coarsely.

2   Blend or process eggplant with remaining ingredients until smooth, cover; refrigerate 3 hours or overnight. Serve with assorted crudités.

SERVES 6
per serving 14.4g carbohydrate; 23.4g fat; 285 cal; 4.5g protein

sweet potato and celeriac chips

PREPARATION TIME 15 MINUTES   COOKING TIME 15 MINUTES

vegetable oil, for deep-frying

1 large sweet potato, sliced thinly

2 pounds celeriac (celery root), trimmed,
**   sliced thinly**

1   Heat oil in wok or large saucepan. Deep-fry sweet potato and celeriac, in batches, until browned and crisp; drain on paper towel.

SERVES 4
per serving   25g carbohydrate; 17.2g fat; 274 cal; 5.2g protein

pineapple and orange frappé

PREPARATION TIME 10 MINUTES

1 medium pineapple, chopped coarsely

½ cup fresh orange juice

3 cups crushed ice

1 tablespoon finely grated orange peel

1   Blend or process pineapple and juice until smooth.

2   Pour into large pitcher with crushed ice and peel. Stir to combine then serve immediately.

SERVES 4
per serving   13.1 carbohydrate; 0.2g fat; 62 cal; 1.6g protein

tuna and tomato pizzas

PREPARATION TIME 10 MINUTES   COOKING TIME 5 MINUTES

2 teaspoons drained capers, chopped finely

1 teaspoon finely chopped fresh dill

1 teaspoon olive oil

1 tablespoon fresh lemon juice

2 multi-grain english muffins

1 medium tomato, seeded, sliced thinly

2 scallions, sliced thinly

3 ounces canned tuna in
**   spring water, drained**

1   Combine capers, dill, oil and juice in small bowl.

2   Halve muffins. Toast both sides.

3   Divide combined tomato and scallion among the four muffin halves; top with tuna. Drizzle with caper mixture.

SERVES 4
per serving   12.8g carbohydrate; 2.1g fat; 104 cal; 8.1g protein

zucchini and eggplant "little shoes"

PREPARATION TIME 15 MINUTES   COOKING TIME 1 HOUR

3 medium green zucchini

3 baby eggplants

1 tablespoon olive oil

1 small onion, chopped finely

2 cloves garlic, crushed in

    garlic press

7 ounces lean ground beef

7 ounces canned crushed

    tomatoes, undrained

2 tablespoons tomato paste

½ cup beef broth

¼ cup short-grain white rice

2 tablespoons finely chopped fresh

    flat-leaf parsley

¼ cup finely grated

    parmesan cheese

SAUCE

2 tablespoons butter

1½ tablespoons all-purpose flour

1 cup milk

1 egg, beaten lightly

pinch ground nutmeg

1   Halve zucchini and eggplants lengthwise, scoop out pulp with spoon, leaving thin shells; chop pulp finely.

2   Heat oil in large skillet; cook onion and garlic, stirring, until onion is soft. Add beef; cook, stirring, until browned. Add chopped pulp, tomatoes, tomato paste and broth. Bring to a boil, add rice; simmer, uncovered, about 15 minutes or until rice is tender and mixture is thick. Stir in parsley.

3   Meanwhile, make sauce.

4   Preheat oven to moderate. Place zucchini and eggplant shells in baking dish, fill with beef mixture. Spoon sauce over beef mixture, sprinkle with cheese. Bake, uncovered, in moderate oven about 35 minutes or until vegetables are tender and tops are browned lightly.

SAUCE   Melt butter in small saucepan, add flour; cook, stirring, until mixture thickens and bubbles. Gradually stir in milk; stir until sauce boils and thickens. Cool, stir in egg and nutmeg.

SERVES 4

per serving   21.7g carbohydrate; 19.8g fat; 330 cal; 16.9g protein

salmon sashimi rolls
with lemon dipping sauce

PREPARATION TIME 25 MINUTES   COOKING TIME 5 MINUTES

Lemon dipping sauce can be made a day ahead. Cover; refrigerate until required.

7 ounces sashimi salmon

¼ medium red bell pepper

½ hothouse cucumber

1 scallion, trimmed

LEMON DIPPING SAUCE

½ cup rice vinegar

¼ cup sugar

2 teaspoons light soy sauce

**½ teaspoon finely grated
    lemon peel**

1 Using sharp knife, cut salmon into paper-thin slices
   (you need 16 slices).

2 Remove and discard seeds and membranes from pepper; halve
   cucumber lengthwise, scoop out seeds. Halve scallion lengthwise.
   Slice pepper, cucumber and scallion into 3-inch-long pieces.

3 Lay salmon slices on board in single layer; divide pepper,
   cucumber and scallion among salmon slices, mounding at one
   of the narrow edges. Roll slices around filling.

4 Meanwhile, make lemon dipping sauce.

5 Serve sashimi rolls with lemon dipping sauce.

   LEMON DIPPING SAUCE Heat vinegar, sugar and sauce in
   small saucepan, stirring, until sugar dissolves. Remove from
   heat, add peel; let stand 10 minutes. Strain sauce into serving
   bowl; discard peel.

   SERVES 4
   per serving 14.6g carbohydrate; 1.9g fat; 119 cal; 10.1g protein

chorizo cheese puffs

PREPARATION TIME **15 MINUTES**   COOKING TIME **10 MINUTES**

Chorizo is a sausage made traditionally of coarsely ground pork and seasoned with garlic and chiles. If you cannot find fresh chorizo, substitute with any spicy sausage.

½ cup self-rising all-purpose flour

¼ cup water

1 egg, beaten lightly

1 chorizo sausage (about
6 ounces), chopped finely

½ small red bell pepper,
chopped finely

¼ cup finely grated
parmesan cheese

2 cloves garlic, crushed in
garlic press

2 tablespoons finely chopped
fresh chives

1 teaspoon ground cumin

vegetable oil, for deep-frying

1   Sift flour into medium bowl, stir in the water, egg, sausage, pepper, cheese, garlic, chives and cumin.

2   Heat oil in large skillet, drop tablespoonfuls of mixture into hot oil; cook until browned, drain on paper towel.

SERVES 4
per serving 15.4g carbohydrate; 18.9g fat; 274 cal; 10.9g protein

ham and tomato pizzas

PREPARATION TIME 10 MINUTES   COOKING TIME 10 MINUTES

2 multi-grain english muffins

1 tablespoon grainy mustard

1 medium tomato, sliced thinly

4 ounces shaved deli ham

**1 tablespoon coarsely chopped
    fresh basil**

¼ small red onion, sliced thinly

**½ cup coarsely grated low-fat
    mozzarella cheese**

1 Preheat oven to moderate. Halve muffins. Toast both sides.

2 Spread mustard on muffins; divide remaining ingredients among four muffin halves, finishing with cheese. Warm in moderate oven 5 minutes. Finish under hot broiler until cheese browns.

SERVES 4
per serving 12.6g carbohydrate; 4.7g fat; 141 cal; 11.9g protein

chicken tikka drumettes

PREPARATION TIME 10 MINUTES   COOKING TIME 25 MINUTES

12 chicken wing drumettes

⅓ cup tikka masala paste

½ cup unflavored yogurt

16 small pappadams

¼ cup coarsely chopped fresh cilantro

1 Preheat oven to moderately hot.

2 Place chicken in large bowl with combined paste and 2 tablespoons of the yogurt; toss to coat chicken in paste mixture. Place chicken, in single layer, on wire rack in large casserole. Roast, uncovered, in moderately hot oven about 20 minutes or until chicken is browned and cooked through.

3 Place three pappadams around edge of microwave oven turntable. Cook on HIGH (100%) about 30 seconds or until puffed. Repeat with remaining pappadams.

4 Combine cilantro and remaining yogurt in small bowl. Serve chicken drizzled with yogurt mixture; accompany with pappadams.

SERVES 4
per serving 20.3g carbohydrate; 26.5g fat; 473 cal; 38g protein

lime and soy wings

PREPARATION TIME 20 MINUTES (PLUS REFRIGERATION TIME)   COOKING TIME 25 MINUTES

8 small chicken wings

   (about 1¼ pounds)

¼ cup lime marmalade, warmed

¼ cup light soy sauce

2 tablespoons dry white wine

1 clove garlic, crushed in

   garlic press

¼ cup barbecue sauce

1 tablespoon fresh lime juice

1 Cut wings into three pieces at joints; discard tips.

2 Combine marmalade, soy sauce, wine and garlic in large bowl. Add chicken; toss to coat chicken all over. Cover; refrigerate 3 hours or overnight.

3 Cook drained chicken, in batches, on heated oiled grill or grill pan, brushing both sides occasionally with barbecue sauce, about 25 minutes or until chicken is cooked through.

4 Serve hot, drizzled with lime juice.

SERVES 4
per serving 20.7g carbohydrate; 5.5g fat; 235 cal; 24.5g protein

Maintaining Weight (no more than 43g carbs per serving)

stewed rhubarb and yogurt cups

PREPARATION TIME 15 MINUTES   COOKING TIME 10 MINUTES (PLUS COOLING TIME)

You will need about two bunches of rhubarb for this recipe.

1 tablespoon butter

7 cups coarsely chopped rhubarb

**⅓ cup firmly packed light
  brown sugar**

2 tablespoons fresh orange juice

2 cups vanilla yogurt

⅔ cup toasted muesli cereal

1 Melt butter in large saucepan; cook rhubarb, sugar and juice, stirring, until sugar dissolves and rhubarb is tender. Let cool.

2 Divide half of the rhubarb mixture evenly among four 10-ounce glasses. Top each glass with ¼ cup of yogurt. Repeat layering with remaining rhubarb mixture and yogurt.

3 Top each glass with 2 tablespoons muesli.

SERVES 4
per serving 40.9g carbohydrate; 10.8g fat; 320 cal; 12.2g protein

wholegrain date loaf

PREPARATION TIME 20 MINUTES   COOKING TIME 1 HOUR

1 cup pitted dates, halved

2 tablespoons boiling water

½ teaspoon baking soda

4 tablespoons margarine

2 teaspoons finely grated lemon peel

**¾ cup firmly packed light
  brown sugar**

7 ounces low-fat cottage cheese

2 eggs

2 cups whole-wheat flour

1 tablespoon baking powder

¼ teaspoon salt

2 tablespoons wheat germ

1 Preheat oven to moderately slow. Grease 9- x 5- x 3-inch loaf pan; line base and two long sides with parchment or wax paper, extending paper 2 inches above edges of pan.

2 Combine dates, the water and baking soda in small bowl, cover; let stand 5 minutes.

3 Using electric mixer, beat margarine, peel and sugar in small bowl until light and fluffy. Add cheese; beat until smooth. Add eggs, one at a time; beat until combined.

4 Stir in flour, baking powder, salt, wheat germ and date mixture; pour into prepared pan.

5 Bake, uncovered, in moderately slow oven about 1 hour. Let stand 10 minutes; turn onto wire rack to cool.

SERVES 14
per serving 30.6g carbohydrate; 3.9g fat; 182 cal; 6.7g protein

grilled mango and ricotta

PREPARATION TIME 10 MINUTES   COOKING TIME 5 MINUTES

1 cup low-fat ricotta cheese

¾ cup low-fat tropical fruit yogurt

3 small mangoes

1　Whisk cheese and yogurt together in medium bowl until mixture is smooth.

2　Slice flesh from mangoes against flat side of pit; remove skin, cut each piece in half.

3　Cook mango on heated oiled grill or grill pan until browned both sides.

4　Top mango with cheese mixture.

SERVES 4
per serving 27.9g carbohydrate; 4.7g fat; 194 cal; 9.5g protein
tips If tropical fruit yogurt is unavailable, you could substitute any fruity yogurt. If mangoes are unavailable, you could substitute fresh pineapple.

pineapple, honeydew and lychee fruit salad

PREPARATION TIME 25 MINUTES (PLUS REFRIGERATION TIME)   COOKING TIME 15 MINUTES

1½ cups water

1 tablespoon light brown sugar

2 star anise

3 tablespoons fresh lime juice

1 small pineapple, chopped coarsely

1 small honeydew melon,
**　chopped coarsely**

20 fresh lychees, pitted

7 ounces seedless red grapes

½ cup loosely packed fresh mint
**　leaves, torn**

1　Stir the water and sugar in small saucepan over low heat until sugar dissolves. Add star anise; bring to a boil then simmer, uncovered, without stirring, 10 minutes. Remove from heat, stir in juice; refrigerate 3 hours or overnight. Strain syrup into medium measuring cup, discard star anise.

2　Just before serving, place fruit and mint in large bowl with syrup; toss gently to combine.

SERVES 4
per serving 39.7g carbohydrate; 0.8g fat; 180 cal; 3.7g protein
tip Star anise is a star-shaped dried pod whose seeds have an astringent aniseed flavor. It can be found at Asian markets and some supermarkets. If you cannot find fresh lychees, substitute canned lychees, drained.

corned beef hash with poached eggs

PREPARATION TIME 10 MINUTES   COOKING TIME 10 MINUTES

1 medium onion, chopped finely

1 large sweet potato, shredded

1 pound cooked corned beef,
  shredded

2 tablespoons finely chopped fresh
  flat-leaf parsley

2 tablespoons all-purpose flour

2 eggs, beaten lightly

1 tablespoon vegetable oil

8 eggs, extra

1   Combine onion, sweet potato, beef, parsley, flour and egg in large bowl; mix well.

2   Divide hash mixture into four portions; flatten to form patties.

3   Heat oil in large heavy-bottomed skillet; cook patties, uncovered, until browned both sides and sweet potato is tender.

4   Half-fill a shallow skillet with water; bring to a boil. One at a time, break eggs into cup, then slide into skillet. When all eggs are in skillet, allow water to return to a boil. Cover skillet, turn off heat; let stand about 4 minutes or until a light film of egg white sets over yolks. One at a time, remove eggs, using spatula, and place on paper towel-lined saucer to blot up poaching liquid.

5   Serve each hash patty topped with two poached eggs; top with shredded basil, if desired.

SERVES 4
per serving 20.6g carbohydrate; 23.4g fat; 446 cal; 38.6g protein

navy beans, bacon and maple syrup with fried eggs

PREPARATION TIME 10 MINUTES (PLUS STANDING TIME)   COOKING TIME 2 HOURS

1 cup dried haricot beans

5 slices bacon, chopped coarsely

1 medium brown onion,
   chopped finely

1 clove garlic, crushed

1 tablespoon tomato paste

14 ounces canned
   crushed tomatoes

1½ cups water

1 tablespoon worcestershire sauce

2 teaspoons dijon mustard

1 tablespoon maple syrup

4 eggs

1   Place beans in medium bowl, cover with water; let stand overnight, drain.

2   Cook bacon, onion and garlic in large saucepan, stirring, until onion softens. Add drained beans, paste, tomato, the water, sauce and mustard; bring to a boil. Reduce heat; simmer, covered, about 1½ hours. Then simmer, uncovered, for a further 15 minutes or until beans are soft. Add maple syrup to beans.

3   Fry eggs, uncovered, in heated, lightly oiled skillet until cooked as desired. Serve beans with eggs.

SERVES 4
per serving 30.7g carbohydrate; 10.9g fat; 307 cal; 23.4g protein
tip Bean mixture can be cooked the day before and reheated.

french fruit toast with maple yogurt

PREPARATION TIME 5 MINUTES   COOKING TIME 10 MINUTES

1 egg white

⅓ cup whole milk

6 slices fruit and grain bread

6 ounces low-fat vanilla yogurt

2 teaspoons maple syrup

1   Whisk egg white and milk in large bowl until combined.

2   Cut bread in half diagonally. Heat oiled large skillet; dip each piece of bread into milk mixture. Cook, in batches, until browned lightly both sides.

3   To serve, place three pieces of toast on each plate, top with combined yogurt and syrup.

SERVES 4
per serving   42.5g carbohydrate; 4.1g fat; 240 cal; 9g protein
tip   If fruit and grain bread is unavailable, you could substitute raisin bread.

peach smoothie

PREPARATION TIME 10 MINUTES

2 cups nonfat soy milk

2 medium bananas, chopped coarsely

4 medium peaches, chopped coarsely

½ teaspoon ground cinnamon

1   Blend or process ingredients, in batches, until smooth.

SERVES 4
per serving   29g carbohydrate; 0.8g fat; 150 cal; 6.8g protein

bircher muesli

PREPARATION TIME **10 MINUTES (PLUS REFRIGERATION TIME)**

1 cup old-fashioned rolled oats

2⅔ cups low-fat unflavored yogurt

2 small apples, grated coarsely

1 tablespoon honey

¼ teaspoon ground cinnamon

1 tablespoon coarsely chopped
   toasted pecans

8 ounces fresh
   strawberries, quartered

1 Combine oats, yogurt, apple, honey, cinnamon and nuts in medium bowl. Cover; refrigerate overnight.

2 Just before serving, stir strawberries into muesli.

SERVES 4
per serving 34.9g carbohydrate; 4.6g fat; 231 cal; 11.2g protein
tips Any berries can be substituted for strawberries.
For a thinner mixture, serve with skim milk.

strawberry smoothie

PREPARATION TIME **10 MINUTES**

8 ounces low-fat strawberry
   frozen yogurt

8 ounces fresh strawberries

4 cups nonfat milk

1 Soften yogurt slightly; cut into pieces. Hull strawberries; cut each in half.

2 Blend or process ingredients, in batches, until smooth.

SERVES 4
per serving 28.3g carbohydrate; 1.4g fat; 177 cal; 13.7g protein

spiced plums with yogurt

PREPARATION TIME 10 MINUTES   COOKING TIME 15 MINUTES (PLUS COOLING TIME)

4 cups water

½ cup fresh orange juice

⅓ cup sugar

2-inch piece orange peel

2 star anise

4 cloves

2 teaspoon ground allspice

1 cinnamon stick

1 vanilla bean, split lengthwise

8 plums, unpeeled

1⅓ cups unflavored yogurt

1   Place the water, juice, sugar, peel and spices in medium saucepan. Scrape vanilla seeds into saucepan then add pod; cook mixture, stirring, until sugar dissolves.

2   Add plums to saucepan, poach, uncovered, over low heat about 10 minutes or until just tender. Using slotted spoon, place two plums in each of four serving dishes (reserve 3 tablespoons of the poaching liquid). Cool plums 20 minutes.

3   Combine yogurt and reserved poaching liquid in small bowl; serve with plums.

SERVES 4
per serving   39.1g carbohydrate; 3.4g fat; 217 cal; 57g protein
tip   Star anise is a star-shaped dried pod whose seeds have an astringent aniseed flavor. It can be found at Asian markets and some supermarkets.

spiced plums with yogurt

tropical fruit salad

tropical fruit salad

PREPARATION TIME 10 MINUTES   COOKING TIME 25 MINUTES (PLUS REFRIGERATION TIME)

2 cups water

¼ teaspoon cardamom seeds

1½-inch piece ginger, quartered

1 teaspoon grated lemon peel

1 tablespoon fresh lemon juice

1 tablespoon fresh lime juice

1 vanilla bean, split lengthwise

½ medium cantaloupe,
    chopped coarsely

1 small papaya, chopped coarsely

3 medium kiwi fruit,
    sliced thickly

1 medium mango,
    chopped coarsely

½ cup frozen concentrated
    passionfruit juice
    cocktail, thawed

1   Place the water, cardamom, ginger, peel and juices into medium
    skillet. Scrape vanilla seeds into skillet, then add pod.

2   Bring to a boil then reduce heat; simmer, uncovered, 20 minutes.
    Strain into medium measuring cup; cool 10 minutes. Refrigerate,
    covered, until liquid is cold.

3   Just before serving, place liquid and remaining ingredients in
    large bowl; toss gently to combine.

SERVES 4
per serving 30.6g carbohydrate; 0.6g fat; 145 cal; 3.4g protein

fresh corn and zucchini chunky salad

PREPARATION TIME 10 MINUTES   COOKING TIME 10 MINUTES

2 fresh ears corn, shucked

4 baby zucchini, halved lengthwise

2 large avocados, chopped coarsely

7 ounces pear tomatoes, halved

1 medium red onion, halved,
sliced thickly

¼ cup coarsely chopped
fresh cilantro

1 tablespoon sweet chili sauce

⅓ cup fresh lime juice

2 red serrano chiles, seeded,
sliced thinly

1 Cook corn and zucchini on heated oiled grill or grill pan until browned lightly and tender. Using a sharp knife, remove corn kernels from cobs.

2 Combine corn and zucchini in large serving bowl with avocado, tomato, onion and cilantro.

3 Place remaining ingredients in screw-top jar; shake well. Drizzle dressing over salad; toss gently to combine.

SERVES 4
per serving 29.8g carbohydrate; 35.3g fat; 482 cal; 11.1g protein
tip You can substitute cherry tomatoes if you cannot obtain the pear variety.

roasted ratatouille with rye toast

PREPARATION TIME 15 MINUTES   COOKING TIME 20 MINUTES

5 baby eggplants, chopped coarsely

4 small green zucchini,
chopped coarsely

4 ounces button mushrooms,
chopped coarsely

8 ounces cherry tomatoes, halved

1 small leek, chopped coarsely

2 cloves garlic, crushed in
garlic press

1 tablespoon olive oil

½ cup coarsely chopped fresh basil

1 tablespoon finely chopped
fresh oregano

2 tablespoons balsamic vinegar

4 thick slices dark rye bread, toasted

1 Preheat oven to hot.

2 Combine eggplant, zucchini, mushroom, tomato, leek, garlic and oil in large shallow casserole; roast, uncovered, in hot oven, stirring occasionally, about 20 minutes or until vegetables are tender.

3 Stir basil, oregano and vinegar into ratatouille. Serve warm on rye bread.

SERVES 4
per serving 25.2g carbohydrate; 6.3g fat; 189 cal; 7.2g protein

tofu burgers with barbecue sauce

PREPARATION TIME 15 MINUTES (PLUS REFRIGERATION TIME)   COOKING TIME 15 MINUTES

1 pound fresh firm tofu

1 clove garlic, crushed in garlic press

¼ cup barbecue sauce

2 tablespoons olive oil

1 medium red onion, sliced thinly

4 wholegrain rolls

½ head romaine lettuce

1 large tomato, sliced thinly

1 tablespoon barbecue sauce, extra

1   Drain tofu; cut into 8 slices. Combine tofu in medium bowl with garlic and sauce; refrigerate, covered, 3 hours or overnight.

2   Heat half of the oil in large skillet; cook onion, stirring, until onion softens. Remove and reserve.

3   Drain tofu; discard marinade. Heat remaining oil in same skillet; cook tofu, uncovered, until browned both sides. Drain on paper towel.

4   Meanwhile, split rolls in half; toast cut sides. To serve, sandwich lettuce leaves, two slices of tofu, tomato, onion and extra sauce between toasted roll halves.

SERVES 4
per serving 40.4g carbohydrate; 19.9g fat; 426 cal; 21.7g protein

grapefruit salad

PREPARATION TIME 30 MINUTES

1 small red onion

6 large grapefruit

2 scallions, sliced thinly

2 red serrano chiles, sliced thinly

¼ cup coarsely chopped
    fresh cilantro

½ cup coarsely chopped roasted
    unsalted peanuts

2 cloves garlic, crushed in
    garlic press

1 tablespoon light brown sugar

¼ cup fresh lime juice

1 tablespoon soy sauce

1   Halve red onion; cut each half into paper-thin wedges.

2   Peel and carefully segment grapefruit; discard membranes. Combine segments in large bowl with red onion, scallion, chile, cilantro and nuts.

3   Combine remaining ingredients in small measuring cup; stir until sugar dissolves. Pour dressing over grapefruit mixture; toss gently to combine.

SERVES 4
per serving 28.3g carbohydrate; 1.1g fat; 156 cal; 5.4g protein

chile tuna pasta salad

PREPARATION TIME 15 MINUTES   COOKING TIME 15 MINUTES

7 ounces large shell pasta

**8 ounces fresh green beans,
   trimmed, halved**

12 ounces canned tuna in oil, drained

1 red serrano chile, chopped finely

**⅓ cup coarsely chopped fresh flat-
   leaf parsley**

**⅓ cup firmly packed fresh basil
   leaves, torn**

2 tablespoons drained baby capers

5 ounces feta cheese, crumbled

**3 cups (5 ounces) baby
   arugula leaves**

¼ cup olive oil

¼ cup fresh lemon juice

**2 cloves garlic, crushed in
   garlic press**

2 teaspoons sugar

1 Cook pasta in large pot of boiling water, uncovered, until just tender; drain. Rinse under cold water; drain.

2 Meanwhile, boil, steam or microwave beans until just tender; drain. Rinse under cold water; drain.

3 Place tuna in large bowl; chunk with fork. Add pasta and beans with chile, herbs, capers, cheese and arugula; toss gently to combine.

4 Place remaining ingredients in screw-top jar; shake well. Drizzle dressing over salad; toss gently to combine.

SERVES 4
per serving 39g carbohydrate; 40.8g fat; 644 cal; 30.3g protein
tip The salad, without the dressing, can be made several hours ahead and refrigerated, covered. Toss the dressing through the salad just before serving.

butternut squash soup

PREPARATION TIME 10 MINUTES   COOKING TIME 30 MINUTES

2 tablespoons butter

1 large leek, chopped coarsely

**2 cloves garlic, crushed in
   garlic press**

**3 pounds butternut squash,
   chopped coarsely**

5 cups chicken broth

½ cup heavy cream

1 Melt butter in soup pot; cook leek and garlic, stirring, until leek softens. Add squash and broth; bring to a boil. Reduce heat; simmer, covered, about 25 minutes or until squash softens.

2 Blend or process squash mixture, in batches, until pureed. Stir in cream.

SERVES 4
per serving 25.6g carbohydrate; 20.4g fat; 331 cal; 12g protein

smoked seafood and mixed vegetable antipasto

PREPARATION TIME 35 MINUTES

⅓ cup sour cream

2 teaspoons raspberry vinegar

1 tablespoon coarsely chopped fresh chives

1 clove garlic, crushed in garlic press

1 large yellow squash

1 tablespoon raspberry vinegar, extra

¼ cup extra virgin olive oil

⅓ cup toasted slivered almonds

¾ cup drained sun-dried tomatoes, halved

1 large avocado

1 tablespoon fresh lemon juice

10 ounces hot-smoked salmon

7 ounces sliced smoked salmon

16 drained caperberries

1 lemon, cut into wedges

6 ounces whole-wheat crackers

1 Combine sour cream, vinegar, chives and garlic in small bowl, cover; refrigerate until required.

2 Meanwhile, using vegetable peeler, slice squash lengthwise into ribbons; combine squash in small bowl with extra vinegar and 2 tablespoons of the oil.

3 Combine nuts, tomatoes and remaining oil in small bowl. Slice avocado thickly into small bowl; sprinkle with juice. Flake hot-smoked salmon into bite-sized pieces.

4 Arrange squash mixture, nut mixture, avocado, both salmons and caperberries on large platter; serve with sour cream mixture, lemon wedges and crackers.

SERVES 4
per serving 40.1g carbohydrate; 56.6g fat; 842 cal; 42.5g protein

fresh salmon and pasta salad

PREPARATION TIME 10 MINUTES   COOKING TIME 20 MINUTES

You need approximately 1¼ pounds fresh peas for this recipe.

1 pound salmon fillets, skinned

7 ounces bow-tie pasta

1 cup shelled fresh peas

½ cup sour cream

1 tablespoon fresh lemon juice

2 teaspoons water

2 tablespoons green peppercorns,
    rinsed, drained

1 tablespoon coarsely chopped fresh dill

2 stalks celery, trimmed, sliced thinly
    on the diagonal

⅓ cup coarsely chopped fresh chives

1 Cook salmon, uncovered, in large heated oiled skillet until lightly browned both sides and cooked as desired. Drain on paper towel.

2 Meanwhile, cook pasta in large pot of boiling water, uncovered, adding peas about halfway through cooking time; drain when pasta is just tender.

3 Combine sour cream, juice, the water, peppercorns and dill in small bowl.

4 Place salmon in large bowl; using fork, chunk salmon. Add celery, chives, sour cream mixture, pasta and peas; toss gently to combine.

SERVES 4
per serving 41.2g carbohydrate; 21.6g fat; 495 cal; 33.4g protein
tip Frozen peas can be thawed and substituted for fresh peas; add them to the pasta just before draining it.

tuna, corn and bean salad with lemon mayonnaise

PREPARATION TIME 15 MINUTES

15 ounces canned tuna in oil, drained

11 ounces canned corn kernels,
    rinsed, drained

14 ounces canned red kidney beans,
    rinsed, drained

3 stalks celery, trimmed, sliced thinly

½ cup coarsely chopped fresh
    flat-leaf parsley

2 cups (3½ ounces) baby
    arugula leaves

⅓ cup mayonnaise

1 tablespoon fresh lemon juice

1 clove garlic, crushed in garlic press

1 Combine tuna, corn, beans, celery, parsley and arugula in large bowl.

2 Place remaining ingredients in small pitcher; whisk to combine dressing.

3 Serve salad drizzled with dressing.

SERVES 4
per serving 27.4g carbohydrate; 11.5g fat; 331 cal; 29g protein

veal and eggplant parmigiana

PREPARATION TIME 10 MINUTES   COOKING TIME 20 MINUTES

4 boneless veal cutlets
    (about 14 ounces)

½ medium eggplant

⅓ cup olive oil

2 cups bottled pasta sauce

1 tablespoon fresh sage leaves

7 ounces bocconcini, sliced thinly

1 Place veal between two pieces wax paper. Flatten each cutlet with flat end of meat mallet until thin.

2 Cut eggplant into four ½-inch slices. Heat 4 tablespoons of the oil in large skillet; cook eggplant, uncovered, until browned both sides and tender. Drain on paper towel.

3 Heat remaining oil in same skillet; cook veal, uncovered, until browned both sides. Remove skillet from heat.

4 Top each piece of veal with eggplant, 1 tablespoon of the pasta sauce, sage and bocconcini. Spoon remaining sauce around veal.

5 Return skillet to heat; simmer, covered, about 5 minutes or until sauce bubbles. Place skillet briefly under hot broiler until cheese melts and browns lightly.

SERVES 4
per serving 34.3g carbohydrate; 28.5g fat; 517 cal; 31.9g protein

hamburger with a twist

PREPARATION TIME 15 MINUTES   COOKING TIME 10 MINUTES

3 ounces gorgonzola cheese,
    crumbled

¼ cup sour cream

14 ounces lean ground beef

4 ounces loose sausage meat

1 small onion, chopped finely

1 tablespoon barbecue sauce

2 teaspoons worcestershire sauce

½ cup drained sun-dried tomatoes in
    oil, chopped finely

4 whole-wheat hamburger buns

1½ cups (2 ounces) baby
    arugula leaves

6 ounces jarred marinated artichoke
    hearts, drained

1   Blend or process half of the cheese with the sour cream until smooth.
    Stir in remaining cheese.

2   Using hands, combine meats, onion, sauces and tomato in medium bowl;
    shape mixture into four hamburger patties.

3   Cook patties in large lightly oiled heated skillet until browned both sides
    and cooked through.

4   Meanwhile, halve buns; toast, cut-side up. Sandwich arugula, patties,
    gorgonzola cream and artichoke in toasted buns.

SERVES 4
per serving 37.7g carbohydrate; 30.5g fat; 571 cal; 36.1g protein

squash wedges with sloppy joe topping

PREPARATION TIME 10 MINUTES   COOKING TIME 30 MINUTES

1¾ pounds butternut squash

2 tablespoons olive oil

1 clove garlic, crushed in garlic press

1 large onion, chopped finely

1 small green bell pepper,
    chopped finely

1 stalk celery, trimmed,
    chopped finely

1½ pounds lean ground beef

2 tablespoons prepared mustard

2 tablespoons cider vinegar

1 cup ketchup

½ cup coarsely grated
    cheddar cheese

2 scallions, sliced thinly

1   Preheat oven to hot.

2   Cut squash into 3-inch by 1-inch wedges; place in large shallow
    casserole, drizzle with half of the oil.

3   Roast, uncovered, in hot oven about 30 minutes or until wedges
    are tender.

4   Meanwhile, heat remaining oil in large skillet; cook garlic, onion,
    pepper and celery, stirring, until vegetables soften. Add beef; cook,
    stirring, until changed in color. Stir in mustard, vinegar and ketchup;
    bring to a boil. Reduce heat; cook, stirring, until sloppy joe is cooked
    through and slightly thickened.

5   Serve wedges topped with sloppy joe mixture; sprinkle with cheese
    and scallion.

SERVES 4
per serving 35.4g carbohydrate; 28.7g fat; 594 cal; 48.7g protein

bun-less steak sandwich

PREPARATION TIME 20 MINUTES   COOKING TIME 1 HOUR 20 MINUTES

four 7-ounce flank steaks

2 cups (3½ ounces) arugula, trimmed

CHILI TOMATO JAM

1 tablespoon olive oil

2 cloves garlic, crushed in garlic press

4 medium tomatoes, chopped coarsely

1 tablespoon worcestershire sauce

¼ cup apple cider vinegar

1 red serrano chile, chopped finely

⅓ cup firmly packed light brown sugar

1 tablespoon coarsely chopped fresh cilantro

CARAMELIZED LEEK

2 tablespoons butter

1 medium leek, sliced thinly

2 tablespoons light brown sugar

2 tablespoons dry white wine

1   Make chili tomato jam and caramelized leek.

2   Cook steaks on heated oiled grill or grill pan until browned both sides and cooked as desired.

3   Top steaks with arugula, chili tomato jam and caramelized leek.

CHILI TOMATO JAM Heat oil in medium saucepan; cook garlic, stirring, until browned lightly. Add tomato, worcestershire, vinegar, chile and sugar; bring to a boil. Reduce heat; simmer, uncovered, about 45 minutes or until mixture thickens. Let stand 10 minutes; stir in cilantro.

CARAMELIZED LEEK Melt butter in medium skillet; cook leek, stirring, until softened. Add sugar and wine; cook, stirring occasionally, about 20 minutes or until leek caramelizes.

SERVES 4
per serving 31.6g carbohydrate; 20g fat; 513 cal; 49.9g protein

lamb and parsley salad pitas

PREPARATION TIME 25 MINUTES   COOKING TIME 10 MINUTES

1 pound trimmed boneless leg of lamb
   in 1 piece

1 tablespoon olive oil

1 teaspoon sesame seeds

1 clove garlic, crushed in garlic press

1 teaspoon finely grated lemon peel

1½ cups coarsely chopped fresh flat-leaf parsley

1 large tomato, seeded, sliced thinly

1 small red onion, sliced thinly

2 tablespoons fresh lemon juice

1 tablespoon olive oil

8 ounces prepared hummus

4 large whole-wheat pitas

½ cup coarsely grated cheddar cheese

1   Place lamb, oil, seeds, garlic and peel in medium bowl; toss to coat lamb. Cook lamb on heated oiled grill or grill pan until browned and cooked as desired. Cover; let stand 5 minutes, slice lamb thickly.

2   Meanwhile, combine parsley, tomato, onion, juice and oil in medium bowl.

3   Spread hummus evenly over one side of each pita. Divide cheese, parsley salad and lamb among pitas; roll to enclose filling. Cut in half to serve.

SERVES 4
per serving 42.6g carbohydrate; 34.8g fat; 653 cal; 42.3g protein

pea and ham soup

PREPARATION TIME 15 MINUTES   COOKING TIME 1 HOUR 10 MINUTES

2 cups dried split peas

1 medium onion, chopped coarsely

2 stalks celery, trimmed,

   chopped coarsely

2 bay leaves

1 meaty ham bone (about 3 pounds)

10 cups water

1 teaspoon cracked black pepper

1 Combine peas in large soup pot with remaining ingredients; bring to a boil. Reduce heat; simmer, covered, about 1 hour or until peas are tender.

2 Remove ham bone; when cool enough to handle, remove meat from bone. Discard bone and fat; shred ham finely.

3 Blend or process half of the pea mixture, in batches, until pureed; return to pot with remaining unprocessed pea mixture and ham. Reheat soup, stirring over heat until hot.

SERVES 6
per serving 31.7g carbohydrate; 4.9g fat; 269 cal; 23.5g protein

warm chicken tabbouleh

PREPARATION TIME 15 MINUTES   COOKING TIME 15 MINUTES

Tabbouleh is a traditional Lebanese salad made with a great deal of chopped flat-leaf parsley and varying amounts of bulgur, scallion, mint, olive oil and lemon juice.

1 cup bulgur

1 pound skinless, boneless chicken

   breasts, sliced thinly

2 cloves garlic, crushed in

   garlic press

⅔ cup fresh lemon juice

¼ cup olive oil

8 ounces cherry tomatoes, halved

3 scallions, chopped coarsely

1 cup loosely packed, coarsely

   chopped fresh flat-leaf parsley

1 cup loosely packed, coarsely

   chopped fresh mint

1 Place bulgur in small bowl; cover with boiling water. Let stand 15 minutes; drain. Using hands, squeeze out as much excess water as possible.

2 Meanwhile, combine chicken, garlic, 3 tablespoons of the juice and 1 tablespoon of the oil in medium bowl; let stand 5 minutes. Drain; discard marinade.

3 Heat 1 tablespoon of the oil in wok or large skillet; stir-fry chicken mixture, in batches, until chicken is browned all over and cooked through. Cover to keep warm.

4 Place bulgur with tomato and scallion in same wok. Stir-fry until scallion softens; remove from heat. Add chicken, parsley, mint, remaining juice and oil; toss gently to combine.

SERVES 4
per serving 27.3g carbohydrate; 17.5g fat; 409 cal; 33.9g protein

mexican burgers

PREPARATION TIME 10 MINUTES   COOKING TIME 10 MINUTES

1 pound lean ground chicken

1 packet taco seasoning mix

⅓ cup sour cream

**1 tablespoon finely chopped
    fresh cilantro**

4 whole-wheat rolls, halved

1 medium avocado, sliced thinly

⅓ cup medium chunky salsa

1 Using hands, combine chicken and seasoning in large bowl. Divide mixture into quarters; using hands, form each portion into burger shape. Cook burgers on heated oiled grill or grill pan until browned both sides and cooked through.

2 Meanwhile, combine sour cream and cilantro in small bowl.

3 Toast rolls, cut-side up, under hot broiler. Spread half of each roll with cream mixture; top each with burger, avocado, salsa and remaining half of roll.

SERVES 4
per serving 25.9g carbohydrate; 24.3g fat; 438 cal; 28.7g protein

sweet and sour chicken

PREPARATION TIME 10 MINUTES   COOKING TIME 10 MINUTES

**4 skinless, boneless chicken breasts
    (about 1½ pounds)**

**15 ounces canned pineapple chunks
    in natural juice**

1 tablespoon peanut oil

1 small onion, sliced thinly

**1 medium red bell pepper,
    chopped coarsely**

**1 large green bell pepper,
    chopped coarsely**

1 stalk celery, trimmed, sliced thickly

¼ cup ketchup

¼ cup plum sauce

2 tablespoons soy sauce

¼ cup white vinegar

1 tablespoon cornstarch

½ cup chicken broth

1 Cook chicken, in batches, on heated oiled grill or grill pan until browned all over and cooked through. Let stand 5 minutes; slice thickly. Cover to keep warm.

2 Meanwhile, drain pineapple; reserve juice. Heat oil in large skillet; cook pineapple, onion, peppers and celery, stirring, 4 minutes. Add reserved juice, sauces, vinegar and blended cornstarch and broth; stir until mixture boils and thickens.

3 Serve chicken topped with sweet and sour sauce.

SERVES 4
per serving 29.9g carbohydrate; 8.9g fat; 371 cal; 42.1g protein

chicken fillets in green peppercorn and tarragon dressing

PREPARATION TIME 10 MINUTES   COOKING TIME 15 MINUTES

2 tablespoons water

2 teaspoons drained green
    peppercorns, crushed

2 teaspoons grainy mustard

2 scallions, sliced thinly

1 tablespoon coarsely chopped
    fresh tarragon

1 tablespoon olive oil

1 tablespoon sugar

⅓ cup white wine vinegar

2 small sweet potatoes

8 skinless, boneless chicken breast halves
    (about 1¼ pounds)

1 tablespoon cracked black pepper

4 large tomatoes, sliced thinly

1 medium red onion, sliced thinly

1   Combine the water, peppercorns, mustard, scallion, tarragon, oil, sugar and vinegar in small bowl. Whisk to combine dressing; reserve.

2   Boil, steam or microwave sweet potatoes until just tender; drain.

3   Meanwhile, coat chicken all over in black pepper; cook chicken, in batches, on heated oiled grill or grill pan until browned both sides and cooked through. Let stand 5 minutes; slice thickly.

4   When sweet potatoes are cool enough to handle, slice thickly. Cook sweet potato, in batches, on same heated oiled grill pan until browned both sides.

5   Arrange chicken, potato, tomato and onion on serving plates; drizzle with reserved dressing.

SERVES 4
per serving 25.7g carbohydrate; 8.4g fat; 340 cal; 38.8g protein

chicken pita pockets

PREPARATION TIME 10 MINUTES   COOKING TIME 15 MINUTES

14 ounces lean ground chicken

1 clove garlic, crushed in garlic press

2 teaspoons ground coriander

2 teaspoons ground cumin

1 tablespoon chili sauce

1 tablespoon olive oil

1 large onion, sliced thinly

½ cup pine nuts

10 ounces (1 bag) spinach, trimmed,
    chopped coarsely

¼ cup loosely packed, coarsely chopped
    fresh mint

4 whole-wheat pocket pitas

1 cup yogurt

1 tablespoon fresh lemon juice

1   Combine chicken, garlic, spices and sauce in large bowl.

2   Heat half of the oil in wok or large skillet; cook chicken mixture until chicken is browned and cooked through. Remove from wok; cover to keep warm.

3   Add remaining oil to same wok; stir-fry onion, pine nuts and spinach until spinach just wilts. Remove from heat. Return chicken mixture to wok with mint; toss gently to combine.

4   Cut pita pockets in half. Open out each half; spoon in chicken mixture. Drizzle combined yogurt and juice into pita pockets or serve separately, as desired.

SERVES 4
per serving 41.7g carbohydrate; 30.9g fat; 580 cal; 33.1g protein

dhal with egg and eggplant

PREPARATION TIME 10 MINUTES   COOKING TIME 1 HOUR

2 cups red lentils

2 teaspoons vegetable oil

1 medium onion, chopped finely

1 clove garlic, crushed in garlic press

2 teaspoons ground cumin

½ teaspoon cumin seeds

1 tablespoon tomato paste

4 cups water

2 cups vegetable broth

1 large tomato, chopped coarsely

3 baby eggplants, chopped coarsely

4 hard-boiled eggs

1 Rinse lentils in large colander under cold water until water runs clear.

2 Heat oil in large heavy-bottomed saucepan; cook onion, garlic, ground cumin, seeds and paste, stirring, 5 minutes. Add lentils with the water and broth; bring to a boil. Reduce heat; simmer, uncovered, stirring occasionally, about 40 minutes or until dhal mixture thickens slightly.

3 Add tomato and eggplant; simmer, uncovered, stirring occasionally, about 20 minutes or until dhal is thickened and eggplant is tender. Add whole eggs; stir gently until eggs are heated through.

SERVES 4
per serving 43.5g carbohydrate 10.5g fat; 395 cal; 33.8g protein
tip Spoon a whole egg into each of four serving bowls, then spoon dhal over the egg.

spicy okra, corn and pepper gumbo

PREPARATION TIME 30 MINUTES   COOKING TIME 1 HOUR

1½ tablespoons olive oil

2 small onions, chopped coarsely

4 cloves garlic, crushed in garlic press

1½ teaspoons cajun seasoning

1 teaspoon ground cumin

¼ teaspoon cayenne

3 stalks celery, trimmed, chopped coarsely

**1 medium green bell pepper,
     chopped coarsely**

2 medium red bell peppers, chopped coarsely

2 fresh ears corn, shucked, sliced thickly

8 baby carrots, chopped coarsely

2 cups vegetable broth

28 ounces canned crushed tomatoes

2 tablespoons worcestershire sauce

⅓ cup basmati rice

1¾ pounds okra, trimmed

¼ cup finely chopped fresh flat-leaf parsley

1 Heat oil in large heavy-bottomed saucepan; cook onion, garlic and spices, stirring, until onion is soft. Add celery, peppers, corn, carrot, broth, undrained crushed tomatoes and sauce; simmer, covered, 30 minutes.

2 Add rice and okra; simmer, covered, about 25 minutes or until rice is tender.

3 Serve sprinkled with parsley.

SERVES 4
per serving 43g carbohydrate; 9.7g fat; 369 cal; 16.6g protein

mixed vegetable salad with roasted eggplant puree

PREPARATION TIME 40 MINUTES   COOKING TIME 1 HOUR 15 MINUTES

1 large green bell pepper

1 large red bell pepper

1 large yellow bell pepper

1 large eggplant

2 cloves garlic, unpeeled

1 tablespoon fresh lemon juice

½ cup olive oil

12 ounces button mushrooms,
   sliced thickly

1 sprig fresh thyme

8 ounces cherry tomatoes

20 baby zucchini,
   halved lengthwise

8 yellow patty-pan squash,
   halved crosswise

2 small bulbs fennel,
   trimmed, quartered

12 shallots, peeled

⅓ cup dry white wine

4 slices pumpernickel bread

½ cup loosely packed fresh
   flat-leaf parsley leaves

1   Preheat oven to hot.

2   Quarter peppers; remove and discard seeds and membranes. Using fork, prick eggplant all over; place on oiled baking sheet with garlic and peppers, skin-side up. Roast vegetables, uncovered, in hot oven about 30 minutes or until skins blister. Cover pepper pieces with plastic wrap or paper for 5 minutes. Peel away skin; slice pepper thickly.

3   When cool enough to handle, peel eggplant and garlic. Blend or process eggplant, garlic and lemon juice until mixture forms a paste. With motor running, pour in half of the oil in a thin, steady stream until eggplant mixture is pureed. Reserve, leaving in blender.

4   Meanwhile, toss mushrooms and thyme with 1 tablespoon of the remaining oil in large shallow casserole. Toss tomatoes, zucchini, squash and 1 tablespoon of the remaining oil in another large shallow casserole. Roast both casseroles, uncovered, in hot oven about 20 minutes or until mushrooms and vegetables are just tender.

5   Heat remaining oil in medium saucepan; cook fennel and shallots, stirring occasionally, about 5 minutes or until vegetables are browned lightly. Add wine; cook, covered, about 20 minutes or until vegetables are tender, stirring occasionally. Drain vegetables; add cooking liquid to processor with eggplant puree, process until smooth.

6   Cut bread slices in half on the diagonal; toast. Divide toast among serving plates; top with combined mushrooms, vegetables and parsley. Serve with eggplant puree.

SERVES 4
per serving 39.3g carbohydrate; 30.5g fat; 502 cal; 14.8g protein

vegetable moussaka

PREPARATION TIME 15 MINUTES
COOKING TIME 1 HOUR 15 MINUTES

2 large eggplants, sliced thickly

1 large red bell pepper,
   chopped finely

4 large tomatoes, chopped finely

1½ tablespoons sugar

2 tablespoons butter

2 tablespoons all-purpose flour

2 cups skim milk

⅓ cup finely grated
   parmesan cheese

⅓ cup finely chopped fresh basil

1   Preheat oven to moderately hot. Place eggplant in single layer on baking sheet. Bake, uncovered, in moderately hot oven 15 minutes; turn. Bake further 15 minutes or until browned lightly; cool 10 minutes. Reduce oven heat to moderate.

2   Meanwhile, combine pepper, tomato and sugar in medium saucepan; cook, stirring occasionally, about 30 minutes or until tomato is soft and liquid almost evaporates.

3   Melt butter in small saucepan; add flour. Cook, stirring, 1 minute. Gradually add milk; stir over medium heat until sauce boils and thickens. Stir in half of the cheese and half of the basil. Stir remaining basil through tomato mixture.

4   Spread a third of the tomato mixture, eggplant and cheese sauce between four 2-cup casseroles; repeat with two more layers. Sprinkle with remaining cheese.

5   Bake, uncovered, in moderate oven, about 15 minutes or until moussaka is browned lightly.

SERVES 4
per serving 26.3g carbohydrate; 7.3g fat; 223 cal; 13.2g protein

vegetable tagine

PREPARATION TIME 20 MINUTES   COOKING TIME 25 MINUTES

Harissa, a North African paste made from dried red chiles, garlic, olive oil and caraway seeds, can be used as a rub for meat, an ingredient in sauces and dressings or eaten on its own, as a condiment. It is available ready-made from Middle-Eastern food shops and some supermarkets.

2 teaspoons olive oil

1 large red onion, chopped coarsely

2 cloves garlic, crushed in
garlic press

2 teaspoons ground ginger

½ teaspoon ground cinnamon

2 teaspoons ground cumin

2 teaspoons ground coriander

1 medium eggplant,
chopped coarsely

1 large red bell pepper,
chopped coarsely

14 ounces canned
crushed tomatoes

2 cups vegetable broth

1 large pear, peeled,
chopped coarsely

2 cups water

8 ounces green beans,
cut into 2-inch lengths

½ cup dried pitted dates

½ cup finely chopped fresh
flat-leaf parsley

½ cup finely chopped mint

1 tablespoon harissa

1 Heat oil in large saucepan; cook onion and garlic, stirring, 5 minutes. Add spices, eggplant and pepper; cook 1 minute or until spices are fragrant. Add undrained tomatoes and broth; bring tagine mixture to a boil. Reduce heat; simmer, covered, until vegetables are just tender.

2 Meanwhile, place pear and the water in a medium saucepan; bring to a boil. Reduce heat; simmer, covered, about 15 minutes or until pear is just tender. Discard cooking liquid; add drained pear to tagine mixture with beans and dates; cook, stirring, 5 minutes. Stir chopped herbs and harissa into tagine off the heat.

SERVES 4
per serving 37.2g carbohydrate; 3.7g fat; 210 cal; 7.4g protein

vegetable and tofu stir-fry

PREPARATION TIME 10 MINUTES   COOKING TIME 15 MINUTES

You need about one and a quarter bunches of baby bok choy for this recipe.

8 ounces fresh firm tofu

10 ounces fresh rice noodles

1 tablespoon peanut oil

1 large onion, sliced thickly

2 cloves garlic, crushed in garlic press

1 teaspoon five-spice powder

10 ounces button mushrooms, halved

7 ounces brown mushrooms, halved

¼ cup soy sauce

1 cup vegetable broth

¼ cup water

1¼ pounds baby bok choy, chopped coarsely

4 scallions, chopped coarsely

2¼ cups (7 ounces) fresh bean sprouts

1   Cut tofu into ¾-inch cubes. Place noodles in large bowl. Rinse under hot water; drain. Separate noodles with fork.

2   Heat oil in wok or large skillet; stir-fry onion and garlic until onion softens. Add five-spice; stir-fry until fragrant. Add mushroom; stir-fry until almost tender.

3   Add combined sauce, broth and the water; bring to a boil. Add bok choy, and scallion; stir-fry until bok choy just wilts. Add tofu, noodles and sprouts; stir-fry until hot.

SERVES 4
per serving 28g carbohydrate; 10.2g fat; 285 cal; 19.4g protein
tip You can use rice stick noodles if fresh noodles are not available. Place rice stick noodles in a large heatproof bowl; cover with boiling water. Let stand until just tender, then drain.

double pea and tofu with pistachios

PREPARATION TIME 10 MINUTES   COOKING TIME 20 MINUTES

2 tablespoons peanut oil

1 pound 5 ounces firm tofu, drained,
    chopped coarsely

1 cup pistachios, shelled

2 tablespoons butter

2 cloves garlic, crushed in garlic press

2 red serrano chiles, seeded, chopped finely

2 teaspoons grated fresh ginger

14 ounces sugarsnap peas

14 ounces snow peas

5 ounces snow pea shoots

¼ cup sweet chili sauce

1   Heat half of the oil in wok or large skillet; stir-fry tofu and nuts, in batches, until tofu is browned lightly.

2   Heat remaining oil with butter in wok; stir-fry garlic, chile and ginger until mixture is fragrant.

3   Add peas to wok; stir-fry until just tender.

4   Add tofu, nuts and pea shoots to wok with sauce; stir-fry, tossing to combine ingredients.

SERVES 4
per serving 28.4g carbohydrate; 45.6g fat; 654 cal; 34.2g protein

japanese omelet salad (see page 28)

chicken, lemon and artichoke skewers (see page 134)

trio of beans in chile-lime sauce

PREPARATION TIME 10 MINUTES   COOKING TIME 20 MINUTES

10 ounces dried rice stick noodles

8 ounces frozen lima beans, thawed

10 ounces green beans, halved

5 ounces yellow beans, halved

vegetable oil, for deep-frying

¼ cup capers, drained

1 tablespoon olive oil

6 cloves garlic, crushed in garlic press

1 small red onion, cut into wedges

4 red serrano chiles, seeded

2 tablespoons finely grated lime peel

1 cup vegetable broth

1   Place noodles in medium heatproof bowl; cover with boiling water. Let stand until just tender; drain. Rinse under cold water; drain.

2   Meanwhile, boil, steam or microwave beans, separately, until just tender; drain. Heat vegetable oil in small skillet; deep-fry capers until crisp. Drain on paper towel.

3   Heat olive oil in wok or large skillet; stir-fry garlic, onion, chile and peel until onion is soft.

4   Add broth, beans and noodles; cook, stirring gently, until sauce thickens and mixture is hot.

5   Serve topped with capers.

SERVES 4
per serving 29.6g carbohydrate; 6.5g fat; 216 cal; 9.1g protein

grilled bream and vegetables with chile-basil butter sauce

PREPARATION TIME 20 MINUTES   COOKING TIME 30 MINUTES

½ small head cauliflower, cut into florets

3 fresh ears corn, shucked, cut into
    1-inch rounds

14 ounces baby carrots, trimmed

2 tablespoons olive oil

four 8-ounce whole bream (or porgies)

CHILE-BASIL BUTTER SAUCE

5 tablespoons butter

2 red serrano chiles, seeded, chopped finely

⅓ cup firmly packed fresh basil leaves,
    shredded finely

1 tablespoon fresh lemon juice

1   Cut cauliflower florets in half. Place vegetables and half of the oil in large bowl; toss to combine. Cook vegetables on heated oiled grill or grill pan about 20 minutes or until browned all over and cooked through.

2   Meanwhile, make chile-basil butter sauce.

3   Score each fish three times both sides; brush all over with remaining oil. Cook fish on heated oiled grill or grill pan about 5 minutes each side or until cooked as desired. Serve fish and vegetables drizzled with sauce.

CHILE-BASIL BUTTER SAUCE Melt butter in small saucepan; add chile, basil and juice, stir until combined.

SERVES 4
per serving 29.8g carbohydrate; 34g fat; 559 cal; 34g protein
tip Substitute fillets for whole fish, if desired.

grilled mahi mahi with roasted corn and chile salad

PREPARATION TIME 30 MINUTES   COOKING TIME 25 MINUTES

4 fresh ears corn, shucked

1 egg yolk

1 clove garlic, crushed in garlic press

2 tablespoons fresh lime juice

1 teaspoon dijon mustard

¾ cup olive oil

1 medium red onion, chopped finely

2 red serrano chiles, chopped finely

1 small avocado, chopped finely

1 medium green bell pepper, chopped finely

⅓ cup coarsely chopped fresh cilantro

four 7-ounce mahi mahi steaks

1 Cook corn on heated oiled grill or grill pan until browned lightly and just tender.

2 Meanwhile, blend or process yolk, garlic, juice and mustard until smooth. With motor running, gradually add oil in a thin, steady stream; process until mayonnaise thickens slightly.

3 Using sharp knife, remove kernels from cobs. Place kernels in large bowl with onion, chile, avocado, pepper, cilantro and half of the mayonnaise; toss gently to combine.

4 Cook fish on heated oiled grill or grill pan until browned both sides and cooked as desired. Divide corn salad among serving plates; top with fish, drizzle with remaining mayonnaise.

SERVES 4
per serving 33.4g carbohydrate; 56.8g fat; 845 cal; 50.7g protein
tips This corn and chile salad goes well with Mexican food too – use it to accompany beef fajitas or bean and cheese burritos.

salmon parcels with fresh mango sauce

PREPARATION TIME 30 MINUTES   COOKING TIME 15 MINUTES

½ small leek

⅓ cup loosely packed fresh cilantro leaves

1 large red bell pepper, sliced thinly

1 teaspoon five-spice powder

½ teaspoon ground coriander

1 tablespoon light brown sugar

1 tablespoon fresh lime juice

four 7-ounce salmon fillets, skinned

four 8-inch square spring roll wrappers

1 tablespoon cornstarch

2 teaspoons water

⅓ cup peanut oil

1 medium mango, chopped coarsely

5 ounces radicchio

1 Cut leek into 3-inch lengths; halve each piece lengthwise, then slice halves into thin strips. Combine leek in small bowl with cilantro and half the pepper.

2 Preheat oven to moderately hot.

3 Heat lightly oiled small skillet; cook five-spice and ground coriander, stirring, until fragrant. Stir in sugar and juice; remove from heat. When cool enough to handle, rub half of the spice mixture into both sides of salmon fillets.

4 Place a salmon fillet on bottom half of one spring roll wrapper; top with a quarter of the leek mixture. Lightly brush edges of wrapper with blended cornstarch and water; roll to enclose salmon, folding in ends. Repeat with remaining salmon, wrappers, leek mixture and cornstarch mixture.

5 Heat oil in large skillet; cook parcels, in batches, until browned lightly. Place on oiled baking sheet; bake parcels in moderately hot oven about 8 minutes or until fish is cooked as desired.

6 Meanwhile, blend or process half of the mango and remaining spice mixture until smooth. Combine remaining mango, remaining pepper and radicchio in large bowl. Serve salmon parcels with salad topped with mango sauce.

SERVES 4
per serving 32.4g carbohydrate; 35g fat; 642 cal; 49.7g protein

blackened cod with sweet tomato relish

PREPARATION TIME 20 MINUTES (PLUS REFRIGERATION TIME)   COOKING TIME 40 MINUTES

We used cod in this recipe, but you can use any firm fish, such as halibut, sea bass or red snapper.

four 7-ounce cod fillets

2 tablespoons olive oil

2 tablespoons grated fresh ginger

1 tablespoon ground turmeric

1 tablespoon garlic powder

1 tablespoon mustard powder

1 tablespoon sweet paprika

1 tablespoon dried basil leaves

1 tablespoon ground fennel

¼ teaspoon cayenne

¼ teaspoon hot chili powder

2 teaspoons salt

2½ cups (5 ounces) mesclun

SWEET TOMATO RELISH

10 medium plum tomatoes, halved

2 cups water

½ cup dry white wine

1 tablespoon fresh lime juice

½ cup firmly packed light

  brown sugar

1 tablespoon grated lime peel

1 tablespoon ground turmeric

1 tablespoon yellow mustard seeds

2 bay leaves

2 stalks fresh lemongrass

1   Place fish in large shallow casserole; pour over combined oil and ginger. Cover; refrigerate 3 hours or overnight.

2   Make sweet tomato relish.

3   Drain fish; discard marinade. Coat fish in combined spices, herbs and salt; cook on heated oiled grill or grill pan, uncovered, until browned both sides and just cooked through. Divide mesclun among serving plates; serve with fish and sweet tomato relish.

SWEET TOMATO RELISH   Combine all ingredients in medium saucepan. Simmer, uncovered, 30 minutes or until most of the liquid has evaporated. Cool, remove and discard leaves and lemongrass.

SERVES 4
per serving 28.8g carbohydrate; 13.7g fat; 428 cal; 42.8g protein

salmon steaks with green apple salad

PREPARATION TIME 20 MINUTES   COOKING TIME 10 MINUTES (PLUS COOLING TIME)

½ teaspoon sea salt

four 6-ounce salmon steaks

2 medium granny smith apples, sliced thinly

2 scallions, sliced thinly

1 medium red onion, sliced thinly

1½ cups loosely packed fresh mint leaves

¾ cup loosely packed fresh cilantro leaves

½ cup fresh lemon juice

¾ cup roasted unsalted cashews

GINGER DRESSING

⅓ cup light brown sugar

2 tablespoons fish sauce

2 teaspoons grated fresh ginger

1   Sprinkle salt evenly over fish. Cook fish on heated oiled grill or grill pan until browned both sides and cooked as desired.

2   Meanwhile, make ginger dressing.

3   Combine apple, scallion, onion, mint, cilantro and juice in large bowl; pour over half of the ginger dressing, toss to combine. Divide fish among serving plates; top with salad, then cashews. Drizzle remaining dressing over fish.

GINGER DRESSING Combine ingredients in small saucepan; bring to a boil. Remove from heat; strain. Cool before using.

SERVES 4
per serving 32.6g carbohydrate; 23.6g fat; 476 cal; 33.9g protein

salmon with grilled corn salsa

PREPARATION TIME 20 MINUTES   COOKING TIME 25 MINUTES

2 fresh ears corn, shucked

2 medium red bell peppers

1 small red onion, chopped finely

1 red serrano chile, seeded, chopped finely

1 tablespoon olive oil

¼ cup coarsely chopped fresh cilantro

four 7-ounce salmon fillets, skin on

1   Place corn on heated oiled grill or grill pan; using metal tongs to roll corn, cook until lightly browned all over. When cool enough to handle, cut kernels from cobs.

2   Meanwhile, quarter peppers; remove and discard seeds and membranes. Cook peppers, skin-side down, on heated oiled grill or grill pan until skin blisters and blackens. Cover pepper pieces with plastic wrap or paper for 5 minutes. Peel away skin; chop pepper finely.

3   Combine corn and pepper in medium bowl with onion, chile, oil and cilantro.

4   Cook salmon on same heated oiled grill or grill pan until browned both sides and cooked as desired. Serve with corn salsa.

SERVES 4
per serving 28.6g carbohydrate; 27.8g fat; 631 cal; 66.4g protein

tahitian fish salad

PREPARATION TIME 40 MINUTES (PLUS REFRIGERATION TIME)   COOKING TIME 10 MINUTES

This delicious fish salad captures the tropical flavor of Tahitian cooking. Unlike that other popular "raw" fish dish, ceviche, where the seafood marinates in citrus juice for such a long time that it is virtually "cooked", here it is assembled quickly and submerged in lime juice only long enough to become slightly opaque on the surface, while remaining raw inside. You need a large bunch of cilantro, with stems and roots intact if possible, for this recipe. If you cannot find cilantro with the root, substitute with ¼ cup extra of leaf and stem.

1¼-pound piece red snapper, skinned

⅔ cup fresh lime juice

1 large sweet potato, sliced thinly

1 large potato, sliced thinly

1 hothouse cucumber

1 tablespoon finely grated lime peel

3 red serrano chiles, sliced thinly

4 scallions, sliced thinly

1½ cups finely chopped cilantro leaf,
    stem and root

1⅔ cups unsweetened coconut milk

2 medium avocados, sliced thinly

1   Slice fish in half lengthwise, remove bones and blood line; slice halves crosswise into ⅛-inch strips. Combine fish with juice in large bowl, cover; refrigerate 20 minutes.

2   Meanwhile, cook potatoes on heated oiled grill or grill pan until browned lightly both sides and just tender.

3   Using vegetable peeler, slice cucumber into ribbons. Add cucumber, peel, chile, scallion, cilantro and coconut milk to undrained fish; toss gently to combine.

4   Divide potatoes among serving plates, top with avocado and fish salad.

SERVES 4
per serving 31.9g carbohydrate; 44.4g fat; 691 cal; 40.4g protein

hot and sour shrimp vermicelli salad

PREPARATION TIME 30 MINUTES (PLUS REFRIGERATION TIME)

2 pounds cooked medium shrimp

8 ounces rice vermicelli

1 lime

1 lemon

1 medium red bell pepper, sliced thinly

1 medium yellow bell pepper, sliced thinly

1 medium red onion, sliced thinly

¼ cup olive oil

¼ cup rice vinegar

1 tablespoon chili sauce (such as
    sambal oelek or sriracha)

1 tablespoon fish sauce

2 tablespoons light brown sugar

1 cup firmly packed fresh cilantro leaves

1   Shell and devein shrimp, leaving tails intact. Place vermicelli in large heatproof bowl of boiling water, let stand until just tender; drain. Rinse under cold water; drain.

2   Meanwhile, halve lime and lemon lengthwise; slice one unpeeled half of each thinly, place in large bowl. Squeeze remaining halves into bowl; add shrimp, vermicelli and remaining ingredients, toss gently to combine. Cover; refrigerate 1 hour before serving.

SERVES 4
per serving 26.4g carbohydrate; 15.4g fat; 383 cal; 33.7g protein

chile-seared tuna
with avocado cream and tortillas

PREPARATION TIME 30 MINUTES (PLUS STANDING AND REFRIGERATION TIMES)   COOKING TIME 25 MINUTES

4 dried chipotle chiles

1 tablespoon olive oil

1 small onion chopped finely

2 cloves garlic, crushed in
garlic press

⅓ cup loosely packed fresh
oregano leaves

2 tablespoons tomato paste

2 tablespoons water

four 7-ounce tuna steaks

8 large flour tortillas

2 limes, cut into wedges

AVOCADO CREAM

2 small avocados

½ cup sour cream

¼ cup coarsely chopped
fresh cilantro

1 tablespoon fresh lime juice

2 scallions, sliced thinly

1   Place chiles in small heatproof bowl of boiling water; let stand 15 minutes. Drain; chop chiles coarsely.

2   Heat oil in small skillet; cook onion and garlic, stirring, until onion softens. Stir in chile, oregano, paste and the water; bring to a boil. Remove from heat; blend or process, pulsing, until mixture forms a thick paste.

3   Place fish, in single layer, in large shallow casserole; using fingers, pat chile paste onto both sides of fish. Cover; refrigerate 15 minutes.

4   Meanwhile, make avocado cream.

5   Cook undrained fish on heated oiled grill or grill pan until browned both sides and cooked as desired. Cover; let stand 5 minutes. Slice fish thickly.

6   Meanwhile, heat tortillas according to directions on packet. Divide fish, avocado cream and tortillas among serving plates. Serve with lime wedges.

AVOCADO CREAM Blend or process avocados and sour cream until smooth; stir in cilantro, juice and scallion.

SERVES 4
per serving 32.2g carbohydrate; 45.6g fat; 769 cal; 57.3g protein

cheese-crumbed fish fillets with stir-fried vegetables

PREPARATION TIME 15 MINUTES   COOKING TIME 15 MINUTES

We used cod in this recipe, but you can use any firm fish, such as halibut, sea bass or red snapper.
Make the breadcrumbs from bread that is at least a day old; grate or process stale bread to make crumbs.

1 cup homemade

wholewheat breadcrumbs

½ cup rolled regular oats

1 tablespoon drained capers,

chopped finely

2 teaspoons finely grated

lemon peel

¼ cup finely grated

pecorino cheese

¼ cup loosely packed, finely

chopped fresh flat-leaf parsley

1 tablespoon sesame oil

four 5-ounce firm white fish fillets

½ cup all-purpose flour

2 egg whites, beaten lightly

1 large carrot, sliced finely

2 stalks celery, trimmed,

sliced thinly

1 medium green bell pepper,

sliced thinly

6 scallions, chopped finely

1 red serrano chile, seeded,

chopped finely

1 tablespoon sesame seeds

1 Preheat oven to hot.

2 Combine breadcrumbs, oats, capers, peel, cheese, parsley and oil in medium bowl. Coat fish in flour, shake off excess; dip in egg white, then in breadcrumb mixture.

3 Place fish, in single layer, in casserole; bake, uncovered, in hot oven about 15 minutes or until cooked through.

4 Meanwhile, cook carrot in heated large nonstick wok or skillet. Add celery, pepper, scallion, chile and sesame seeds; cook until vegetables are just tender.

5 Serve sliced fish on stir-fried vegetables.

SERVES 4
per serving 36.6g carbohydrate; 12.8g fat; 430 cal; 41.6g protein
tip Fish can be crumbed several hours ahead; store, covered, in refrigerator.
serving suggestion Serve with wedges of lime or lemon.

crusted halibut with herbs and caper mayonnaise

PREPARATION TIME 25 MINUTES (PLUS REFRIGERATION TIME)   COOKING TIME 10 MINUTES

2 eggs, beaten lightly

2 tablespoons water

1 cup stale breadcrumbs

¾ cup finely grated parmesan cheese

½ cup toasted sliced almonds

1½ pounds halibut fillets

½ cup all-purpose flour

1 cup loosely packed fresh basil leaves

1 cup loosely packed fresh parsley leaves

1 cup loosely packed baby arugula leaves

vegetable oil, for shallow-frying

lemon wedges

CAPER MAYONNAISE

¾ cup mayonnaise

1 tablespoon capers, drained, chopped finely

1 tablespoon coarsely chopped fresh basil

1 clove garlic, crushed in garlic press

1 tablespoon fresh lemon juice

1 Combine eggs and water in small bowl. Combine breadcrumbs, cheese and almonds in medium bowl. Coat fish in flour, shaking off excess; coat fish in egg mixture then in breadcrumb mixture. Place fish on baking sheet; refrigerate, covered, about 30 minutes or until crust firms.

2 Make caper mayonnaise.

3 Place herbs and arugula in medium bowl; toss to combine.

4 Heat oil in large skillet; shallow-fry fish, in batches, until lightly browned both sides and cooked through. Top with herbs; drizzle with caper mayonnaise. Serve with lemon wedges.

CAPER MAYONNAISE Combine ingredients in small bowl.

SERVES 4
per serving 36.6g carbohydrate; 72.9g fat; 1015 cal; 54.5g protein
tips Mayonnaise can be prepared a day ahead and refrigerated, covered. Fish can be coated and refrigerated up to 2 hours ahead of cooking time.

steaks with spinach and mashed parsnip

PREPARATION TIME 10 MINUTES (PLUS REFRIGERATION TIME)   COOKING TIME 20 MINUTES

four 7-ounce new york strip steaks

⅓ cup plum sauce

⅓ cup ketchup

⅓ cup worcestershire sauce

2 cloves garlic, crushed in garlic press

2 scallions, chopped finely

5 medium parsnips, chopped coarsely

1 tablespoon butter, chopped

¼ cup heavy cream

10 cups (16 ounces) baby spinach leaves

1 Combine steaks in large bowl with sauces, garlic and scallion; toss to coat steaks all over in marinade. Cover; refrigerate 30 minutes.

2 Meanwhile, boil, steam or microwave parsnip until just tender; drain. Mash with butter and cream in large bowl until smooth. Cover to keep warm.

3 Drain steaks; discard marinade. Cook steaks on heated oiled grill or grill pan until browned both sides and cooked as desired.

4 Boil, steam or microwave spinach until just wilted; drain. Serve steaks with mashed parsnips and spinach.

SERVES 4
per serving 37.4g carbohydrate; 26g fat; 586 cal; 51.3g protein

beef roulade

PREPARATION TIME 20 MINUTES (PLUS REFRIGERATION TIME)   COOKING TIME 1 HOUR

1 pound lean ground beef

1 small onion, chopped finely

2 cloves garlic, crushed in garlic press

1 egg

1 tablespoon tomato paste

1 tablespoon coarsely chopped fresh basil

2 cups homemade breadcrumbs

1½ cups (2 ounces) baby spinach leaves

6 slices prosciutto

9 cherry tomatoes

5 ounces radicchio

2 tablespoons fresh lemon juice

TOMATO AND MUSTARD SAUCE

½ cup ketchup

2 tablespoons barbecue sauce

2 tablespoons dijon mustard

¼ cup water

1   Grease 10- x 15-inch jelly roll pan (or flat baking sheet); line with parchment or wax paper, extending paper 2 inches over the edge of both long sides.

2   Using hands, combine beef, onion, garlic, egg, paste, basil and breadcrumbs in large bowl; press mixture into prepared pan, top with spinach leaves then prosciutto.

3   Place cherry tomatoes along one long side. Starting with this side, lift paper and roll, holding filling in place as you roll away from you, pressing roll gently but tightly around filling. Discard paper, wrap roll in foil; refrigerate 20 minutes. Preheat oven to hot.

4   Make tomato and mustard sauce.

5   Place roulade, still wrapped in foil, on baking sheet; bake in hot oven 40 minutes. Unwrap roulade; bake on baking sheet in hot oven about 15 minutes or until browned.

6   Meanwhile, place radicchio in medium bowl. Just before serving, drizzle with lemon juice; serve roulade, sliced, with tomato and mustard sauce, and radicchio salad.

TOMATO AND MUSTARD SAUCE Combine ingredients in small saucepan; cook, stirring, until heated through.

SERVES 4
per serving 41.6g carbohydrate; 13.1g protein; 440 cal; 38.8g protein

veal marsala

PREPARATION TIME 10 MINUTES   COOKING TIME 20 MINUTES

2 fresh ears corn, shucked, sliced thickly

10 ounces frozen lima beans

eight 4-ounce veal scallopine

3 tablespoons butter

1 large onion, sliced thinly

1 tablespoon all-purpose flour

¼ cup marsala

¾ cup beef broth

1 tablespoon finely chopped fresh
**   flat-leaf parsley**

1   Boil, steam or microwave corn and beans separately until tender; drain.

2   Meanwhile, cook veal in heated oiled large skillet, in batches, until browned both sides and cooked as desired. Remove veal from skillet; cover to keep warm.

3   Add butter and onion to same skillet; cook, stirring, until onion is soft. Add flour; cook, stirring, until mixture thickens and bubbles. Gradually stir in combined marsala and broth; stir until mixture boils and thickens. Stir in the parsley. Serve veal with sauce and vegetables.

SERVES 4
per serving 37.3g carbohydrate; 15.3g fat; 500 cal; 52.5g protein

beef fajitas

PREPARATION TIME 20 MINUTES (PLUS REFRIGERATION TIME)   COOKING TIME 20 MINUTES

1 pound skirt steak, sliced thinly

⅓ cup barbecue sauce

1 teaspoon ground cumin

1 teaspoon ground coriander

½ teaspoon chili powder

1 small red bell pepper,
  sliced thinly

1 small green bell pepper,
  sliced thinly

1 small yellow bell pepper,
  sliced thinly

8 large flour tortillas

½ cup sour cream

AVOCADO TOPPING

2 small avocados

1 tablespoon fresh lime juice

1 clove garlic, crushed in
  garlic press

TOMATO SALSA

2 small tomatoes, seeded,
  chopped finely

1 small red onion, chopped finely

1 tablespoon olive oil

2 teaspoons finely chopped
  fresh cilantro

1   Place beef in medium bowl with sauce, cumin, coriander and chili. Cover; refrigerate 15 minutes.

2   Cook pepper slices on heated oiled grill or grill pan until browned and tender. Cook beef on heated oiled grill or grill pan until browned and cooked as desired.

3   Meanwhile, wrap tortillas in foil in parcels of four and heat on grill. Make avocado topping. Make tomato salsa. Remove tortillas from foil and divide beef and peppers among them. Top with sour cream, avocado topping and tomato salsa.

AVOCADO TOPPING   Mash avocados coarsely in a medium bowl with a fork; add juice and garlic.

TOMATO SALSA   Combine all ingredients in a small bowl.

SERVES 4
per serving 40.3g carbohydrate; 42g fat; 675 cal; 34.5g protein

veal souvlaki
with tomato and onion salsa

PREPARATION TIME 40 MINUTES (PLUS REFRIGERATION TIME)   COOKING TIME 10 MINUTES

Soak eight bamboo skewers in water for at least an hour prior to use to prevent splintering or scorching.

2-pound whole piece boneless veal

1 small onion, chopped coarsely

2 cloves garlic, crushed in
** garlic press**

2 tablespoons yogurt

1 tablespoon fresh lemon juice

1 tablespoon olive oil

¼ cup firmly packed fresh mint
** leaves, chopped coarsely**

3 teaspoons white wine vinegar

3 pitas, cut into 4 wedges each

TOMATO AND ONION SALSA

4 small plum tomatoes, seeded,
** chopped finely**

1 small white onion, chopped finely

2 tablespoons finely chopped
** fresh mint**

1 teaspoon sweet paprika

YOGURT SAUCE

½ cup unflavored yogurt

2 teaspoons tahini

1 tablespoon hot water

1 Cut veal into 1-inch pieces; thread onto eight skewers.

2 Combine onion, garlic, yogurt, juice, oil, mint and vinegar in large shallow casserole; add veal skewers. Cover; refrigerate 3 hours or overnight.

3 Make tomato and onion salsa. Make yogurt sauce.

4 Cook veal on heated oiled grill or grill pan until browned all over and cooked as desired. Wrap pita in foil parcel and heat on grill.

5 Serve veal with tomato and onion salsa, yogurt sauce and warm pita bread.

TOMATO AND ONION SALSA Combine ingredients in small bowl.

YOGURT SAUCE Whisk ingredients in small bowl until combined.

SERVES 4
per serving 34.7g carbohydrate; 13.9g fat; 517 cal; 61.9g protein
tip If using metal skewers, oil them first to prevent veal from sticking.

beef, squash and mushroom salad with onion chutney

PREPARATION TIME 25 MINUTES   COOKING TIME 40 MINUTES

You could use beef already cut into thin strips by the butcher in this recipe.

4 large plum tomatoes, quartered

8 large mushrooms

1 clove garlic, chopped finely

1 tablespoon olive oil

3 tablespoons butter

2 tablespoons light brown sugar

1 large onion, sliced thinly

2 pounds butternut squash

1½ pounds london broil

2 tablespoons balsamic vinegar

2 cups (3½ ounces) baby arugula leaves

1   Preheat oven to moderately hot. Place tomato and mushrooms on large baking sheet; sprinkle with garlic, drizzle with oil. Bake, uncovered, in moderately hot oven about 40 minutes or until tomato is browned lightly.

2   Meanwhile, heat butter and sugar in medium skillet, stirring, until sugar dissolves. Add onion; cook, stirring, until onion is soft. Simmer mixture, uncovered, about 10 minutes or until onion caramelizes, stirring frequently.

3   Cut eight ⅛-inch-thick slices from squash. Heat oiled medium nonstick skillet; cook squash, in batches, until browned both sides. Drain on paper towel.

4   Cook beef in same skillet until browned all over and cooked as desired. Remove beef from skillet, cover; let stand 10 minutes, slice thinly.

5   Add vinegar to skillet juices; simmer, uncovered, 2 minutes. Add onion mixture to skillet; stir until chutney is mixed and heated through.

6   Divide squash and mushrooms among serving plates; stack with beef, tomato, onion chutney and arugula.

SERVES 4
per serving 25.7g carbohydrate; 26.7g fat; 549 cal; 51.6g protein

beef with brandied walnuts and prunes

PREPARATION TIME 10 MINUTES (PLUS REFRIGERATION TIME)   COOKING TIME 50 MINUTES

1¼ pounds round roast

⅓ cup walnut oil

⅓ cup cider vinegar

¼ cup light brown sugar

1 cup pitted prunes, halved

¾ cup walnut pieces, chopped coarsely

⅓ cup brandy

3 tablespoons butter

2½ cups (5 ounces) mesclun

1   Place beef in large bowl with combined walnut oil, vinegar and sugar. Cover; refrigerate 3 hours or overnight.

2   Drain beef over medium bowl; reserve marinade. Cook beef on heated oiled grill or grill pan until browned all over. Place beef on roasting rack or in disposable roasting pan. Cook in covered grill, using indirect heat, following manufacturer's instructions, about 40 minutes or until cooked as desired. Remove from heat, cover; let stand 10 minutes before slicing and serving.

3   Meanwhile, combine reserved marinade with prunes, nuts, brandy and butter. Bring to a boil; simmer, uncovered, for 5 minutes.

4   Divide mesclun among serving plates. Serve brandied walnuts and prunes with beef and salad.

SERVES 4
per serving 29g carbohydrate; 61.4g fat; 856 cal; 38.5g protein

veal chops with pear relish and spinach

PREPARATION TIME 15 MINUTES   COOKING TIME 55 MINUTES

four 7-ounce veal chops

3 tablespoons butter

1 pound baby spinach leaves

PEAR RELISH

4 small pears

1 medium red onion, chopped coarsely

1 tablespoon butter

1 tablespoon red wine vinegar

¼ cup firmly packed light brown sugar

4 cloves

¼ teaspoon ground allspice

1 Make pear relish.

2 Cook chops on heated oiled grill or grill pan until browned both sides and cooked as desired.

3 Meanwhile, melt butter in large saucepan; cook spinach, tossing, until just wilted.

4 Serve chops with spinach and pear relish.

PEAR RELISH Peel and core pears; chop coarsely. Combine pear in medium nonreactive saucepan with onion, butter and vinegar; bring to a boil. Reduce heat; simmer, covered, about 20 minutes or until mixture is pulpy. Add sugar, cloves and allspice, stir over low heat until sugar dissolves; bring to a boil. Reduce heat; simmer, uncovered, stirring occasionally, about 20 minutes or until mixture thickens slightly.

SERVES 4
per serving 36.4g carbohydrate; 16.8g fat; 425 cal; 33.4g protein

steak with roast pepper relish

PREPARATION TIME 10 MINUTES   COOKING TIME 20 MINUTES

3 medium red bell peppers

1 teaspoon olive oil

1 large onion, sliced thinly

2 cloves garlic, sliced thinly

2 tablespoons light brown sugar

2 tablespoons sherry vinegar

3 red serrano chiles, seeded, chopped finely

four 7-ounce new york strip steaks

10 ounces tiny new potatoes, halved

7 ounces broccoli

14 ounces baby carrots

2 tablespoons finely chopped fresh
    flat-leaf parsley

1 Quarter peppers; remove and discard seeds and membranes. Roast under broiler, skin-side up, until skin blisters and blackens. Cover with plastic wrap or paper for 5 minutes. Peel away skin; slice pepper thinly.

2 Heat oil in medium skillet; cook onion and garlic, stirring, until soft. Add sugar, vinegar, chile and roasted pepper; cook, stirring, 5 minutes.

3 Meanwhile, cook steaks on heated oiled grill or grill pan until browned and cooked as desired.

4 Boil, steam or microwave vegetables, separately, until just tender; drain.

5 Top steaks with roast pepper relish; serve with vegetables, sprinkle with parsley.

SERVES 4
per serving 27.3g carbohydrate; 14.7g fat; 451 cal; 51.9g protein
tip You can make the roast pepper relish a day ahead; store, covered, in refrigerator. Reheat just before serving.

borscht with meatballs

PREPARATION TIME 20 MINUTES   COOKING TIME 2 HOURS

Borscht is a fresh beet soup, originally from Poland and Russia, made with meat or cabbage,
or both. Serve it cold or hot, but always with a dollop of sour cream. Ask your butcher to cut
the shanks into thirds. You will need about a quarter of a head of savoy cabbage for this recipe.

1 tablespoon olive oil

1 small onion, chopped coarsely

1 small carrot, chopped coarsely

1 small leek, chopped coarsely

**8 ounces savoy cabbage,
     chopped coarsely**

1 large tomato, chopped coarsely

**2 medium beets, peeled,
     chopped coarsely**

**2 veal shanks (about 3 pounds),
     trimmed, cut into thirds**

5 cups water

1 pound lean ground beef

**½ cup cooked medium-grain
     brown rice**

1 teaspoon sweet paprika

1 small onion, chopped finely

**3 cloves garlic, crushed in
     garlic press**

**½ cup finely chopped fresh
     flat-leaf parsley**

2 eggs, beaten lightly

½ cup sour cream

**2 tablespoons finely chopped
     fresh dill**

1   Heat oil in large saucepan; cook coarsely chopped onion, carrot,
    leek, cabbage, tomato and beet, stirring, 15 minutes. Add veal
    and the water; bring to a boil. Reduce heat; simmer, covered,
    1½ hours. Remove veal; remove and reserve meat from shank
    for another use, if desired.

2   Meanwhile, using hands, combine ground beef, cooked rice,
    paprika, finely chopped onion, garlic, parsley and egg in large
    bowl; shape rounded teaspoons of mince mixture into meatballs.

3   Return borscht to a boil; add meatballs. Reduce heat; simmer,
    uncovered, until meatballs are cooked through.

4   Divide borscht and meatballs among serving bowls; dollop with
    combined sour cream and dill.

SERVES 4
per serving   33.9g carbohydrate; 31.4g fat; 729 cal; 77.5g protein
tips   Make the meatballs the day before; refrigerate them, uncooked,
covered on a tray. Drop meatballs in reheated soup to cook.
Make soup a day ahead to allow the flavors to intensify.

soupe au pistou

PREPARATION TIME 15 MINUTES (PLUS STANDING TIME)
COOKING TIME 1 HOUR 50 MINUTES

Soupe au pistou is a classic Provençale recipe, usually made with white and green beans, and flavored with pistou, a French spin-off of its near-neighbour, Italy's pesto. Not dissimilar to Italian minestrone, this soup also benefits from being made a day in advance.

1 cup dried cannellini beans

⅓ cup olive oil

2 veal shanks

   (about 3 pounds), trimmed

1 large leek, sliced thinly

8 cups water

2 cups chicken broth

2 tablespoons toasted pine nuts

1 clove garlic, quartered

¼ cup finely grated

   parmesan cheese

½ cup firmly packed fresh

   basil leaves

2 medium carrots,

   chopped coarsely

7 ounces green beans,

   chopped coarsely

1 Cover cannellini beans with cold water in large bowl; let stand, covered, overnight.

2 Heat 1 tablespoon of the oil in large saucepan; cook shanks, until browned all over. Remove from saucepan. Cook leek in same saucepan, stirring, about 5 minutes or until just softened. Drain beans. Return shanks to saucepan with the water, beans and broth; bring to a boil. Reduce heat; simmer, covered, 1 hour.

3 Meanwhile, blend or process remaining oil, nuts, garlic and cheese until combined. Add basil; process until pistou mixture forms a paste.

4 Remove shanks from soup. When cool enough to handle, remove meat from bones. Discard bones; chop meat coarsely. Return meat to soup; bring to a boil. Reduce heat; simmer, uncovered, 30 minutes. Add carrot; simmer, uncovered, 10 minutes. Add green beans and pistou; simmer, uncovered, 5 minutes. Divide soup among serving bowls.

SERVES 4
per serving 27.5g carbohydrate; 29.6g fat; 600 cal; 58.1g protein

mexican meatballs with guacamole

PREPARATION TIME 25 MINUTES   COOKING TIME 25 MINUTES

2 tablespoons vegetable oil

1 medium onion, chopped finely

1 clove garlic, crushed in garlic press

1 teaspoon ground cumin

1 teaspoon ground coriander

½ teaspoon chili powder

1½ pounds lean ground beef

¼ cup packaged breadcrumbs

28 ounces canned crushed tomatoes

15 ounces canned kidney beans

⅓ cup sour cream

GUACAMOLE

2 medium avocados

1 large tomato, seeded, chopped finely

1 small red onion, chopped finely

2 teaspoons fresh lemon juice

1   Heat half of the oil in large skillet; cook onion, garlic and spices, stirring, until onion softens.

2   Combine beef, breadcrumbs and onion mixture in medium bowl; using hands, roll level tablespoons into balls. Heat remaining oil in same skillet; cook meatballs, in batches, until browned all over.

3   Add tomato and beans to same skillet; bring to a boil. Reduce heat; simmer, uncovered, about 5 minutes or until mixture thickens slightly. Return meatballs to skillet; simmer, uncovered, about 10 minutes or until meatballs are cooked through.

4   Meanwhile, make guacamole.

5   Serve meatballs topped with guacamole and sour cream.

GUACAMOLE Mash avocados with fork in medium bowl; stir in remaining ingredients.

SERVES 4
per serving 26g carbohydrate; 52.2g fat; 763 cal; 48g protein

veal goulash with braised red cabbage

PREPARATION TIME 20 MINUTES   COOKING TIME 1 HOUR 30 MINUTES

You need about half a head of red cabbage for this recipe.

1 tablespoon olive oil

1 medium onion, sliced thickly

1 medium red bell pepper, sliced thickly

2 cloves garlic, crushed in garlic press

1¾ pounds boneless veal leg, cut into
**   1-inch cubes**

1 tablespoon sweet paprika

½ teaspoon cayenne

14 ounces canned crushed tomatoes

1½ cups beef broth

¾ cup long-grain brown rice

2 tablespoons butter

14 ounces red cabbage, chopped coarsely

1   Heat oil in large saucepan; cook onion, pepper and garlic until onion softens. Add veal, paprika, cayenne, undrained tomato and ½ cup of the broth; bring to a boil, stirring. Reduce heat; simmer, uncovered, about 1 hour or until veal is tender and sauce thickens slightly.

2   Meanwhile, cook rice in medium saucepan of boiling water until just tender; drain.

3   Melt butter in large skillet; cook cabbage, stirring, about 5 minutes or until just softened. Add remaining broth; bring to a boil. Reduce heat; simmer, covered, 10 minutes.

4   Serve goulash with rice and braised red cabbage.

SERVES 4
per serving 39.9g carbohydrate; 16.1g fat; 525 cal; 54.7g protein

hoisin beef stir-fry (see page 240)

lamb shanks with five-spice, tamarind and ginger (see page 122)

mint and lime lamb with salsa

PREPARATION TIME 20 MINUTES (PLUS REFRIGERATION TIME)   COOKING TIME 10 MINUTES

½ cup olive oil

2 cloves garlic, crushed in garlic press

2 teaspoons grated lime peel

2 tablespoons fresh lime juice

2 tablespoons chopped fresh mint leaves

8 lamb rib chops

WATERMELON AND MANGO SALSA

2 pounds chopped seeded watermelon

3 small mangoes, chopped

2 red serrano chiles, seeded, chopped

¼ cup shredded fresh cilantro leaves

2 tablespoons grated lime peel

¼ cup raspberry vinegar

1 Combine oil, garlic, peel, juice and mint in medium bowl, add chops; mix well. Cover, refrigerate 3 hours or overnight.

2 Make watermelon and mango salsa.

3 Cook chops on heated oiled grill or grill pan until browned both sides and cooked as desired. Serve with watermelon and mango salsa.

WATERMELON AND MANGO SALSA Combine all ingredients in large bowl; toss gently to combine.

SERVES 4
per serving 33.4g carbohydrates; 38.9g fat; 606 cal; 30.5g protein

curried lamb shanks

PREPARATION TIME 20 MINUTES   COOKING TIME 2 HOURS 15 MINUTES

To "french trim" meat is to remove the excess gristle and fat from the end of a shank, chop or rack to expose the bone. Ask your butcher to prepare the lamb shanks for this recipe.

4 french-trimmed lamb shanks

    (about 4 pounds)

¼ cup all-purpose flour

2 tablespoons peanut oil

1 medium onion, chopped finely

2 cloves garlic, crushed in garlic press

½ cup curry paste

2 cups water

14 ounces canned crushed tomatoes

1 teaspoon sugar

2 cups beef broth

¼ small head cauliflower (14 ounces),

    chopped coarsely

14 ounces butternut squash, chopped coarsely

½ cup red lentils

¼ cup coarsely chopped fresh cilantro

1 Toss lamb in flour; shake away excess. Heat oil in large deep saucepan; cook lamb, in batches, until browned all over.

2 Cook onion and garlic in same saucepan, stirring, until onion softens. Add paste; cook, stirring, until fragrant. Return lamb to saucepan with the water, undrained tomatoes, sugar and broth; bring to a boil. Reduce heat; simmer, covered, 1½ hours.

3 Add cauliflower and squash to curry; bring to a boil. Reduce heat; simmer, covered, 15 minutes. Stir in lentils; simmer, covered, about 10 minutes or until lentils are tender. Remove from heat; stir in cilantro.

SERVES 4
per serving 31.9g carbohydrate; 40.1g fat; 774 cal; 71.9g protein
tip You can use any type of curry paste from mild tikka to fiery vindaloo, depending on how spicy you want your lamb to be.

lemon and artichoke rack of lamb with moroccan orange and radish salad

PREPARATION TIME 20 MINUTES   COOKING TIME 40 MINUTES

1 french-trimmed rack of lamb with 8 chops
 (1¼ pounds)

2 medium onions, sliced thinly

1 medium lemon

14 ounces canned, drained, artichoke hearts

2 tablespoons drained capers

1 tablespoon butter

1 teaspoon light brown sugar

4 medium seedless oranges, peeled, sliced thinly

3 large red radishes, sliced thinly

½ small red onion, sliced thinly

¾ cup niçoise olives, pitted

LEMON DRESSING

1 clove garlic, crushed in garlic press

½ teaspoon sweet paprika

½ teaspoon ground cumin

2 tablespoons fresh lemon juice

2 tablespoons olive oil

2 tablespoons finely chopped fresh flat-leaf parsley

½ teaspoon ground cinnamon

1 Cook lamb and onion on heated oiled grill pan until lamb is browned all over and onion soft.

2 Cut lemon into eight wedges. Place lamb, onion and lemon in disposable roasting pan with artichokes, capers, butter and sugar. Cook in covered grill, using indirect heat, following manufacturer's instructions, about 30 minutes or until lamb is cooked as desired.

3 Make lemon dressing.

4 Overlap alternate slices of orange and radish around edge of serving plate; overlap remaining slices in center. Top with red onion and olives; drizzle with dressing. Serve lamb, vegetables and lemon with salad.

LEMON DRESSING Combine all ingredients in screw-top jar; shake well.

SERVES 4
per serving 27.5g carbohydrate; 29.1g fat; 454 cal; 20.2g protein

mango chutney lamb with arugula and sugarsnap salad

PREPARATION TIME 10 MINUTES   COOKING TIME 10 MINUTES

⅓ cup unflavored yogurt

⅓ cup mango chutney

⅓ cup hot chili sauce

12 french-trimmed single lamb
 rib chops (2 pounds)

8 ounces sugarsnap peas

3 cups (5 ounces) arugula

¼ cup olive oil

2 tablespoons balsamic vinegar

2 whole wheat pitas, cut into 4 wedges each

1 Combine yogurt, chutney and sauce in large bowl.

2 Cook lamb on heated oiled grill or grill pan, brushing with yogurt mixture frequently, until browned on both sides and cooked as desired.

3 Meanwhile, boil, steam or microwave peas until just tender. Rinse peas under cold water; drain. Toss peas and arugula in large bowl with combined oil and vinegar.

4 Wrap pitas in foil parcel and heat on grill. Serve arugula and sugarsnap salad with lamb and warmed pitas.

SERVES 4
per serving 38.8g carbohydrate; 36g fat; 602 cal; 27.4g protein

lamb and haloumi kebabs

PREPARATION TIME 30 MINUTES (PLUS REFRIGERATION TIME)   COOKING TIME 15 MINUTES

Soak 12 bamboo skewers in water for at least an hour prior to use to prevent splintering or scorching.

2½ pounds leg of lamb, cut into 1-inch cubes

10 ounces sun-dried tomatoes

1½ pounds haloumi or white frying cheese,
    cut into 1-inch cubes

½ cup red wine vinegar

2 cloves garlic, crushed in garlic press

⅓ cup olive oil

2½ cups (5 ounces) mesclun

1   Thread lamb, tomatoes and cheese onto 12 skewers.

2   Place kebabs in shallow casserole; pour over combined vinegar, garlic and oil. Cover; refrigerate 3 hours or overnight.

3   Drain kebabs; discard marinade. Cook kebabs on heated oiled grill or grill pan until browned all over and cooked as desired. Serve with mesclun.

SERVES 4
per serving 29.3g carbohydrate; 73.7g fat; 1195 cal; 103.2g protein
tip If using metal skewers, oil them first to prevent lamb from sticking.

lamb and dhal with minted cucumber yogurt

PREPARATION TIME 20 MINUTES   COOKING TIME 35 MINUTES

2 cups water

1¼ cups red lentils

1 teaspoon ground turmeric

1 teaspoon cumin seeds

1 teaspoon black mustard seeds

1 tablespoon butter

2 scallions, sliced thinly

1 red serrano chile, chopped finely

1 tablespoon grated fresh ginger

1 clove garlic, crushed in garlic press

1 small tomato, seeded, chopped finely

1 teaspoon garam masala

1 tablespoon olive oil

1 pound butterflied leg of lamb,
    cut into ½-inch strips

MINTED CUCUMBER YOGURT

2 hothouse cucumbers, seeded, chopped finely

1 cup unflavored yogurt

½ cup loosely packed fresh mint leaves, sliced thinly

¼ cup fresh lime juice

1   Combine the water, lentils and turmeric in large saucepan; bring to a boil. Reduce heat; simmer, uncovered, about 15 minutes or until lentils are tender, stirring occasionally.

2   Meanwhile, make minted cucumber yogurt.

3   Cook seeds in large deep heated skillet, stirring until fragrant. Add butter, scallion, chile, ginger, garlic and tomato; cook, stirring, 5 minutes. Add lentil mixture to skillet; stir over low heat until heated through. Remove from heat; stir in garam masala.

4   Heat oil in large skillet; add lamb. Cook until browned all over and cooked as desired. Serve dhal topped with lamb and minted cucumber yogurt.

MINTED CUCUMBER YOGURT   Combine ingredients in small bowl.

SERVES 4
per serving 28.9g carbohydrate; 12.6g fat; 417 cal; 46.5g protein
tip Garam masala, a blend of spices favored by cooks in North India, is based on varying proportions of cardamom, cinnamon, cloves, coriander, fennel and cumin, roasted and ground together. Black pepper and chile can be added for a spicier version.

slow-roasted lamb shanks with caramelized red onion and white bean puree

PREPARATION TIME 20 MINUTES   COOKING TIME 4 HOURS 30 MINUTES

1 tablespoon olive oil

4 french-trimmed lamb shanks
    (about 4 pounds)

2 teaspoons sugar

1½ cups dry red wine

2 cups beef broth

3 cloves garlic, crushed in
    garlic press

1 tablespoon butter

1 small onion, chopped finely

1 stalk celery, trimmed,
    chopped finely

1 tablespoon all-purpose flour

1 tablespoon tomato paste

4 sprigs fresh rosemary,
    chopped coarsely

WHITE BEAN PUREE

28 ounces canned cannellini beans,
    rinsed, drained

1 cup chicken broth

4 cloves garlic, quartered

1 tablespoon fresh lemon juice

2 tablespoons olive oil

CARAMELIZED ONION

3 tablespoons butter

2 small red onions, sliced thinly

2 tablespoons light brown sugar

¼ cup raspberry vinegar

1   Preheat oven to slow.

2   Heat oil in large roasting pan; cook shanks until browned all over. Stir in sugar, wine, broth and garlic; bring to a boil. Transfer lamb to slow oven; roast, covered, about 4 hours, turning twice during cooking.

3   Meanwhile, make white bean puree. Make caramelized onion.

4   Remove lamb from roasting pan; cover to keep warm. Pour pan liquids into large heatproof measuring cup. Skim off fat.

5   Return pan to heat, melt butter; cook onion and celery, stirring, until celery is just tender. Stir in flour; cook, stirring, 2 minutes. Add reserved pan liquids, tomato paste and rosemary; bring to a boil. Simmer, uncovered, stirring until mixture boils and thickens; strain sauce into large heatproof measuring cup.

6   Serve lamb with wine sauce, white bean puree and caramelized onion.

WHITE BEAN PUREE   Combine beans and broth in medium saucepan, bring to a boil; simmer, covered, 20 minutes. Uncover; simmer, stirring occasionally, about 10 minutes or until liquid is absorbed. Blend or process beans, garlic and juice until almost smooth; with motor running, gradually add oil until mixture forms a smooth puree.

CARAMELIZED ONION   Melt butter in medium saucepan; cook onion, stirring, about 15 minutes or until browned and soft. Stir in sugar and vinegar; cook, stirring, about 15 minutes or until onion is caramelized.

SERVES 4
per serving 35g carbohydrate; 43.9g fat; 879 cal; 72.3g protein

mustard lamb chops
with basil cream and mixed vegetables

PREPARATION TIME 25 MINUTES (PLUS REFRIGERATION TIME)   COOKING TIME 40 MINUTES

**1 french-trimmed rack of lamb with
   8 chops (1¼ pounds)**

¾ cup olive oil

½ cup coarsely chopped fresh basil

**2 cloves garlic, crushed in
   garlic press**

2 medium potatoes

2 medium yellow squash

2 medium green zucchini

1 large red bell pepper

1 large yellow bell pepper

4 medium baby eggplants

4 spring onions

**7 ounces haloumi or white frying
   cheese, sliced thinly**

**1 tablespoon caraway
   seeds, toasted**

1 tablespoon grated lemon peel

2 teaspoons ground cumin

**1 tablespoon finely chopped fresh
   lemon thyme**

**2 tablespoons finely
   chopped capers**

2 tablespoons grainy mustard

BASIL CREAM

2 teaspoons olive oil

1 medium white onion, sliced thinly

**1 clove garlic, crushed in
   garlic press**

½ cup dry white wine

1¼ cups heavy cream

½ cup coarsely chopped fresh basil

1 Cut lamb rack into double chops. Combine ¼ cup of oil, basil and half of the garlic in large bowl, add chops; mix well. Cover; refrigerate 3 hours or overnight.

2 Slice all vegetables thickly lengthwise. Cook vegetables on heated oiled grill or grill pan 25 minutes or until browned both sides and tender. Add cheese to grill until browned both sides. Transfer vegetables and cheese to large serving platter; drizzle with combined remaining oil, seeds, peel, remaining garlic, cumin, thyme and capers.

3 Meanwhile, drain chops; discard marinade. Cook chops on heated oiled grill or grill pan until browned all over and cooked as desired.

4 Make basil cream.

5 Spread lamb with mustard; serve with basil cream and mixed vegetables.

BASIL CREAM Heat oil in medium skillet; cook onion and garlic, stirring, until tender. Add wine, simmer, uncovered, 5 minutes or until reduced by half. Add cream; boil 5 minutes or until sauce thickens. Remove from heat, stir in basil; serve immediately.

SERVES 4
per serving 28.7g carbohydrate; 99.1g fat; 1155 cal; 35g protein

merguez, beet and lentil salad

PREPARATION TIME 30 MINUTES   COOKING TIME 50 MINUTES

Merguez sausages, from North Africa, are traditionally made with lamb and seasoned with garlic and hot spices. If you cannot find merguez sausages, replace with any spicy sausages.

1 cup brown lentils

2 sprigs fresh thyme

6 merguez sausages

1 medium onion, chopped finely

2 teaspoons yellow mustard seeds

2 teaspoons ground cumin

1 teaspoon ground coriander

½ cup chicken broth

1 pound spinach, trimmed, chopped coarsely

15 ounces canned beets, drained,
    cut into large chunks

THYME DRESSING

1 teaspoon finely chopped fresh thyme

1 clove garlic, crushed in garlic press

½ cup red wine vinegar

¼ cup extra virgin olive oil

1   Make thyme dressing.

2   Cook lentils with thyme sprigs, uncovered, in large pot of boiling water until tender; drain lentils, discard thyme sprigs. Place lentils in large bowl with half of the dressing; toss gently to combine.

3   Meanwhile, cook sausages in heated large nonstick skillet until browned and cooked through. Cool 5 minutes; slice thickly.

4   Reheat same skillet; cook onion, mustard seeds, cumin and coriander, stirring, until onion softens. Add broth; bring to a boil. Remove from heat; stir in spinach.

5   Add spinach mixture, beets, sausages and remaining dressing to lentil mixture; toss gently to combine.

THYME DRESSING Combine ingredients in screw-top jar; shake well.

SERVES 4
per serving 35.7g carbohydrate; 41.3g fat; 687 cal; 44.7g protein

tex-mex ribs with sage-and-bacon corn

PREPARATION TIME 10 MINUTES (PLUS REFRIGERATION TIME)   COOKING TIME 55 MINUTES

4 fresh ears corn

5 quarts water

¼ cup milk

⅓ cup barbecue sauce

1 teaspoon chili powder

1¼ ounces taco seasoning

2 pounds pork spareribs

2 tablespoons chopped fresh sage leaves

3 slices bacon, chopped finely

1   Peel husks back from corn, leaving them attached at base; remove silk, fold husks back over corn. Soak corn in combined water and milk. Cover; refrigerate 3 hours or overnight.

2   Combine sauce, chili powder and seasoning in large bowl; add ribs, mix well. Cover; refrigerate 3 hours or overnight.

3   Place ribs in disposable roasting pan. Cook in covered grill, using indirect heat, following manufacturer's instructions, about 55 minutes or until tender. During cooking, brush ribs occasionally with pan juices.

4   Meanwhile, gently peel husk back from corn, press combined sage and bacon onto corn; tie husks with kitchen string to enclose filling. Cook in covered grill, using indirect heat, following manufacturer's instructions, about 40 minutes or until tender. Serve with ribs.

SERVES 4
per serving 40.5g carbohydrate; 17.1g fat; 494 cal; 44.4g protein

sweet and spicy pork skewers with celeriac and apple salad

PREPARATION TIME 40 MINUTES (PLUS REFRIGERATION TIME)   COOKING TIME 10 MINUTES

1½ pounds pork medallions

6 cloves garlic, crushed in garlic press

2 tablespoons honey

2 teaspoons ground hot paprika

½ cup chopped fresh flat-leaf parsley

1½ cups olive oil

2 egg yolks

1 teaspoon finely grated lemon peel

2 tablespoons fresh lemon juice

1 teaspoon prepared white horseradish

1 pound celeriac (celery root),
**   trimmed, peeled**

1 large red apple

2 medium carrots, grated coarsely

1 cup walnuts, toasted,
**   chopped coarsely**

1 bunch fresh chives,
**   cut into 2½-inch lengths**

1   Cut pork into 1-inch cubes, combine with all but 1 tablespoon of garlic, honey, paprika, half of the parsley and ½ cup oil in large bowl. Cover; refrigerate 3 hours or overnight.

2   Blend or process yolks, reserved tablespoon of garlic, peel and juice until combined. With motor running, gradually add remaining oil; process until dressing thickens and is smooth. Stir in horseradish. Store in refrigerator until needed.

3   Using a mandoline, V-slicer or sharp knife, cut celeriac and apple into very thin slices; cut slices into matchstick-sized pieces. Place in large bowl of water to prevent discoloration.

4   Thread pork onto skewers; discard remaining marinade. Cook skewers, in batches, on heated oiled grill or grill pan until browned and cooked through.

5   Place drained celeriac and apple in large bowl with carrot, nuts, remaining parsley, chives and horseradish dressing; toss gently to combine. Serve with sweet and spicy pork.

SERVES 4

per serving 26.3g carbohydrate; 109.9g fat; 1273 cal; 48.7g protein

tips It's worth investing in a mandoline if you're a serious cook. This hand-operated machine has adjustable razor-sharp blades for precise cutting, julienning and slicing. Soak 12 bamboo skewers in water for at least an hour prior to use to prevent splintering or scorching. If using metal skewers, oil them first to prevent pork from sticking.

pork chops valenciana with roasted garlic celeriac

PREPARATION TIME 15 MINUTES   COOKING TIME 1 HOUR

1 large celeriac (celery root)

1 large bulb garlic

2 tablespoons olive oil

four 6-ounce boneless pork chops

¼ cup orange marmalade

2 tablespoons hot chili sauce (such
**   as sambal oelek or sriracha)**

1 tablespoon cider vinegar

1 teaspoon finely grated fresh ginger

1 teaspoon ground cumin

3 scallions, sliced finely

⅓ cup chopped fresh flat-leaf parsley

1   Peel celeriac; cut into 1-inch pieces. Combine celeriac and garlic in disposable baking dish; add oil.

2   Cook in covered grill, using indirect heat, following manufacturer's instructions, about 1 hour or until celeriac is golden brown and tender, turning occasionally during cooking.

3   Meanwhile, cook pork in large heated oiled skillet until browned both sides and cooked through. Remove pork from skillet; cover to keep warm.

4   Cook marmalade, sauce, vinegar, ginger and cumin in small skillet, stirring, until sauce thickens slightly; stir scallion into sauce.

5   Cut garlic in half crosswise; squeeze pulp over celeriac. Toss with parsley.

6   Drizzle pork with sauce; serve with celeriac.

SERVES 4

per serving 33.1g carbohydrate; 29.6g fat; 550 cal; 38.7g protein

pork with orange-mustard sauce on mashed sweet potatoes

PREPARATION TIME 10 MINUTES (PLUS REFRIGERATION TIME)   COOKING TIME 30 MINUTES

four 5-ounce boneless pork chops

1 clove garlic, crushed in garlic press

1 teaspoon grated fresh ginger

1 tablespoon orange marmalade

1 teaspoon finely grated orange peel

2 tablespoons fresh orange juice

2 tablespoons olive oil

1¼ pounds sweet potato, chopped coarsely

1 tablespoon butter

1 tablespoon maple syrup

3 tablespoons butter, extra

2 tablespoons grainy mustard

½ cup fresh orange juice, extra

½ cup dry white wine

¼ cup chicken broth

¼ cup sour cream

1   Combine pork in large bowl with garlic, ginger, marmalade, peel, juice and half of the oil. Cover; refrigerate 3 hours or overnight.

2   Boil, steam or microwave sweet potato until tender; drain. Mash sweet potato in large bowl with butter and maple syrup; cover to keep warm.

3   Meanwhile, drain pork; reserve marinade. Heat remaining oil in large skillet; cook pork, in batches, until browned both sides and cooked as desired. Cover to keep warm.

4   Heat extra butter in same skillet; cook mustard, extra juice, wine, broth and reserved marinade. Bring to a boil; reduce heat. Simmer, uncovered, about 5 minutes or until sauce reduces by half. Remove sauce from heat; stir in sour cream. Serve sweet potato with pork; drizzle with sauce.

SERVES 4
per serving 34.4g carbohydrate; 33.7g fat; 597 cal; 34.8g protein

baked mustard pork with caramelized apples

PREPARATION TIME 10 MINUTES   COOKING TIME 30 MINUTES

1 medium red onion, cut into thin wedges

1 tablespoon olive oil

1½ pounds boneless pork loin, trimmed

½ cup honey dijon mustard

½ cup apple juice

⅓ cup vegetable broth

¼ cup coarsely chopped fresh
   flat-leaf parsley

4 tablespoons butter

3 large apples, peeled, cored, sliced thinly

1 tablespoon light brown sugar

5 cups (5 ounces) trimmed watercress

1   Preheat oven to very hot.

2   Combine onion and oil in large casserole. Brush pork all over with mustard; place on onion in casserole. Bake, uncovered, in very hot oven about 20 minutes or until cooked as desired. Remove pork from dish, cover; let stand 5 minutes.

3   Place dish over heat; add juice and broth, bring to a boil. Reduce heat; simmer, uncovered, about 3 minutes or until sauce thickens slightly. Stir in parsley.

4   Meanwhile, melt butter in large skillet. Add apple and sugar; cook, stirring occasionally, about 10 minutes or until almost caramelized. Cover to keep warm.

5   Divide watercress among serving plates. Slice pork thickly; serve with onion sauce and caramelized apple.

SERVES 4
per serving 35.4g carbohydrate; 22.6g fat; 523 cal; 45.6g protein

pork loin with fresh peach chutney and crackling

PREPARATION TIME 35 MINUTES   COOKING TIME 3 HOURS

3 pounds boneless pork loin roast, rind on

1 tablespoon olive oil

½ teaspoon celery seeds

1 teaspoon sea salt

4½ cups (7 ounces) baby spinach leaves

FRESH PEACH CHUTNEY

1 large peach, chopped coarsely

1 large onion, chopped coarsely

1 tablespoon coarsely chopped raisins

1 teaspoon grated fresh ginger

½ cup sugar

½ cup apple cider vinegar

1 cinnamon stick

¼ teaspoon ground clove

1 Make fresh peach chutney.

2 Preheat oven to hot. Remove rind from loin; reserve. Rub pork with half of the oil; sprinkle with seeds.

3 Place pork on wire rack in large roasting pan; roast in hot oven, about 50 minutes or until juices run clear when pierced with skewer. Remove from oven; place pork on cutting board, cover to keep warm.

4 Increase oven temperature to very hot.

5 Remove excess fat from underside of reserved rind; score rind, rub with remaining oil and sea salt. Place rind, fatty-side up, on wire rack in casserole; bake, uncovered, in very hot oven about 15 minutes or until crisp and browned. Drain on paper towel.

6 Serve thickly sliced pork and rind with fresh peach chutney. Accompany with baby spinach leaves.

FRESH PEACH CHUTNEY Combine ingredients in medium nonreactive saucepan, stir over heat, without boiling, until sugar dissolves; bring to a boil. Reduce heat; simmer, uncovered, stirring occasionally, about 1¾ hours or until mixture thickens.

SERVES 4
per serving 36.8g carbohydrate; 27g fat; 833 cal; 110g protein
tip The chutney can be made up to a week ahead. Place in a sterilized jar while still hot; seal, cool, then refrigerate until required.

pork with pear chutney and mashed butternut squash

PREPARATION TIME 30 MINUTES   COOKING TIME 30 MINUTES

1 tablespoon vegetable oil

1½ pounds boneless pork chops

1 pound butternut squash, chopped coarsely

2 tablespoons milk

1 medium head broccoli (1 pound)

PEAR CHUTNEY

2 small pears

1 small onion, chopped finely

¼ cup apple cider vinegar

2 tablespoons bourbon

¼ cup firmly packed light brown sugar

1 Make pear chutney.

2 Heat oil in large skillet; cook pork, in batches, over medium heat until browned all over and cooked as desired.

3 Meanwhile, boil, steam or microwave squash until soft; drain. Mash squash with milk in large bowl until smooth.

4 Separate broccoli into florets. Boil, steam or microwave until just tender; drain. Serve pork with pear chutney, mashed pumpkin and broccoli.

PEAR CHUTNEY Peel, core and thinly slice pears. Combine pears with remaining ingredients in medium nonreactive saucepan; bring to a boil. Reduce heat; simmer, uncovered, about 25 minutes or until liquid has almost evaporated.

SERVES 4
per serving 40.7g carbohydrate; 10.1g fat; 445 cal; 48.1g protein

honey-soy pork with spinach and snow pea salad

PREPARATION TIME 10 MINUTES (PLUS REFRIGERATION TIME)   COOKING TIME 2 HOURS

You need about three limes for this recipe.

1¾ pounds pork shoulder

2 cloves garlic, crushed in garlic press

2 tablespoons olive oil

1 tablespoon light brown sugar

¼ cup honey

2 teaspoons grated fresh ginger

2 tablespoons light soy sauce

2 tablespoons fresh lime juice

SPINACH AND SNOW PEA SALAD

4½ cups (7 ounces) baby spinach leaves

4 ounces snow peas, trimmed, sliced thinly

4 scallions, sliced thinly

⅓ cup roasted pine nuts, chopped coarsely

½ cup shaved parmesan cheese

⅓ cup olive oil

1 teaspoon finely grated lime peel

¼ cup fresh lime juice

1 tablespoon sugar

1   Place pork in large shallow casserole; pour combined remaining ingredients over pork. Cover; refrigerate 3 hours or overnight, turning pork occasionally in marinade.

2   Preheat oven to moderate.

3   Drain pork; reserve marinade. Wrap pork tightly in three layers of foil. Bake in moderate oven about 2 hours or until cooked as desired. Let stand 10 minutes; slice thinly.

4   Meanwhile, place reserved marinade in small saucepan; bring to a boil. Reduce heat; simmer, uncovered, 5 minutes.

5   Make spinach and snow pea salad. Drizzle pork with marinade; accompany with spinach and snow pea salad.

SPINACH AND SNOW PEA SALAD Place spinach, snow peas, scallion, nuts and cheese in large bowl. Just before serving, add combined remaining ingredients; toss gently to combine.

SERVES 4
per serving 28.8g carbohydrate; 55.6g fat; 812 cal; 50.7g protein

grilled pork with green apple salad

PREPARATION TIME 20 MINUTES   COOKING TIME 10 MINUTES (PLUS COOLING TIME)

four 8-ounce boneless pork chops

3 medium granny smith apples, sliced thinly

4 scallions, sliced thinly

2 cups loosely packed fresh mint leaves

1 cup loosely packed fresh cilantro leaves

½ cup fresh lemon juice

¾ cup toasted unsalted cashews

GINGER DRESSING

¼ cup firmly packed light brown sugar

2 tablespoons fish sauce

1-inch piece fresh ginger, grated

1   Make ginger dressing.

2   Cook pork on heated oiled grill or grill pan until browned both sides and cooked as desired.

3   Meanwhile, combine apple, scallion, mint, cilantro and juice in large bowl; pour over half of the ginger dressing, toss to combine. Divide pork among serving plates. Top with salad, sprinkle with nuts then drizzle with remaining dressing.

GINGER DRESSING Combine ingredients in small saucepan; bring to a boil. Remove from heat; strain. Cool before using.

SERVES 4
per serving 35.8g carbohydrate; 34.4g fat; 583 cal; 33.7g protein

marmalade chicken with asparagus-walnut salad

PREPARATION TIME 15 MINUTES   COOKING TIME 1 HOUR 30 MINUTES

½ cup orange marmalade

2 tablespoons Grand Marnier

¼ cup fresh orange juice

3¼-pound whole chicken

ASPARAGUS-WALNUT SALAD

2 bunches asparagus

¼ cup finely chopped walnuts, toasted

2 teaspoons grainy mustard

1 tablespoon red wine vinegar

1 small shallot, chopped finely

¼ cup extra virgin olive oil

2 cups (3½ ounces) baby arugula leaves

1 Combine marmalade, liqueur and juice in small saucepan. Bring to a boil, simmer, uncovered, about 5 minutes or until glaze thickens. Divide glaze into two portions. Wash chicken under cold water; pat dry with paper towel. Place chicken on roasting rack or in disposable roasting pan. Cook in covered grill, using indirect heat, following manufacturer's instructions, 1 hour. Brush chicken with one portion of glaze, cook 20 minutes more or until browned all over and tender.

2 Meanwhile, make asparagus-walnut salad. Just before serving, brush chicken with remaining glaze. Serve with asparagus-walnut salad.

ASPARAGUS-WALNUT SALAD Cut asparagus spears into 3½-inch lengths. Boil, steam or microwave asparagus until tender. Blend or process half the walnuts with mustard, vinegar, shallot and oil until smooth. Just before serving, combine asparagus with arugula and walnut dressing, sprinkle with remaining walnuts.

SERVES 4
per serving 36.9g carbohydrate; 47.7g fat; 765 cal; 43.8g protein

open-face chicken burgers with avocado cream

PREPARATION TIME 30 MINUTES   COOKING TIME 10 MINUTES

1¾ pounds lean ground chicken

3 slices bacon, chopped finely

⅓ cup grated parmesan cheese

3 scallions, chopped finely

1 tablespoon finely chopped fresh thyme

1 egg, beaten lightly

⅓ cup packaged breadcrumbs

4 thick slices rye bread

1 cup (3 ounces) alfalfa sprouts

2 medium tomatoes, sliced thinly

1 medium carrot, sliced thinly

AVOCADO CREAM

1 medium avocado, chopped coarsely

4 ounces cream cheese, softened

1 tablespoon fresh lemon juice

1 Combine chicken, bacon, cheese, scallion, thyme, egg and breadcrumbs in medium bowl. Using hands, shape mixture into four patties.

2 Cook patties on heated oiled grill or grill pan, uncovered, until browned and cooked through.

3 Meanwhile, make avocado cream.

4 Place bread on grill; cook until lightly toasted.

5 Top bread with sprouts, patties, tomato, avocado cream and carrot.

AVOCADO CREAM Combine ingredients in bowl; mash with a fork until well combined.

SERVES 4
per serving 40.4g carbohydrate; 44.2g fat; 792 cal; 58.4g protein

roast chicken on mashed parsnips with tomato chutney

PREPARATION TIME 20 MINUTES   COOKING TIME 1 HOUR 20 MINUTES

3¾-pound whole chicken

1 tablespoon olive oil

2 teaspoons sea salt

2 pounds large parsnips,
    chopped coarsely

2 cloves garlic, crushed in
    garlic press

3 tablespoons butter, chopped

½ cup milk

TOMATO CHUTNEY

1 tablespoon olive oil

1 small red onion,
    chopped coarsely

4 small tomatoes, chopped coarsely

1 clove garlic, crushed in
    garlic press

¼ cup firmly packed light
    brown sugar

1 tablespoon balsamic vinegar

1 Preheat oven to hot.

2 Wash chicken under cold water; pat dry with paper towel. Using kitchen scissors, cut along both sides of backbone of chicken; discard backbone. Place chicken, skin-side up, on cutting board; using heel of hand, press down on breastbone to flatten chicken.

3 Rub oil all over chicken, sprinkle with salt; place chicken, skin-side up, on oiled wire rack over roasting pan. Roast, uncovered, in hot oven 20 minutes. Reduce oven to moderate; roast, uncovered, 1 hour or until chicken is browned and cooked through. Cover with foil halfway through cooking if chicken starts to overbrown.

4 Meanwhile, make tomato chutney.

5 Boil, steam or microwave parsnip until tender; drain. Mash parsnip in large bowl until smooth; stir in garlic, butter and milk. Push parsnip mash through fine strainer or food mill back into same bowl. Serve parsnip with chicken; top with tomato chutney.

TOMATO CHUTNEY Combine ingredients in medium nonreactive saucepan; stir over heat until sugar dissolves. Bring to a boil; simmer, uncovered, about 1 hour or until chutney is thickened, stirring occasionally.

SERVES 4
per serving 39.9g carbohydrate; 59.8g fat; 1004 cal; 69.8g protein
tip Tomato chutney can be stored in sterilized jars up to one month in refrigerator.

spicy caribbean-style chicken stew

PREPARATION TIME 45 MINUTES   COOKING TIME 50 MINUTES

2 pounds skinless, boneless chicken thighs

2 teaspoons ground allspice

1 teaspoon ground cinnamon

pinch ground nutmeg

1 tablespoon finely chopped fresh thyme

¼ cup olive oil

2 medium onions, sliced thinly

2 cloves garlic, crushed in garlic press

1 tablespoon grated fresh ginger

1 teaspoon chili sauce (such as sambal oelek
    or sriracha)

5 medium tomatoes, peeled, seeded, chopped finely

2 tablespoons light brown sugar

2 teaspoons grated orange peel

2 tablespoons soy sauce

1 medium sweet potato, chopped coarsely

2 fresh ears corn, shucked, sliced thickly

2½ cups (4 ounces) baby spinach leaves

1   Cut chicken into ¾-inch strips. Toss chicken in combined spices and thyme.

2   Heat half of the oil in large saucepan; cook chicken, in batches, stirring, until browned. Drain on paper towel.

3   Heat remaining oil in same cleaned saucepan. Cook onion, garlic, ginger and chili sauce, stirring, until onion is soft.

4   Add tomato, sugar, peel, soy sauce, sweet potato, corn and chicken; cook, covered, about 15 minutes or until chicken and vegetables are tender. Remove cover; simmer 5 minutes.

5   Remove from heat. Add spinach; stir until spinach is wilted.

SERVES 4
per serving 37.2g carbohydrate; 33g fat; 661 cal; 54.5g protein

baked chicken, sweet potato and spinach

PREPARATION TIME 15 MINUTES   COOKING TIME 45 MINUTES

8 ounces feta cheese

10 ounces frozen chopped spinach, thawed

2 medium sweet potatoes, sliced thinly

four 6-ounce skinless, boneless chicken
    breasts, sliced thinly

1 medium onion, chopped finely

2 teaspoons finely chopped fresh thyme

¼ cup light sour cream

½ cup chicken broth

2 teaspoons all-purpose flour

1 tablespoon water

2 cups shredded mozzarella cheese

1   Crumble feta into medium bowl. Using hands, squeeze excess moisture from spinach; mix spinach with feta.

2   Boil, steam or microwave sweet potato until just tender; drain.

3   Meanwhile, cook chicken, in batches, in heated oiled medium skillet until just cooked through and browned all over.

4   Cook onion and thyme in same skillet, stirring, until onion is soft; stir into feta mixture. Cook sour cream, broth and blended flour and water in same skillet, stirring, until mixture boils and thickens.

5   Layer half the sweet potato, half the chicken and all of the feta mixture in oiled 3-quart casserole. Repeat layering with remaining sweet potato and chicken; pour cream mixture over the top. Sprinkle with mozzarella; bake, uncovered, in moderately hot oven about 30 minutes or until cheese melts and is browned lightly.

SERVES 4
per serving 28.5g carbohydrate; 41.4g fat; 774 cal; 72.5g protein

chicken with mushrooms and celeriac

PREPARATION TIME 35 MINUTES   COOKING TIME 1 HOUR 30 MINUTES

2 large red bell peppers

8 skinless, boneless chicken thighs
    (about 2½ pounds)

¼ cup all-purpose flour

1 tablespoon olive oil

1 teaspoon caraway seeds

5 juniper berries

1 medium celeriac (celery root),
    chopped coarsely

8 ounces button mushrooms, halved

1½ cups chicken broth

1 tablespoon tomato paste

1 tablespoon cornstarch

1 tablespoon water

1 tablespoon finely chopped fresh
    flat-leaf parsley

1   Quarter peppers; remove and discard seeds and membranes. Cook
    pepper, skin-side down, on heated oiled grill until skin blisters and
    blackens. Cover pepper pieces with plastic wrap or paper for 5 minutes;
    peel away skin, slice thickly.

2   Preheat oven to moderate. Toss chicken in flour; shake away excess
    flour. Heat oil in 3-quart casserole; cook chicken, in batches, until
    browned. Drain on paper towel.

3   Add seeds, berries, celeriac and mushrooms to casserole; cook, stirring,
    until mushrooms are just soft.

4   Return chicken to casserole with pepper, broth and paste; mix well. Cook,
    covered, in moderate oven about 45 minutes or until chicken is tender.

5   Stir in blended cornstarch and water. Stir over heat until mixture boils
    and thickens slightly.

6   Serve sprinkled with parsley.

SERVES 4
per serving 26.4g carbohydrate; 35.9g fat; 604 cal; 44.2g protein

honey-soy chicken salad

PREPARATION TIME 20 MINUTES   COOKING TIME 15 MINUTES

1¼ pounds skinless, boneless chicken
    breasts, sliced thinly

2 tablespoons soy sauce

⅓ cup honey

1 clove garlic, crushed in garlic press

4 red serrano chiles, seeded, chopped finely

10 ounces snow peas

1 small carrot

1 tablespoon peanut oil

2 cups finely shredded savoy cabbage

1 medium yellow bell pepper, sliced thinly

1 medium red bell pepper, sliced thinly

1 hothouse cucumber, seeded, sliced thinly

4 scallions, sliced thinly

½ cup loosely packed fresh mint leaves

2 tablespoons fresh lime juice

2 teaspoons sesame oil

1   Place chicken in medium bowl with sauce, honey, garlic and half of
    the chile; toss to coat chicken in chile mixture. Cover; refrigerate
    until required.

2   Boil, steam or microwave snow peas until just tender; drain. Rinse
    immediately under cold water; drain. Using vegetable peeler, slice carrot
    into ribbons.

3   Heat peanut oil in wok or large skillet; stir-fry drained chicken, in batches,
    until browned and cooked through.

4   Place chicken, snow peas and carrot in large serving bowl with remaining
    ingredients and remaining chile; toss gently to combine.

SERVES 4
per serving 33.7g carbohydrate; 15.6g fat; 422 cal; 37.6g protein
tip You need about a quarter of a small head of savoy cabbage for this recipe.

chicken jambalaya

PREPARATION TIME 15 MINUTES   COOKING TIME 30 MINUTES

One of the most well-known American creole dishes, jambalaya is believed to have been devised when a New Orleans cook named Jean tossed together – or "balayez" in the dialect of Louisiana – various leftovers and came up with such a delicious dish that diners named it "Jean Balayez".

1 tablespoon olive oil

1 medium onion, chopped coarsely

1 medium red bell pepper, chopped coarsely

1 clove garlic, crushed in garlic press

2 stalks celery, trimmed, sliced thinly

2 red serrano chiles, seeded, sliced thinly

1½ cups basmati rice

½ cup dry white wine

2½ cups chicken broth

14 ounces canned crushed tomatoes

1 tablespoon tomato paste

1½ pounds chicken and herb sausages

⅓ cup coarsely chopped fresh cilantro

1   Heat oil in large saucepan; cook onion, pepper, garlic, celery and chile, stirring, until vegetables soften. Stir in rice, wine, broth, undrained tomatoes and paste; bring to a boil. Reduce heat; simmer, covered, about 20 minutes or until liquid is absorbed.

2   Meanwhile, cook sausages in large skillet until browned and cooked through. Drain on paper towel; slice thickly.

3   Stir sausage and cilantro into jambalaya mixture just before serving.

SERVES 4
per serving 33g carbohydrate; 45.5g fat; 837 cal; 26.3g protein

oven-baked parmesan chicken

PREPARATION TIME 15 MINUTES   COOKING TIME 10 MINUTES

You need about half a head of frisée for this recipe.

1 tablespoon all-purpose flour

2 eggs, beaten lightly

2 cups homemade breadcrumbs

⅓ cup coarsely grated parmesan cheese

2 tablespoons finely chopped fresh flat-leaf parsley

12 chicken tenderloins (about 1 pound)

1 cup firmly packed fresh basil leaves

½ cup olive oil

¼ cup fresh lemon juice

1 clove garlic, quartered

¾ cup kalamata olives, pitted

7 ounces frisée

1 cup (1½ ounces) baby arugula leaves

1   Preheat oven to hot.

2   Combine flour and egg in medium bowl; combine breadcrumbs, cheese and parsley in another medium bowl. Coat chicken, one piece at a time, first in flour mixture then in breadcrumb mixture. Place chicken, in single layer, on oiled baking sheet; roast, uncovered, in hot oven about 5 minutes or until chicken is lightly browned and cooked through.

3   Meanwhile, blend or process basil, oil, juice and garlic until dressing is well combined.

4   Serve chicken with combined olives, frisée and arugula; drizzle with basil dressing.

SERVES 4
per serving 31.5g carbohydrate; 40g fat; 738 cal; 63g protein

spiced chicken legs with green mango salad

PREPARATION TIME 40 MINUTES   COOKING TIME 30 MINUTES

2 teaspoons sesame oil

8 chicken drumsticks

   (about 2½ pounds)

½ cup chicken broth

3 teaspoons honey

2 tablespoons rice vinegar

1 teaspoon five-spice powder

6 cloves garlic, crushed in

   garlic press

¼ cup soy sauce

½ cup water

GREEN MANGO SALAD

2 green mangoes, sliced thinly

4 scallions, sliced thinly

1 cup loosely packed fresh

   cilantro leaves

5 ounces snow peas, halved

2 hothouse cucumbers, seeded,

   sliced thinly

1½ cups (4½ ounces) fresh

   bean sprouts

LIME AND VINEGAR DRESSING

¼ cup fresh lime juice

¼ cup rice vinegar

2 teaspoons peanut oil

1 Heat oil in large deep skillet, cook chicken, in batches, about 5 minutes or until browned all over.

2 Meanwhile, combine broth, honey, vinegar, five-spice, garlic, soy sauce and the water in medium measuring cup.

3 Return chicken to skillet with broth mixture, bring to a boil; simmer, covered, about 20 minutes or until chicken is cooked through.

4 Meanwhile, make green mango salad. Make lime and vinegar dressing.

5 Add dressing to salad; toss to combine. Divide salad among serving plates; top with chicken and remaining skillet juices.

GREEN MANGO SALAD Combine ingredients in large bowl.

LIME AND VINEGAR DRESSING Combine ingredients in screw-top jar; shake well.

SERVES 4
per serving 26g carbohydrate; 27g fat; 510 cal; 40.2g protein

spiced chicken legs with green mango salad

asian chicken broth (see page 48)

green peppercorn chicken with creamy avocado and mango salad

PREPARATION TIME 20 MINUTES   COOKING TIME 20 MINUTES

eight 5-ounce skinless, boneless chicken thighs

¼ cup grainy mustard

2 tablespoons drained green peppercorns, chopped

2 cloves garlic, crushed in garlic press

2 tablespoons fresh lemon juice

¼ cup chopped fresh chives

¼ cup olive oil

1 small onion, chopped finely

1 cup (3½ ounces) mung bean sprouts

12 ounces snow pea shoots

1 medium avocado, sliced thinly

2 stalks celery, trimmed, sliced thinly

1 medium mango, sliced thinly

CREAMY AVOCADO DRESSING

½ small avocado

½ cup buttermilk

1 teaspoon grainy mustard

1 tablespoon olive oil

1 tablespoon fresh lemon juice

1 teaspoon wasabi paste

1   Place chicken in large bowl, coat with combined mustard, peppercorns, garlic, juice, chives and 2 tablespoons of the oil.

2   Make creamy avocado dressing.

3   Heat remaining oil in large nonstick skillet; cook onion, stirring, until soft. Add chicken to skillet; cook, brushing chicken with peppercorn mixture occasionally, until chicken is browned both sides and cooked through.

4   Meanwhile, combine sprouts, snow pea shoots, avocado, celery and mango in large bowl; drizzle with creamy avocado dressing. Serve with chicken.

CREAMY AVOCADO DRESSING Blend or process all ingredients until smooth.

SERVES 4
per serving 36.3g carbohydrate; 64.3g fat; 915 cal; 48.4g protein

coronation chicken

PREPARATION TIME 15 MINUTES   COOKING TIME 20 MINUTES

Invented by renowned British cook Constance Spry, this salad was originally served at the 1953 coronation of Queen Elizabeth II.

1¾ pounds skinless, boneless chicken breasts

1 cup mayonnaise

½ cup sour cream

1 teaspoon curry powder

2 cups loosely packed fresh basil leaves

5 ripe nectarines, cut into wedges

1 cup toasted unsalted cashews

1   Poach chicken, covered, in large skillet of boiling water about 10 minutes or until cooked through. Cool chicken in liquid 10 minutes; slice thinly.

2   Combine mayonnaise, cream and curry powder in large bowl. Add chicken, basil, nectarine and three-quarters of the nuts; toss gently to combine.

3   Divide chicken mixture among serving plates, sprinkle with remaining nuts.

SERVES 4
per serving 40.4g carbohydrate; 66.7g fat; 968 cal; 52.7g protein

duck liver salad
with candied ginger and wasabi-soy dressing

PREPARATION TIME 20 MINUTES (PLUS REFRIGERATION TIME)   COOKING TIME 10 MINUTES

Wasabi is a pungent root vegetable also known as japanese horseradish. You need half a head of frisée for this recipe.

8 duck livers (1 pound)

3 cups milk

16-inch piece fresh ginger, sliced thinly

½ cup confectioners' sugar mixture

vegetable oil, for deep-frying

¼ cup peanut oil

6 ounces frisée

4 cups (4 ounces) trimmed watercress

⅓ cup light soy sauce

2 teaspoons sesame oil

1 teaspoon wasabi paste

1   Trim and wash livers. Place in medium bowl with milk, cover; refrigerate overnight.

2   Drain livers, rinse under cold water, dry on paper towel; cut each liver into three pieces.

3   Coat ginger in confectioners' sugar. Heat vegetable oil in wok or medium skillet; deep-fry ginger, in batches, until crisp. Drain on paper towel.

4   Heat half of the peanut oil in large nonstick skillet over high heat; sear liver quickly, in batches, both sides, until pieces are well browned but quite rare. Cover to keep warm.

5   Place frisée and watercress in large bowl with combined remaining peanut oil, sauce, sesame oil and wasabi; toss to combine. Divide salad among serving plates; top with liver and ginger.

SERVES 4
per serving 41g carbohydrate; 24.7g fat; 639 cal; 33g protein
tip Chicken livers can be substituted for the duck in this recipe.

chile quail, tangerine and grape salad

PREPARATION TIME 30 MINUTES (PLUS REFRIGERATION TIME)   COOKING TIME 20 MINUTES

eight 7-ounce whole quails

4 red serrano chiles,
   chopped coarsely

2 cloves garlic, halved

¼ cup olive oil

2 tablespoons fresh lemon juice

4 medium tangerines

10 ounces snow peas, halved

14 cups (14 ounces) trimmed
   watercress

1 cup toasted blanched
   whole almonds

7 ounces seedless red grapes, halved

1   Wash quail under cold water; pat dry with paper towel. Using kitchen scissors, cut along both sides of each quail's backbone; discard backbones. Place each quail flat on cutting board, skin-side down; remove and discard ribcage. Cut into quarters.

2   Blend or process chile, garlic, oil and half of the lemon juice until smooth; combine with quail pieces in large bowl. Cover; refrigerate 20 minutes.

3   Meanwhile, segment peeled tangerines over large bowl to save juice. Reserve segments with juice.

4   Cook undrained quail on heated oiled grill or grill pan until browned both sides and cooked through.

5   Meanwhile, boil, steam or microwave snow peas until just tender; drain.

6   Place quail and peas in large bowl with tangerine segments and juice, watercress, nuts, grapes and remaining lemon juice; toss gently to combine.

SERVES 4
per serving 25.1g carbohydrate; 63.6g fat; 917 cal; 61.8g protein
tip You can also cook the quail in a moderately hot oven for about 15 minutes, if you prefer.

chicken enchiladas with corn salsa

PREPARATION TIME 30 MINUTES   COOKING TIME 35 MINUTES

2 tablespoons vegetable oil

1 large red onion, chopped finely

2 cloves garlic, crushed in garlic press

1 tablespoon tomato paste

¼ cup drained pickled jalapeño chiles,
   chopped coarsely

14 ounces canned crushed tomatoes

1 cup chicken broth

1 pound skinless, boneless chicken breasts,
   sliced thinly

10 corn tortillas

2 cups coarsely shredded cheddar cheese

½ cup sour cream

CORN SALSA

1 small red bell pepper, chopped finely

10 ounces canned corn kernels, drained

1 tablespoon fresh lime juice

1 cup loosely packed, coarsely chopped
   fresh cilantro

1 Preheat oven to moderate.

2 Heat oil in large skillet; cook three-quarters of the onion with garlic, stirring, until onion softens. Add paste, chile, undrained tomatoes, broth and chicken; bring to a boil. Reduce heat; simmer, uncovered, until chicken is cooked through. Remove chicken from skillet; cover to keep warm.

3 Warm tortillas in oven or microwave. Dip tortillas, one at a time, in tomato mixture in skillet; place on flat surface. Divide chicken and half of the cheese among tortillas, placing along edge; roll tortilla to enclose filling. Place enchiladas, seam-side down, in oiled 3-quart shallow casserole; enchiladas should fit snugly, without overcrowding.

4 Pour remaining tomato mixture over enchiladas; top with sour cream, sprinkle with remaining cheese. Bake, uncovered, in moderate oven about 15 minutes or until heated through.

5 Meanwhile, make corn salsa.

6 Divide enchiladas among serving plates; serve with corn salsa.

CORN SALSA Place remaining onion in small bowl with pepper, corn, juice and cilantro; toss to combine.

SERVES 4
per serving 42.8g carbohydrate; 51.8g fat; 842 cal; 51.4g protein

waldorf salad

PREPARATION TIME 15 MINUTES   COOKING TIME 15 MINUTES

four 6-ounce skinless, boneless
   chicken breasts

2 tablespoons fresh lemon juice

1 tablespoon honey

2 teaspoons olive oil

4 medium red delicious apples

¼ cup fresh lemon juice

5 stalks celery, trimmed, chopped coarsely

1 cup coarsely chopped walnuts

MAYONNAISE

2 egg yolks

2 teaspoons fresh lemon juice

1 teaspoon dijon mustard

¾ cup olive oil

1 tablespoon warm water

1 Place chicken in large bowl with juice, honey and oil; toss to coat chicken in mixture. Cook chicken on heated oiled grill or grill pan until browned and cooked through. Cover to keep warm.

2 Make mayonnaise.

3 Core and coarsely chop unpeeled apples. Combine apple in small bowl with juice.

4 Combine apple, celery and walnuts in large serving bowl with mayonnaise; top with chicken.

MAYONNAISE Blend or process egg yolks, juice and mustard until smooth; with motor running, add oil in thin stream, process until mayonnaise thickens. Stir in the water.

SERVES 4
per serving 25.5g carbohydrate; 71.1g fat; 915 cal; 45.7g protein
tip Use warm water if the mayonnaise needs to be thinned, because it will blend into the mixture more easily.

chicken with prunes and honey

PREPARATION TIME 20 MINUTES   COOKING TIME 1 HOUR

3-pound whole chicken

¼ cup olive oil

1 medium onion, sliced thinly

1 teaspoon ground cinnamon

pinch saffron threads

¼ teaspoon ground turmeric

2 teaspoons ground ginger

1¼ cups water

⅓ cup honey

½ cup pitted prunes

3 teaspoons sesame seeds

2 tablespoons butter

½ cup blanched almonds

1 tablespoon thinly sliced preserved
   lemon peel

1 Wash chicken under cold water; pat dry with paper towel. Halve chicken lengthwise. Cut each half crosswise through the center; separate breasts from wings and thighs from legs. You will have eight pieces.

2 Heat oil in large deep skillet; cook chicken, in batches, until well browned all over. Drain all but 1 tablespoon of the oil from skillet.

3 Cook onion in same skillet, stirring, until soft. Add spices; cook, stirring, until fragrant. Return chicken to skillet; stir to coat chicken in onion mixture. Add the water; bring to a boil. Reduce heat; simmer, covered, about 30 minutes or until chicken is tender.

4 Remove chicken from skillet; cover to keep warm. Add honey and prunes to skillet; simmer, uncovered, about 15 minutes or until sauce thickens slightly.

5 Meanwhile, toast sesame seeds in small saucepan, stirring, until lightly browned. Remove from saucepan immediately.

6 Melt butter in same saucepan; cook almonds, stirring, until almonds are lightly browned. Remove from saucepan immediately.

7 Return chicken to skillet; stir over heat until chicken is heated through. Divide chicken and sauce among serving plates; sprinkle with seeds, nuts and preserved lemon.

SERVES 4
per serving 34.5g carbohydrate; 60.4g fat; 849 cal; 44.9g protein

warm duck, orange and mushroom salad

PREPARATION TIME 25 MINUTES   COOKING TIME 15 MINUTES

2 tablespoons honey

¼ cup fresh orange juice

2 tablespoons soy sauce

1 clove garlic, crushed in garlic press

four 5-ounce boneless duck breasts

10 ounces oyster mushrooms

7 ounces button mushrooms, sliced thickly

10 ounces shiitake mushrooms,
   stemmed, halved

3 large oranges, segmented

2 cups (3½ ounces) mâche

1 Preheat oven to moderately hot.

2 Combine honey, juice, sauce and garlic in small bowl. Score each piece of duck shallowly; brush with about ¼ cup of the honey mixture.

3 Combine mushrooms with remaining honey mixture in large roasting pan. Place duck on wire rack over mushrooms in pan; roast, uncovered, in moderately hot oven 10 minutes.

4 Remove duck and wire rack from pan; drain mushrooms, reserving about a third of the pan juices. Place mushrooms in large bowl. Preheat broiler.

5 Replace duck on wire rack over same dish; brown under broiler until skin crisps. Slice duck thickly.

6 Add orange, mâche and reserved pan juices to mushrooms; toss gently to combine. Divide salad among serving plates; top with duck slices.

SERVES 4
per serving 28.2g carbohydrate; 9g fat; 339 cal; 36.3g protein

salt and lemon-pepper squid with lemon mayonnaise

PREPARATION TIME 15 MINUTES   COOKING TIME 15 MINUTES

1¼ pounds cleaned squid
   (calamari), bodies only
½ cup all-purpose flour
2 teaspoons kosher salt
1 tablespoon lemon-pepper
vegetable oil, for deep-frying
6 cups (12 ounces) mesclun

LEMON MAYONNAISE

1 cup mayonnaise
¼ cup fresh lemon juice
1 tablespoon boiling water

1 Halve squid lengthwise, score the insides in crosshatch pattern, then cut each half lengthwise into five pieces. Toss squid in medium bowl with combined flour, salt and lemon-pepper until coated; shake off excess.

2 Make lemon mayonnaise.

3 Heat oil in wok or large saucepan; deep-fry squid, in batches, until tender and browned lightly. Drain on paper towel.

4 Place mesclun with a quarter of the lemon mayonnaise in medium bowl; toss gently to combine. Serve squid and mesclun salad with remaining lemon mayonnaise.

LEMON MAYONNAISE Whisk ingredients in small bowl until well combined.

SERVES 4
per serving 28.5g carbohydrate; 25.8g fat; 550 cal; 28.2g protein

blue cheese and scallion mini-pizzas

PREPARATION TIME 20 MINUTES   COOKING TIME 10 MINUTES

12-inch packaged pizza base

2 tablespoons tomato paste

2 scallions, sliced thinly

3 ounces blue cheese,

    crumbled coarsely

1 Preheat oven to moderately hot.

2 Using 2-inch round cutter, cut 24 rounds from pizza base.

3 Place rounds on baking sheet. Divide paste evenly over rounds; top with scallion and cheese. Bake, uncovered, in moderately hot oven about 5 minutes or until pizzas are heated through.

4 Serve hot.

SERVES 4
per serving 41.2g carbohydrate; 9g fat; 291 cal; 11g protein

greek mini-pizzas

PREPARATION TIME 20 MINUTES   COOKING TIME 10 MINUTES

12-inch packaged pizza base

2 tablespoons tomato paste

2 tablespoons halved pitted

    kalamata olives

4 ounces feta cheese, crumbled

24 small fresh basil leaves

1 Preheat oven to moderately hot.

2 Using 2-inch round cutter, cut 24 rounds from pizza base.

3 Place rounds on baking sheet. Divide paste evenly over rounds; top with olives and cheese. Bake, uncovered, in moderately hot oven about 5 minutes or until pizzas are heated through. Top with basil.

4 Serve hot.

SERVES 4
per serving 42.7g carbohydrate; 8.8g fat; 298 cal; 11.6g protein

lamb and arugula mini-pizzas

PREPARATION TIME 20 MINUTES   COOKING TIME 10 MINUTES

12-inch packaged pizza base

2 tablespoons tomato paste

3 ounces firm goat cheese,
  sliced thinly

6 sun-dried tomatoes, quartered

5 ounces cooked boneless
  leg of lamb, sliced thinly

24 baby arugula leaves, sliced thinly

1 Preheat oven to moderately hot.

2 Using 2-inch round cutter, cut 24 rounds from pizza base.

3 Place rounds on baking sheet. Divide paste evenly over rounds; top with cheese. Bake, uncovered, in moderately hot oven about 5 minutes or until pizzas are heated through. Top with tomato, lamb and arugula.

4 Scrve hot.

SERVES 4
per serving 41.2g carbohydrate; 10.7g fat; 346 cal; 20.8g protein

mascarpone and ham mini-pizzas

PREPARATION TIME 20 MINUTES COOKING TIME 10 MINUTES

12-inch packaged pizza base

2 tablespoons tomato paste

4 ounces shaved deli ham

2 tablespoons mascarpone
  cheese, softened

2 teaspoons finely chopped
  fresh chives

1 Preheat oven to moderately hot.

2 Using 2-inch round cutter, cut 24 rounds from pizza base.

3 Place rounds on baking sheet. Divide paste evenly over rounds; top with ham, cheese and chives. Bake, uncovered, in moderately hot oven about 5 minutes or until pizzas are heated through.

4 Serve hot.

SERVES 4
per serving 41.1g carbohydrate; 9.4g fat; 298 cal; 11.9g protein

roast beef with caramelized onion on rye

PREPARATION TIME 20 MINUTES   COOKING TIME 30 MINUTES

½ **pound beef fillet**

1 **tablespoon olive oil**

1 **large red onion, sliced thinly**

2 **teaspoons light brown sugar**

2 **teaspoons red wine vinegar**

½ **loaf bakery rye bread**

2 **tablespoons olive oil, extra**

1 **tablespoon mild prepared mustard**

20 **fresh flat-leaf parsley sprigs**

1   Preheat oven to moderate. Cook beef in medium heated oiled skillet until browned all over; place in small casserole. Roast, uncovered, in moderate oven 20 minutes or until cooked as desired. Wrap beef in foil.

2   Meanwhile, heat oil in same skillet; cook onion until soft. Add sugar and vinegar; cook, stirring, until caramelized.

3   Discard ends from bread. Cut bread into ½-inch slices; cut each slice into quarters. Brush bread both sides with extra oil; toast both sides.

4   Slice beef thinly. Spread mustard on bread; top with parsley, beef and onion. Serve at room temperature.

SERVES 4
per serving 41.1g carbohydrate; 19.5g fat; 427 cal; 21.9g protein

chicken tandoori pockets with raita

PREPARATION TIME 10 MINUTES   COOKING TIME 10 MINUTES

2 **teaspoons fresh lime juice**

¼ **cup tandoori paste**

2 **tablespoons unflavored yogurt**

8 **ounces chicken tenderloins**

4 **large flour tortillas**

1 **cup snow pea shoots**

RAITA

½ **cup unflavored yogurt**

½ **hothouse cucumber, halved,**
    seeded, chopped finely

2 **teaspoons finely chopped**
    fresh mint

1   Combine juice, paste and yogurt in medium bowl; add chicken, toss to coat chicken in marinade.

2   Cook chicken, in batches, on heated oiled grill or grill pan until cooked through. Let stand 5 minutes; slice thickly.

3   Make raita.

4   Meanwhile, heat tortillas according to manufacturer's instructions.

5   Place equal amounts of each of the chicken, pea shoots and raita on a quarter section of each tortilla; fold tortilla in half and then in half again to enclose filling and form triangle-shaped pockets.

RAITA Combine ingredients in small bowl.

SERVES 4
per pocket 28.4g carbohydrate; 12.1g fat; 313 cal; 21.6g protein

thanksgiving open sandwich

PREPARATION TIME 30 MINUTES

10 ounces brie

**4 ounces thinly sliced smoked
    turkey breast**

24 cocktail pumpernickel rounds

¼ cup cranberry sauce

**1 tablespoon coarsely chopped
    fresh chives**

1   Cut cheese into small, thin slices.

2   Divide cheese and turkey equally among pumpernickel rounds; top each
    with cranberry sauce and chives.

3   Serve at room temperature.

SERVES 4
per serving 39.6g carbohydrate; 24g fat; 485 cal; 28.1g protein

tandoori chicken on naan

PREPARATION TIME 30 MINUTES (PLUS REFRIGERATION TIME)   COOKING TIME 15 MINUTES

Naan is an Indian specialty. It is a leavened bread that is baked on the inside wall of a tandoor or clay oven.

**½ pound skinless, boneless
    chicken breasts**

2 tablespoons tandoori paste

4 ounces unflavored yogurt

**2 tablespoons coarsely chopped
    fresh mint**

1 tablespoon fresh lemon juice

2 pieces naan

16 small fresh mint leaves

1   Combine chicken, paste and a quarter of the yogurt in medium bowl; toss
    to coat chicken all over. Cover; refrigerate 3 hours or overnight.

2   Cook chicken on heated oiled grill or grill pan until browned and cooked
    through; let stand 10 minutes. Slice chicken; cut into small pieces.

3   Combine remaining yogurt, mint and juice in small bowl. Cut sixteen
    1½-inch rounds from naan. Spread about ½ teaspoon of the yogurt
    mixture on each round; top with chicken, another ½ teaspoon of the
    yogurt mixture, and mint leaf.

4   Serve cold.

SERVES 4
per serving 34g carbohydrate; 14.9g fat; 414 cal; 35.3g protein

chocolate-rum mini-mousse

PREPARATION TIME 10 MINUTES   COOKING TIME 5 MINUTES

6 egg yolks

⅓ cup sugar

½ cup dark rum, warmed

2 ounces dark (semisweet) chocolate, grated finely

1   Beat egg yolks and sugar in small deep heatproof bowl with electric mixer until light and fluffy.

2   Place bowl over small saucepan of simmering water; whisk egg mixture constantly while gradually adding rum. Continue to whisk until mixture is thick and creamy. Add chocolate, in two batches, whisking gently to melt chocolate between additions.

3   Pour mousse mixture into four ⅓-cup serving glasses.

SERVES 4
per serving 26.7g carbohydrate; 25.6g fat; 444 cal; 12.8g protein
tip The mousse can be served chilled if desired; refrigerate about 2 hours.

ricotta and berry trifle

PREPARATION TIME 15 MINUTES (PLUS REFRIGERATION TIME)

This traditional English favorite is given a new look with this summery update. If you prefer, trifle can be served in a large glass bowl.

8 ounces fresh raspberries

8 ounces fresh blueberries

8 ounces fresh strawberries, quartered

2 cups low-fat ricotta cheese

⅓ cup fresh orange juice

⅓ cup maple syrup

3 meringue drops, crumbled

1 tablespoon toasted sliced almonds

1   Combine berries in medium bowl.

2   Blend or process combined cheese, juice and maple syrup until smooth.

3   Divide a quarter of the cheese mixture among four 1-cup dessert glasses; sprinkle with some of the berries. Repeat layering with remaining cheese mixture and berries, finishing with berries.

4   Sprinkle meringue and nuts over trifles. Refrigerate, covered, for at least 3 hours.

SERVES 4
per serving 38.8g carbohydrate; 10.7g fat; 303 cal; 13.3g protein

pink grapefruit granita with hazelnut wafers

PREPARATION TIME 20 MINUTES (PLUS FREEZING TIME)   COOKING TIME 20 MINUTES (PLUS COOLING TIME)

You will need two large pink grapefruit for this recipe.

1 cup water

1 cup sugar

1 cup fresh pink grapefruit juice

¼ cup fresh lemon juice

2 egg whites

HAZELNUT WAFERS

1 egg white

¼ cup sugar

2 tablespoons very finely
   ground hazelnuts

1 tablespoons margarine, melted

1 Stir the water and sugar in small saucepan over heat, without boiling, until sugar dissolves. Bring to a boil; boil 5 minutes without stirring. Remove from heat; stir in juices, cool.

2 Using electric mixer, beat egg whites in small bowl until soft peaks form. Fold grapefruit syrup into egg whites; pour into metal loaf pan. Cover; freeze 3 hours or overnight.

3 Blend or process granita until pale and creamy. Return to pan, cover; freeze 3 hours or overnight.

4 Make hazelnut wafers. Serve granita with hazelnut wafers.

HAZELNUT WAFERS Preheat oven to moderate. Grease two baking sheets; line each with parchment or wax paper. Using electric mixer, beat egg white in small bowl until soft peaks form; gradually add sugar, beating until sugar dissolves between additions. Add hazelnut meal and margarine; stir until combined. Trace sixteen 3-inch circles, 1 inch apart, on lined trays. Spread a teaspoon of mixture in each circle. Bake in moderate oven about 5 minutes or until lightly browned. Cool wafers on baking sheets before carefully peeling away paper.

SERVES 8
per serving 37g carbohydrate; 2.8g fat; 176 cal; 2.0g protein

pears poached in cranberry syrup

PREPARATION TIME 5 MINUTES   COOKING TIME 45 MINUTES (PLUS COOLING TIME)

2 cups cranberry juice

½ cup dry white wine

pinch cardamom seeds

½ vanilla bean, halved lengthwise

4 small anjou pears

1 Combine juice, wine, cardamom and vanilla bean in large saucepan.

2 Add peeled pears to pan; bring to a boil. Reduce heat; simmer, covered, about 25 minutes or until tender. Cool pears in syrup.

3 Remove pears from syrup; strain syrup into medium heatproof bowl. Return 2 cups of the strained syrup to same pan (discard remaining syrup); bring to a boil. Boil, uncovered, about 15 minutes or until syrup is reduced by half. Serve pears, hot or cold, with syrup.

SERVES 4
per serving 31.2g carbohydrate; 0.7g fat; 163 cal; 2.3g protein
tip Pears can be poached a day ahead; reduce the syrup just before serving.

fruit salad with star anise syrup

PREPARATION TIME 30 MINUTES (PLUS REFRIGERATION TIME)   COOKING TIME 5 MINUTES

1 small honeydew melon

8 ounces fresh strawberries

10 ounces fresh cherries

¼ teaspoon cardamom seeds

3 star anise

¼ cup sugar

2 tablespoons fresh lemon juice

2 tablespoons water

1 Halve, peel and chop melon coarsely. Hull strawberries; cut in half. Pit cherries; place fruit in large bowl.

2 Place cardamom seeds in small saucepan with star anise, sugar, juice and the water. Stir over heat, without boiling, until sugar dissolves.

3 Pour warm syrup over fruit; refrigerate, covered, about 30 minutes or until cold.

SERVES 4
per serving 33.4g carbohydrate; 0.7g fat; 150 cal; 2.9g protein
tip Star anise is a star-shaped dried pod whose seeds have an astringent aniseed flavor. It can be found at Asian markets and some supermarkets.

yogurt and strawberry kiwi mousse

PREPARATION TIME 10 MINUTES (PLUS REFRIGERATION TIME)

You need half of a packet of gelatin mix for this recipe.

3 ounces strawberry kiwi gelatin mix

1 cup boiling water

1¾ cups low-fat fruit yogurt

1 medium mango, chopped finely

1 medium banana, sliced thinly

1 medium kiwi fruit, halved,
    sliced thinly

1 Stir gelatin with the water in small heatproof bowl until dissolved; refrigerate about 20 minutes or until cold (do not allow to set).

2 Add yogurt and mango to gelatin; stir to combine. Divide yogurt mixture among six 1-cup serving glasses. Cover; refrigerate about 2 hours or until set. Just before serving, top each with equal amounts of banana and kiwi fruit.

SERVES 6
per serving 35.9g carbohydrate; 1g fat; 169 cal; 5.3g protein

mocha smoothie

PREPARATION TIME 5 MINUTES

4 cups nonfat milk

1 cup prepared chocolate pudding

1 cup whole milk

   chocolate ice-cream

1 tablespoon instant coffee powder

½ teaspoon vanilla extract

1 Blend or process ingredients, in batches, until smooth.

SERVES 4
per serving 29.7g carbohydrate; 7.1g fat; 233 cal; 13.8g protein

rhubarb galette

PREPARATION TIME 10 MINUTES   COOKING TIME 20 MINUTES

You need about four trimmed large stalks of rhubarb for this recipe.

1 tablespoon butter, melted

2½ cups coarsely chopped rhubarb

⅓ cup firmly packed light

   brown sugar

1 teaspoon finely grated orange peel

1 sheet frozen puff pastry, thawed

2 tablespoons finely ground almonds

2 teaspoons butter, melted, extra

1 Preheat oven to hot. Line baking sheet with parchment or wax paper.

2 Combine butter, rhubarb, sugar and peel in medium bowl.

3 Cut 10-inch round from pastry, place on prepared baking sheet; sprinkle almonds evenly over pastry. Spread rhubarb mixture over pastry, leaving a 1½-inch border. Fold ¾ inch of pastry edge up and around filling. Brush edge with extra butter.

4 Bake galette, uncovered, in hot oven about 20 minutes or until browned lightly.

SERVES 4
per serving 34.5g carbohydrate; 18.2g fat; 317 cal; 4.3g protein

glossary

ALLSPICE also known as pimento or jamaican pepper; so-named because it tastes like a combination of nutmeg, cumin, clove and cinnamon – all spices. It is available whole (a dark brown berry) or ground, and is used in both sweet and savory dishes.

ARTICHOKES

globe large flower-bud of a member of the thistle family; having tough petal-like leaves, edible in part when cooked.

hearts tender center of the globe artichoke, itself the large flower-bud of a member of the thistle family; having tough petal-like leaves, edible in part when cooked. Artichoke hearts can be harvested fresh from the plant or purchased in brine canned or in glass jars.

jerusalem neither from Jerusalem nor an artichoke, this crunchy tuber, also known as sunchoke, tastes a bit like a fresh water chestnut and is related to the sunflower family.

BAKING POWDER a raising agent consisting mainly of two parts cream of tartar to one part baking soda.

BAMBOO SHOOTS the tender shoots of bamboo plants, available in cans; must be drained and rinsed before use.

BARBERRIES long red berries; rarely eaten raw due to their high acidity. Available from specialist food outlets.

BARLEY a nutritious grain used in soups and stews (often as a thickener) as well as in whisky- and beer-making. Hulled barley is the least processed form of the grain, making it particularly high in fiber. Pearl barley has had the husk discarded and been hulled and polished, much the same as rice.

BEANS

cannellini small white dried bean similar in appearance and flavor to other *Phaseolus vulgaris* varieties – great northern and navy or haricot beans.

haricot similar in appearance and flavor to other small dried white beans such as great northern, navy and cannellini; sold dried, good in soups and casseroles.

mung tiny dried green beans available from Asian food stores, whole, skinned and split. A good source of fiber, protein, iron, folate, niacin and thiamin, mung beans are commonly used for sprouting.

wax a yellow-colored variety of fresh green bean.

BOK CHOY also known as bak choy, pak choi, chinese white cabbage or chinese chard, has a fresh, mild mustard taste; use stems and leaves, stir-fry or braise. Baby bok choy, also known as pak kat farang or shanghai bok choy, is a smaller variety and is more tender than bok choy.

BROCCOLINI a cross between broccoli and chinese kale, it is milder and sweeter than broccoli. Each long stem is topped by a loose floret that closely resembles broccoli; from floret to stem, broccolini is completely edible.

BULGUR also called bulghur wheat; hulled, steamed wheat kernels that, once dried, are crushed into various-sized grains. Not the same as cracked wheat. Used in Middle-Eastern dishes such as kibbeh and tabbouleh.

CAJUN SEASONING used to give an authentic Deep South spicy cajun flavor to food, this packaged blend of assorted herbs and spices can include paprika, basil, onion, fennel, thyme, cayenne and tarragon.

CAPERBERRIES fruit formed after the caper buds have flowered; caperberries are pickled usually with stalks intact.

CARAWAY SEEDS a member of the parsley family, available in seed or ground form and suitable for both sweet and savory dishes.

CARDAMOM native to India and used extensively in its cuisine; can be purchased in pod, seed or ground form. It has a distinctive, aromatic, sweetly rich flavor and is one of the world's most expensive spices.

CELERIAC tuberous root with brown skin, white flesh and a celery-like flavor.

CHARD also known as swiss chard; a leafy, dark green vegetable with thick, crisp white or red stems and ribs. The leaves, often trimmed from the stems and ribs, are used raw or cooked.

CHEESE

bocconcini walnut-sized baby mozzarella, a delicate, semi-soft, white cheese traditionally made in Italy from buffalo milk. Spoils rapidly so must be kept under refrigeration, in brine, for 1 or 2 days at most.

brie Often referred to as the 'queen of cheeses', brie originated in France. It has a bloomy white rind and a creamy center which becomes runnier as it ripens.

goat made from goat milk, has an earthy, strong taste; available in both soft and firm textures, in various shapes and sizes, sometimes rolled in ash or herbs.

gorgonzola a creamy Italian blue cheese having a mild, sweet taste; good as an accompaniment to fruit or to flavor sauces.

gruyère a Swiss cheese having small holes and a nutty, slightly salty flavor.

haloumi a firm, cream-colored sheep milk cheese matured in brine; somewhat like a minty, salty feta in flavor, haloumi can be grilled or fried, briefly, without breaking down. If unavailable, it can be substituted with any white frying cheese.

mascarpone a cultured cream product made in much the same way as yogurt. It's whitish to creamy yellow in color, with a soft, creamy texture.

pecorino is the generic Italian name for cheeses made from sheep milk. It's a hard, white to pale yellow cheese, usually matured for eight to 12 months and known for the region in which it's produced – Romano from Rome, Sardo from Sardinia, Siciliano from Sicily and Toscano from Tuscany.

CHILE use rubber gloves when seeding and chopping chiles as they can burn your skin. Removing seeds and membranes lessens the heat.

chipotle hot, dried, smoked jalapeño, available in cans.

green either an unripened chile or one of several varieties that are ripe when green, such as habanero, poblano or serrano chiles.

guajillo also called travieso; the dried form of the mirasol chile. Deep red to almost black in color, this medium-hot chile must be soaked in boiling water before use.

jalapeño fairly hot green chile, available bottled in brine or fresh from specialty greengrocers.

long green/red long, medium hot chile.

serrano, green/red small, very hot chile.

CHORIZO a sausage of Spanish or Mexican origin, made of coarsely ground pork and highly seasoned with garlic and chiles. Can be purchased fresh or smoked.

CHOY SUM also known as pakaukeo or flowering cabbage, a member of the bok choy family; easy to identify with its long stems, light green leaves and yellow flowers. It is eaten, stems and all, steamed or stir-fried.

CLOVES dried flower buds of a tropical tree; can be used whole or in ground form. They have a strong scent and taste so should be used minimally.

CORNICHON French for gherkin, a very small variety of cucumber. Pickled, they are a traditional accompaniment to pâté; the Swiss always serve them with fondue (or raclette).

CUMIN also known as zeera, available in ground or seed form; can be purchased from supermarkets.

CURRY PASTES some recipes in this book call for commercially prepared pastes of various strengths and flavors. Use whichever one you feel suits your spice-level tolerance best.

rogan josh a spicy paste made from fresh chiles or paprika, tomato and spices.

tandoori consisting of garlic, tamarind, ginger, coriander, chile and spices.

tikka consisting of chile, coriander, cumin, lentil flour, garlic, ginger, oil, turmeric, fennel, pepper, cloves, cinnamon and cardamom.

CURRY POWDER a blend of ground spices used for convenience when making Indian food. Can consist of some of the following spices: dried chile, cinnamon, coriander, cumin, fennel, fenugreek, mace, cardamom and turmeric.

CRÈME FRAÎCHE a naturally fermented cream (minimum fat content 35%) having a velvety texture and tangy taste.

DAIKON has a sweet, fresh flavor. The daikon's flesh is crisp, juicy and white, while the skin can be either creamy white or black. It can range from 6 to 15 inches in length with an average diameter of 2 to 3 inches. Refrigerate, wrapped in a plastic bag, for up to a week.

EGGS some recipes in this book call for raw or barely cooked eggs; exercise caution if there is a salmonella problem in your area.

FARFALLE bow-tie shaped short pasta; sometimes known as butterfly pasta.

FENUGREEK hard, dried seed usually sold ground as an astringent spice powder. Good with seafood and in chutneys, fenugreek helps mask unpleasant odors.

FIVE-SPICE POWDER a fragrant mixture of ground

cinnamon, cloves, star anise, sichuan pepper and fennel seeds.

FRISEE also known as curly endive; a curly-leafed green vegetable, mainly used in salads.

GAI LARN also known as kanah, gai lum, chinese broccoli and chinese kale; appreciated more for its stems than its coarse leaves. Can be served steamed or stir fried, in soups and noodle dishes.

GARAM MASALA a blend of spices, originating in northern India, based on varying proportions of cardamom, cinnamon, cloves, coriander, fennel and cumin, roasted and ground together. Black pepper and chile can be added for a hotter version.

GARBANZOS also called chickpeas; irregularly round, sandy-colored legumes used extensively in Mediterranean and Latin cooking.

GINGER

ground also known as powdered ginger; used as a flavoring in cakes, pies and puddings but cannot be substituted for fresh ginger.

pickled pink available, packaged, from Asian grocery stores; pickled paper-thin shavings of ginger in a mixture of vinegar, sugar and natural coloring.

GRAND MARNIER French orange-flavored liqueur.

GRAPEVINE LEAVES available fresh or cryovac-packed in brine. Can be purchased from Middle-Eastern food stores.

GREEN PEPPERCORN soft, unripe berry of the pepper plant, usually sold packed in

brine (occasionally found dried, packed in salt in health food stores and delicatessens). Has a distinctive fresh taste that goes well with mustard or cream sauces.

pickled has a fresh herbal 'green' flavor without being extremely pungent; early harvested unripe pepper that needs to be dried or pickled to avoid fermentation. We used pickled thai green peppercorns, which are canned, still strung in clusters, but an equivalent weight from a bottle of green peppercorns in brine can be substituted.

GUAVA PASTE made from guava pulp and sugar, cooked to a paste-like consistency. Available in cans from gourmet food stores.

HARISSA sauce or paste made from dried red chiles, garlic, oil and sometimes caraway seeds.

HERBS 1 teaspoon dried herbs equals 4 teaspoons (1 tablespoon) chopped fresh herbs.

marjoram sweet and mild tasting, used to season meats and fish.

tarragon has a strong anise-like flavor, use sparingly.

thai basil has small leaves and purplish stems with a slight licorice or aniseed taste.

HUMMUS a Middle-Eastern salad or dip made from softened dried garbanzos, garlic, lemon juice and tahini (sesame seed paste); can be purchased, ready-made, from most supermarkets.

INDIRECT METHOD a barbecue cooking method where the heat beads or coals are placed around the outside perimeter of the bottom grill, surrounding the food being cooked rather than burning directly under it.

JUNIPER BERRIES dried berries of an evergreen tree; they are the main flavoring ingredient in gin.

KAFFIR LIME wrinkled, bumpy-skinned green fruit of a small citrus tree originally grown in South Africa and Southeast Asia. Gives Thai food a unique aromatic flavor; usually only the zest is used.

KAFFIR LIME LEAVES look like two glossy dark green leaves joined in a rounded hourglass shape. Used fresh or dried in many Asian dishes and used like bay leaves or curry leaves, especially in Thai cooking.

KECAP MANIS a dark, thick, sweet soy sauce used in most Southeast-Asian cuisines.

KIRSCH cherry-flavored brandy from Germany.

KOSHER SALT coarser than table salt, but not as large-grained as sea salt.

LEMONGRASS a tall, clumping, lemon-smelling and tasting, sharp-edged grass; the white lower part of the stem is used, finely chopped, in cooking.

LETTUCE

boston also called butterhead lettuce; a soft, slightly curly lettuce with a sweet flavor.

mâche also known as corn salad or lamb's tongue, the tender, narrow, dark-green leaves have a mild, almost nutty flavor.

mizuna Japanese in origin; frizzy green salad leaf having a delicate mustard flavor.

red leaf frilly leaf lettuce, also available in a crinkly green-leafed variety.

MAPLE SYRUP a thin syrup distilled from the sap of the maple tree.

MARSALA a sweet fortified wine originally from Sicily.

MESCLUN a salad mix of assorted young lettuce and other green leaves, including baby spinach leaves, mizuna and frisée.

MIRIN is a Japanese champagne-colored wine made of glutinous rice and alcohol and used expressly for cooking. It should not be confused with sake.

MIXED SPICE a blend of ground spices usually consisting of cinnamon, allspice and nutmeg.

MUSHROOMS

brown light-to-dark brown mushrooms with full-bodied flavor; also known as roman or cremini.

button small, cultivated white mushrooms with a mild flavor.

dried cloud ear also known as wood ear or dried black fungus; it is popular in Asian cooking. Sold dried, it is black on one side and pale gray on the other.

dried shiitake also known as donko or dried chinese mushrooms; they have a unique meaty flavor.

enoki long, thin white mushrooms with a delicate, fruity flavor.

oyster also known as abalone; gray-white mushrooms that are shaped like a fan. Prized for their smooth texture and subtle, oyster-like flavor.

portobello large, dark brown mushrooms with a full-bodied flavor.

shiitake also known as chinese black, forest or golden oak mushrooms; although cultivated, have the earthiness and taste of wild mushrooms.

MUSTARD

dry powdered yellow mustard seeds.

powder finely ground white (yellow) mustard seeds.

seeds, black also known as brown mustard seeds; more pungent than the white (or yellow) seeds.

NAAN is that delicious leavened bread we associate with the tandoori dishes of northern India.

NIGELLA also known as kalonji or black onion seeds, these are angular seeds, black on the outside and creamy within, having a sharp nutty flavor.

NOODLES

bean thread also known as cellophane or glass noodles because they are transparent when cooked. White in color (not off-white like rice vermicelli), very delicate and fine.

rice stick especially popular Southeast-Asian dried rice noodles. Come in different widths, but all should be soaked in hot water until soft.

rice vermicelli similar to bean threads, only they're longer and made with rice flour instead of mung bean starch.

NORI a type of dried seaweed used in Japanese cooking as a flavoring, garnish or for sushi. Sold in thin sheets.

OKRA also known as bamia or lady fingers, a green, ridged, oblong pod with a furry skin. Native to Africa, this vegetable is used in Indian, Middle-Eastern and southern United States cooking, and is used to thicken stews.

PANCETTA an Italian bacon cured in spices and salt. Can be purchased from gourmet food stores.

PAPPADUMS sun-dried wafers made from a combination of lentil and rice flours, oil and spices.

PASTRAMI a seasoned, cured and smoked beef, usually cut from the brisket; ready to eat when purchased.

PATTYPAN SQUASH a round, slightly flat summer squash being yellow to pale green in color and having a scalloped edge. It has firm white flesh and a distinct flavor.

PEA

black-eyed small beige bean with a black circular 'eye' at its inner curve. Can be purchased fresh or dried.

PEPITAS dried pumpkin seeds with a delicate flavor.

PERNOD an aniseed-flavored liqueur from France.

PITA also known as lebanese bread. This flour pocket bread is sold in small thick pieces called pocket pita.

POLENTA also known as cornmeal; a flour-like cereal made of dried corn (maize) sold ground in several different textures; also the name of the dish made from it.

PRESERVED LEMON salted lemons preserved in a mixture of olive oil and lemon juice. They are available from gourmet food stores and are a common flavoring in Moroccan cooking. Rinse preserved lemon well under cold water before using.

PROSCIUTTO cured, air-dried (unsmoked), pressed ham; usually sold thinly sliced. Available from most delicatessens.

RADICCHIO a member of the chicory family used in Italian cooking as well as salads. Has dark burgundy leaves and a strong bitter flavor.

RIGANI Greek oregano, is a stronger, sharper version of the familiar herb we use in Italian cooking and is available from gourmet food shops and Mediterranean food stores.

SAKE Japan's favorite rice wine, is used in cooking, marinating and as part of dipping sauces. If sake is unavailable, dry sherry, vermouth or brandy can be used as a substitute.

SAMBAL OELEK also ulek or olek; Indonesian in origin, a salty paste made from ground chiles and vinegar.

SANSHO PEPPER a hot Japanese seasoning ground from the pod of the prickly ash tree. Closely related to chinese sichuan pepper.

SAUCES

char siu a dark, thick sauce made from sugar, water, salt, fermented soy bean paste, honey, soy sauce, malt syrup and spices.

chinese barbecue a thick, sweet and salty sauce made from fermented soy beans, vinegar, garlic, pepper and various spices. Available from Asian food stores.

fish made from pulverized salted fermented fish (most often anchovies); has a

pungent smell and strong taste. There are many versions of varying intensity, so use according to your taste.

hoisin a thick, sweet and spicy Chinese paste made from salted fermented soy beans, onions and garlic; used as a marinade or baste, or to accent stir-fries and barbecued or roasted foods.

plum a thick, sweet and sour sauce made from plums, vinegar, sugar, chiles and spices.

sweet chili comparatively mild, thin Thai sauce made from red chiles, garlic and vinegar; used as a condiment more often than in cooking.

SHALLOT small, elongated, brown-skinned member of the onion family. Grows in tight clusters similarly to garlic.

fried usually served as a condiment on the Thai table or sprinkled over just-cooked dishes. Can be purchased packaged in jars or cellophane bags at Asian grocery stores.

SHERRY fortified wine consumed as an aperitif or used in cooking. Sold as fino (light, dry), amontillado (medium sweet, dark) and oloroso (full-bodied, very dark).

SICHUAN PEPPERCORN also known as szechuan or chinese pepper. A mildly hot spice that comes from the prickly ash tree. Although not related to the peppercorn family, the small, red-brown aromatic sichuan berries look like black peppercorns and have a distinctive peppery-lemon flavor and aroma.

SMOKING CHIPS small pieces of various wood chips packaged and available from barbecue outlets.

SRIRACHA hot Thai sauce.

STAR ANISE a dried star-shaped pod whose seeds have an astringent aniseed flavor; used to flavor stocks and marinades.

STOCK 1 cup stock is the equivalent of 1 cup water plus 1 crumbled stock cube (or 1 teaspoon stock powder).

SUMAC a purple-red, astringent spice ground from berries growing on shrubs that flourish wild around the Mediterranean; it adds a tart, lemony flavor to dips and dressings and goes well with barbecued meat. It can be found in Middle-Eastern food stores.

TACO SEASONING MIX a packaged seasoning meant to duplicate the Mexican sauce made from oregano, cumin, chiles and other spices.

TAHINI sesame seed paste available from Middle-Eastern food stores; most often used in hummus, baba ghanoush and other Lebanese recipes.

TAMARIND CONCENTRATE (OR PASTE) the commercial result of the distillation of tamarind juice into a condensed, compacted paste. Thick and purple-black, it is ready to use, with no soaking or straining required; it can be diluted with water according to taste. Use tamarind concentrate to add zing to sauces, chutneys, curries and marinades.

TARAMASALATA a Greek dip made from the salted, dried roe of the orange carp blended with olive oil, lemon juice and soaked breadcrumbs. It can be purchased from most delicatessens.

TOFU also known as bean curd, an off-white, custard-like product made from the 'milk' of crushed soy beans.

firm made by compressing bean curd to remove most of the water. Good used in stir-fries because it can be tossed without falling apart.

fried pieces available in Asian specialty stores.

silken refers to the manufacturing method of straining the soy bean liquid through silk.

TORTILLA thin, round unleavened bread originating in Mexico; can be made at home or purchased frozen, fresh or vacuum-packed. Available in two varieties: flour and corn.

TURMERIC also known as kamin, this is a rhizome related to ginger, and must be grated or pounded to release its somewhat acrid aroma and pungent flavor. Known for the golden color it imparts to dishes, it can be substituted with the more common dried powder (use 2 teaspoons of ground turmeric plus a teaspoon of sugar for every tablespoon of fresh turmeric).

WASABI an Asian horseradish used to make the pungent, green-colored sauce traditionally served with Japanese raw fish dishes; sold in powdered or paste form.

WATERCRESS one of the cress family, a large group of peppery greens used raw in salads, dips and sandwiches, or cooked in soups. Highly perishable, so must be used as soon as possible after purchase.

WHEAT GERM flakes milled from the embryo of wheat.

facts & figures

These easy-to-follow conversions will help you to use our recipes wherever you live. While these conversions are approximate only, the difference between an exact and the approximate conversion of various liquid and dry measures is minimal and will not affect your cooking results.

dry measures

imperial	metric
½oz	15g
1oz	30g
2oz	60g
3oz	90g
4oz (¼lb)	125g
5oz	155g
6oz	185g
7oz	220g
8oz (½lb)	250g
9oz	280g
10oz	315g
11oz	345g
12oz (¾lb)	375g
13oz	410g
14oz	440g
15oz	470g
16oz (1lb)	500g
24oz (1½lb)	750g
32oz (2lb)	1kg

liquid measures

imperial	metric
1 fluid oz	30ml
2 fluid oz	60ml
3 fluid oz	100ml
4 fluid oz	125ml
5 fluid oz (¼ pint/1 gill)	150ml
6 fluid oz	190ml
8 fluid oz	250ml
10 fluid oz (½ pint)	300ml
16 fluid oz	500ml
20 fluid oz (1 pint)	600ml
1¾ pints	1000ml (1 litre)

helpful measures

imperial	metric
⅛in	3mm
¼in	6mm
½in	1cm
¾in	2cm
1in	2.5cm
2in	5cm
2½in	6cm
3in	8cm
4in	10cm
5in	13cm
6in	15cm
7in	18cm
8in	20cm
9in	23cm
10in	25cm
11in	28cm
12in (1ft)	30cm

measuring equipment

The difference between one country's measuring cups and another's is, at most, within a 2 or 3 teaspoon variance. The most accurate way of measuring dry ingredients is to weigh them. When measuring liquids, use a clear glass or plastic jug with graduated markings.

how to measure

When using graduated measuring cups, shake dry ingredients loosely into the appropriate cup. Do not tap the cup on a bench or tightly pack the ingredients unless directed to do so. Level top of measuring cups and measuring spoons with a knife. When measuring liquids, place a clear glass or plastic jug with graduated markings on a flat surface to check accuracy at eye level.

Note: The United States, Canada, New Zealand and the United Kingdom use 15ml tablespoons. All cup and spoon measurements are level. We use large eggs having an average weight of 2oz.

oven temperatures

These oven temperatures are only a guide. Always check the manufacturer's manual.

	°C (Celsius)	°F (Fahrenheit)	Gas Mark
Very slow	120	250	½
Slow	140 – 150	275 – 300	1 – 2
Moderately slow	170	325	3
Moderate	180 – 190	350 – 375	4 – 5
Moderately hot	200	400	6
Hot	220 – 230	425 – 450	7 – 8
Very hot	240	475	9

index

Page numbers in italics refer to photographs.